The Moment of Death in Early Modern Europe, c. 1450–1800

Intersections

INTERDISCIPLINARY STUDIES IN EARLY MODERN CULTURE

General Editor

Karl A.E. Enenkel (*Chair of Medieval and Neo-Latin Literature
Universität Münster*
e-mail: kenen_01@uni_muenster.de*)

Editorial Board

W. de Boer (*Miami University*)
S. Bussels (*University of Leiden*)
A. Dlabačová (*University of Leiden*)
Chr. Göttler (*University of Bern*)
J.L. de Jong (*University of Groningen*)
W.S. Melion (*Emory University*)
A. Montoya (*Radboud University Nijmegen*)
R. Seidel (*Goethe University Frankfurt am Main*)
P.J. Smith (*University of Leiden*)
J. Thompson (*Queen's University Belfast*)
A. Traninger (*Freie Universität Berlin*)
C. Zittel (*Ca' Foscari University of Venice / University of Stuttgart*)
C. Zwierlein (*Berlin*)

VOLUME 89 – 2024

The titles published in this series are listed at *brill.com/inte*

The Moment of Death in Early Modern Europe, c. 1450–1800

Contested Ideals, Controversial Spaces, and Suspicious Objects

Edited by

Benedikt Brunner
Martin Christ

BRILL

LEIDEN | BOSTON

Cover illustrations: (central image) *Ars moriendi*, demons tempt the dying man with crowns (a medieval allegory to earthly pride) under the disapproving gaze of Mary, Christ and God, *c.*1460, Netherlands, woodblock seven (4a) of eleven, public domain; (background image) Images from Peter Isselburg, *Bericht: wie es gehe/Gar nach dem A,B,C, Welche sich zur Ehe/Vnbesonnen geben///Da jhr gantzes Leben/Hat zu widerstreben* (Nuremberg: 1616), UB Erlangen-Nürnberg, A II 8 (see also page 6 in this volume).

Library of Congress Cataloging-in-Publication Data

Names: Brunner, Benedikt, 1986- editor. | Christ, Martin, 1991- editor.
Title: The moment of death in early modern Europe, c. 1450–1800 : contested ideals, controversial spaces, and suspicious objects / edited by Benedikt Brunner, Martin Christ.
Other titles: Moment of death in early modern Europe, circa 1450–1800
Description: Leiden ; Boston : Brill, 2024. | Series: Intersections, 1568-1181 ; volume 89 | Includes bibliographical references and index.
Identifiers: LCCN 2024002817 (print) | LCCN 2024002818 (ebook) | ISBN 9789004517738 (hardback) | ISBN 9789004517745 (ebook)
Subjects: LCSH: Death—Social aspects—Europe—History—16th century. | Death—Social aspects—Europe—History—17th century. | Death—Symbolic aspects—Europe—History—16th century. | Death—Symbolic aspects—Europe—History—16th century.
Classification: LCC GT3242 .M66 2024 (print) | LCC GT3242 (ebook) | DDC 306.09409/031—dc23/eng/20240307
LC record available at https://lccn.loc.gov/2024002817
LC ebook record available at https://lccn.loc.gov/2024002818

Typeface for the Latin, Greek, and Cyrillic scripts: "Brill". See and download: brill.com/brill-typeface.

ISSN 1568-1181
ISBN 978-90-04-51773-8 (hardback)
ISBN 978-90-04-51774-5 (e-book)
DOI 10.1163/9789004517745

Copyright 2024 by Benedikt Brunner and Martin Christ. Published by Koninklijke Brill BV, Leiden, The Netherlands.
Koninklijke Brill BV incorporates the imprints Brill, Brill Nijhoff, Brill Schöningh, Brill Fink, Brill mentis, Brill Wageningen Academic, Vandenhoeck & Ruprecht, Böhlau and V&R unipress.
Koninklijke Brill BV reserves the right to protect this publication against unauthorized use. Requests for re-use and/or translations must be addressed to Koninklijke Brill BV via brill.com or copyright.com.

This book is printed on acid-free paper and produced in a sustainable manner.

Contents

List of Figures   VII
Notes on the Editors   VIII
Notes on the Contributors   IX

1 Introduction: the Moment(s) of Death in Early Modern Europe   1
  Benedikt Brunner and Martin Christ

PART 1
Approaching the Last Moments

2 Ambiguity and Authenticity: the 'Good Death' on the Scaffold   21
  Hillard von Thiessen

3 Privacy in Death? Early Modern French Accounts of Death and Huguenots' *Last Hours*   36
  Michaël Green

4 Urbanity around the Deathbed: Considerations from Early Modern London   61
  Martin Christ

PART 2
Ideal Deathbeds

5 Deathbed Scenes in the Early Modern Atlantic World: Cross-Cultural Perspectives   81
  Erik R. Seeman

6 Confessing in the Contexts of Dying and Narratives of Death   101
  Irene Dingel

7 The Catholic Reformation and the Dying: Confraternities and Preparations for Death in France 1550–1700   119
  Elizabeth Tingle

8   Dying in Communities: the Ideal Death between Individual and
    Communal Requirements in Early Modern Protestantism   142
       Benedikt Brunner

PART 3
Objects and the Moments of Death

9   Candles of Death and the Death of the Virgin Mary as a Model of the
    Ideal Death on the Threshold of the Early Modern Era   165
       Vera Henkelmann

10 Contested Kingship – Controversial Coronation: York's Paper
    Crown   193
       Imke Lichterfeld

11 *Miseraciones eius super omnia opera eius*: Lucas Cranach the
    Elder's 'Der Sterbende' on the Brink of Reformation?   211
       Friedrich J. Becher

PART 4
Violence and Diseases

12 The Moment of Death during the Thirty Years' War   235
       Sigrun Haude

13 Death Disrupted: Heresy Executions and Spectators in the
    Low Countries, 1550–1566   257
       Isabel Casteels

14 Deaths in Hospitals and Care Institutions in Sixteenth- and
    Seventeenth-Century London   288
       Vanessa Harding

15 Fleeing the Deathbed: Sensory Anxieties and the Persecution of
    Non-Catholic Dying Practices in Antwerp, 1560s–1570s   302
       Louise Deschryver

Index Nominum   327

Figures

1.1 Detail from Peter Isselburg, *Bericht: wie es gehe/Gar nach dem A,B,C, Welche sich zur Ehe/Vnbesonnen geben///Da jhr gantzes Leben/Hat zu widerstreben* (Nuremberg: Peter Isselburg, 1616), Universitätsbibliothek Erlangen-Nürnberg: EINBLATTDRUCK.A-II 8   5

1.2 Peter Isselburg, *Bericht: wie es gehe/Gar nach dem A,B,C, Welche sich zur Ehe/Vnbesonnen geben///Da jhr gantzes Leben/Hat zu widerstreben* (Nuremberg: Peter Isselburg, 1616), Universitätsbibliothek Erlangen-Nürnberg: EINBLATTDRUCK.A-II 8   6

3.1 Gaultier Leonard, "Portrait of Philippe du Plessis-Mornay at the age of 62 [1611]", engraving, 1611–1641   40

3.2 Dagen Henrick Rochuszn van, "Portret of André Rivet", engraving, 1644–1652   44

3.3 Schweizer Johann, "Portrait of Pierre du Moulin", engraving, 1638–1670 [1658]   52

4.1 John Dunstall, Nine scenes from the 1665 plague that ravaged London, 1666, engraving, 45 × 33.3 cm, Museum of London, ID no. 42.39/142   67

9.1 Israhel van Meckenem after Hans Holbein the Elder, The Death of the Virgin, 1490/1500, engraving. Washington, National Gallery of Art (Rosenwald Collection)   173

9.2 Hugo van der Goes, The Death of the Virgin, 1475–1482, oil on panel, 147.8 × 122.5 cm. Bruges, Groeningemuseum   174

9.3 Michael Pacher, The Death of the Virgin, right inner wing of Pacher-Altar, 1471–1481, oil on panel, Sankt Wolfgang (Austria), parish church. Image kindly provided by Peter Böttcher, Institut für Realienkunde, Universität Salzburg   175

9.4 Joos van Cleve, The Death of the Virgin, 1515, oil on panel, 65 × 125.5 cm. Cologne, Wallraf-Richartz-Museum   178

9.5 Joos van Cleve, The Death of the Virgin, after 1515, oil on panel, 130 × 154 cm. Munich, Alte Pinakothek   178

9.6 Martin Schongauer, The Death of the Virgin, before 1475, engraving, 27 × 17.8 cm. Berlin, Kupferstichkabinett (SMPK)   182

9.7 Joos van Cleve, Altar retable with the death of the Virgin, 1515, oil on panel, 65 × 243.5 cm. Cologne, Wallraf-Richartz-Museum   184

9.8 Rembrandt (Harmenszoon van Rijn), The Death of the Virgin Mary [one of three states of the etching], 1639, etching, 41 × 31.5 cm. Amsterdam, Rijksprentenkabinet (Rijksmuseum)   186

9.9 The Grace of the Sacrament of Death, 1734, oil painting, 150 × 175 cm. Vreden, parish church St George (possession of the brotherhood of the Fear of the Death)   187

11.1 Lucas Cranach the Elder, *Der Sterbende*, 1518, oil on limewood, 93 × 36.2 cm. Leipzig, Museum der bildenden Künste, Inv.Nr. 40   213

Notes on the Editors

Benedikt Brunner
is a Research Associate at the Leibniz-Institute for European History in Mainz. He received his PhD from the University of Münster in 2017 with a conceptual history of the term "Volkskirche" in German Protestantism. Since then, he worked on several aspects of the history of Early Modern Protestantism in Europe and beyond. He is currently finishing a book-length project about coping practices among Protestants in the cities of Nuremberg, Basel, London and Boston. He is the author of *Volkskirche. Zur Geschichte eines evangelischen Grundbegriffs (1918–1960)* (2020) and several articles about death in early modern Europe.

Martin Christ
is a Junior Fellow and post-doctoral researcher in the project "Religion and Urbanity: Reciprocal Formations", based at the Max Weber Centre for Advanced Cultural and Social Studies at the University of Erfurt, Germany. He has worked on religious coexistence in early modern central Europe, conversions to Lutheranism and urban history. He is currently working on a project about death and burials in Munich and London, *c.*1550–1870. He is the author of *Biographies of a Reformation. Religious Change and Confessional Coexistence in Upper Lusatia, 1520–1635* (2022) and co-editor, together with Carmen González Gutiérrez, of *Death in the City in Premodern Europe* (2022).

Notes on the Contributors

Friedrich J. Becher

has a Master in European Art History and defended his PhD thesis, in 2023, in which he elaborated on the cultural practice(s) of displaying human bones. The research was funded by the Gerda Henkel Stiftung.

Isabel Casteels

works as a PhD researcher at the KU Leuven and Leiden University, where she is preparing a dissertation on the role of spectators in public executions during the Dutch Revolt. Her research interests are in the fields of cultural history and the history of knowledge of the early modern Low Countries. Together with Louise Deschryver and Violet Soen she recently edited a thematic issue of the journal *Early Modern Low Countries, Divided by Death? Staging Mortality in the Early Modern Low Countries* (2021).

Louise Deschryver

is a PhD fellow of the FWO at the KU Leuven. She is preparing a dissertation on death, the senses and the Reformation in the sixteenth-century Low Countries, investigating how new sensory repertoires and conflicts on embodied funerary rites co-shaped the course of the Revolt in Antwerp. Together with Isabel Casteels and Violet Soen, she edited the volume *Divided by Death? Staging Mortality in the Early Modern Low Countries* (2021) for the journal *Early Modern Low Countries*.

Irene Dingel

is the former director of the Leibniz-Institute of European History, Mainz (department of European Religious History), and Professor Emerita at the University of Mainz. She has worked extensively on Protestantism, Lutheran confessional cultures, the Reformation and the early Enlightenment religious peace agreements in Ealy Modern Europe. Her books include *Concordia controversa. Die öffentlichen Diskussionen um das lutherische Konkordienwerk am Ende des 16. Jahrhunderts* (1996), and *Vielfalt – Ordnung – Einheit. Kirchengeschichtliche Studien zur Frühen Neuzeit* (2021).

Michaël Green

is a historian of early modern religion, society and culture. He completed his PhD at the University of Groningen (Netherlands). Since then he has held research and teaching positions in Switzerland, Germany, Denmark, Spain and Poland. He is currently professor at the University of Łódz (Poland) and works on notions of privacy, history of religious minorities, and epistolary exchanges in the early modern world. He is the author of *An Interreligious Dialogue: Portrayal of Jews in Dutch French-Language Periodicals (1680–1715)* (2022), and *The Huguenot Jean Rou (1638–1711): Scholar, Educator, Civil Servant* (2015). He is the editor of *Le Grand Tour 1701–1703. Lettres de Henry Bentinck et de son précepteur Paul Rapin-Thoyras, à Hans Willem Bentinck* (2021).

Vanessa Harding

is Emeritus Professor of London History at Birkbeck, University of London. Her research focuses on London between c. 1300 and 1700, and specifically on mortality, death and burial, and urban space. Publications include *The Dead and the Living in London and Paris, 1500–1700* (2002).

Sigrun Haude

is Walter C. Langsam Professor of European History at the University of Cincinnati. Her research focuses on the Reformation from its roots in the later Middle Ages to the Thirty Years' War (1618–1648). She has published on the Radical Reformation, the role of Gender among Anabaptists and Spiritualists, on society and the Thirty Years' War. Her most recent publication book is *Coping with Life during the Thirty Years' War* (2021).

Vera Henkelmann

is a fellow at the Max Weber Centre, University of Erfurt, and a freelance lecturer at the Universities of Tübingen and Greifswald. Her areas of expertise include light and lighting devices in the Christian and Jewish Middle Ages, medieval jewellery and its relation to the body, object cultures of medieval hunting, and textiles in profane-sacral networks. She is the author of *Spätgotische Marienleuchter. Formen, Funktionen, Bedeutungen* (2014).

Imke Lichterfeld

teaches English Literature at Bonn University, Germany, where she currently holds a position as Studies Coordinator at the Department of English, American and Celtic Studies. She has contributed to publications on the English Renaissance, Modernism, and contemporary literature. She is the author of *When the Bad Bleeds – Mantic Elements in English Renaissance Revenge Tragedy*. Her current research focuses on early modern drama, and Shakespeare and his contemporaries.

Erik R. Seeman

is Professor of History at the University at Buffalo (SUNY). A specialist in the history of religion and death practices in the early modern Atlantic world, he is the author of *Death in the New World: Cross-Cultural Encounters, 1492–1800* (2010), *The Huron-Wendat Feast of the Dead: Indian-European Encounters in Early North America* (2011), and *Speaking with the Dead in Early America* (2019). His current book project is *Boston's Pox of 1721: A People's History*.

Elizabeth Tingle

is Professor of History at De Montfort University, Leicester, UK. She has written extensively on the Wars of Religion and the Catholic Reformation in France. Her recent book-size publications are *Sacred Journeys: Long Distance Pilgrimage in North-Western Europe in the Counter Reformation* (2020) and, together with Philip Booth the edited volume, *A Companion to Death, Burial and Remembrance in Late Medieval and Early Modern Europe c.1300–c.1700* (2021). Currently she is working on cathedral chapters in early modern France.

Hillard von Thiessen

is professor for early modern history at the University of Rostock (since 2013), formerly, he was substitute professor for early modern history at the University of Cologne. His research interests include norms, values and the culture of ambiguity in premodern Europe, diplomacy in early modern Europe, corruption and patronage in early modern political culture. Among his book-length publications are *Das Zeitalter der Ambiguität. Vom Umgang mit Werten und Normen in der Frühen Neuzeit* (2021); *Normenkonkurrenz in historischer Perspektive* (edited volume, together with Arne Karsten, 2015); *Diplomatie und Patronage. Die spanisch-römischen Beziehungen 1605–1621 in akteurszentrierter Perspektive* (2010); *Die Kapuziner zwischen Konfessionalisierung und Alltagskultur. Vergleichende Fallstudie am Beispiel Freiburgs und Hildesheims 1599–1750* (2002).

CHAPTER 1

Introduction: the Moment(s) of Death in Early Modern Europe

Benedikt Brunner and Martin Christ

In September 1663, 'citizen and comb-maker' of London, Edward Dun, was dying. As he had been sick for some time, he had been thinking about his last moments for a while. His moment of death was actually a protracted process, as he was in bed for more than a week, until he finally died. However, this also gave him time to participate in some of the processes associated with the last moments, such as bringing his affairs in order. And so, 'to prevent all further strife between his children and relations, he caused a will to be made'.[1] In the will, Dun not only reflected on his own last moments, but used it as an opportunity to consider the moment of death more generally, writing that

> One of the most Important Mysteries in the world, is to dye well. It is never done but once, and if one fail to perform it well, he is lost without recovery. It is the last lineament of the Table of our Life, the last blaze of the Torch Extinguished, the last Lustre of the setting Sun, the end of the Race, which gives a period to the Course, and the great Seal which signeth all our Actions. One may in Death correct all the defects of an ill Life, and all the virtues of a good are defaced, and polluted by an evil Death. The Art of dying well, being of so great Consequence, let it therefore teach every one to prize it, For all Affairs of the World, end in one great Affair of the other Life, which is that of the Judgment God will give upon our Soul, at its passage out of the Body.[2]

As Dun pointed out, a good death was just as important as a good life. Perhaps even more so.

---

1 Anonymous, *The Last will and testament of Squire Dun, late executioner for the city of London who was buried on Saturday night last, with his several legacies bequeathed to his friends upon his death-bed: as also an elegie, touching his life, death, and burial* (London, George Horton: 1663) 5.
2 Ibidem 3.

But Dun was not just any London citizen. Besides being a comb-maker, he was also the executioner of the city and therefore had spent his life surrounded by a different kind of death. This special position also resulted in the publication of an elegy on the occasion of the death of Dun, who seems to have been a well-known figure in London.[3] The deaths on the execution site were nothing like the death he experienced in his home.[4] Yet what connected them is that in both cases, how someone behaved during their last moments was of great importance, as Dun indicated with his assessment that a good life could be undone by a bad death. And in both cases, those who expected to die spent a considerable amount of time reflecting on how to shape their final moments in this world. These careful preparations already point at the issues connected to a sudden or unexpected death, and the anxieties surrounding a difficult death.

Both in our time and in the past, death was one of the most important aspects of anyone's life. The early modern period saw drastic changes in rites of death, burials and commemoration. The Reformation, European expansion, scientific advances and changes in public health and hygiene all contributed to the changing ways in which men and women in this period experienced death. Philippe Ariès, Michel Vovelle and other scholars researching *mentalités* gave important initial pointers for a historical analysis of death's cultural meanings.[5] More recently, Thomas Laqueur's *The Work of the Dead* provides another example of a wide-ranging analysis of the importance of death for human societies.[6] Besides such general studies, there have been a number of contributions on death and burial.[7] Many such works focus on a particular region or city in order to illuminate broader patterns of change.

Alongside such important studies came master narratives that fitted death into broader patterns of change. One particularly powerful such narrative is that of the "disenchantment of the world". It argues that the Enlightenment brought about a rational approach to death. Peter Marshall argued that the period saw 'a larger process of conceptual reorientation, one of desacralization

---

3 Anonymous, *Groanes from Newgate; OR, AN ELEGY UPON Edvvard Dun Esq: The Cities Common Hangman, who Dyed Naturally in his bed, the 11th. of September* (London, Edward Crowch: 1663).
4 For a recent discussion of an executioner in the German context, see Harrington J.F., *The Faithful Executioner: Life and Death in the Sixteenth Century* (London: 2013).
5 Ariès P., *Geschichte des Todes* (Stuttgart: 2015) 713–770; Vovelle M., *La mort et l'Occident de 1300 à nos jours* (Paris: 1983).
6 Laqueur T.W., *The Work of the Dead: A Cultural History of Mortal Remains* (Princeton: 2015).
7 Cf. Malone H., "New Life in the Modern Cultural History of Death", *Historical Journal* 62.3 (2019) 833–852; Christ M. – González Gutiérrez C., "Death and the City in Premodern Europe", Special Issue of *Mortality* (2022).

or secularization'.[8] However, the question of how much the religious, political and cultural upheavals of the early modern period changed the meanings and patterns of experience of death has by no means been answered conclusively. Current research on how death was dealt with in the Enlightenment period is still strongly influenced by French *mentalité* research. The image of 'death reversed into the opposite' (in the original: 'mort inversée') developed by Ariès requires further differentiation, even if the model he sketched still has a stimulating effect on research.[9] Erik R. Seeman has provided a nuanced and convincing account of the continued relevance of "irrational" beliefs that the living and dead could communicate centuries after the Enlightenment.[10] Thus, studies on death continue to shed new light on historiographical debates on the early modern period, such as modernisation, rationalisation and secularisation.

One particularly fruitful avenue of research is not to focus on death in general, but the moment of death specifically. This volume investigates this transitionary moment between life and death.[11] In many cases, this was a death on a deathbed, but it also included the scaffold, battlefield or death in the streets. Early modern sources indicate the importance attached to these final moments in the context of a "good" dying process. By focusing on this particular moment in a range of European countries and in North America, the volume investigates how men and women prepared for their death, how friends and family experienced the death of a person and what an early modern deathbed, understood as a social event, looked like.

The deathbed is particularly revealing, as it can be understood as a "normative threshold" and thus as a place where diverse transformation processes culminated.[12] How, where and when someone died was highly scrutinised in the early modern period. Keith Luria therefore described the behaviour on the

---

8   Marshall P., "After Purgatory: Death and Remembrance in the Reformation World", in Rasmussen T. – Øygarden Flaeten J. (eds.), *Preparing for Death, Remembering the Dead* (Göttingen: 2015) 25–43, at 28; see also Walsham A., "The Reformation and the 'Disenchantment of the World' Reassessed", *Historical Journal* 51.2 (2008) 497–528, especially 506, 515–517.
9   Ariès, *Geschichte des Todes* 713–770.
10 Seeman E.R., *Speaking with the Dead in Early America* (Philadelphia: 2019).
11 We thank our institutions, the Leibniz-Institute for European History in Mainz and Humanities Centre in Advanced Studies "Religion and Urbanity: Reciprocal Formations", funded by the German Research Foundation (DFG, FOR 2779) for their support.
12 See von Thiessen H., "Das Sterbebett als normative Schwelle. Der Mensch in der Frühen Neuzeit zwischen irdischer Normenkonkurrenz und göttlichem Gericht", *Historische Zeitschrift* 295 (2012) 625–659; Brunner B., "York", in *Ortstermine. Umgang mit Differenz in Europa* (Mainz: 2020), URL: http://ieg-differences.eu/ortstermine/benedikt-brunner-york, URN: urn: nbn:de:0159-2020102935.

deathbed as a 'moment of truth'.[13] Contemporaries observed closely how a person behaved on his or her deathbed. For example, in the account of Archduke Charles of Austria's (1590–1624) death, we find a description of how he kept the image of a saint with him, received the sacrament and extreme unction, gave confession and instructed the priest to speak loudly and clearly so that he could follow all the ceremonies. Even when the archduke was no longer able to speak, he hit his breast and lifted his hands in order to show contrition for his sins and continued to try to pray. Clerics and political advisors surrounded him.[14] This semi-public display of Catholic piety, combined with dynastic symbols, served purposes that went beyond the confines of the death chamber.

Dying people, according to Hillard von Thiessen, 'gradually moved from a contradictory horizon of norms, characterised by competing expectations of action, to one that was generally expected to be characterised by unambiguity and in which there could be no conflicting norms'.[15] The deathbed is thus a prime example of the competition of norms in the early modern period and allows for 'fundamental statements about systems of norms and values'.[16] In pre-modern Europe, religiously based competing norms came to a head in a special way, but at the same time people's abilities to deal with them developed and they were adapted to specific situations.[17]

The last moments formed the focus of early modern literature, art, poetry and music as well as in scholarly discourse and theology, as shown, for example, in the illustration by Peter Isselburg [Figs. 1.1 and 1.2]. Around the deathbed, one can find family members and a clerics as well as a range of objects. The image was accompanied by a poem and forms part of a larger narrative on a married life that ends with the burial, which is also illustrated in the copperplate engraving. It shows that the fraught moments before death can only be properly understood if they are analysed in an interdisciplinary way. The current volume therefore combines perspectives from theology, art history, literary studies and history. In this way, it is also possible to integrate deathbed discourses and practices into more recent research directions, such as

---

13 Luria K.P., "The Embodiment of Truth and Sanctity: Women's Deathbed Conversions and Confessional Conflict in Seventeenth-Century France", *COLLeGIUM: Studies across Disciplines in the Humanities and Social Sciences* 2 (2007) 210–33, at 210.
14 Scholz B.W., *Erzherzog Karl von Österreich (1590–1624), Bischof von Breslau am Vorabend und zu Beginn des Dreißigjährigen Krieges* (Cologne: 2021) Quellenanhang.
15 Thiessen, "Sterbebett" 626.
16 Ibidem. See also von Thiessen H. – Karsten A. (eds.), *Normenkonkurrenz in historischer Perspektive* (Berlin: 2015).
17 See also von Thiessen H., *Das Zeitalter der Ambiguität. Vom Umgang mit Werten und Normen in der Frühen Neuzeit* (Cologne – Weimar – Vienna: 2021).

INTRODUCTION: THE MOMENT(S) OF DEATH IN EARLY MODERN EUROPE 5

FIGURE 1.1 Detail from Peter Isselburg, *Bericht: wie es gehe/Gar nach dem A,B,C, Welche sich zur Ehe/Vnbesonnen geben///Da jhr gantzes Leben/Hat zu widerstreben* (Nuremberg: 1616)
UB ERLANGEN-NÜRNBERG, A II 8

material culture studies. A focus on the moments of death is particularly fruitful because it enables comparisons across traditional disciplinary boundaries.

Although there are individual studies dealing with the deathbed and the last moments, comparative research is still lacking.[18] Yet the fact that everyone

---

18   For example, Tankard D., "The Reformation of the Deathbed in Mid-Sixteenth-Century England", *Mortality* 8.3 (2003) 251–267; Luria, "Embodiment"; Hallam E.A., "Turning the Hourglass: Gender Relations at the Deathbed in Early Modern Canterbury", *Mortality* 1.1 (1996) 61–82; Wunderli R. – Broce G., "The Final Moment Before Death in Early Modern England", *Sixteenth Century Journal* 20.2 (1989) 259–275; Cross M.C., "The Third Earl of Huntingdon's Death-Bed: A Calvinist Example of the Ars Moriendi", *Northern History* 21 (1985) 80–107; Attreed L.C., "Preparation for Death in Sixteenth-Century Northern England", *Sixteenth Century Journal* 13.3 (1982) 37–66.

FIGURE 1.2
Peter Isselburg,
*Bericht: wie es gehe
Gar nach dem A,B,C,
Welche sich zur Ehe
Vnbesonnen geben
Da jhr gantzes Leben
Hat zu widerstreben*
(Nuremberg: 1616)
UB ERLANGEN-
NÜRNBERG, A II 8

has to die makes it possible to compare the moment of death across geographical, gender and class boundaries. At least in theory, all deaths were equal, as was expressed in medieval dances of death as well as theological tracts by Martin Luther and others.[19] While this was undoubtedly an exaggeration, all members of early modern communities were concerned about a proper death. We find sources that describe the death of the poor during times of plague, for instance, just as there are sources on the deathbeds of kings and queens.

The possibilities to compare the same phenomenon enables the detection of similarities and differences across traditional geographical, chronological

---

19 Luther Martin, *Ob man vor dem Sterben fliehen möge* (Wittenberg, Hans Luft: 1527); Pesch O.H., "Theologie des Todes bei Martin Luther", in Becker H. – Einig B. – Ullrich P.-O. (eds.), *Im Angesicht des Todes. Ein interdisziplinäres Kompendium*, vol. II, Pietas Liturgica 4 (St. Ottilien: 1987) 709–789.

and disciplinary boundaries. For example, as the chapter by Erik Seeman shows, considering the deathbed in a trans-Atlantic perspective opens up new possibilities of comparison. He shows how this focus can bridge historiographical divides and integrate scholarship that focuses on Europe with work on North America. This volume therefore expands previous approaches to include cross-religious perspectives in a trans-Atlantic and global frame.[20]

In our understanding, the "moment of death" has to be broadly defined in order to enable comparisons and understand its true significance. Therefore, the authors of this volume discuss the normative instructions for an ideal deathbed alongside other forms of death, which were sudden or unexpected and therefore deviated from the norms. Likewise, the temporality of the moment of death is understood broadly and includes both the few seconds when someone realised they were about to die on the battlefield, just as much as the long time someone had to prepare when they heard a death sentence pronounced.[21] Even in the cases when death was sudden or unexpected, previous preparations for a good death show how important these final moments were for those living in the early modern period.

Already in the late medieval period, the genre of the *ars moriendi* literature instructed men and women on how to die a "good" death. These instructions included advice on how to behave during the final moments, what prayers to say, who to talk to and, ultimately, how to avoid the temptations of the devil and prepare the soul for divine judgment. These notions of a good death continued to be very influential in the early modern period, although they were adapted after the Reformation and other major religious changes.[22] But as

---

20 See Seeman E.R., "Death in Early America", *History Compass* 17.10 (2019); idem, "Reading Indians' Deathbed Scenes: Ethnohistorical and Representational Approaches", *Journal of American History* 88.1 (2001) 17–47; and idem, *Death in the New World: Cross-Cultural Encounters, 1492–1800* (Philadelphia: 2010).

21 See Kaiser M., "Zwischen 'ars moriendi' und 'ars mortem evitandi'. Der Soldat und der Tod in der Frühen Neuzeit", in idem – Kroll S. (eds.), *Militär und Religiosität in der Frühen Neuzeit* (Münster: 2004) 323–343; Kästner A., "Die Ungewissheit überschreiten. Erzählmuster und Auslegungen unverhoffter Todesfälle in Leichenpredigten", in Dickhaut E.-M. (ed.), *Leichenpredigten als Medien der Erinnerungskultur im europäischen Kontext* (Stuttgart: 2014) 147–172; Casteels I. – Deschryver L. – Soen V., "Divided by Death? Staging Mortality in the Early Modern Low Countries", *Early Modern Low Countries* 5.1 (2021) 1–16; Casteels I., "Death on Display: Execution Prints on the Eve of the Dutch Revolt", *Nederlands Kunsthistorisch Jaarboek Online / Netherlands Yearbook for History of Art* 72 (2022).

22 There is a large body of scholarship on this topic. See, for example, Resch C., *Trost im Angesicht des Todes. Frühe reformatorische Anleitungen zur Seelsorge an Kranken und Sterbenden* (Tübingen – Basel: 2006); Reinis A., *Reforming the Art of Dying: The Ars Moriendi in the German Reformation, 1519–1528* (Aldershot: 2007); Schottroff L., *Die*

Friedrich J. Becher's contribution illustrates, the Reformation changes were initially limited, while Irene Dingel shows the impact of Lutheran theology on normative instructions for a deathbed. Elizabeth Tingle focuses on the Catholic context and especially the role that fraternities played in the preparations for the final moments. She shows how the moment of death and burial rituals were closely intertwined and that in Catholicism, too, major changes occurred in the ideas about a good death in the early modern period. These contributions argue that there was no single Christian response to death and dying, but that different groups found different interpretations of the moments of death.[23] They speak to another major debate in the history of death, namely the question whether there was a specifically denominational way of dealing with death at all, or whether, apart from the modifications to the ritual, mourning and coping mechanisms have great similarities.[24] This volume is a first step in the investigation of the complex and multi-faceted topic of the moments of death that shows how different Christian communities interpreted and coped with their last moments in this world. We hope that the contributions in this volume will lead to further studies on this topic that expand these discussions beyond Christian denominations, particularly to Judaism and Islam, and to more areas beyond Europe.[25]

The preparations for a proper deathbed were crucial in the early modern period, as there were fixed norms and rules on what a deathbed was supposed to look like. Theologians argued about the best way to depart this life in a range of genres. Their visions of an ideal death influenced people lower down the

---

Bereitung zum Sterben. Studien zu den frühen reformatorischen Sterbebüchern (Göttingen: 2012); Leppin V., "Die Transformation der mittelalterlichen ars moriendi zur reformatorischen Leichenpredigt", in Deiters M. – Slenczka R. (eds.), *Häuslich – persönlich – innerlich: Bild und Frömmigkeitspraxis im Umfeld der Reformation* (Berlin – Boston: 2020) 165–178.

23 On this topic, see Brunner B., "Was passiert mit dem 'stinkenden Madensack'? Der Umgang mit dem Tod als Lackmustest der reformatorischen Bestimmung von Leib und Seele", *Theologische Zeitschrift* 76.2 (2020) 164–190.

24 On a confessional death, see Marshall P., "Was There a Protestant Death?", in Angel S. et al. (eds.), *Were We Ever Protestants? Essays in Honor of Tarald Rasmussen* (Berlin – Boston: 2019) 143–160; Karant-Nunn S., *The Reformation of Ritual: An Interpretation of Early Modern Germany* (London: 1997); Koslofsky C., *The Reformation of the Dead: Death and Ritual in Early Modern Germany, c. 1450–1700* (Basingstoke: 2000).

25 On Jewish deathbeds, see Bar-Levav A., "Games of Death in Jewish Books for the Sick and the Dying", *Kabbalah: Journal for the Study of Jewish Mystical Texts* 5 (2000) 11–33; Goldberg S.A., *Crossing the Jabbok: Illness and Death in Ashkenazi Judaism in Sixteenth through Nineteenth-Century Prague*, trans. Cosman C. (Berkeley: 1996); Horowitz E., "The Jews of Europe and the Moment of Death in Medieval and Modern Times", *Judaism* 44 (1995) 271–281.

social scale, just as they influenced the elites.[26] At the same time, the everyday practices of simple town-dwellers and artisans changed how scholars and urban elites interpreted the moments of death. Visual sources played an important role for ideas about an ideal deathbed and as early as the fifteenth century, woodcuts show different kinds of deathbeds. Depending on confession, social status and gender, ideas about an ideal death could be different and the contributions in this volume explore these differences as well as similarities.

Through the last moments before death, it is possible to retrace broader processes of change in the early modern period. The dynamics around the deathbed illustrate what role different groups of actors played when it came to crucial rites of passage. Families, doctors, friends and clerics assembled around the deathbed and they help us to understand the complexity of early modern societies more generally. As the deathbed was a liminal space, somewhere between life and death, those from other worlds could also attend the final moments.[27] As we know from the works of Alexandra Walsham and Peter Marshall, this could include angels.[28] The London diarist Samuel Pepys recorded another example on 8 January 1663/4: '[Luellin's] wife upon her death-bed […] dreamt of her uncle Scobell, and did foretell, from some discourse she had with him, that she should die four days thence, and not sooner, and did all along say so, and did so'.[29]

As Benedikt Brunner argues in his contribution, notions of community between all these different groups of people came to the fore around the deathbed. This included both groups in this world, and in the next. The wide variety of actors involved in the final moments has also been observed in Ashkenazi Judaism.[30] Whether dying in one's bedchamber could be considered private, domestic or public, urban or rural, or ambiguous or not are questions that concern not only the final moments, but early modernity more generally. While all chapters in this volume speak to broader themes, three papers deal explicitly with key concepts of early modernity. Michaël Green uses the moment of death as a vantage point to investigate French manuals on the final moments. He finds that privacy in a modern sense was not one of the features of early modern deathbeds, instead arguing for a definition of privacy derived from a

---

26   Cf. Houlbrooke R., *Death, Religion and the Family in England, 1480–1750* (Oxford: 1998).
27   On this topic in a modern context, see Berger P. – Kroesen J., *Ultimate Ambiguities: Investigating Death and Liminality* (Oxford – New York: 2015).
28   Marshall P. – Walsham A.M. (eds.), *Angels in the Early Modern World* (Cambridge: 2006), especially Marshall P., "Angels Around the Deathbed: Variations on a Theme in the English Art of Dying", in ibidem, 83–103.
29   Pepys' Diary, online version, entry for 8 January 1663/64.
30   Bar-Levav, "Games of Death" 19–24.

close analysis of the early modern sources.[31] Hillard von Thiessen goes even further in his argument that the early modern period can be understood as an age of ambiguity and that this becomes especially clear during the moments of death, in this case during executions. Finally, Martin Christ asks how far urbanity, usually associated with large-scale buildings or features of city life, can be detected around the deathbed.

Another indication of the importance of the last moments was that they were rarely free of strong emotions. This included sadness, of course, but also relief or happiness about the soul's journey to heaven. The fear of a violent or especially painful death was heightened by stories about such last moments. One particularly influential example from the sixteenth century was the death of the convert Francis Spiera, who was born as a Catholic, then became a Protestant and eventually returned to Catholicism in 1548. On his deathbed he expressed his regret at this decision and was certain of his own damnation because of the way he lived. Contemporary accounts included ones by a law teacher from Padua, a Roman Catholic priest, who later converted himself, and Spiera's nephew, who argued that his uncle was insane rather than guilt-ridden. Protestant commentators interpreted Spiera's painful death as a sign of divine disapproval of Catholicism. The story of Spiera's last moments was especially popular in England, as an example of a bad death, but also made its way to other regions, such as Germany and Bohemia.[32] Or, to name another example, the deathbed of the Huguenot scholar Isaac Casaubon (1559–1614) was the subject of medical treatises and learned exchanges because his was an especially painful death.[33] The printed letter on his death even included an engraving of the deceased's infected bladder, which presumably led to his death and caused

---

31   Cf. on this topic Schlögl R., "Politik beobachten. Öffentlichkeit und Medien in der Frühen Neuzeit", *Zeitschrift für Historische Forschung* 35.4 (2008) 581–616 and idem, "Öffentliche Gottesverehrung und privater Glaube in der Frühen Neuzeit. Beobachtungen zur Bedeutung von Kirchenzucht und Frömmigkeit für die Abgrenzung privater Sozialräume", in Melville G. – von Moos P. (eds.), *Das Öffentliche und das Private in der Vormoderne* (Köln – Weimar – Wien: 1998) 165–209.

32   Overell M.A., "The Exploitation of Francesco Spiera", *The Sixteenth Century Journal* 26.3 (1995) 619–637.

33   Miert D. van, "The Curious Case of Isaac Casaubon's Monstrous Bladder: The Networked Construction of Learned Memory within the Seventeenth-Century Reformed World of Learning", in Scholten K. – van Miert D. – Enenkel K.A.E., *Memory and Identity in the Learned World: Community Formation in the Early Modern World of Learning and Science*, Intersections 81 (Leiden: 2022) 307–341. The depiction can be found in Thorius Raphael, *Epistola medici Londinensis R. T. de viri celeberrimi Isaaci Casauboni morbi mortisque causa, edita ex museo Joachimi Morsi* (Leiden, Jacobus Marcus: 1619) fol. A2r.

his suffering on the deathbed. By comparison, the importance of martyrs shows that the moments of death were highly context-specific. In these cases, a painful death was interpreted by their followers not as a sign of divine disapproval, but rather as an indication that the dying person followed God's wishes.

An important element when preparing for death was to have the appropriate objects at hand. In Judaism, a prayer shawl (*tallith*) and bowl for the washing of hands were important objects present at the deathbed.[34] Catholic priests took a host to the house of a person who was dying. Once there, holy water, oil, a crucifix and candles were used. In Lutheranism, some of these objects were kept, while theologians adapted or abandoned others. In some Reformed confessions, objects were consciously rejected around the deathbed. Vera Henkelmann draws our attention to one such object that had symbolic and practical functions: the candle. She shows the many layers of candles around the deathbed, especially connected to the death of the Virgin Mary. Imke Lichterfeld's analysis goes in a different direction, as she focuses on another object: the paper crown used in the mock coronation of Richard, Duke of York. She underlines how the paper crown was closely tied to the last moments of Richard and turned an honourable death into a mockery.

Besides objects, place was another important component of the final moments. While much scholarship has focused on the location of burial spaces and the movement of cemeteries, much less attention has been paid to the spaces of the last moments.[35] Indeed, even the bedchamber, where most people died, was more than just a room. Here, the dying said prayers and received sacraments, read and wrote books, dictated their wills and hoped for their souls to move on to the afterlife. As Vanessa Harding shows in her contribution, hospitals were a crucial part of early modern infrastructure and many poor individuals died there, in many cases with limited access to clerics. As a point of comparison, the violence on battlefields and attempts to flee plague prevented an ordered deathbed for many inhabitants of early modern Europe.

Another example of the importance of the space of the last moments is the execution site. In the diary of Samuel Pepys, we find the author record on 14 June 1662 how he and some friends watched the execution of Sir Henry Vane:

---

34   Horowitz, "The Jews of Europe" 274.
35   On early modern spaces generally, see Rau S., *History, Space and Place* (London: 2019). On the early modern bedchamber, cf. Christ M., "Co-Spatiality in the Early Modern European Bedchamber", in Rau S. – Rüpke J. (eds.), *Religion and Urbanity Online* (Berlin – Boston: 2022). https://doi.org/10.1515/urbrel.17261275.

> A very great press of people. He [Vane] made a long speech, many times interrupted by the Sheriff and others there; and they would have taken his paper out of his hand, but he would not let it go. But they caused all the books of those that writ after him to be given the Sheriff; and the trumpets were brought under the scaffold that he might not be heard […] Then he prayed, and so fitted himself, and received the blow; but the scaffold was so crowded that we could not see it done.[36]

Pepys observed minutely how Vane, after giving his speech in which he criticised the trial and explained himself, eventually died:

> he changed not his colour or speech to the last, but died justifying himself and the cause he had stood for; and spoke very confidently of his being presently at the right hand of Christ; and in all, things appeared the most resolved man that ever died in that manner, and showed more of heat than cowardize, but yet with all humility and gravity.[37]

The account in Pepys' Diary illustrates that the moments of death reached far beyond the deceased and their immediate families. Isabel Casteels explores these dynamics further in her contribution, which shows how audiences interfered in executions. Even if people were not immediately assembled around the deathbed, they still participated and heard about the death of relatives and friends.

Finally, temporalities played a crucial role in a person's final moments on earth. A quick death could mean less suffering, but also deprived a person of important deathbed rituals. Many accidents resulted in a unexpected death, but their sudden nature could also mean that theologians interpreted them as a sign of divine disapproval. To name just one example, when the residence of the French ambassador collapsed in 1623 and 95 people died, many Protestant commentators blamed this on divine disapproval of Catholicism.[38] It was not just that the people died, but that their death was unexpected and violent, many of them being buried underneath the rubble. During certain times, death was especially prevalent and the moments of death changed accordingly. In times of war and disease, as the contributions by Sigrun Haude and

---

36 Pepys' Diary, online version, entry for 14 June 1662.
37 Ibidem.
38 Walsham A., "'The Fatall Vesper': Providentialism and Anti-Popery in Late Jacobean London", *Past and Present* 144 (1994) 36–87. For another example of a similar kind of interpretation, see Oetzel L., "Der Tod und die Gesandten. Tod als politischer und persönlicher Faktor auf dem Westfälischen Friedenskongress", *Frühneuzeit-Info* 29 (2018) 75–87.

Louise Deschryver show, rituals were adapted and a quick disposal of the dead was a priority. However, this did not mean that those living in the early modern period simply accepted their fate, as they attempted to avoid diseases and could flee their cities if plague broke out.

Paying close attention to different groups of people, their spaces, objects and temporalities of death also helps us avoid analytical pitfalls. It is all too easy to argue that death was ever-present in the early modern period and therefore everyone prepared for death in the same way. This would obscure the very real differences that the moments of death contained for a range of people. Women are a case in point for the specificity of deaths in the early modern period. As childbirth was a dangerous occasion, women's mortality was especially high during this point in time. As we know from a funeral sermon from 1692, which tells the story of Maria Eleonora, whose childbed turned into a coffin as she died during her lying-in period, the boundary between a happy and a sad occasion could be fluid.[39]

The sheer number of sources produced on the moments of death in the early modern period indicate their importance. Theologians argued about the right way to die, diarists wrote about the deathbeds of their friends and relatives, executioners prepared for the most appropriate way to end a convict's life, painters depicted a blessed death and playwrights included minute details on the last breaths of their protagonists. Underlying all these works was the idea that a good death mirrored a good life. Likewise, a painful and violent death was an indication that the soul of the departed may end up in Hell. If we take these concerns of the inhabitants of the early modern world seriously, then we see that the final moments not only teach us about death, but just as much about life.

Bibliography

Primary Printed Sources

Anonymous, *The Last will and testament of Squire Dun, late executioner for the city of London who was buried on Saturday night last, with his several legacies bequeathed*

---

39   Schreiber, Michael, *Das in einen Sarg verkehrte Wochen-Bett/ Der Hochwolgebohrnen Frauen/ Fn. Maria Eleonora* (Königsberg, Reusner: 1692). Cf. Jarzebwoski C., "Loss and Emotion in Funeral Works on Children in Seventeenth-Century Germany", in Tatlock L. (ed.), *Enduring Loss in Early Modern Germany: Cross Disciplinary Perspectives* (Leiden – Boston: 2008) 187–213; and Struckmeier E., *'Vom Glauben der Kinder im Mutter-Leibe'. Eine historisch-anthropologische Untersuchung frühneuzeitlicher Seelsorge und Frömmigkeit im Zusammenhang mit der Geburt*, Kontexte 31 (Frankfurt am Main: 2000).

to his friends upon his death-bed: as also an elegie, touching his life, death, and burial* (London, George Horton: 1663).

Anonymous, *Groanes from Newgate; OR, AN ELEGY UPON Edvvard Dun Esq: The Cities Common Hangman, who Dyed Naturally in his bed, the 11th. of September* (London, Edward Crowch: 1663).

Luther Martin, *ob man vor dem Sterben fliehen möge* (Wittenberg, Hans Luft: 1527).

Schreiber Michael, *Das in einen Sarg verkehrete Wochen-Bett/ Der Hochwolgebohrnen Frauen/ Fn. Maria Eleonora* (Königsberg, Reusner: 1692).

Thorius Raphael, *Epistola medici Londinensis R.T. de viri celeberrimi Isaaci Casauboni morbi mortisque causa, edita ex museo Joachimi Morsi* (Leiden, Jacobus Marcus: 1619).

Online Edition

Samuel Pepys, The Diary of Samuel Pepys. Daily entries from the 17th century London Diary, published by Phil Gyford, https://www.pepysdiary.com/, last accessed 07/01/2024.

Secondary Literature

Ariès P., *Geschichte des Todes* (Stuttgart: 2015).

Attreed L.C., "Preparation for Death in Sixteenth-Century Northern England", *Sixteenth Century Journal* 13.3 (1982) 37–66.

Bar-Levav A., "Games of Death in Jewish Books for the Sick and the Dying", *Kabbalah: Journal for the Study of Jewish Mystical Texts* 5 (2000) 11–33.

Berger P. – Kroesen J., *Ultimate Ambiguities: Investigating Death and Liminality* (Oxford – New York: 2015).

Brunner B., "Was passiert mit dem 'stinkenden Madensack'? Der Umgang mit dem Tod als Lackmustest der reformatorischen Bestimmung von Leib und Seele", *Theologische Zeitschrift* 76.2 (2020) 164–190.

Brunner B., "York", in *Ortstermine. Umgang mit Differenz in Europa* (Mainz: 2020), URL: http://ieg-differences.eu/ortstermine/benedikt-brunner-york, URN:urn:nbn:de:0159-2020102935.

Casteels I. – Deschryver L. – Soen V., "Divided by Death? Staging Mortality in the Early Modern Low Countries", *Early Modern Low Countries* 5.1 (2021) 1–16.

Casteels I., "Death on Display: Execution Prints on the Eve of the Dutch Revolt", *Nederlands Kunsthistorisch Jaarboek Online / Netherlands Yearbook for History of Art* 72 (2022).

Christ M. – González Gutiérrez C., "Death and the City in Premodern Europe", Special Issue of *Mortality* (2022).

Christ M., "Co-Spatiality in the Early Modern European Bedchamber", in Rau S. – Rüpke J. (eds.), *Religion and Urbanity Online* (Berlin – Boston: 2022). https://doi.org/10.1515/urbrel.17261275.

Cross M.C., "The Third Earl of Huntingdon's Death-Bed: A Calvinist Example of the Ars Moriendi", *Northern History* 21 (1985) 80–107.

Goldberg S.A., *Crossing the Jabbok: Illness and Death in Ashkenazi Judaism in Sixteenth through Nineteenth-Century Prague*, trans. Cosman C. (Berkeley: 1996).

Hallam E.A., "Turning the Hourglass: Gender Relations at the Deathbed in Early Modern Canterbury", *Mortality* 1.1 (1996) 61–82.

Harrington J.F., *The Faithful Executioner: Life and Death in the Sixteenth Century* (London: 2013).

Horowitz E., "The Jews of Europe and the Moment of Death in Medieval and Modern Times", *Judaism* 44 (1995) 271–281.

Houlbrooke R., *Death, Religion and the Family in England, 1480–1750* (Oxford: 1998).

Jarzebwoski C., "Loss and Emotion in Funeral Works on Children in Seventeenth-Century Germany", in Tatlock L. (ed.), *Enduring Loss in Early Modern Germany: Cross Disciplinary Perspectives* (Leiden – Boston: 2008) 187–213.

Kästner A., "Die Ungewissheit überschreiten. Erzählmuster und Auslegungen unverhoffter Todesfälle in Leichenpredigten", in Dickhaut E.-M. (ed.), *Leichenpredigten als Medien der Erinnerungskultur im europäischen Kontext* (Stuttgart: 2014) 147–172.

Kaiser M., "Zwischen 'ars moriendi' und 'ars mortem evitandi'. Der Soldat und der Tod in der Frühen Neuzeit", in idem – Kroll S. (eds.), *Militär und Religiosität in der Frühen Neuzeit* (Münster: 2004) 323–343.

Karant-Nunn S., *The Reformation of Ritual: An Interpretation of Early Modern Germany* (London: 1997).

Koslofsky C., *The Reformation of the Dead: Death and Ritual in Early Modern Germany, c. 1450–1700* (Basingstoke: 2000).

Laqueur T.W., *The Work of the Dead: A Cultural History of Mortal Remains* (Princeton: 2015).

Leppin V., "Die Transformation der mittelalterlichen ars moriendi zur reformatorischen Leichenpredigt", in Deiters M. – Slenczka R. (eds.), *Häuslich – persönlich – innerlich: Bild und Frömmigkeitspraxis im Umfeld der Reformation* (Berlin – Boston: 2020) 165–178.

Luria K.P., "The Embodiment of Truth and Sanctity: Women's Deathbed Conversions and Confessional Conflict in Seventeenth-Century France", *COLLeGIUM: Studies across Disciplines in the Humanities and Social Sciences* 2 (2007) 210–33.

Malone H., "New Life in the Modern Cultural History of Death", *Historical Journal* 62.3 (2019) 833–852.

Marshall P., "After Purgatory: Death and Remembrance in the Reformation World", in Rasmussen T. – Øygarden Flaeten J. (eds.), *Preparing for Death, Remembering the Dead* (Göttingen: 2015) 25–43.

Marshall P. "Angels Around the Deathbed: Variations on a Theme in the English Art of Dying", in idem – Walsham A.M. (eds.), *Angels in the Early Modern World* (Cambridge: 2006) 83–103.

Marshall P. – Walsham A.M. (eds.), *Angels in the Early Modern World* (Cambridge: 2006).

Marshall P., "Was There a Protestant Death?", in Angel S. et al. (eds.), *Were We Ever Protestants? Essays in Honor of Tarald Rasmussen* (Berlin – Boston: 2019) 143–160.

Miert D. van, "The Curious Case of Isaac Casaubon's Monstrous Bladder: The Networked Construction of Learned Memory within the Seventeenth-Century Reformed World of Learning", in Scholten K. – van Miert D. – Enenkel K.A.E., *Memory and Identity in the Learned World: Community Formation in the Early Modern World of Learning and Science*, Intersections 81 (Leiden: 2022) 307–341.

Oetzel L., "Der Tod und die Gesandten. Tod als politischer und persönlicher Faktor auf dem Westfälischen Friedenskongress", *Frühneuzeit-Info* 29 (2018) 75–87.

Overell M.A., "The Exploitation of Francesco Spiera", *The Sixteenth Century Journal* 26.3 (1995) 619–637.

Pesch O.H., "Theologie des Todes bei Martin Luther", in Becker H. – Einig B. – Ullrich P.-O. (eds.), *Im Angesicht des Todes. Ein interdisziplinäres Kompendium*, vol. II, Pietas Liturgica 4 (St. Ottilien: 1987) 709–789.

Rau S., *History, Space and Place* (London: 2019).

Reinis A., *Reforming the Art of Dying: The Ars Moriendi in the German Reformation, 1519–1528* (Aldershot: 2007).

Resch C., *Trost im Angesicht des Todes. Frühe reformatorische Anleitungen zur Seelsorge an Kranken und Sterbenden* (Tübingen – Basel: 2006).

Seeman E.R., "Death in Early America", *History Compass* 17.10 (2019).

Seeman E.R., *Death in the New World: Cross-Cultural Encounters, 1492–1800* (Philadelphia: 2010).

Seeman E.R., "Reading Indians' Deathbed Scenes: Ethnohistorical and Representational Approaches", *Journal of American History* 88.1 (2001) 17–47.

Seeman E.R., *Speaking with the Dead in Early America* (Philadelphia: 2019).

Schlögl R., "Öffentliche Gottesverehrung und privater Glaube in der Frühen Neuzeit. Beobachtungen zur Bedeutung von Kirchenzucht und Frömmigkeit für die Abgrenzung privater Sozialräume", in Melville G. – von Moos P. (eds.), *Das Öffentliche und das Private in der Vormoderne* (Köln – Weimar – Wien: 1998) 165–209.

Schlögl R., "Politik beobachten. Öffentlichkeit und Medien in der Frühen Neuzeit", *Zeitschrift für Historische Forschung* 35.4 (2008) 581–616.

Scholz B.W., *Erzherzog Karl von Österreich (1590–1624), Bischof von Breslau am Vorabend und zu Beginn des Dreißigjährigen Krieges* (Cologne: 2021).

Schottroff L., *Die Bereitung zum Sterben. Studien zu den frühen reformatorischen Sterbebüchern*, Refo500 Academic Studies 5 (Göttingen: 2012).

Struckmeier E., *'Vom Glauben der Kinder im Mutter-Leibe'. Eine historisch-anthropologische Untersuchung frühneuzeitlicher Seelsorge und Frömmigkeit im Zusammenhang mit der Geburt*, Kontexte 31 (Frankfurt am Main: 2000).

Tankard D., "The Reformation of the Deathbed in Mid-Sixteenth-Century England", *Mortality* 8.3 (2003) 251–267.

von Thiessen H., "Das Sterbebett als normative Schwelle. Der Mensch in der Frühen Neuzeit zwischen irdischer Normenkonkurrenz und göttlichem Gericht", *Historische Zeitschrift* 295 (2012) 625–659.

von Thiessen H. – Karsten A. (eds.), *Normenkonkurrenz in historischer Perspektive* (Berlin: 2015).

von Thiessen H., *Das Zeitalter der Ambiguität. Vom Umgang mit Werten und Normen in der Frühen Neuzeit* (Cologne – Weimar – Vienna: 2021).

Vovelle M., *La mort et l'Occident de 1300 à nos jours* (Paris: 1983).

Walsham A., "'The Fatall Vesper': Providentialism and Anti-Popery in Late Jacobean London", *Past and Present* 144 (1994) 36–87.

Walsham A., "The Reformation and the 'Disenchantment of the World' Reassessed", *Historical Journal* 51.2 (2008) 497–528.

Wunderli R. – Broce G., "The Final Moment Before Death in Early Modern England", *Sixteenth Century Journal* 20.2 (1989) 259–275.

PART 1

Approaching the Last Moments

∴

CHAPTER 2

Ambiguity and Authenticity: the 'Good Death' on the Scaffold

Hillard von Thiessen

1 Rodrigo Calderón's Conversion before His Execution as an Act of Authenticity

On the 21st of October 1621, Rodrigo Calderón, a former client of the Duke of Lerma, Philip III's overthrown minister-favourite, was executed in Madrid.[1] He had been found guilty of murder and corruption. Calderón had already been arrested in February 1619 and charged with several crimes. After most of the charges had turned out to be unfounded and lacking evidence, he was expected to be released in the spring of 1621. However, at the end of March, the king died, and with his successor, Philip IV, a new faction with the Count-Duke of Olivares at its centre came into power. They accused Lerma of having led a regime characterised by corruption and political decline. Calderón was the negative symbol of Lerma's reign: he had been the favourite's client and hatchet man and had, with the help of his patron, moved up the social ladder from lower to higher nobility, an ascension which had been accompanied by material and symbolic benefits on a big scale. Due to this advancement, which was commonly regarded as illegitimate, he was hated by many.[2] The new regime under Philip IV, keen to present itself as the opposite of the unpopular

---

1 For Calderón's life and the proceedings against him see: Boyden J.M., "The Worst Death becomes a Good Death: the Passion of Don Rodrigo Calderón", in Gordon B. – Marshall P. (eds.), *The Place of the Dead. Death and Remembrance in Late Medieval and Early Modern Europe* (Cambridge: 2000) 240–265; Diallo K., *La figura de don Rodrigo Calderón a través de la literature (s. 17–21)* (Ph.D. dissertation, Universidad Complutense de Madrid: 2009) 39–45; Juderías J., "Un proceso político en tiempo de Felipe III. Don Rodrigo Calderón, Marqués de Siete Iglesias, Su vida, su proceso y su Muerte", *Revista de Archivos, Bibliotecas y Museos* 13 (1905) 334–365 and 14 (1906) 1–31; Martínez Hernández S., *Rodrigo Calderón. La sombra del valido. Privanza, favor y corrupción en la corte de Felipe III* (Madrid: 2009).
2 For Calderón's role in the system of the Duke of Lerma's reign see: Juderías, "Proceso" 336–364; Martínez Hernández, "Rodrigo Calderón"; von Thiessen H., "Herrschen mit Verwandten und Klienten. Aufstieg und Fall des Herzogs von Lerma, Günstling-Minister Philipps III. von Spanien", in Karsten A. – id. (eds.), *Nützliche Netzwerke und korrupte Seilschaften* (Göttingen: 2006) 181–207, in particular 194–195.

old reign,[3] resumed the proceedings against Calderón, which ended with the death sentence. The public execution of Calderón in the central Plaza Mayor in Madrid was meant to symbolise the monarchy's purification and cleansing of the corrupt regime.

But it turned out differently: 'The worst death becomes a good death', as James M. Boyden sums up the proceedings prior to and during the execution.[4] The crowd did not perceive the execution as an act of political purification but as an exemplary death of an inwardly converted Christian, which completely counteracted the intended political and symbolical effects of the execution. Already Calderón's ride to the place of execution on a black mule became a triumphal procession. The crowd was deeply moved by his exemplary demeanour. The execution was barely over, when even some of Calderón's former enemies hastened to compose eulogies, praising his composure on the scaffold. How did Calderón accomplish this complete change of image from the hated agent of a corrupt regime to a Christian dying in an exemplary manner? He employed a dramatic composition which began on the 9th of July 1621, the day of the proclamation of the sentence, and ended on the day of his execution three and a half months later. In this period, Calderón received religious instruction by Carmelites. He prayed and fasted, read devotional books, only wore plain clothes and grew a beard and long hair as symbols of his newly acquired humility. On the day of the execution, he appeared ostentatiously calm and humble; he staged his role in this drama of the good death with great consistency which did not fail to impress the witnesses of his execution.[5] Indeed, his transformation into a humble sinner, appreciative of God's grace, was considered credible.

In a way, the crowd watching Calderón's decapitation witnessed the result of a conversion – not in the sense of changing from one belief system to another, but as a fundamental transformation of a person or, in other words, as a radical change of identity of an individual who, in the opinion of those watching the change, would finally gain salvation. Within a period of a few months, a sinner obviously condemned to hell had become a candidate for direct access to heaven whose death even bore the features of martyrdom. The poet Luis de Góngora chose the metaphor of the phoenix in a sonnet about Calderón's execution: the seemingly doomed delinquent was reborn in the place of execution and died as a symbol of Christian values and of the power of a fervent

---

3 Elliott J.H., *The Count-Duke of Olivares. The Statesman in an Age of Decline* (New Haven: 1986) 101–115.
4 Boyden, "Death".
5 Boyden, "Death" 254–263.

belief. In other words: Calderón's change of identity before his execution was perceived as authentic – bearing an authenticity that would, in the opinion of many witnesses, convince even God himself.[6]

In this chapter, I will discuss the question of the authenticity of conversion-like changes of identity immediately before death, and indeed necessarily sealed by death. I will do so by contrasting the transformations of delinquents condemned to death from ungodly criminals to poor sinners with conversions from one religious denomination to another. Why were the former often perceived as credible and moved by religious insight – indeed, Calderón's case is not an exception,[7] and I will present another example –, whereas the latter in many cases were suspected of being based on opportunistic instead of religious motives?

"Authenticity" has only quite recently evolved as an analytical term prominent in historical research.[8] It is a multifaceted expression which is used in various contexts.[9] Authenticity, with regard to identity, means a basic attitude of a person towards him- or herself or others. It is revealed in the correlation of a person's way of living and his or her beliefs: an authentic person acts in accordance with the norms he or she regards valid.[10] Authenticity, therefore, is a positive evaluative term which assumes that a person takes a point of view with conviction and acts accordingly. Therefore, antonyms for authenticity are lie, deception and scheming. Thus, to act authentically means to act for the sake of one's own conviction and not based on strategic or opportunistic considerations.[11]

---

6   On the deathbed as a space of authenticity see von Thiessen H., "Das Sterbebett als normative Schwelle. Der Mensch in der Frühen Neuzeit zwischen irdischer Normenkonkurrenz und göttlichem Gericht", *Historische Zeitschrift* 295 (2012) 625–659; for Góngora's sonnet see: Boyden, "Death" 263–264.

7   Martschukat J., *Inszeniertes Töten. Eine Geschichte der Todesstrafe vom 17. bis zum 19. Jahrhundert* (Cologne: 2000) 15–40.

8   See for example the following collections of essays: Lindholm C. (ed.), *Culture and Authenticity* (Malden: 2008); Vannini P. – Williams P.J. (eds.), *Authenticity in Culture, Self, and Society* (Farnham: 2009); Sabrow M. – Saupe A. (eds.), *Historische Authentizität* (Göttingen: 2016); Sabrow M. – Saupe E. (eds.), *Handbuch Historische Authentizität* (Göttingen: 2022).

9   Theodor W. Adorno's employment of this term as an attribute of 'aesthetic modernity' is particularly prominent: Adorno T.W., *Philosophie der neuen Musik* (Frankfurt:1958).

10 Jüngel E., "Wahrhaftigkeit/Authentizität: I. Fundamentaltheologisch", in Betz H.-D. (ed.), *Religion in Geschichte und Gegenwart. Handwörterbuch für Theologie und Religionswissenschaft, Volume 8* (Tübingen: 2005) col. 1242–44, here 1242.

11 Amrein U., "Einleitung", in ead., (ed.), *Das Authentische. Referenzen und Repräsentationen* (Zurich: 2009) 9–24, here 16; Knaller S., "Einleitung", in ead. – Müller H. (eds.), *Authentizität. Diskussion eines ästhetischen Begriffs* (Munich: 2006) 7–16, here 8–9.

Whereas in modern societies a person's authenticity is widely considered to be the self-fulfilment of an individual,[12] this cannot be transferred easily to the early modern period. Furthermore, the term "authenticity" was quite unfamiliar in the early modern period; it is traceable only from the 16th century onwards and was not in general use before the 18th century.[13] Hence, I do use "authenticity" as an analytical term. However, steadfastness, purity, sincerity and honesty are terms frequently appearing in the sources, describing an authentic disposition. They were virtues highly valued in public discourse.[14] Hence, authentic behaviour was demanded in many cases – but was it really expected? For the early modern period was an era of casuistry and of normative ambiguity, of compromising with regard to normative expectations, to religious norms or to political ethics. The daily experience of ambiguity stood against highly strung virtues of authenticity.[15] The question to be answered now therefore is: Why was, in contrast to many cases of religious conversion, the transformation of a criminal convict into a repentant candidate for heaven frequently regarded as authentic, i. e. in accordance with the inner self of a person who had been judged to be a criminal?

2 Conversion and Change of Persona

The conversion of a person condemned to death and the ideal religious conversion have one important feature in common: the concept of fundamental inner change, which can be found in many reports on conversions. That concept is, however, not necessarily an actual description of the process of a change of religion and its motives, but primarily a representation serving as its legitimisation. To represent the conversion in this way fulfils the expectations of the religious group to which the convert is admitted. In these model-like reports the decision to make a basic change is the result of having realised that one had led a life determined by the wrong faith. This stage of insight is

---

12 Kohler G., "Rolle, Maske, Person oder: echt falsch", in Amrein (ed.), *Das Authentische* 198–208, here 198–200; Krückeberg E., "Authentizität", in Ritter J. (ed.), *Historisches Wörterbuch der Philosophie, Volume 1* (Basel: 1971) 692–693, here 693.

13 Knaller S., "Genealogie des ästhetischen Authentizitätsbegriffs", in ead. and Müller H. (eds.), *Authentizität* 17–35, here 18; Saupe A., Historische Authentizität: Individuen und Gesellschaften auf der Suche nach dem Selbst – ein Forschungsbericht, in H-Soz-Kult 2017/08/15 (http://hsozkult.geschichte.hu-berlin.de/forum/2017-08-00).

14 See e. g. John Martin, "Inventing Sincerity, Refashioning Prudence: The Discovery of the Individual in Renaissance Europe", *American Historical Review* 102 (1997) 1309–1342.

15 von Thiessen H., *Das Zeitalter der Ambiguität. Vom Umgang mit Werten und Normen in der Frühen Neuzeit* (Cologne – Weimar – Vienna: 2021).

followed by one of liminality[16] in which the person adjusts to a life characterised by new, fundamentally different values and assumes a new identity. At the end of this phase, which is often marked by dissociation and accompanied by religious instruction, there is a ritual rebirth which accomplishes the integration into the new religious community.[17] While a person willing to convert is instructed by clerics in the fundamental truths of the denomination he or she wishes to adopt,[18] a person condemned to death is expected to sincerely repent his or her sins. Like in the case of a religious conversion, this is achieved by religious instruction and contemplative reflection, thus creating the basic requirements needed to attain salvation. In both cases the conversion represents a clear biographical disruption, which can be seen as, using Heinz-Dieter Kittsteiner's term, a 'change of persona'. This term refers to a one-time act through which a sinner, whose soul is seemingly lost already, becomes a 'saint' who is sure of God's grace.[19]

However, there is one striking difference between the change of religion and the "good death" on the scaffold. The change of religious confession ideally leads to a new phase of earthly life, marked by a new identity. From the point of view of the convert and also of the religious community he or she joins, this change towards a new life was instrumental to the salvation of his or her soul. By contrast, the conversion of a convicted criminal to a humble Christian who hoped for God's grace was sealed with his or her death on the scaffold. The delinquent's death at a specified time was a constitutive element of his or her soul's salvation: The liminal phase came to a definite end in his or her death.

---

16 For liminality see: van Gennep A., *The Rites of Passage* (Chicago: 1960) 26–27 and 113–14.
17 Leone M., *Religious Conversion and Identity. The Semiotic Analysis of Texts* (London: 2004); Pollack D., "Überlegungen zum Begriff und Phänomen der Konversionen aus religionssoziologischer Perspektive", in Lotz-Heumann U. – Mißfelder F. – Pohlig M. (eds.), *Konversion und Konfession in der Frühen Neuzeit* (Heidelberg: 2007) 33–55. For the self in reports of conversions in the early decades after the Reformation see: Bremer K., "Conversus, confirma fratres tuos. Zum 'Ich' in Konversionsberichten in den ersten Jahrzehnten nach der Reformation", *zeitenblicke* 1 (2002), No. 2, http://deposit.ddb.de/ep/netpub/67/20/57/975572067/_data_stat//02/bremer/index.html; Lotz-Heumann U. – Mißfelder F. – Pohlig M., "Ästhetische und rhetorische Strategien: Einführung", in iid. (eds.), *Konversion und Konfession* 425–429. For conversions in an intercultural perspective see Mills K. – Grafton A. (eds.), *Conversion. Old Worlds and New* (Rochester: 2003).
18 von Thiessen H., "Konversionsbereitschaft als Lebensunterhalt. Der Fall der vermeintlichen Konvertitin Catharina Baumännin vor dem Freiburger Stadtgericht (1730/31) und seine Bedeutung für unser Verständnis der Konfessionalisierung", *Zeitschrift des Breisgau-Geschichtsvereins 'Schau-ins-Land'* 119 (2000) 87–101, here 90.
19 Kittsteiner H.-D., "Die Buße auf dem Schafott. Weltliches Urteil und göttliche Gnade im 18. Jahrhundert", in Saurer E. (ed.), *Die Religion der Geschlechter. Historische Aspekte religiöser Mentalitäten* (Vienna: 1995) 213–243, here 222.

It secured his or her inner transformation because death eliminated any possibility of committing more sins in earthly life. Being aware of the exact hour of his death the delinquent could prepare himself, in terms of a variant of the *ars moriendi*,[20] for the "good death". This meant that the converted and therefore purified delinquent could die humbly and piously and therefore deliver a model for other Christians.[21]

The notion of allowing a delinquent the opportunity of a good death was widespread in early modern Europe, among Protestants as well as Catholics.[22] Benedikt Carpzov, the influential Saxon scholar of criminal law, considered a period of at least three days between the proclamation and the execution of the death sentence to be indispensable in order to allow the delinquent to repent, instructed by clerics, and to assume the role of the "poor sinner". If the conversion was not accomplished by the time the execution was scheduled, but the process of transformation of the soul already underway, the execution could be postponed. Secular justice was not allowed to interfere with the workings of divine grace.[23] Many examples show that these guidelines were indeed put into practice.[24]

---

20 For ars moriendi see: Beaty N.L., *The Craft of Dying. A Study in the Literary Tradition of the Ars Moriendi in England* (New Haven: 1970); Imhof A.E., *Ars moriendi. Die Kunst des Sterbens einst und heute*, Vienna: 1991; Mohr R., "Ars moriendi II: 16.–18. Jahrhundert", in Müller G. (ed.), *Theologische Realenzyklopädie, Volume 4* (Berlin: 1979) 149–54; O'Connor M.C., *The Art of Dying Well. The Development of the Ars Moriendi* (New York: 1942); Reinis A., *Reforming the Art of Dying. The "Ars moriendi" in the German Reformation (1519–1528)* (Aldershot: 2007); Rudolf R., *Ars moriendi. Von der Kunst des heilsamen Lebens und Sterbens* (Cologne: 1957); Schottroff L., *Die Bereitung zum Sterben. Studien zu den frühen reformatorischen Sterbebüchern*, (Göttingen: 2012).

21 Kittsteiner, "Buße".

22 Although Calvin's doctrine of predestination rules out a change in the status of salvation on the deathbed as God had already decided the soul's fate at the beginning of time, preparing for a good death as a point of culmination of a Christian life was an important issue in Calvinist pastoring: Blitzel A. "Vom Trost der Erwählung. Wie calvinistische Theologen der frühen Neuzeit vor dem Hintergrund der Lehre von der doppelten Prädestination Seelsorge betrieben", in Lekebusch S. – Ulrichs H.-G. (eds.), *Historische Horizonte. Vorträge der dritten Emder Tagung zur Geschichte des Refromierten Protestantismus* (Wuppertal: 2002) 159–169; Hahn A., "Tod und Sterben in soziologischer Sicht", in Assmann J. – Trauzettel R. (eds.), *Tod, Jenseits und Identität. Perspektiven einer kulturwissenschaftlichen Thanatologie* (Freiburg: 2002) 55–89, here 82; Selderhuis H., "Ars moriendi in Early Modern Calvinism", in Rasmussen T. – Flaeten J.O. (eds.), *Preparing for Death, Remembering the Dead* (Göttingen 2015) 109–122.

23 Carpzov B., *Peinlicher Sächsischer Inquisitions- und Achtsprozess* [...] (Frankfurt – Leipzig: 1638; reprint, St. Ingbert:1996) 185–6. With regard to Carpzov's argumentation see also: Martschukat, *Inszeniertes Töten* 15 and 37–39.

24 Evans R.J., *Rituals of Retribution. Capital Punishment in Germany 1600–1987* (Berlin: 2001) 65–108.

The essential point is that death was not seen as the end of life but as its most important transition, namely the one from the short, earthly life to the eternal one. Thus, death signified the beginning of the second phase of life. Between these two phases, the particular judgment took place where, as was generally accepted by Catholics and Protestants alike, the fate of the soul was decided.[25] This means that the dying person or the delinquent condemned to death was expecting imminently the judgment of his soul's fate by an incorruptible authority – an authority which would no doubt see through a feigned conversion. Hence, the main recipient of the "good death" was God himself. It was *his* judgment the doomed person had to face primarily. The contemporaries were aware of this; therefore, delinquents on the scaffold in most cases were not suspected to have pragmatic reasons for their role play like better treatment or a less cruel execution. Furthermore, it was commonly believed that the scaffold (as well as the deathbed) were places where divine signs could be perceived. If a dying person found the strength to master the good death, he or she did not just accomplish this of his or her own accord, but also because God had given him or her that strength, thereby hinting at a favourable verdict to be expected from the particular judgment.[26] Consequently, the hour of death was a short time of unquestioned authenticity in the life of an early modern person in which the omniscient God sometimes revealed his judgment on the soul of the dying.[27]

---

25   Imhof A.E., "Unsere Lebensuhr. Phasenverschiebungen im Verlaufe der Neuzeit", in Borscheid P. – Teuteberg H.J. (eds.), *Ehe, Liebe, Tod. Zum Wandel der Familie, der Geschlechts- und Generationenbeziehungen in der Neuzeit* (Münster: 1983) 170–198, here 195; Jezler P., "Jenseitsmodelle und Jenseitsvorsorge – eine Einführung", in id. (ed.), *Himmel Hölle Fegefeuer. Das Jenseits im Mittelalter. Eine Ausstellung des schweizerischen Landesmuseums in Zusammenarbeit mit dem Schnütgen-Museum und der Mittelalter-Abteilung des Wallraf-Richartz-Museums der Stadt Köln* (Munich: 1994) 13–26, here 17–18; Kessel M., "Sterben / Tod: Neuzeit", in Dinzelbacher P. (ed.), *Europäische Mentalitätsgeschichte* (Stuttgart: 1993) 260–273, here 261; Wollgast S., *Zum Tod im späten Mittelalter und in der frühen Neuzeit* (Berlin: 1992) 16–17. For Calvinists, according to the concept of predestination, the fate of each soul had been determined by God since the beginning of time.

26   For example, King Philip II's long and torturous, but patiently borne death was interpreted in this manner; consequently, it was documented in detail in publicized reports due to its exemplary and legitimating functions promoting the ideal of sovereign of the Spanish Crown. The king's enemies shared the view that the deathbed was a place of divine signs, but they interpreted the 53 days of illness as divine punishment: Eire C., *From Madrid to Purgatory. The Art and Craft of Dying in Sixteenth-Century Spain* (Cambridge: 1995) 257–366.

27   von Thiessen, "Sterbebett".

3 The Case of Catharina Baumännin

Another example shall illustrate the contrast of the credibility of the converted sinner on the scaffold to that of the religious convert: the execution of Catharina Baumännin on the 5th of January 1731 in Freiburg in the Breisgau.[28] Her case combines religious conversions and the change of persona before an execution. She was charged with having earned her living by committing a kind of conversion fraud for several years while travelling the south-western part of the Holy Roman Empire and the Alsace. Every time she came to a new place, she pretended to be a Jew or Christian of the denomination not practised there, coming from a place at a certain distance, now willing to convert. She was usually lodged at the local rectory, monastery or – in centralised Protestant territories – with the superintendent or court chaplain. There she was instructed in the articles of faith and provided for during that time. Most of the authorities dealing with her were not prepared to believe the sincerity of her intentions without a check. Therefore, in most cases a letter was sent to her alleged hometown to ask whether the statements she had made about her origins were correct. Her trick was to turn this procedure of suspicion to good account for her: she stayed and enjoyed board and lodging for a while, only to slip away before the authorities would receive the answer which revealed her fraud. She did not always manage to escape in time and in two cases, where no verification had taken place, she was baptised a Catholic. Since she had already been baptised a Catholic after her birth, she had received this sacrament of one and the same denomination three times – a repetition which cost her her life in Freiburg, where the authorities had prisoned her. In their survey on this case, the Faculty of Law of the University of Freiburg regarded the repeated reception of baptism a capital offence. The court of the city of Freiburg followed this legal opinion and punished her accordingly.

Catharina Baumännin, facing her imminent death by execution, also performed a fundamental change of roles similar to that of Calderón. At first, she tried to conceal her repeated baptisms, but after they had been revealed, she asked for the vita of a saint who had been converted at an advanced age to lead a pious life afterwards. She received the vita of Margaret of Cortona (ca. 1247–1297), who had been canonised in 1728. That saint was the perfect role model for the delinquent: being of humble birth, she had spent nine years as mistress to a nobleman until he died. Finding his body caused her sudden conversion. She joined the Third Order of St. Francis, lived the isolated life of a

---

28 For the following events see: Stadtarchiv Freiburg, C1 Criminalia 37; see also: von Thiessen, "Konversionsbereitschaft".

recluse for some time, experienced mystic visions and finally engaged in nursing the sick in Cortona.[29] This saint provided the model of a change of persona which Catharina Baumännin tried to emulate during the remaining days before her execution. It turned into a big public event which was commented on at unusual length in the city council reports of Freiburg. Therein, the composure with which she had faced her death sentence as well as her demeanour on the scaffold were praised. According to this report, she had moved the crowd to tears as they were certain to have witnessed an act of God's grace.[30]

Like Calderón, Catharina Baumännin could hope to have achieved a state of grace by means of an immediate fundamental change of roles before her death. She managed to convey an authentic impression of her change of roles. "Authenticity" in this context means that the witnesses of the event were convinced that her change of roles had been undertaken for religious reasons alone, in the knowledge that her particular judgment was imminent, and that it had been successfully achieved with God's help. This means that the delinquent gave the impression of being completely committed to her newly acquired role of the penitent sinner and not just playing it superficially. After the change of persona, her self-image matched the behaviour that was expected of her. One has to take into account that this impression of authenticity was evoked by the behaviour of a woman who had led a life full of fraud, again and again cunningly pretending to wish to change her religious faith. Furthermore, she had lied repeatedly to the judges right until her final change of roles just when there was no escape anymore. In this case, too, the place of execution was seen as a place of divine signs which were considered as proof of the credibility of the conversion. God Himself had pronounced the sentence by showing his mercy and this was sealed with the execution. The imminence of death and of the particular judgment made all the difference.

4   Authenticity and Ambiguity

Catharina Baumännin's change of persona is particularly spectacular, and it is difficult to understand on the basis of a modern concept of authenticity. We tend to be more distrustful of rapid changes of persona than early modern contemporaries were. As mentioned before, in modern discourses of authenticity, individuals are expected to live according to their particular personality, to act in a way consistent with one's core values and with one's character.

---

29   Marchese F., *Vita di Santa Margarita di Cortona* (Venice: 1752).
30   Stadtarchiv Freiburg, B5 XIIIa 135, 788–789.

A fundamental change of persona is a disturbing or at least exceptional feature in such an understanding of human personality. In contrast, in early modern societies, changes of social roles were rather common and indeed were expected to occur quite frequently. Early modern individuals were – at least up to the mid-18th century – not expected to follow the path of self-realisation. In contrast, in a society in which the individual was primarily dependent on groups, it was crucial to reconcile the self to the identity of the group to which one belonged and with the social position one had taken.[31] Early modern individuals were much less constrained by expectations of individual uniqueness than their modern descendants; hence, changes of social roles or switching between them was not or at least to a much lesser extent disturbed by expectations of individual authenticity. Therefore, early modern individuals were much more at ease with accepting changes of social roles, even though they might come abruptly. This explains the general acceptance of role changes in early modern times.

However, early modern individuals were not just living under the expectations of the respective social group to which they belonged. They also had to navigate between different, at times contradictory, normative expectations. From the late medieval period on, the church admonished the faithful, in a more demanding way than ever, to follow religious norms in life in order to avoid hell or a long stay in purgatory; after the Reformation, the competing confessional churches encouraged their flock to comply with the rules of confessionally correct behaviour. On the other hand, the rising states increasingly regulated the scope of action of their subjects. In the early modern period, both state and church gained authority, created and wrote rules, demanded their observance and built up means and forces to impose order.[32] This process has been described in German historiography as "Sozialdisziplinierung" ("social disciplining"), a concept which nevertheless overestimated the disciplinary forces of church and state as well as the result of the disciplining process: before the mid-18th century at least, no society of thoroughly disciplined confessionalized Christians and obedient subjects had been created. Belonging to a Christian confessional church and believing in fundamental elements of doctrine was a self-evident matter of fact for most early modern

---

31   Davis N.Z., "Boundaries and the Sense of the Self in Sixteenth-Century France", in Heller T.C. – Sosna M. – Wellbery D.E. (eds.), *Reconstructing Individualism. Autonomy, Individuality, and the Self in Western Thought* (Stanford/CA: 1986) 53–63.

32   von Thiessen H., "Normenkonkurrenz. Handlungsspielräume, Rollen, normativer Wandel und normative Kontinuität vom späten Mittelalter bis zum Übergang zur Moderne", in Karsten A. – von Thiessen H. (eds.), *Normenkonkurrenz in historischer Perspektive* (Berlin: 2015) 241–286, here 255–265.

individuals, and political power exercised by princes and a number of republics was generally accepted as part of God's order. However, this does not mean that subjects or citizens were just obeying orders from those who governed them in a top-down manner. In contrast, political rule meant constant negotiation between the governing and the governed; the subjects therefore were producers of political norms as well and communicated to their authorities what they expected from them and what they regarded as politically legitimate and viable.[33] Accordingly, the confessional churches tended to listen carefully to the expectations of their flock; the faithful tended to follow religiously legitimised rules of conduct selectively.[34]

Consequently, the result of the rise of normative demands of social, religious and political origins was not a thoroughly disciplined society. Quite the contrary, disciplinary demands from different sources and contradictions between them resulted in cultural ambiguity. In many aspects of life, compromises had to be made between social, religious and political norms. If, for example, the honour of a person was in question, that person was expected to defend his reputation in order to avoid a loss of honour and social standing. If necessary, this had to be done with force, even though such a reaction violated both Christian norms as well as law and order. Everyday life in a constellation of coexistent, and partly competing norms meant, for most early modern actors, practicing casuistry, which meant to live in a way that secured social reputation and that would not accrue too many serious sins in order to uphold the prospect of Eternal Life. Consequently, life required frequent changes or combinations of social roles: as a family member, a neighbour, a confessionalized Christian, a loyal subject – and finally as a Christian awaiting death and leaving worldly ambiguity behind.[35]

With regard to conversions, those changing confession were expected to play the role of the sincere and convinced Christian who had realised an error in his beliefs and therefore turned to the religion he, with the help of God, finally recognised as the true one. Converts had to play that role which implied

---

[33] Brakensiek S., "Akzeptanzorientierte Herrschaft. Überlegungen zur politischen Kultur der Frühen Neuzeit", in Neuhaus H. (ed.), *Die Frühe Neuzeit als Epoche* (Munich: 2009) 395–406; Holenstein A., "Introduction: Empowering Interactions. Looking at Statebuilding from Below", in Blockmans W. – Holenstein A. – Mathieu J. (eds.), *Empowering Interactions. Political Cultures and the Emergence of the State in Europe 1300–1900* (Aldershot: 2009) 1–31; Weber N., "Praktiken des Verhandelns – Praktiken des Aushandelns. Zur Differenz und Komplementarität zweier politischer Interaktionsmodi am Beispiel der preußischen Monarchie im 18. Jahrhundert", in Brendecke A. (ed.), *Praktiken in der Frühen Neuzeit. Akteure – Handlungen – Artefakte* (Cologne – Weimar – Vienna 2015) 560–570.

[34] von Thiessen, *Zeitalter* 61.

[35] von Thiessen, *Zeitalter*.

the discourse of a fundamental change of persona in order to be accepted by their new religious community and its social networks and to claim the sincerity and authenticity of their motives – meaning that they asserted to have changed confession for religious reasons only.[36] Early modern contemporaries knew from their own experience of living in a society of ambiguity that the credibility of this very claim was rather implausible for many.[37] It was implausible in a society, where orientation on just one class of norms (in this case, religious norms) was rare. It might be obvious that a conversion was administered with the aim of a marriage or of gaining patronage or getting an income, but for the members of the receiving confession it was essential to be presented with a display of sincerity – a sincerity that was nonetheless open to attack from members of the confession the convert left. The argument that the conversion was done primarily out of opportunistic (i.e., non-religious) motives, whether right or wrong, was almost always more or less plausible in a world marked by the concurrence of norms and roles.[38]

Furthermore, the integration of converts into a new social environment was accompanied by the termination of old social relationships and religious practices to a far lesser extent than has generally been assumed. In everyday dealings the confessional border was blurred and religiously hybrid practices remained possible, if not the rule.[39] On this account, Kim Siebenhüner has suggested to consider the 'border' between the religious denominations as a

---

36 Horowski L., "Konfession und dynastische Strategie: Turenne und das Ende des französischen Hochadelscalvinismus", in Lotz-Heumann – Mißfelder – Pohlig (eds.), *Konversion und Konfession* 171–211, here 206; Lotz-Heumann – Mißfelder – Pohlig, "Strategien" 427; Schunka A., "Transgressionen: Revokationspredigten von Konvertiten im mitteldeutschen Raum im 17. Jahrhundert", in Lotz-Heumann – Mißfelder – Pohlig (eds.), *Konversion und Konfession* 491–516.

37 Deventer J., "'Zu Rom übergehen'. Konversion als Entscheidungshandlung und Handlungsstrategie. Ein Versuch", in Leeb R. – Pils S.C – Winkelbauer T. (eds.), *Staatsmacht und Seelenheil. Gegenreformation und Geheimprotestantismus in der Habsburgermonarchie* (Vienna – Munich: 2007) 168–180, here 176–178.

38 Lotz-Heumann U. – Mißfelder F. – Pohlig M., "Religiöse Authentizität und Politik: Einführung", in iid. (eds.), *Konversion und Konfession* 59–61, here 59. See also Mißfelder J.F., "Die allzu politische Konversion des Duc de Lesdiguières. Zur diskursiven Produktion von Aufrichtigkeit", in Pietsch A. – Stollberg-Rilinger B. (eds.), *Konfessionelle Ambiguität. Uneindeutigkeit und Verstellung als religiöse Praxis in der Frühen Neuzeit* (Heidelberg: 2013) 170–182.

39 Grochowina N., "Bekehrung und Indifferenz in Ostfriesland im 16. Jahrhundert", in Lotz-Heumann – Mißfelder – Pohlig (eds.), *Konversion* 243–270; Kooi C., "Converts and Apostates. The Competition for Souls in Early Modern Holland", *Archiv für Reformationsgeschichte* 92 (2001) 195–214; Luria K.P., *Sacred Boundaries. Religious Coexistence and Conflict in early-modern France* (Washington, D.C.: 2005); Pollmann J., "A Different Road to God. The Protestant Experience of Conversion in the Sixteenth Century",

contact zone rather than a separative gulf.[40] She points out: 'The normative guidelines of clerical authorities often did not or only partially correspond to the convert's faith'.[41] Fulfilling the role of a sincere convert in the act of conversion in most cases did not induce a life characterised by confessional zeal. The act of conversion from one denomination to another was followed by life in a normatively ambiguous society. In contrast, criminals sentenced to death imminently expected to be judged by a completely unambiguous and incorruptible authority. This prospect made all the difference with regard to the credibility and authenticity of a change of persona.

To conclude, in the ambiguous normative horizon of early modern society, changes of roles and identities were an everyday matter and did not collide with expectations of individual authenticity. However, in mundane life it was difficult to follow exclusively one normative system. This was a path open only to a few normative overachievers like mendicants or, in Protestantism, Pietists for example.[42] The common sinners were bound to follow the path of pragmatism and casuistry. Whilst in modern societies individual authenticity is regarded by many as an achievable and desirable goal, most early modern individuals, regarding themselves and most of their contemporaries as moderate sinners, lacked this optimism in a world tainted by original sin. In that world, the core dilemma of conversions – i.e., that converts had to display a sincerity which was almost always questionable – could only be evaded successfully immediately before death. On the brink of death, an exclusive and pure orientation towards religious norms was plausible in light of the imminent judgment of God. Criminals sentenced to death could exploit the knowledge of the hour of their death in order to accomplish a change of persona which was convincing because they were in the liminal situation of leaving the mortal world, characterized by a plurality of norms and roles, and heading to

in van der Veer P. (ed.), *Conversion and Modernities. The Globalization to Christianity* (New York – London: 1996) 47–64.

40   Siebenhüner K., "Glaubenswechsel in der Frühen Neuzeit. Chancen und Tendenzen einer historischen Konversionsforschung", in *Zeitschrift für historische Forschung* 34 (2007) 243–272, 250f. Also see the collective volume: von Greyerz K. – Jakubowski-Tiessen M. – Kaufmann T. – Lehmann H. (eds.), *Interkonfessionalität – Transkonfessionalität – binnenkonfessionelle Pluralität. Neue Forschungen zur Konfessionalisierungsthese* (Gütersloh: 2003).

41   ,Dem normativen Vorgehen kirchlich-religiöser Obrigkeiten entsprach der Glaube der Konvertiten oft gar nicht oder nur partiell'. Siebenhüner, "Glaubenswechsel" 262.

42   See for an example of a protestant overachiever Schwerhoff G., "Transzendenz ohne Gemeinsinn. Ein religiöser 'Übererfüller' im 17. Jahrhundert", in Brodocz A. – Hermann D. – Schmidt R. – Schulz D. – Schulze Wessel J. (eds.), Die Verfassung des Politischen. Festschrift für Hans Vorländer (Wiesbaden: 2014) 45–62.

the transcendent world where deception would inevitably be uncovered. This particular prospect created a moment of sincerity hardly to be gained in the earthly world. In a world marked by ambiguity and concurrence of norms, the moment of death was a rare time of authenticity.

Bibliography

Amrein U. (ed.), *Das Authentische. Referenzen und Repräsentationen* (Zurich: 2009).

Boyden J.M., "The Worst Death becomes a Good Death: the Passion of Don Rodrigo Calderón", in Gordon B. – Marshall P. (eds.), *The Place of the Dead. Death and Remembrance in Late Medieval and Early Modern Europe* (Cambridge: 2000) 240–65.

Davis N.Z., "Boundaries and the Sense of the Self in Sixteenth-Century France", in Heller T.C. – Sosna M. – Wellbery D.E. (eds.), *Reconstructing Individualism. Autonomy, Individuality, and the Self in Western Thought* (Stanford/CA: 1986) 53–63.

Eire C., *From Madrid to Purgatory. The Art and Craft of Dying in Sixteenth-Century Spain* (Cambridge: 1995).

Elliott J.H., *The Count-Duke of Olivares. The Statesman in an Age of Decline* (New Haven: 1986).

Imhof A.E., *Ars moriendi. Die Kunst des Sterbens einst und heute*, Vienna: 1991.

Kessel M., "Sterben / Tod: Neuzeit", in Dinzelbacher P. (ed.), *Europäische Mentalitätsgeschichte* (Stuttgart: 1993) 260–73.

Kittsteiner H.-D., "Die Buße auf dem Schafott. Weltliches Urteil und göttliche Gnade im 18. Jahrhundert", in Saurer E. (ed.), *Die Religion der Geschlechter. Historische Aspekte religiöser Mentalitäten* (Vienna: 1995) 213–43.

Knaller S. – Müller H. (eds.), *Authentizität. Diskussion eines ästhetischen Begriffs* (Munich: 2006).

Leone M., *Religious Conversion and Identity. The Semiotic Analysis of Texts* (London: 2004).

Lindholm C. (ed.), *Culture and Authenticity* (Malden: 2008).

Lotz-Heumann U. – Mißfelder F. – Pohlig M. (eds.), *Konversion und Konfession in der Frühen Neuzeit* (Heidelberg: 2007).

Luria K.P., *Sacred Boundaries. Religious Coexistence and Conflict in early-modern France* (Washington, D.C.: 2005).

Martschukat J., *Inszeniertes Töten. Eine Geschichte der Todesstrafe vom 17. bis zum 19. Jahrhundert* (Cologne: 2000).

Mills K. – Grafton A. (eds.), *Conversion. Old Worlds and New* (Rochester: 2003).

Pietsch A. – Stollberg-Rilinger B. (eds.), *Konfessionelle Ambiguität. Uneindeutigkeit und Verstellung als religiöse Praxis in der Frühen Neuzeit* (Heidelberg: 2013).

Sabrow M. – Saupe E. (eds.), *Handbuch Historische Authentizität* (Göttingen: 2022).

Sabrow M. – Saupe A. (eds.), *Historische Authentizität* (Göttingen: 2016).

Siebenhüner K., "Glaubenswechsel in der Frühen Neuzeit. Chancen und Tendenzen einer historischen Konversionsforschung", in *Zeitschrift für historische Forschung* 34 (2007) 243–272.

von Thiessen H., "Das Sterbebett als normative Schwelle. Der Mensch in der Frühen Neuzeit zwischen irdischer Normenkonkurrenz und göttlichem Gericht", *Historische Zeitschrift* 295 (2012) 625–659.

von Thiessen H., *Das Zeitalter der Ambiguität. Vom Umgang mit Werten und Normen in der Frühen Neuzeit* (Cologne – Weimar – Vienna: 2021).

Van Gennep A., *The Rites of Passage* (Chicago: 1960).

Vannini P. – Williams P.J. (eds.), *Authenticity in Culture, Self, and Society* (Farnham: 2009).

CHAPTER 3

Privacy in Death? Early Modern French Accounts of Death and Huguenots' *Last Hours*

Michaël Green

1 Introduction*

> Je m'en vay a ton Dieu, & a mon Dieu, Nous avons tout gagné Amen, Ainsi soit il, Adieu mon Filz. Adieu ma chere Niepce. Ne craignez point, jay prie pour vous, Vous serez tous bien-heureux.[1]
>
> I am going to your God, & to my God, we have gained everything, Amen, so be it, farewell my Son. Farewell my dear Niece. Do not be afraid, I have prayed for you, you will all be blessed [...].

The passage above recounts the last words of André Rivet (1572–1651), a prominent Huguenot theologian, Professor at the University of Leiden and a close friend of the Stadtholder Frederik Hendrik of Holland (1584–1647). The description goes on to portray his last moments, and the reader learns that the room in which he lies is full of people coming and going. We see his wife, his son and niece, his pastor, his household members, and possibly others who are not named. It is hard to imagine a more public way to die – in full view of everybody. Or so it seems at first glance. Yet, was it indeed so? Can we speak of "privacy in death" when one is surrounded by so many people? In the following pages, I will argue that this was very much the case: I will demonstrate based on several other examples that this public death was in fact very much private.

There is no fully developed methodology that allows us to trace instances of privacy for the early modern period. Mette Birkedal Bruun suggests using

---

* The writing of this article has been supported by National Centre for Science of Poland Grant Miniatura 6, #2022/06/X/HS3/00697, which was conducted at the University of Lodz. The various sources I found during my archival research for this project, allowed me to get a better understanding of the sources examined here. I am grateful to the editors of this volume for inviting me to reflect on two of my research specialisations: history of early modern privacy and Huguenot intellectual history.

1 Du Moulin Marie, *Les dernières heures de Monsieur Rivet vivant Docteur & Professeur honoraire en l'Université de Leyden, & Currateur de l'Eschole Illustre, & College d'Orange à Breda* (Breda, Jean Waesberguf: 1651) 81.

heuristic zones of privacy as a tool to navigate through the early modern world in order to pinpoint such instances, when talking about soul/mind, body, chamber/bedroom, house/household, community and state.[2] Privacy instances can be traced where these zones overlap, when for example members of the household observe the bedroom, or when the state imposes a certain religion on its entire population. I further supplement these zones with those relating to the realm of personal relationships – couple, family, friends, and colleagues.[3] One could also include God as a privacy category: for example, in Christianity each of the entities of the Trinity is God, and is separate.[4] One indeed has a very private relationship with God, who is always there, omnipresent, so that the person is never actually alone.

Finally, to have a working definition of what could be considered private, I will use the definition of Stephen T. Margulis, which speaks of regulating access by an individual to him or herself.[5] I extend this idea also to a community, which can regulate access to itself by various means, such as making itself difficult to join, or expelling its members. This is often the case with religious communities, such as for example the Jews.[6] In the case of the French-speaking Calvinists, better known by their nickname Huguenots, community seemingly was less private than was the case for the Jews, who traditionally did not welcome gentiles to participate in, or even witness, their prayers. For the Huguenots, their community was a safe place, communal prayers were common, and the community provided strong support for its members. This was especially important because persecution was rampant in France. It was through the community that the members managed to escape into the neighbouring United Provinces, the Reformed German States, England, Switzerland and beyond.[7]

---

2 Birkedal Bruun M., 'Towards an Approach to Early Modern Privacy: The Retirement of the Great Condé', in Green M. – Nørgaard L.C. – Birkedal Bruun M. (eds.) *Early Modern Privacy: Sources and Approaches* (Leiden: 2022) 12–60.

3 Read more in Green M. – Huysman I., in collaboration with Bakić J. – Klein Käfer N. "The Low Countries, Private Life, and Privacy", in Green M. – Huysman I. (eds.), *Private Life and Privacy in the Early Modern Low Countries* (Turnhout: 2023) 13–26.

4 I would like to thank Jonas Kjøller-Rasmussen from the University of Copenhagen for this suggestion.

5 Margulis S.T., "Privacy as a Social Issue and Behavioral Concept", *Journal of Social Issues* 59/2 (2003) 243–261.

6 More on the Jewish community and its privacy practices is in Green M., *An Interreligious Dialogue: Portrayal of Jews in Dutch French-Language Periodicals (1680–1715)* (Lodz – Cracow: 2022); Green M., "Privacy in Jewish Egodocuments of Amsterdam (1600–1830)", in Green M. – Nørgaard L.C. – Birkedal Bruun M. (eds.), *Early Modern Privacy: Sources and Approaches* (Leiden – Boston: 2022) 213–242.

7 Yardeni M., *Le refuge protestant* (Paris: 1985); Yardeni M., *Le refuge huguenot: Assimilation et culture* (Paris: 2002); Stanwood O., *The Global Refuge: Huguenots in an Age of Empire* (Oxford: 2020).

In the United Provinces of the Netherlands, it was through the so-called Walloon Churches, i.e. Reformed churches established by the first wave of refugees from the Southern Netherlands and French after the St. Bartholomew's Day massacre in 1572, that help for Huguenots was provided. This continued to be the case until the second massive wave of refugees following the revocation of the Edict of Nantes in 1685 by Louis XIV.[8] In this article, we will examine several important Huguenots whose last days and minutes were recorded, both in France and in the United Provinces.

2   The Last Hours

The last moments of a famous person were quite often recorded, and frequently bore the French title "Les dernières heures" (The last hours). The records we will examine date from the late sixteenth to late seventeenth centuries. The structure of these texts is quite often the same. It starts with a major event, either the outbreak of an illness (as in the case of Rivet) or the signing of a testament (as in the case of Duplessis-Mornay, which we will examine below). The illness progresses, and the person usually retires to bed to suffer under unsuccessful medical treatment, all the while performing acts of devotion and piety in front of family and friends. At this time the dying person, severely ill, suddenly gets the strength to engage in very long conversations and discussions about death and the nature of the Reformed religion, all in preparation for passing into the better world. In the third stage, the situation of the person worsens, and he or she is expected to die. At this point there is usually one more expression of the person's piety. The family usually comes to bid the dying farewell and receives their last blessings. In the fourth stage, the person actually dies; the hour and the circumstances are recorded, often with an account of those who were present at his or her death.[9]

---

8   On the Huguenot refuge in the United Provinces, see van Ruymbeke B. – Sparks R.J. (eds.), *Uncertain Brotherhood: The Huguenots in the Dutch Republic* (Columbia, SC: 2003).

9   Barros P. et al. (eds.), *Prêcher la mort à l'époque moderne: Regards croisés sur la France et l'Angleterre* (Paris: 2020); Lahtinen A. – Korpiola M. (eds.), *Dying Prepared in Medieval and Early Modern Northern Europe* (Leiden – Boston: 2018); Wunderli R. – Broce G., "The Final Moment before Death in Early Modern England", *The Sixteenth Century Journal* 20/2 (1989) 259–275. See also: Regent-Susini A., "How to Make Exemplarity with Secret Virtues: Funeral Sermons and Their Challenges in Early Modern France", in Green – Nørgaard – Bruun (eds.), *Early Modern Privacy* 179–193; Nørgaard L.C., "Making Private Public: Representing Private Devotion in an Early Modern Funeral Sermon", in Ibidem 378–400.

It is not my goal here to judge the reliability of the accounts of death, the words said, or the actions performed. What is important for this study is the death itself, its circumstances, spatial location, the people present and how they were connected with each other. In the following, I will analyse three accounts one by one, while reconstructing the network that is made visible from the account of those who witnessed the last hours of the deceased.

3   Philippe Duplessis-Mornay (1549–1623)

The first treatise that I would like to address is that recounting the last hours of Philippe Duplessis-Mornay. He was one of the major French Protestant figures of the second half of the sixteenth century, known as the "Pope of the Huguenots". While a military commander, associated with Henry de Bourbon (1553–1610), king of Navarre and future King Henry IV of France, he also promoted education and scholarship and was behind the establishment of the Huguenot Academy of Saumur. An author in his own right, he wrote essays on ecclesiastical matters.[10] As such, he served as an example to other prominent Huguenots and therefore it is not surprising that an account of his last hours was written. As Hugues Daussy asserts, it was Jean Daillé (1594–1670) who undertook the task of writing this record, probably because of his familiarity with the man, whose two granddaughters he tutored. The booklet was published a year after Duplessis's death, in 1624.[11] This account is the shortest of the three accounts under consideration in this article, comprising only eighteen pages (without dedication) in the eighteenth-century edition.[12]

The text begins with an opening event pointing to the approaching death of Duplessis-Mornay: on 24 October 1623 he wrote his "Codicile", which was a kind of testament containing his last wishes. It took over ten days to accomplish and

[10]   Among his publications are: *De la verité de la religion Chrestienne: contre les Athées, Epicuriens, Payens, Juifs, Mahumedistes, & autres Infidels* (Antwerpen, Christofle Plantin: 1581); *De sacra evcharistia, in qvatuor libros* (Hanover, Claude Marnius: 1605).

[11]   Daussy H., *Les huguenots et le roi: combat politique de Philippe Duplessis-Mornay (1572–1600)* (Geneva: 2002) 245 n. 88.

[12]   Daillé J., "Des dernières heures de Mr. Du Plessis", in Salchi J.J. (ed.), *Recueil des dernières heures de Messieurs de Mornay du Plessis, Gigord, Rivet, Du Moulin, Drelincourt & Fabri, nouvelle edition augmentée d'un Discours premininaire sur l'utilité de cet ouvrage, & sur le fondement de nôtre Salut & de nos espérances dans la vie & dans la mort* (1725), 4 pages of unpaginated introduction, 1–18. An exemplar of the original publication from 1624 is located in the British Library, under shelf mark General Reference Collection 3900.aa.40. (2.). For the convenience of the reader, references here will be made to the 1725 edition, which is easily accessible online and is not different in its content from the original one.

FIGURE 3.1 Gaultier Leonard, "Portret of Philippe du Plessis-Mornay at the age of 62 [1611]", engraving, 1611–1641
©RIJKSMUSEUM AMSTERDAM. OBJ. NUM. RP-P-1920-1732

it was only on 3 November that he finally signed it, saying that he was 'décharge d'un grand souci, et désormais il ne me reste plus qu'à mourir' ('relieved of a great worry, and now all that is left for me is to die').[13] The next day he developed a fever and was put to bed, and by 9 November his condition was declared hopeless. This also resulted in a close monitoring of these "last" hours by the author. Indeed, he states that '[d]epuis ce tems là Dieu nous le laisse encore pendant quarante-huit heures, qu'il ménagea si bien à penser à soi même et à son salut [...]' ('since that moment God leaves him to us for another forty-eight hours, which he spends so well to reflect upon himself and his salvation').[14]

What do we learn about his entourage during this period? Who were the people present near him and who interacting with him? On 9 November, Madame de Villarnoül (his daughter with Charlotte Albaleste (1548–1606), whom he had married in 1576) came by and having been informed about his condition remained there in silence. Duplessis-Mornay demanded to talk, probably about things that were on his mind at the time, and a pastor of the Reformed church was sent to prepare him for his death. According to Daillé, this pastor was in a very disturbed mood and rough in his ways, but Duplessis was firm and determined. However, the narrator states that he had difficulty speaking, although this did not prevent him from testifying about his faith and other matters.[15] We see here that he was certainly not dying alone. We have identified two people present: Madame de Villarnoül and the unnamed pastor, who could have been Daillé himself.

Soon afterwards, Duplessis-Mornay blessed his daughters and his sons-in-law, i.e., the aforementioned Marthe de Villarnoül and her husband Jean de Jaucourt, Elisabeth and her husband Jacques de Saint-Germain, and Anne and her husband Jacques de Nouhes de La Tabarière.[16] Besides them, he also gave his blessing to his immediate family, his "domestiques", i.e., members of his household, his "nephew" (as Daillé puts it) who was in fact his brother-in-law – Anthony de Sendchal, seigneur d'Auberville – and his wife, Françoise de Mornay, Duplessis-Mornay's sister. He also blessed the pastor who informed him of his approaching death and was taking care of the preparations for his departure. Further blessings were bestowed upon his

---

13 Ibidem, 1. Orthography of the original texts is kept throughout the article.
14 Ibidem, 1–2.
15 Ibidem, 3.
16 Ibidem, 5; Kuperty-Tsur N., "Charlotte Arbaleste", *Dictionnaire des femmes de l'Ancien Régime*, 2003. Online edition. [Accessed 1 September 2022. <http://siefar.org/dictionnaire/fr/Charlotte_Arbaleste >].

physician Mr. Dissaudean[17] and, *in absentia*, Samuel Bouchereau (1600–1630), the Huguenot minister from Saumur, as well as the churches of Saumur and St. Jovin located near Duplessis-Mornay's home. Saumur Academy was founded by Duplessis-Mornay in 1600 and Samuel Bouchereau was its first rector until his death in 1630; this blessing of course shows the importance of this institution for its founder.[18]

While Duplessis-Mornay was dying, the pastor administering pastoral care took upon himself the role of secretary and wrote letters with his blessing to his various acquaintances.[19] This demonstrates the close relationship the two had and strengthens the assumption that Daillé himself was the pastor in question. However, death was slowly approaching, and in the afternoon, 'on l'entendit prier en particulier & dire d'une voix entrecoupée, *Je vole, je vole au ciel* [...]' ('we heard him praying in private and saying in a broken voice, *I am flying, I am flying to heaven*').[20] The pastor approached to console and calm him. According to Merlin-Kajman, French words such as "particulier" refer directly to the private domain, meaning that Duplessis-Mornay prayed without anyone participating in his prayer, thus in private.[21] This is contrary to the Huguenot idea of communal prayer that was meant to unite the community by being said together, along with singing the Psalms in unison.[22] It was probably Duplessis's conscious decision to pray in private, as his family and friends were nearby. Therefore, we can see that although the dying person was surrounded by many people, there was still time for private prayer. Yet this idea of "private" differs from what we would consider to be private nowadays; Duplessis-Mornay was overheard in his prayer to such an extent that his words were recorded, yet for a person in the seventeenth century being heard did not always mean that there was no privacy. On some occasions, a visual separation between the person and others would have been sufficient to create this private space.[23] Here we also see that Duplessis-Mornay was looking forward to being reunited with his Creator, in a way that can also be seen as private: he would not be solitary, he would be with God. At the same time, the fact that it

---

17   It has been impossible to trace any information about him.
18   Samuel Bouchereau is the author of *Disputationum theologicarum tertia de essentia Dei et attributis illius* (Leiden: 1602).
19   Daillé, "Des dernières heures de Mr. Du Plessis" 6–10.
20   Ibidem.
21   Merlin-Kajman H., "'Privé' and 'Particulier' (and Other Words) in Seventeenth-Century France", in Green, Nørgaard, Bruun (eds.), *Early Modern Privacy* 79–104.
22   Wheeler K.J.-L., "Rabaut Saint-Étienne and the Huguenot Fight for Religious Freedom", in Messer P.C. – Taylor W.H., *Revolution as Reformation: Protestant Faith in the Age of Revolutions, 1688–1832* (Tuscaloosa, Al.: 2021) 96–112, here 97.
23   Green M., "Sex and Privacy: The Case of Hans Barhow (1704–1754)", currently in review.

was noted in the account of his last hours demonstrates that this act of praying alone also had public symbolism – to set an example to his followers, but also to present him as a pious believer.

Next, we learn that at midnight Duplessis-Mornay was no longer able to speak, at two o'clock in the morning he was no longer able to hear, and between six and seven o'clock in the morning he stopped breathing.[24] Daillé stresses that during the forty-eight hours preceding his death, Duplessis-Mornay did not suffer. He spent his time on discussions on salvation.

If one considers early modern notions of privacy and the story of the last hours of Duplessis-Mornay, there are several aspects to note. I have already mentioned above the most obvious – the linguistic reference to privacy with the word "particulier", which points to Duplessis praying in private. Yet this is the only such reference. When we look at his entourage in the final days, we see that it consisted of close family – his daughters, their husbands, the pastor, also Moris de Bressuire his Catholic doctor, and members of his household. When considering privacy, besides remembering that everyone was gathered in the house of the dying, we should also keep in mind interpersonal connections. The people present were all part of Duplessis-Mornay's inner circle – his family and friends, those whom the dying man knew and possibly invited or allowed to be present or, to use Margulis's definition, allowed to have access to him. This point will be clarified with our second account, that of the last hours of André Rivet.

4   André Rivet (1572–1651)

André Rivet was perhaps one of the best-known Huguenot theologians residing in the United Provinces in the first half of the seventeenth century. After studying theology, he became pastor to the Duke de La Trémouille in the city of Thouars. Because of his scholarly reputation, he was invited to the University of Leiden, where he became professor in 1620, and in 1632 was appointed head tutor to Prince Willem II of Orange (1626–1650), the son of the stadtholder of Holland, Frederik Hendrik (1584–1647). He was a prolific writer whose theological thought influenced his contemporaries and corresponded with many prominent scholars of his time, such as Claude Saumaise. His proximity to the princely family, to the stadtholder Frederik Hendrik and then his son Willem II, made him also an important political figure. Overall, he was held in

---

24   Daillé, "Des dernières heures de Mr. Du Plessis" 15–16.

FIGURE 3.2 Dagen Henrick Rochuszn van, "Portret of André Rivet", engraving, 1644–1652
© RIJKSMUSEUM AMSTERDAM. INV. NUM. RP-P-1905-2036

high regard both by his French Reformed compatriots and by his Dutch peers, which explains why an account of his last hours was written.[25]

The author of *Récit des dernières heures de Monsieur Rivet* is Marie du Moulin (1622–1699), who was the daughter of the Huguenot minister Pierre du Moulin (1568–1658) (whose last hours were also authored by her, and which we will discuss below). She was André Rivet's niece-in-law through Rivet's wife Marie, who was Pierre du Moulin's sister from the second marriage of his father to Guillaumette d'Avrigny. Marie du Moulin was a scholar in her own right, who corresponded with other writers such as Anna Maria van Schurman (1607–1678),[26] Madelaine de Scudéry (1607–1701)[27] and Valentin Conrart (1603–1675).[28] Although she did not publish the text under her own name, according to Carol Pal, 'Marie's status as the author of these works was an open secret in the republic of letters; their authorship was veiled with a

---

[25] There is no recent biography of André Rivet, but two older works give a good overview of his life: Opstal A.G., *André Rivet: Een invloedrijk hugenoot aan het hof van Frederik Hendrik* (Harderwijk: 1937); Honders H.J., *Andreas Rivetus als invloedrijk gereformeerd theoloog in Hollands bloeitijd* (The Hague: 1930). His educational work is explored in my articles: Green M. – Nørgaard L.C. – Birkedal Bruun M., "*En privé & en public*: The Epistolary Preparation of the Dutch Stadtholders", *Journal of Early Modern History* 24 (2020) 253–279; Green M., "The Orange-Nassau family at the educational crossroads of the Stadholder's position (1628–1711)", *Dutch Crossing: Journal of Low Countries Studies* 43/2 (2019) 99–126. See also Strickland F.C., "Building a Library in the Dutch Golden Age: André Rivet and His Books", in der Weduwen A. – Pettegree A. – Kemp G. (eds.), *Book Trade Catalogues in Early Modern Europe*, Library of the Written Word 93 (Leiden – Boston: 2021) 161–192.

[26] Anna Maria van Schurman is one of the most renowned Dutch female scholars. She is considered to be the first female university student in the United Provinces, having been allowed to attend Utrecht University. She was part of a circle of more radical devotees around the mystic Antoinette Bourignon and others. See: de Baar M. – Loewenstein M. – Monteiro M. – Sneller A.A., *Choosing the better part. Anna Maria van Schurman (1607/1678)* (Dordrecht – Boston – London: 1996); de Baar M., "'En onder het hennerot het haantje zoekt te blijven': de betrokkenheid van vrouwen bij het huisgezin van Jean de Labadie, 1669–1732", *Vrouwenlevens 1500–1800. Achtste jaarboek voor vrouwengeschiedenis* (Nijmegen: 1987) 11–43; Aronson N., *Mademoiselle de Scudéry* (Boston: 1978); Albrecht R., "Konfessionsprofil und Frauen: Anna Maria van Schurman (1607–1678) und Antoinette Bourignon (1616–1680)", *Jahrbuch der Gesellschaft für Niedersächsische Kirchengeschichte* 96 (1998) 61–75. On Bourignon and her circle see de Baar M., *'Ik moet spreken': Het spiritueel leiderschap van Antoinette Bourignon (1616–1680)* (Zutphen: 2004).

[27] Madame de Scudéry as she was known to her contemporaries, was famous for holding intellectual salons and for her written work, particularly concerned philosophical questions. See: Niderst A., *Madeleine de Scudéry, Paul Pellisson et leur monde* (Paris: 1976).

[28] Valentin Conrart, a Huguenot, was secretary to Louis XIV and the founder of the Academie Française. Not an author in his own right, he occupied himself with connecting scholars to patrons, and to the king himself. See: Schapira N., *Un professionnel des lettres au XVIIe siècle. Valentin Conrart: une histoire sociale* (Seyssel: 2003).

transparent anonymity, which has only become opaque with the passage of time'.[29] According to her, Rivet's *Dernières heures* was her first publication. Therefore, what can we deduce from her account in relation to privacy during death?

The text begins with Marie du Moulin expressing the hope of giving a true account of events, but fearing the feeble memory of a living person. This is of course nothing but a rhetorical tool, since she was only about twenty-nine years of age at the time of writing the text. As we have seen in the death account of Duplessis-Mornay, there is a contextual background given for the approaching end: for Rivet the major blow was the death of his pupil, Prince Willem II of Orange, who died suddenly of smallpox at the age of twenty-four. She stresses that his sorrow was not provoked by the loss of benefits that Rivet expected from this connection, but by his love for his pupil, who he had hoped would live long to serve God and the State. Indeed, she states, 'il a paru plus destaché que jamais des choses du monde' ('he seemed to be detached more than ever from the world').[30]

We have a further description of Rivet's final healthy days: he went for a walk with a friend in the garden and said that if he lived to see the spring, he would be delighted, and if not, he would enter a nicer garden. He also said that he was at the age when he would need to be ready for death any day, not tomorrow, but today. Then Antonius Hulsius (1615–1685), the German minister of the Walloon Church of Leiden, invited Rivet to preach on Christmas Sunday.[31] He chose to speak about Psalm 144 verses 3 and 4, which directly reference the brevity of one's days:[32]

> Lord, what is man, that thou takest knowledge of him! or the son of man, that thou makest account of him! Man is like to vanity: his days are as a shadow that passeth away.[33]

---

29 Carol P., *Republic of Women: Rethinking the Republic of Letters in the Seventeenth Century* (Cambridge: 2012) 102.
30 Du Moulin, *Les dernières heures de Monsieur Rivet* 5.
31 Nauta D. (ed.), "Hulsius, Antonius", in *Biografisch lexicon voor de geschiedenis van het Nederlands protestantisme*, vol. 2 (Kampen: 1983) 266–269. He was the author of *Scrutinium memoriae Generosioribus dicatum ingeniis, quae liguarum Reginam, non in limine cum theologastrorumvulgo sed in intimis penetralibus salutare gestiunt* (Breda, Subbingius: 1650); *Theologiae Judaïcae pars prima, de Messia: addito breviario locorum Scripturae, quae a vanis rabbinorum glossematis repurgata veritati restituuntur* (Breda, Subbingius: 1653).
32 Du Moulin, *Les dernières heures de Monsieur Rivet* 7.
33 KJV, Psalm 144: 3–4.

What follows is a rather specific description of a particular medical procedure. Marie du Moulin gives a detailed account of Rivet's illness: on Tuesday 27 December 1650, he complained of pain under his navel, refused to eat and requested an enema, which could not be given to him successfully. He passed the night in pain and on Wednesday morning his complaints doubled; he again requested an enema, and again it was unsuccessful, though two doctors were called to his side. They attempted an enema once more, but were again unsuccessful. The reader receives even more detail on the cause of Rivet's suffering: a sticky, hardened obstruction in the lower part of his intestinal tract did not allow for a remedy. At this point the reader understands that Rivet was to die a painful death. Although on Thursday he was prescribed pilules of aloe and on Friday an infusion of rhubarb, the passage remained blocked. His stomach began to bloat, causing him to refuse to eat or drink for fear of aggravating his situation. Despite attempts to give him more enemas and baths, he died on the twelfth day of his illness.[34] According to the author of this account, all this time Rivet, though suffering, was meditating and reflecting on his situation from a theological perspective, just like Duplessis-Mornay.[35] The precise descriptions of his meditations are likely meant to emphasise the religious devotion that Rivet had.

Who were the people surrounding him in these last days? The text speaks of his wife and son, who were told by Rivet to go and eat something, while his niece, i.e., Marie du Moulin, the author, remained at his side. 'S'estans donc retirez pour un peu dans la chambre voisine, on apporta un oeuf a sa niepce, qu'il encouragea a le prendre *Pour moy*, disoit il [...]' ('While they had thus retired for a while to the adjoining room, an egg was brought to his niece, whom he encouraged to take it, *For me*, he said').[36] Here we see a reference to what could be considered spatial privacy – Rivet asked his wife and son Frederik[37] to leave in order to be alone with his niece: she is presented here as

---

34 Du Moulin, *Les dernières heures de Monsieur Rivet* 8–9.
35 Ibidem, 9.
36 Ibidem, 74.
37 Frederik Rivet (1617–1666) is one of the presumed authors of *De l'éducation des enfants*, while it is considered that it was in fact Marie du Moulin who wrote the original version published in 1654: *De la premiere education d'un Prince, depuis sa naissance* (Rotterdam, Arnout Leers: 1654). The second edition, which is more widely available, is: [Anonymous], *De l'éducation des enfants et particulièrement de celle des princes* (Amsterdam, chez Daniel Elsevier: 1679). Du Moulin's authorship is stated in a letter from Pierre Bayle to his brother Jacob on 15 June 1679. See Labrousse E., *Pierre Bayle: Tome 1: Du Pays de Foix à la Cité d'Erasme*, 2nd edition (Dordrecht – Boston – Lancaster: 1985) 143, n. 52; Labrousse E., "Marie du Moulin éducatrice", *Bulletin de la Société de l'Histoire du Protestantisme Français* 139 (1993) 255–268. On Frederik Rivet, see Rang B., "Letters Across the North Sea: A Dutch

his spiritual disciple, with whom he exchanged some words in private. After the conversation ended, his wife and son returned to the room. Perhaps this clause was added by Du Moulin to point to her closeness to her uncle, to her status as his follower and to herself as the author, since the text was anonymous. Yet privacy here is created by establishing a closed space, where only two people were present to have a conversation. Once the family is back, the personal tone of the conversation is gone and Rivet addresses all those present and asks them to pray for him: 'Priez tous pour moy, *leur disoit il* [...]' ('You all pray for me, *he told them*').[38] It is no longer a private setting, where two people exchange personal ideas. We see that once Rivet invites others to join him, the place loses a degree of privacy. Yet was it still private? We will come back to this question later.

In fact, this conversation is only known to us because one of its participants chose to tell it to the reader. As with the rest of the account, it is difficult to assess the extent of correlation between reality and the author's imagination in this situation. Although by revealing the content of this conversation Du Moulin effectively makes this private conversation public, the privacy of the situation remains intact.

Besides family members, the Dutch minister Jacob Lydius (1610–1679) of Dordrecht was also called upon to keep Rivet company.[39] Du Moulin mentions that they conversed in Latin and duly records the conversation to show how capable her uncle was in his last moments.[40] Subsequently, from the description we learn that at three o'clock in the morning Rivet's wife Marie approached him only to see that his death was imminent. The words she used are dramatic: 'Adieu, mon cher ami, va t'en Joyeux a la vie eternelle' ('Goodbye, my dear friend, go with happiness to the eternal life'). His reply, which we have already seen in the introductory section of this chapter, was merely:

Source of John Locke's Letters Concerning Education", Roding J. – van Voss L.H. (eds.), *The North Sea and Culture (1550–1800): Proceedings of the International Conference held at Leiden 21–22 April 1995* (Hilversum: 1996) 378–395, here 381–383. The author of this entry claims that it was Frederik Rivet who authored the 1679 edition of *De l'éducation des enfants et particulièrement de celle des princes*.

38 Du Moulin, *Les dernières heures de Monsieur Rivet* 75.
39 Jacobus Lydius was the author of, among others, *Agonistica sacra sive syntagma vocum & phrasium agonisticarum quae in S. Scriptura, imprimis vero in Epistolis S. Pauli Apostoli, occurrunt* (Rotterdam, Arnold Leers: 1657).
40 He was the author of *Agonistica Sacra, sive Syntagma vocum et phrasium agonisticarum quae in Scriptura occurrunt* (Rotterdam, 1657); *Florum Sparsio ad historium passionis Jesu Christi* (Rotterdam: 1672). See "Lydius, Johannes", *McClintock and Strong Biblical Cyclopedia*, 1880. Online edition. [Accessed on 2 September 2022. <https://www.biblical cyclopedia.com/L/lydius-johannes.html>].

Ouy [...], Je m'en vay a ton Dieu, & a mon Dieu, Nous avons tout gagné[,] Amen, Ainsi soit il, Adieu mon Filz. Adieu ma chere Niepce. Ne craignez point, j'ay prie pour vous, Vous serez tous bien-heureux [...] Vien Seigneir Iesus, vien, prens ta creature, j'aspire, j'espere, je frappe a la porte : Ouvre, ouvre, Seigneur a ton pauvre Serviteur.

Yes [...], I am going to your God, & to my God, we have gained everything, Amen, so be it, farewell my Son. Farewell my dear Niece. Do not be afraid, I have prayed for you, you will all be blessed [...] Come, Lord Jesus, come, take your creature, I yearn, I hope, I knock at the door: open, open, Lord to your poor servant.

Rivet does not respond to his wife directly, but rather bids goodbye to his son Frederik and his niece Marie, who probably used this passage to once again show her closeness to him. It seems as if in addition to these two, only his wife was there. But this was not the case. Rivet asks God to open the gate for him and accept him. Once again, the gate symbolises a passage to a secluded place – into Heaven. Its doors are closed, and only those who are admitted by God can enter there. Once again, the relationship with God plays a role in this constellation: he is not alone, he is with God.

The description of his death continues by stating that 'une grande faiblesse' ('deadly weakness') descended upon him, and indeed many people were present in the room where he lay dying. Someone, probably his physician, advised them not to speak to him anymore, since there would be nothing that he could add to any conversation. At five o'clock in the morning everyone left, with the exception of the minister Lydius, who awaited his last breath in silence, in order to say the last prayers. Despite this, at eight o'clock in the morning Rivet was still alive; assuming that he would not die immediately, Lydius left, planning to return in the evening.[41]

We learn an interesting detail from the next sentence. Previously it was said that everyone left besides Lydius, who now was gone too. But then it turns out that '[s]es domestiques demeurerent seulement pres de luy' ('members of his household stayed alone with him') – the most inner circle remained with him.[42] They did not dare talking to him, and it was not clear whether he could speak, although his mouth was open as if in attempt to say something. We then learn that not only household members, but also certain friends of his wife,

---

41   Du Moulin, *Les dernières heures de Monsieur Rivet* 81–82.
42   Ibidem, 82.

who did what they could to reduce his agony, were there. His son and niece were also present, next to him.

From the text we learn that suddenly at half past eight his face changed colour and some visible little contractions could be seen. He was asked by his niece whether he was still able to hear, and he replied that he could.[43] He said a few words of devotion. At some point his son told him that they were there alone, yet since these words were recorded, it seems that Marie du Moulin was present too, unless it was second hand information. But Rivet replied that he was not alone, that God was with him.[44] He was receiving the last rites, and at the end of the preparation and prayers, Rivet raised his hands towards Heaven, and someone present said aloud that it seemed that Rivet now saw a vision of God. Rivet replied "Yes", and expired calmly in the same moment, at half past nine on Saturday morning, 7 January 1651. The text states that he was aged 78 years and 6 months.[45]

This account of Rivet's last days reveals several circles of privacy: the circle of Rivet's and his wife's acquaintances, dignitaries from Huguenot and possibly Dutch communities, who were paying their last respects to him while he was alive, is the broadest one. We then move into the circle of closer friends, among them the minister Lydius. We also learn that besides the pastor, Moris de Bressuire, a Catholic physician, also stayed with Duplessis at all times. This of course does not mean staying physically in the same room, but rather in the house. Even closer are his "domestiques", i.e. members of his household, who stayed with him when everyone else had gone. His son and wife should be the closest to Rivet, as his immediate family, but we see from the description above that he had a very private conversation with his niece, Marie du Moulin, who presents herself as his closest associate. It was with her that he shared the most significant reflections and wished to speak alone, in private. We also see that the idea of "alone" does not necessarily mean that there was no one present other than those specifically mentioned, such as Rivet and his son, as it always turns out that there were more people present. The only exception was indeed the one-on-one conversation with his niece. These privacy circles demonstrate to us the different degrees of privacy that existed in the last hours of Rivet's life. The death occurs inside a room within the house of the dying person. The person enjoys a degree of privacy even when there is a large number of

---

43   Ibidem.
44   Ibidem, 84.
45   Ibidem, 84–85. Medical testimony, in Latin, of Dr. Balthasar van der Cruyce is added as appendix. In Gigord's later edition which included the *Receuil* of De Mornay, the editor this last section is omitted.

people present – these are people who were allowed by Rivet or his family to be in either his room or the house. All uninvited or unwanted people were excluded from this setting, and therefore it is possible to claim a degree of privacy. Being private does not necessarily mean to be alone; it means to control access, to use Margulis's definition, which seems appropriate within this context. Whether it was Rivet himself or his family who controlled the situation remains an open question.

5   Pierre du Moulin (1568–1658)

The final account that I would like to analyse is *Recit des dernières heures de Monsieur du Moulin*.[46] Just like the account of the death of Rivet, it was written by Marie du Moulin. Once again it is a relative that she writes about: in this case, her own father. Pierre du Moulin is a renowned Huguenot theologian, who held prominent positions in the Reformed milieu – he was one of the ministers of the Huguenot Temple in Charenton, which was the centre of Huguenot life in France. He also held the position of professor of theology at the Huguenot academy of Sedan, established, as we already know, by Philippe Duplessis-Mornay. His son-in-law was the hard-line Huguenot theologian Pierre Jurieu (1637–1713), also professor at Sedan and later at the Illustrious School of Rotterdam, where he arrived by invitation of Adriaen Paetz, mayor of the city.[47] Du Moulin spent several years in the United Provinces as professor at Leiden University, some years before André Rivet came there.[48] The exact reason Marie du Moulin had for writing this account is unknown, but because of the status of her father both within the Huguenot community and beyond, it seems that it was as an obvious choice for creating a piece of devotional literature that would set an example of piety.

As with the other accounts, Marie du Moulin begins her story of the final days of her father with a turning point. Three and a half years before Pierre du Moulin died in Sedan on 10 March 1658, he had an accident (of which we learn nothing from the text) that significantly damaged his health. The first

---

46   Du Moulin Marie, *Récit des dernières heures de Monsieur du Moulin, Decedé à Sedan le 10 Mars, 1658* (Sedan, François Chayer: 1658).

47   On Jurieu, see Howels R.J., *Pierre Jurieu: Antinomian Radical* (Durham: 1983); Knetsch F.R.J., *Pierre Jurieu, theoloog en politikus der Refuge* (Kampen: 1967).

48   On Pierre du Moulin, see Gordon Tait L., *Pierre Du Moulin (1568–1658): Huguenot Theologian* (doctoral dissertation, University of Edinburgh: 1955); Borvan D., *Fighting for the Faith: Pierre Du Moulin's Polemical Quest* (doctoral dissertation, University of Oxford: 2019).

FIGURE 3.3 Schweizer Johann, "Portrait of Pierre du Moulin", engraving, 1638–1670[1658]
©RIJKSMUSEUM AMSTERDAM. INV. NUM. RP-P-1920-1426

signs of the approaching end appeared on Tuesday 26 February, on which he woke up feeling very weak. According to the author, he suffered from pneumonia, which caused a fever.[49] The last Thursday of February, the 28th, his health declined so much that it was expected that he would die soon. We are told that his colleagues came to see him (and probably to bid their farewells), but he encouraged them and spoke to them about virtue.

During the first few days Du Moulin dedicated his time to prayers, some of which his daughter recounts in the text. Yet the disease progressed and brought him a lot of suffering. It seems that he was surrounded by people at all times: "L'un des Pasteurs le voyant souffrir, l'exhorta qu'il prît courage, que le tems de sa deliverance approchoit" (one of the ministers, seeing him suffering, exhorted that he had some courage because the time of his liberation was approaching).[50] Throughout the week of his final illness, people continued to visit Du Moulin. On Sunday, 3 March, the minister who was to preach at the Huguenot church in Sedan came to visit him. This seems rather similar to what we have seen in previous accounts, in which the dying were frequently visited by their peers until their death.

The text presents us with one more dimension of what could be considered private in this context. Having suffered greatly, Du Moulin actually expresses his physical pain in his prayer, which could be seen as some sort of complaint to God: "O Seigneur, [...] n'appesa[n]tis point avantage ta main sur ton pauvre Serviteur, tu m'as chatié suffusamme[n]t, pour me faire sentir mon péché" (O Lord, [...] do not weigh your hand any more on your poor servant, you have chastened me sufficiently, to make me feel my sin).[51] This reference to the two most inner zones of privacy – the body, which feels the physical pain inflicted by God, and the mind/soul, which feels the mental pain and accepts being punished by God for the sins committed. God as a part of the private constellation of Du Moulin's emotions, hopes and aspirations manifests himself once again.

Just like in the account of Rivet, we see that he was "tout entouré de sa Famille, & de ses principaux amis" (wholly surrounded by his family and by his closest friends).[52] The imminent death was expected to occur at any hour. The description goes on to depict how clearly he was speaking in the hours that he was not affected by fever, how much he prayed and how he dedicated his time to his pastoral duties.

---

49   Du Moulin, *Récit des dernières heures de Monsieur du Moulin* 3.
50   Ibidem, 11.
51   Ibidem, 12.
52   Ibidem, 22.

> La Chambre estoit iour & nuict [sic] pleine de monde; un soir ouvrant ses yeux, il dit, *Voila bien des gens*: On lui répondit, ce sont vos brebis, qui demandent vostre Bénédiction, *Dieu les benisse*, dit-il, *& leur donne sa crainte, & le salut qu'il a promis*.[53]

> The Chamber was full of people day and night; one evening opening his eyes, he said, "Here are many people": He was answered, "It is your sheep, whom your blessing asks", "God bless them", he said, "& give them his fear, & the salvation he has promised".

The text tells us that Du Moulin was dying in a room full of people – yet we must keep in mind that these were nonetheless only those who were allowed to be present. One can only imagine how much energy was spent by the dying man to entertain the crowd awaiting his death. However, it seems to be of particular importance to have been blessed by a dying person. We must also keep in mind that these were not random people, but those who were counted as his friends or close colleagues, just as his daughter suggested in her text: the inner circle. Furthermore, contrary to Duplessis-Mornay and Rivet, the family is almost absent in the description. There is little doubt that they were present, but their place is much less prominent. Curiously, it seems that appearing feeble and in pain was not considered a private sentiment that could not be shared with these people, whom he knew well and with whom he spent a considerable part of his life.

Saturday 9 March was passed in agony and with heavy convulsions; Du Moulin's friends tried to console him in this moment of approaching death. He prayed one more time, his final intelligible words being "je le croy" (I believe in it), and for the following quarter of an hour he continued mumbling without anyone being able to understand what he was saying. He died at ten minutes past midnight on 10 March 1658.[54]

This account demonstrates several instances of privacy. First of all, the particular emphasis on personal pain, both bodily and of the soul. Pierre du Moulin revealed his most personal sentiments in this text – appearing hurt both mentally and physically – his words seem to be duly transcribed (meant in fact to appear as if he pronounced them) thus demolishing any borders between the reader and the dying man. Yet, at the time, those who witnessed his agony were his closest (and perhaps some less close) friends and acquaintances. The emphasis in this text on the presence of this large group of friends,

---

53   Ibidem, 29.
54   Ibidem, 31.

rather than family, shows another dimension of dying – it was possible to die within a close circle of friends, rather than only next to one's wife and children or other relatives.

6   Conclusion

In this article I have analysed three texts recounting the "last moments" of three prominent Huguenot theologians: Philippe Duplessis-Mornay, André Rivet and Pierre du Moulin. While the standard goal of such accounts was to teach a moralistic and religious lesson to their co-religionists, they serve as an excellent source for the level of privacy in early modern death. Surely, the target audience of these three accounts was a broader public, and as such they provide us with an idea of how a person of their status would want to be imagined or seen dying – dignified, in the right mind, pious and in control. As with any other case of written text, the reader has to rely on the account told by the author, who selects the information to be presented and can change the portrayal of the situation according to his or her wish. Yet even here there are certain moments which seem to be trivial, but which tell the researcher of a common situation that could occur in that situation. Based on these depictions, several depictions and conceptions of privacy as presented by the authors can be deduced.

First of all, we learn that there were different degrees of privacy. Particularly enlightening in this matter is the account of Rivet, where he explicitly asks to be left alone with his niece Marie du Moulin in order to discuss theological matters with her. This shows the intimate, close relationship between them, which in its turn allows for such a discussion. The symbolic re-entry of his family into the room terminates this private moment, while creating a new, wider circle of privacy, which still excludes uninvited guests. God, either as God the Father or as Jesus Christ, is nonetheless always there, meaning the person is never alone: He is the one who regulates the degree of pain and comfort and access to Heaven, and is seen as a constant part of one's life and afterlife.

Secondly, the family circle – wife, children, their spouses, and other relatives – create another private zone. This zone is especially visible in the accounts of Duplessis-Mornay and Rivet, where on a number of occasions various family members are left alone with the dying. Members of the family were often joined by members of the household, servants or maids who were also allowed into the presence of their master and supported him. One needs to keep in mind that a household as such was a private zone, where family secrets were kept (or not), and in which those who lived there shared a bond with each other.

Thirdly, the circle of friends and colleagues is the broadest and least private, but once again private enough, in the sense of excluding all those who did not belong. In all three accounts we see that a large number of people attended to the needs of the dying person. In the late Middle Ages and the early modern period, it was common to assume that family, friends and community needed to be present to assure a good death.[55] According to Philippe Ariès "[i]t was essential for parents, friends and neighbours to be present".[56] Many were looking for a blessing, others were there to support, a third group was probably just standing and gazing. Most of the intellectual exchanges were undertaken with the second group. Yet they were witnessing how the person was suffering and then dying. This brings us to two more zones of privacy.

The chamber and the house are the final spaces of privacy to be discussed. As Mette Birkedal Bruun explained, the home is the fourth zone of privacy of the early modern world, and the chamber or alcove is the third.[57] Aided by Margulis's definition of privacy, we can assume that access to both of these zones was regulated, either by the person dying or by his family members. It would not be possible to participate in any these spaces of people of such stature as the theologians in question here, without permission. This regulation of access is in fact a regulation of privacy. Some were allowed to sit outside the bedroom (but we do not know who), and others, whose names are often mentioned, were allowed to be present inside the room, alongside the family.

The moment of death had both private and public aspects to it, and sometimes, these were intertwined. This is because while only select people were allowed to attend the house of the dying person, their presence also ensured that the way he or she died would be known to others. This is also why the accounts of the last hours are important: they convey knowledge about the private setting in which a person died to a large and undefined public. The careful editing of such accounts and selection of facts was aimed at presenting

---

55 For discussion on death preparation and the role of community, see the aforementioned Lahtinen A. – Korpiola M. (eds.), *Dying Prepared in Medieval and Early Modern Northern Europe*, and in particular the following chapters within this work: Lahtinen A. – Korpiola M., "Introduction: Preparing for a Good Death in Medieval and Early Modern Norther Europe" 1–17; Kanerva K., "Restless Dead or Peaceful Cadavers? Preparations for Death and Afterlife in Medieval Iceland" 18–43; Korpiola M. "'At Death's Door': The Authority of Deathbed Confessions in Medieval and Early Modern Swedish Law" 65–104.

56 Ariès P., *Western Attitudes Toward Death from the Middle Ages to the Present*, trans. by Patricia M. Ranum (London: 1974) 12. Ariès continues the sentence by saying that until the eighteenth century there was no description of a deathbed without mentioning children in attendance, but the text discussed here shows that Ariès's assertation about the presence of children in such texts was incorrect.

57 Bruun, "Towards an Approach to Early Modern Privacy".

the deceased as a good Christian, an example of piety and devotion. Therefore, the fact of sharing what seems to be private information after the death of the person, does not necessarily breach his or her privacy of these last moments, but rather uses them to convey a particular message to the broader public.

The heuristic zones of privacy used in this article have helped to investigate what could be considered private – the self, the alcove, the house and the community. All of these present various degrees of privacy: that of one person, that of two people, of a household, etc. Through the prism of heuristic zones, aided by the category of God and family relations, it is possible to establish that privacy existed not only in seclusion, but also when a large group of people was present. Further research is needed to determine how common these practices were among other Huguenots and beyond, as well as how different they were for lower and higher classes of society, and for more private people who were not well known beyond their own social circle.

Bibliography

Primary Printed Sources

[Anonymous], *De l'éducation des enfants et particulièrement de celle des princes* (Amsterdam, chez Daniel Elsevier : 1679).

du Moulin Marie, *Les dernières heures de Monsieur Rivet vivant Docteur & Professeur honoraire en l'Université de Leyden, & Currateur de l'Eschole Illustre, & College d'Orange à Breda* (Breda, Jean Waesberguf: 1651).

du Moulin Marie, *Récit des dernières heures de Monsieur du Moulin, Decedé à Sedan le 10 Mars, 1658* (Sedan, François Chayer: 1658).

Hulsius Antonius, *Scrutinium memoriae Generosioribus dicatum ingeniis, quae liguarum Reginam, non in limine cum theologastrorumvulgo sed in intimis penetralibus salutare gestiunt* (Breda, Subbingius: 1650).

Hulsius Antonius, *Theologiae Judaïcae pars prima, de Messia: addito breviario locorum Scripturae, quae a vanis rabbinorum glossematis repurgata veritati restituuntur* (Breda, Subbingius: 1653).

Lydius Jacobus, *Agonistica sacra sive syntagma vocum & phrasium agonisticarum quae in S. Scriptura, imprimis vero in Epistolis S. Pauli Apostoli, occurrunt* (Rotterdam, Arnold Leers: 1657).

Lydius Jacobus, *Florum Sparsio ad historium passionis Jesu Christi* (Rotterdam: 1672).

Rivet Frederick, *De la premiere education d'un Prince, depuis sa naissance* (Rotterdam, Arnout Leers: 1654).

Bouchereau Samuel, *Disputationum theologicarum tertia de essentia Dei et attributis illius* (Leiden, Ex officina I. Patii: 1602).

Carol P., *Republic of Women: Rethinking the Republic of Letters in the Seventeenth Century* (Cambridge: 2012).

Daillé Jean, "Des dernières heures de Mr. Du Plessis", in Salchi J.J. (ed.), *Recueil des dernières heures de Messieurs de Mornay du Plessis, Gigord, Rivet, Du Moulin, Drelincourt & Fabri, nouvelle edition augmentée d'un Discours premininaire sur l'utilité de cet ouvrage, & sur le fondement de nôtre Salut & de nos esprérances dans la vie & dans la mort* (Laisanne, Jean Zimmerli: 1725).

Secondary Literature

Albrecht R., "Konfessionsprofil und Frauen: Anna Maria van Schurman (1607–1678) und Antoinette Bourignon (1616–1680)", *Jahrbuch der Gesellschaft für Niedersächsische Kirchengeschichte* 96 (1998) 61–75.

Ariès P., *Western Attitudes Toward Death from the Middle Ages to the Present*, trans. by P.M. Ranum (London: 1974).

Aronson N., *Mademoiselle de Scudéry* (Boston: 1978).

Barros P. et al. (eds.), *Prêcher la mort à l'époque moderne: Regards croisés sur la France et l'Angleterre* (Paris: 2020).

Birkedal Bruun M., 'Towards an Approach to Early Modern Privacy: The Retirement of the Great Condé', in Green M. – Nørgaard L.C. – Birkedal Bruun M. (eds.) *Early Modern Privacy: Sources and Approaches* (Leiden: 2022) 12–60.

Borvan D., *Fighting for the Faith: Pierre Du Moulin's Polemical Quest* (doctoral dissertation, University of Oxford: 2019).

Daussy H., *Les huguenots et le roi: combat politique de Philippe Duplessis-Mornay (1572–1600)* (Geneva: 2002).

de Baar M. – Loewenstein M. – Monteiro M. – Sneller A.A., *Choosing the better part. Anna Maria van Schurman (1607/1678)* (Dordrecht – Boston – London: 1996).

de Baar M., *'Ik moet spreken': Het spiritueel leiderschap van Antoinette Bourignon (1616–1680)* (Zutphen: 2004).

de Baar M., "'En onder het hennerot het haantje zoekt te blijven': de betrokkenheid van vrouwen bij het huisgezin van Jean de Labadie, 1669–1732", *Vrouwenlevens 1500–1800. Achtste jaarboek voor vrouwengeschiedenis* (Nijmegen: 1987) 11–43.

Gordon Tait L., *Pierre Du Moulin (1568–1658): Huguenot Theologian* (doctoral dissertation, University of Edinburgh: 1955).

Green M. – Nørgaard L.C. – Birkedal Bruun M., "*En privé & en public*: The Epistolary Preparation of the Dutch Stadtholders", *Journal of Early Modern History* 24 (2020) 253–279.

Green M. – Huysman I., in collaboration with Bakić J. – Klein Käfer N. "The Low Countries, Private Life, and Privacy", in Green M. – Huysman I. (eds.), *Private Life and Privacy in the Early Modern Low Countries* (Turnhout: 2023) 13–26.

Green M., "Privacy in Jewish Egodocuments of Amsterdam (1600–1830)", in Green M. – Nørgaard L.C. – Birkedal Bruun M. (eds.), *Early Modern Privacy: Sources and Approaches*, Intersections 78 (Leiden – Boston: 2022) 213–242.

Green M., "The Orange-Nassau family at the educational crossroads of the Stadholder's position (1628–1711)", *Dutch Crossing: Journal of Low Countries Studies* 43/2 (2019) 99–126.

Green M., *An Interreligious Dialogue: Portrayal of Jews in Dutch French-Language Periodicals (1680–1715)* (Lodz – Cracow: 2022).

Honders H.J., *Andreas Rivetus als invloedrijk gereformeerd theoloog in Holland's bloeitijd* (The Hague: 1930).

Howels R.J., *Pierre Jurieu: Antinomian Radical* (Durham: 1983).

Kanerva K., "Restless Dead or Peaceful Cadavers? Preparations for Death and Afterlife in Medieval Iceland", in Lahtinen A. – Korpiola M. (eds.), *Dying Prepared in Medieval and Early Modern Northern Europe* (Leiden – Boston: 2018) 18–43.

Knetsch F.R.J., *Pierre Jurieu, theoloog en politikus der Refuge* (Kampen: 1967).

Korpiola M. "'At Death's Door': The Authority of Deathbed Confessions in Medieval and Early Modern Swedish Law", in Lahtinen A. – Korpiola M. (eds.), *Dying Prepared in Medieval and Early Modern Northern Europe* (Leiden – Boston: 2018) 65–104.

Kuperty-Tsur N., "Charlotte Arbaleste", *Dictionnaire des femmes de l'Ancien Régime*, 2003. Online edition. [Accessed 1 September 2022. <http://siefar.org/dictionnaire/fr/Charlotte_Arbaleste>].

Labrousse E., "Marie du Moulin éducatrice", *Bulletin de la Société de l'Histoire du Protestantisme Français* 139 (1993) 255–268.

Labrousse E., *Pierre Bayle: Tome 1: Du Pays de Foix à la Cité d'Erasme*, 2nd edition (Dordrecht – Boston – Lancaster: 1985).

Lahtinen A. – Korpiola M., "Introduction: Preparing for a Good Death in Medieval and Early Modern Norther Europe", in Lahtinen A. – Korpiola M. (eds.), *Dying Prepared in Medieval and Early Modern Northern Europe* (Leiden – Boston: 2018) 1–17.

Lahtinen A. – Korpiola M. (eds.), *Dying Prepared in Medieval and Early Modern Northern Europe* (Leiden – Boston: 2018).

Margulis S.T., "Privacy as a Social Issue and Behavioral Concept", *Journal of Social Issues* 59/2 (2003) 243–61.

Merlin-Kajman H., "'Privé' and 'Particulier' (and Other Words) in Seventeenth-Century France", in Green M. – Nørgaard L.C. – Birkedal Bruun M. (eds.) *Early Modern Privacy: Sources and Approaches* (Leiden: 2022) 79–104.

Mornay P.D., *De sacra evcharistia, in qvatuor libros* (Hanover, Claude Marnius: 1605).

Mornay P.D., *De la verité de la religion Chrestienne: cotnre les Athées, Epicuriens, Payens, Juifs, Mahumedistes, & autres Infidels* (Antwerpen, Christofle Plantin: 1581).

Nauta D. (ed.), "Hulsius, Antonius", in *Biografisch lexicon voor de geschiedenis van het Nederlands protestantisme*, vol. 2 (Kampen: 1983) 266–269.

Niderst A., *Madeleine de Scudéry, Paul Pellisson et leur monde* (Paris: 1976).

Nørgaard L.C., "Making Private Public: Representing Private Devotion in an Early Modern Funeral Sermon", in Green M. – Nørgaard L.C. – Birkedal Bruun M. (eds.), *Early Modern Privacy: Sources and Approaches*, Intersections 78 (Leiden – Boston: 2022) 378–400.

Opstal A.G., *André Rivet: Een invloedrijk hugenoot aan het hof van Frederik Hendrik* (Hardewijk: 1937).

Rang B., "Letters Across the North Sea: A Dutch Source of John Locke's Letters Concerning Education", Roding J. – van Voss L.H. (eds.), *The North Sea and Culture (1550–1800): Proceedings of the International Conference held at Leiden 21–22 April 1995* (Hilversum: 1996) 378–395.

Regent-Susini A., "How to Make Exemplarity with Secret Virtues: Funeral Sermons and Their Challenges in Early Modern France", in Green M. – Nørgaard L.C. – Birkedal Bruun M. (eds.), *Early Modern Privacy: Sources and Approaches*, Intersections 78 (Leiden – Boston: 2022) 179–193.

Schapira N., *Un professionnel des lettres au XVIIe siècle. Valentin Conrart: une histoire sociale* (Seyssel: 2003).

Stanwood O., *The Global Refuge: Huguenots in an Age of Empire* (Oxford: 2020).

Strickland F.C., "Building a Library in the Dutch Golden Age: André Rivet and His Books", in der Weduwen A. – Pettegree A. – Kemp G. (eds.), *Book Trade Catalogues in Early Modern Europe*, Library of the Written Word 93 (Leiden – Boston: 2021) 161–192.

van Ruymbeke B. – Sparks R.J. (eds.), *Uncertain Brotherhood: The Huguenots in the Dutch Republic* (Columbia, SC: 2003).

Wheeler K.J.-L., "Rabaut Saint-Étienne and the Huguenot Fight for Religious Freedom", in Messer P.C. – Taylor W.H., *Revolution as Reformation: Protestant Faith in the Age of Revolutions, 1688–1832* (Tuscaloosa, Al.: 2021) 96–112.

Wunderli R. – Broce G., "The Final Moment before Death in Early Modern England", *The Sixteenth Century Journal* 20/2 (1989) 259–275.

Yardeni M., *Le refuge huguenot: Assimilation et culture* (Paris: 2002).

Yardeni M., *Le refuge protestant* (Paris: 1985).

CHAPTER 4

Urbanity around the Deathbed: Considerations from Early Modern London

Martin Christ

1   Introduction[1]

On 5 January 1642, Sir James Cambell was dying in London. Cambell became Lord Mayor of the English capital in 1630 and was knighted in the same year.[2] He held various other administrative positions, such as Colonel of the Trained Band and alderman. Additionally, he was a member of the Worshipful Company of Ironmongers and a successful businessman. He was also on the committee of the East India Company for two periods, between 1631 to 1634 and 1635 to 1640, and held the post of Governor of the French Company. According to his funeral sermon, delivered by Edward Browne and printed in London soon after, his life was a blessed one and although he described Cambell as an "austere, and hard man", his life could serve as an example to others.[3]

The funeral sermon also mentions the last moments of Sir James. Although the description only covers a few pages, it is nonetheless telling. Browne points out that Cambell had prepared for his final moments for quite some time, as he 'prepare[d] himselfe for death, shall I say a month or two? nay I may affirme a yeare or two before he died' by 'having set his house in order, by composing of his Will'. Moreover, he spent 'his spare time in reading the Bible, and other good bookes, and in singing of Psalmes'. Finally, 'perceiving his houre draw neere', he 'sealed his Will, and went quietly to bed, as to his grave, from which

---

1   This chapter was written as part of the Humanities Centre in Advanced Studies "Religion and Urbanity: Reciprocal Formations", funded by the German Research Foundation (DFG, FOR 2779).
2   On Cambell, see Lang R.G., "Social Origins and Social Aspirations of Jacobean London Merchants", *The Economic History Review* 27/1 (1974). I thank Benedikt Brunner for drawing my attention to Cambell's case. See also his forthcoming *Den Tod ins Leben ziehen. Vergleichende Perspektiven auf den protestantischen Umgang mit dem Tod und Sterben in der Frühen Neuzeit* (1580–1750).
3   Browne Edward, *A Rare Paterne of Iustice and Mercy; Exemplified in the Many Notable, and Charitable Legacies of Sr. Iames Cambel, Knight, and Alderman of London, Deceased: Worthy Imitation. Whereunto Is Annexed a Meteor, and a Starre: Or, Briefe and Pleasant Meditations of Gods Providence to His Chosen, of the Education of Children and of the Vertue of Love; with Other Poems. / by Edw: Browne.* (London, William Ley: 1642) 43.

© MARTIN CHRIST, 2024 | DOI:10.1163/9789004517745_005

place he would not be removed till the houre of his death, which was upon the Wednesday following betweene six and seven of the clocke in the morning'. While visitors came to his deathbed, he remained steadfast in his faith and 'hoped [his soul] should shortly bee delivered, and carried by the Angels of God into a heavenly habitation, to enjoy everlasting freedome'.[4]

In his life and death, Cambell was closely connected to London. The will he wrote in preparation for his death and sealed in his final moments distributed 50,000 pounds to relatives, friends, London hospitals and other city institutions. Poems by other urban dignitaries formed part of the printed funeral sermon, an epitaph and further paratexts praising Cambell and his virtuous life were added as well.[5] The sermon also contained illustrations, which was rare for such publications. The piety of Cambell could be confirmed by the citizens, aldermen and dignitaries of London, but also by the French merchants with whom Cambell had interacted.[6]

Many of the preparations for the final moments and the process of dying itself were related to London's urbanity. During his death, a period that spanned four days, visitors likely included urban dignitaries and physicians, both groups of people especially common in cities. Sir James' donation to the city's charitable foundations illustrate the local administration of poor relief, while his involvement in overseas ventures during his life and a gift for the ransom of soldiers in Ottoman captivity indicate a global dimension to death in the early modern metropolis. Finally, the quick publication of the funeral sermon, including copper plate engravings of Sir James and his grave monument, testify to the lively print industry of London at the time.

London was one of the largest and most important early modern cities, growing from 80,000 to 700,000 inhabitants between 1550 and 1750.[7] But urbanity was not tied to fixed population numbers or a certain density.[8]

---

4 Ibidem 50–52.
5 On the different elements associated with the funeral sermon, see Lenz R. "Leichenpredigten – eine Quellengattung", *Blätter für deutsche Landesgeschichte* 111 (1975) 15–30, especially his definition on 15. See also Brunner B., Die gedruckte Leichenpredigt als Erbauungsbuch – eine Erfolgsgeschichte des 17. Jahrhunderts?, *Medium Buch. Wolfenbütteler interdisziplinäre Forschungen* 1 (2019) 87–105.
6 Browne, *A Rare Paterne of Iustice and Mercy* 39.
7 For a general introduction to the English context, see Gittings C., *Death, Burial and the Individual in Early Modern England* (London: 1984). On the development of London, see Griffiths P. – Jenner M.S.R. (eds.), *Londinopolis. Essays in the Cultural and Social History of Early Modern London* (Manchester – New York: 2000).
8 On this approach and definitions of urbanity, see Rau S. – Rüpke J., "Religion Und Urbanität: Wechselseitige Formierungen Als Forschungsproblem", *Historische Zeitschrift* 310/3 (2020) 654–680; Rüpke J. – Rau S., "Religion and Urbanity: Reciprocal Formations", *Religion and Urbanity Online* (Berlin – Boston, 2020), online database.

Rather, urbanity was highly dependent on specific circumstances and individual interpretations. Cities were dynamic and ever-changing, in the case of London defined by growth and expansion, though also with temporary setbacks, such as the great fire of 1666.[9] Urban spaces could both include ones outside the city and imagined spaces. Following Susanne Rau and Jörg Rüpke in their definition of urbanity, I understand urbanity 'not only as a historical concept but also as an analytical instrument for understanding and describing the temporally and regionally distinct characteristics of the urban'.[10] This also means that "urbanity" is used in this chapter to describe the features of city life, and not primarily in the sense of cultured or urbane. At the same time, I understand urbanity as the mode of life characteristic of cities, in the words of Louis Wirth, a way of life.[11] However, there was not only an urban way of life, but also an urban way of death.[12]

Vanessa Harding has argued in a comparative way that the urban setting in London and Paris changed how burials were conducted.[13] Her research reflects on the ways in which urbanity influenced the placing and treatment of the dead. For instance, urban density and the increasing demand for space influenced the accommodation of the dead. Harding showed that not only do we need to consider urbanity in order to understand the treatment of the dead, but that beyond this, the dead 'can make an important contribution to our understanding of urban culture and experience'.[14] Further aspects related to death more generally could be added here, for example the wide range of *ars moriendi* literature[15] that was produced in urban print centres like London or

---

9   Ross S., *The Plague and the Fire of London* (London: 1965).
10 Rüpke – Rau, "Religion and Urbanity".
11 Wirth L., "Urbanism as a Way of Life", *American Journal of Sociology* 44 (1938) 1–24.
12 Christ M. – González Gutiérrez C., "Introduction: Death and the City in Premodern Europe", *Mortality* 27/2 (2022) 129–143.
13 Harding V., *The Dead and the Living in Paris and London, 1500–1670* (Cambridge: 2002). See also her contribution in this volume.
14 Ibidem, 3.
15 For example, Becon Thomas, *The sycke mans salue VVherin the faithfull christians may learne both how to behaue them selues paciently and thankefully, in the tyme of sickenes, and also vertuously to dispose their temporall goodes, and finally to prepare them selues gladly and godly to die. Made and newly recognised by Maister Tho. Becon* (London, no printer: 1561); Taylor Jeremy, *The rule and exercises of holy dying in which are described the means and instruments of preparing our selves and others respectively, for a blessed death, and the remedies against the evils and temptations proper to the state of sicknesse: together with prayers and acts of vertue to be used by sick and dying persons, or by others standing in their attendance: to which are added rules for the visitation of the sick and offices proper for that ministery* (London, Printed for R.R. and are to be sold by Edward Martin, bookseller: 1651); Kettlewell John, *Death made comfortable, or, The way to dye well consisting of directions for an holy and an happy death: together with an office for the sick and for certain kinds of*

the establishment of large-scale urban cemeteries and the logistical problems that came with such major building projects in dense urban settings.[16]

But while urbanity has been explored in some of these contexts, less attention has been paid to urbanity in smaller spaces, such as the bedchamber.[17] Consequently, there is also little work on the ways in which urbanity impacted the early modern deathbed. While in modern societies the bedroom is a space understood as personal or private, in early modern Europe this was not the case. The bedchamber was no space that was sealed or locked in most instances, so people were entering and passing through. This included friends, but also uninvited visitors. Bedchambers used as sources of income in inns and taverns add to this already complex picture of a highly frequented and easily permeated space. In this way, a single bedchamber could be a site of interaction and exchange, frequently crossing age, gender and class boundaries. Many of the visitors to bedchambers would frequent them periodically or during special points in the lifecycle of a person, including during death.[18]

In general, this multi-functional nature of bedchambers did not change drastically during the last moments and a range of actors assembled, came, and went during a person's dying moments.[19] Clerics would enter the bedchamber during a person's last moments and in many cases also apothecaries, barber surgeons or others with medical knowledge. But death is unpredictable. For example, when women died in childbirth, midwives, friends and family were present. But the bedchamber was not only a space for actors from this world, especially during times of crisis. In Catholic belief, saints could help a dying person and guide their souls.[20] Alexandra Walsham has pointed out that angels remained a constant presence around early modern English deathbeds.[21]

---

bodily illness, and for dying persons, and proper prayers upon the death of friends (London, Printed for Robert Kettlewell: 1695); Perneby William, *A direction to death: teaching man the way to die well, that being dead, he may liue euer. Made in the forme of a dialogue, for the ease and benefite of him that shall reade it. The speakers therein are Quirinus and Regulus* (London: Imprinted for Thomas Man, 1599).

16 On the London cemeteries, see Meller H. – Parsons B., *London Cemeteries. An Illustrated Guide and Gazetteer* (London: 2008); Bard R., *Graveyard London: Lost and Forgotten Burial Grounds* (London: 2008). Still important is also: Holmes B., *The London Burial Grounds* (London: 1897).

17 See also, Christ M., "Co-Spatiality in the Early Modern European Bedchamber", *Religion and Urbanity Online* (Berlin – Boston, 2020), online database.

18 Ibidem.

19 On this topic, see also the contribution of Benedikt Brunner in this volume.

20 Marshall P., *Beliefs and the Dead in Reformation England* (Oxford: 2004); Marshall P. – Walsham A. (eds.), *Angels in the Early Modern World* (Cambridge, 2006).

21 Walsham A., *Catholic Reformation in Protestant Britain* (London: 2014), 209. See also Marshall – Walsham, *Angels*.

So while the complex and multi-layered nature of the last moments in early modern bedchambers has received some scholarly attention, this chapter draws attention to the fact that urbanity also changed how people experienced the end of their lives.

2   Health and Hygiene

Urban density led to the quick spread of diseases and outbreaks of plague tended to be especially severe in urban environments, something that also influenced the urban deathbed.[22] Visiting the sick was an important part of the work of clerics, as we know from urban ordinances of the early modern period in many parts of Europe. In some cases, clerics could refuse to visit the sick, when they feared that they might catch the disease themselves. In some towns, plague preachers were employed precisely for this purpose in order to ensure that the sick were taken care of, if it was too dangerous for the regular clergy to visit them.[23] Medical theories of the spread of diseases meant that in order to contain diseases, it was especially important to limit the time spent by the dying in close proximity with others.[24]

The danger of plague and other diseases resulted in systems that assessed and recorded those who had just died in order to determine if there was danger for the city at large. In London, this role of assessing those who had just died fell primarily to widowed or unemployed women, called searchers.[25] These semi-professional women were employed by the parish and had to swear an oath to the city.[26] The statistics were passed on to the parish and

---

[22]   Champion J.A.I. (ed.), *Epidemic Disease in London* (London: 1993).
[23]   Mauelshagen F., "Pestepidemien im Europa der Frühen Neuzeit", in Meier M. (ed.), *Pest. Die Geschichte eines Menschheitstraumas* (Stuttgart, 2005) 237–266. See also Christ M., "Preaching during Plague Epidemics in Early Modern Germany, c.1520–1618" *Studies in Church History* 58 (2022) 91–111.
[24]   Cole L., "Of Mice and Moisture: Rats, Witches, Miasma, and Early Modern Theories of Contagion", *Journal for Early Modern Cultural Studies* 10/2 (2010) 65–84.
[25]   Henry W.S., "Women Searchers of the Dead in Eighteenth- and Nineteenth-Century London", *Social History of Medicine* 29/3 (2015) 445–466; Munkhoff R., "Poor Women and Parish Public Health in Sixteenth-Century London", *Renaissance Studies* 28/4 (2014) 579–596.
[26]   Munkhoff R., "Searchers of the Dead: Authority, Marginality, and the Interpretation of Plague in England, 1574–1665", *Gender & History* 11/1 (1999) 1–29; Eadem, "Reckoning Death: Women Searchers and the Bills of Mortality in Early Modern London" in Vaught J.C. (ed.), *Rhetorics of Bodily Disease and Health in Medieval and Early Modern England* (Surrey: 2010).

then entered into the Bills of Mortality, which were published weekly and informed Londoners of the spread of diseases and the city's general health.[27] For the deathbed in London, this meant that through the tolling of the bells or the call of family and friends, searchers entered the house soon after a person had died in order to find out the cause of death.[28] Searchers as urban actors were intimately connected to the dead and their relatives.

How closely connected London's urbanity was with the moments of death during plague becomes apparent in a 1665 broadsheet illustration by John Dunstall.[29] In it, we see a sick person, including objects and personnel that surrounded the sick and dying during such times of crisis. Of the nine images, it is the only one that shows the interior of a house. Visually, it forms part of a tableau of depictions of plague in the city, which illustrate urban mortality, quick burials and other features connected to London's density and the rapid spread of diseases in the metropolis. The sickbed turned deathbed was an important feature of the imagination of early modern urbanity, where an individual's life was quickly lost to the ravages of disease [Fig. 4.1].

London was also especially dangerous due to a prevalence of accidental deaths that went beyond the dangers in other places. Partly this was the case in all cities, where major building projects increased the number of fatalities and busy streets, where humans, animals and vehicles came together, posed risks. Moreover, the rivers that flowed through major European cities posed serious health risks and many inhabitants died an unexpected death through drowning. But, as Craig Spence has argued, London's demographic features led to a particularly high mortality rate through accidental deaths. As the city contained large numbers of young and unskilled workers, the streets of London were especially dangerous and many of the people living and working there died in unexpected ways, depriving them of a preparation for their moments of death.[30]

---

27   For a recent treatment of the Bills of Mortality, see Slack P., "Counting People in Early Modern England: Registers, Registrars, and Political Arithmetic Get access Arrow", *The English Historical Review* 137/587 (2022) 1118–1143.

28   Clark O., "The Ancient Office of Parish Clerk and the Parish Clerks Company of London", *Ecclesiastical Law Journal* 8/38 (2006) 307–322; Murel J., "Print, Authority, and the Bills of Mortality in Seventeenth-Century London", *The Seventeenth Century* 36/ 6 (2021), 935–959.

29   Thorpe L.E., *'In Middest of Death': Medical Responses to the Great Plague of 1665 with Special Reference to John Allin* (Ph.D. dissertation, Royal Holloway, University of London: 2017), 216–219.

30   Spence C., *Accidents and Violent Death in Early Modern London, 1650–1750* (Cambridge: 2016), 23–41.

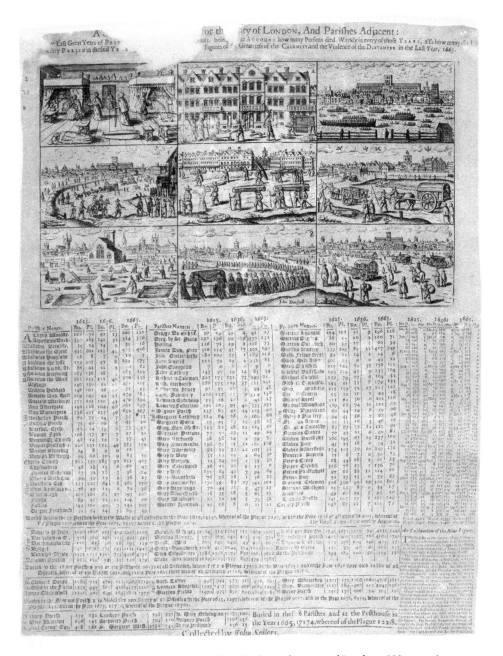

FIGURE 4.1 John Dunstall, Nine scenes from the 1665 plague that ravaged London, 1666, engraving, 45 × 33.3 cm, Museum of London, ID no. 42.39/142
© MUSEUM OF LONDON

3 Diversity and Expertise

Another feature of urban life that impacted directly on the deathbed was the presence of diversity in terms of professions, including city administrators, religious experts, artisans, artists, grieving families and the deceased person, all of whom helped shape the way people experienced death in the city.[31] The people present around an urban deathbed formed part of a microcosm that indicates features of urban life more generally, such as a greater diversity of trades or religious personnel. In John Dunton's (1659–1733) fictional dialogue concerning the deathbed from 1627, the author makes explicit references to the appropriate behavior during the last moments and the roles of those surrounding the dying person. Dunton was an English bookseller and author, and he points out that there are more friends around the deathbed in the city. Yet, just like in other cases, this is not necessarily a good thing, as they can also distract from God.

> Stranger. Sir But what shall I do if in my sickness my friends will not come at me?
> Minister. O, but God will never forsake you: and (especially in Cities) you shall have so many, as can do you any good: the fewer you have to gaze upon you, the fitter you are to look up to God.[32]

Urban diversity also extended to medical professionals. While in the countryside it may have been difficult to receive treatment through a physician and many inhabitants of villages had to rely on travelling doctors or local healers, it was possible in the early modern period in towns to receive treatment from barber surgeons, doctors or others. In some cases, medical professionals or certain clerics travelled between smaller settlements or came to the countryside from a nearby city, meaning that there were fewer options outside of major urban centres to receive certain kinds of treatments or rituals. However, the availability of personnel also depended on income and status, as not everyone could afford such services. But this, too, could be identified as a feature of an

---

31 Litten J., *The English Way of Death: The Common Funeral since 1450* (London: 2002); Houlbrooke R., *Death, Religion and the Family in England 1480–1750* (Oxford: 2000).

32 Dunton John, *The pilgrims guide from the cradle to his death-bed with his glorious passage from thence to the New-Jerusalem, represented to the life in a delightful new allegory, wherein the Christian traveller is more fully and plainly directed than yet he hath been by any, in the right and nearest way to the celestial paradice: to which is added The sick-mans passing-bell: with no less than fifty several pleasant treatises ...: to these are annext, The sighs and groans of a dying man* (London, Printed for John Dunton: 1684), 167.

urban deathbed: there was great diversity in terms of how much money was spent on treatments or elaborations of rituals, as major cities contained very poor inhabitants as well as wealthy citizens. Many of the urban poor did not have access to medical care, but it was certainly possible, also for people lower down the social scale, to call on surgeons, wise women or others who had some medical knowledge.[33]

Both medical professionals and clerics agreed that, ultimately, suffering and death was a divine punishment and so medical tracts could also include passages, which emphasized this dimension of the early modern deathbed. And there was one example, one of the better researched ones, where medical professionals could take over religious functions, and that was during emergency baptisms. If a child seemed too sick to survive, midwives sometimes performed these. As David Cressy, Emily Vine and others have shown for baptisms amongst the social elites, particularly in London, these were increasingly performed in domestic settings, though normally with the participation of a cleric.[34]

Not only in terms of personnel, but also regarding knowledge, urban settings functioned as focal points for novel developments. Medical advances led to different treatment of the sick on their deathbed. The expertise present in urban settings also led to higher expectations of what doctors could achieve. This was especially true for the elites. In an entry in the diary of the navy official and MP Samuel Pepys about the death of the English princess from 26 December 1660, we can read:

> so I went up to his chamber, and there having made an end of the business I returned to White Hall by water, and dined with my Lady Sandwich, who at table did tell me how much fault was laid upon Dr. Frazer and the rest of the Doctors, for the death of the Princess![35]

---

33 On the impact of disease and death on the poor, see Newton G. – Smith R., "Convergence or divergence? Mortality in London, its suburbs and its hinterland between 1550 and 1700", *Annales de démographie historique* 126/2 (2013), 17–49, especially 20.

34 Vine E., "'Those Enemies of Christ, If They Are Suffered to Live among Us': Locating Religious Minority Homes and Private Space in Early Modern London", *The London Journal* 43/3 (2018) 197–214; Cressy D., *Birth, Marriage and Death: Ritual, Religion and the Life-Cycle in Tudor and Stuart England* (Oxford: 1997); Bowden C., Vine E., Whitehouse E. (eds.), *Religion and Lifecycles in Early Modern England* (Manchester: 2021).

35 Gyford P. (ed.), *The Diary of Samuel Pepys. Daily entries from the 17th century London diary* (https://www.pepysdiary.com/about/), entry for 26 December 1660 (last accessed 03 January 2023).

These concerns about incompetent doctors around the deathbed were not just rhetoric. In a 1672 tract on the Royal College of Physicians, the author described 'a Reverend Divine, who upon his deathbed complained that this medicine had killed him'.[36] Normally, the division between clerics and medical professionals was clearly demarcated and both agreed that, ultimately, death was inevitable and in God's hands. However, in rare cases, clerics complained of unwarranted meddling by medics in the divine will, when those suffering on their deathbed should rather gratefully accept God's plan, even if it meant death. Jeremy Taylor in his tract *Holy Dying*, for instance, complained that when people died they were conversing with 'Surgeons and Physicians, Mourners and Divines', but what they should really be worried about is their souls.[37]

The urban diversity also included 'religious experts' that belonged to a variety of different religious and confessional groups. As the English monasteries were dissolved after the Henrician Reformation, this did not include monks or nuns, which is a marked difference to Catholic urban contexts. However, ambassadors from Catholic countries like Spain still had members of Catholic orders with them, and they could also perform deathbed rituals for Catholics in London, especially members of ambassadorial households. In other cases, London's Catholics found different ways to try and have a Catholic deathbed in an otherwise Protestant city.[38]

London offers a particularly striking example for urban diversity because it was connected globally.[39] Just like the actors, the objects present in an urban bedchamber would have been more diverse than in their rural counterparts. As cities had more trade networks than villages or the rural hinterland, the availability of cures from overseas was much greater in urban centres, as was the knowledge circulating about such good.[40] This can also be traced beyond the moments of death in funerals and commemoration. The global exchange of goods, where, for example, luxury goods such as coffee were increasingly

---

36　Charles Goodall, *The Royal College of Physicians of London, founded and established by law as appears by letters patents, acts of Parliament, adjudged cases, &c.: and An historical account of the College's proceedings against empiricks and unlicensed practisers, in every princes reign from their first incorporation to the murther of the royal martyr, King Charles the First* (London, printed by M. Flesher for Walter Kettilby: 1684).

37　Taylor, *The rule and exercises of holy dying*.

38　Vine, "Locating Religious Minority Homes".

39　On trade connections, see, for instance, Oldland J., "The Wealth of the Trades in Early Tudor London" *London Journal* 31/2 (2006) 127–155.

40　One disease where cures could be imported was syphilis, see Boehrer B.T., "Early Modern Syphilis", *Journal of the History of Sexuality* 1/2 (1990), 197–214.

consumed at funerals was more common in London than in the countryside or villages.[41] Elements of global exchange also increasingly came into play in *memento mori* and, for example, epitaphs in important London churches referred to sea voyages of the deceased.[42] The precise impact of London's global entanglements on deathbed rituals still awaits further investigations, but it becomes increasingly clear that global connections also impacted how people died in urban centres.[43]

4 Discourses

Innovations and new trends in the changing treatment of the dead became visible in the cities and could then be exported to the surrounding rural areas. One expression of these discourses around death in urban settings was in regulations on the proper treatment and behaviour when a person was dying. This was frequently linked to the urban commonweal. If people disobeyed rules by the magistrates, the city as a whole would be punished by God.[44] While divine wrath could also be inflicted on villages, the discourses on cities as centres of sin, rife with drinking, gambling and prostitution, made the city a particularly popular target of divine punishment.

Not only were certain themes especially popular in urban deathbed narratives, but in cities we also find a particularly large variety of how people died. For example, the preacher Ralph Robinson waited until his final moments until he authorized his family to print his sermons, as, according to the print, he was too modest to do so before.[45] Or, as Alexandra Walsham has pointed out, 'a woman present at the deathbed of John Reeve, co-founder of the Muggletonian movement, in 1658 cut off a lock of his hair to keep', providing

---

41 On the broader implications of this, see Harris J., "The Grecian Coffee House and Political Debate in London 1688–1714", *The London Journal* 25/1 (2000), 1–13.

42 See Lang, "Social Origins and Social Aspirations of Jacobean London Merchants".

43 On this topic from a trans-Atlantic perspective, see the contribution of Erik Seeman in this volume.

44 On this topic in relation to the Bills of Mortality, see Weinreich S.J., "Sums Theological: Doing Theology with the London Bills of Mortality, 1603–1666", *Church History. Studies in Christianity and Culture* 90/4 (2022) 799–823.

45 Robinson Ralph, *Christ All and in All. Or, Several Significant Similitudes by Which the Lord Jesus Christ Is Described in the Holy Scriptures Being the Substance of Many Sermons Preached by That Faithful and Useful Servant of Christ Mr. Ralph Robinson, Late Pastor at Mary Wolnoth London. Which Were Appointed by the Reverend Author on His Death-Bed (If His Brethren Should Think Fit) to Be Published* (London, printed for John Rothwel: 1656).

a different kind of focus for a deathbed and sanctifying Reeves.[46] While prints produced in London circulated throughout England and Europe, these different narratives of deathbeds were especially readily available for those living in the English capital and served to show recipients different ways of dying, both through exemplary and bad deaths.

Once more, London's global connections played a role in the discourses on the last moments. Travel accounts, particularly common in urban settings, included descriptions of deathbeds in regions beyond Europe. In his description of the world, Samuel Purchas wrote about a king of Japan:

> His name before was Faxiba, called after, Quabacondonus, the highest Title next to the Dairi, and signifieth the chiefe of the treasure: next borrowing a kingly Stile from China, would (mad folly) on his deathbed bequeath Godhead to a man, and immortalitie to a carkasse: when hee could no longer hold out his pride, cruelty, and other wicked courses, which made his presence.[47]

Traders and citizens interested in foreign countries consumed such descriptions in London, shaping their own ideas about what a deathbed might look like.

Urbanity also influenced what was told to Londoners on their deathbeds, most notably through discussion of the "Heavenly Jerusalem". This common description of a heaven contained elements of urbanity and is referred to in Revelation 3.12 and Revelation 21.2. It was 'a City that hath foundations, whose Builder and maker is God'.[48] Authors linked the ideas about the Heavenly Jerusalem to biblical passages, especially Hebrews 13.14, which reads 'For this world is not our permanent home; we are looking forward to a home yet to

---

46   Walsham A., *Charitable Hatred: Tolerance and Intolerance in England, 1500–1700* (Manchester – New York: 2006), 172.
47   Purchas Samuel, *Purchas his pilgrimage. Or Relations of the vvorld and the religions obserued in all ages and places discouered, from the Creation vnto this present In foure partes. This first containeth a theologicall and geographicall historie of Asia, Africa, and America, with the ilands adiacent. Declaring the ancient religions before the Flood … With briefe descriptions of the countries, nations, states, discoueries, priuate and publike customes, and the most remarkable rarities of nature, or humane industrie, in the same. By Samuel Purchas, minister at Estwood in Essex* (London, Printed by William Stansby for Henrie Fetherstone: 1613), 442.
48   Doolittle Samuel, *The righteous man's hope at death consider'd and improv'd for the comfort of dying Christians, and the support of surviving relations: to which is added Death-bed reflections, &c. proper for a righteous man in his last sickness* (London, Printed for Thomas Cockerill: 1693) 160.

come'. Many of the authors adjusted this text to mean that there is no permanent city on this earth, only the Heavenly Jerusalem in eternity. In various funeral sermons and deathbed accounts these imagined cities are evoked and they shaped ideas about the afterlife. In Paul Lorrain's *The Dying Man's Assistant: Or, Short Instructions how to Prepare the Sick*, we read: 'Let him [= the dying person] remember with St. Paul, that God's children have no abiding and continuing City upon Earth; but ought to long for the New Jerusalem, which is above'.[49]

In Samuel Doolittle's tract on the hopes of a dying man, he wrote about the Heavenly Jerusalem that 'They [=true believers] are Citizens of the new Jerusalem; in it are Mansions designed, purchas'd, prepared, and standing empty for them; but they must dip there feet in the cold fatal stream that runs beween this World, and that, before they can get thither'.[50] Linking the passage to biblical descriptions of the afterlife, he pointed out that 'In short, Gods Children die; that they may go home' and at another point 'To be a stranger upon Earth is your character; to get an hope of an abiding City should be your endeavour: and this cannot be had without Gospel-righteousness'.[51] He described a procession entering the Heavenly Jerusalem: 'the Lord marching in triumph to the City above, and the glorious, blessed Jesus leading the way: I shall not be left asleep, or stay behind, but accompany them to the everlasting Kingdom'.[52] In John Dunton's *The pilgrims guide from the cradle to his death-bed* (1684), the author elaborated on the long and hard way of a pilgrim to Jerusalem, but the text had a second layer of meaning, namely the progress of the soul to the New Jerusalem or, as it is called in the text, the 'Celestial City'.[53] He praised the 'beauty and the pleasant Scituation of that City'.[54]

But in Dunton's account, not all aspects of the city were good, the pilgrim also went to travel into the

> Destructive City called Debauchery, where they had like to have been destroyed and burnt alive, but that one called sincere Repentance, and

---

49 Lorrain Paul, *The Dying man's assistant, or, Short instructions for those who are concern'd in the preparing of sick persons for death being also no less worthy the consideration of all good Christians in time of health, as shewing the importance of an early preparation for their latter end, with regard as well to their temporal, as eternal state* (London, Printed for John Lawrence: 1697) 37.
50 Doolittle, *The righteous man's hope at death consider'd and improv'd* 29.
51 Ibidem 29 and 98.
52 Ibidem 79.
53 Dunton, *The pilgrims guide from the cradle to his death-bed*.
54 Ibidem 3.

several other honest Souls hastily came to their assistance, and delivered them out of this City, and set them in their right way again that lead to Jerusalem.[55]

Dunton's description of urbanity was therefore an ambiguous one. On the one hand, it was present in the Heavenly Jerusalem, but on the other hand, he also described debauchery as a city. Both descriptions were connected to the moments of death of London's inhabitants and they show an interpretation of cities as the place of both sin and redemption.

5 Conclusion

Urbanity shaped how men and women died in early modern London. The presence of a range of professions, denominations and variety of friends are indicative of an urban diversity that was already recognized by early modern authors. This diversity was especially important during times of crisis, such as outbreaks of disease, when different medical professionals assembled around the deathbed, trying to prevent deaths. When they failed, one of the numerous clerics was consulted. London's status as an international trade centre and hub for the exchange of goods and movement of people resulted in further diversity around the early modern deathbed. Bearing this in mind, it is not surprising that discourses on death, including ones that recommended certain behaviours or rituals on the deathbed, included tropes such as the Heavenly Jerusalem or a City of Debauchery, illustrating the ambivalence of urbanity.

The case of London illustrates how thinking about concepts such as urbanity in connection to the moments of death can lead to fruitful results. Undoubtedly, some of the features described here can also be found in rural contexts. Some villages also had a range of medical or clerical professions and many of the prints that shaped discourses in London were also consumed elsewhere. But taken together, this chapter has argued that there were fundamental differences in the ways an inhabitant of the early modern world died in London or a rural village. In order to fully understand the impact urbanity had on those living (and dying) in the early modern period, urbanity has to be taken into account as an analytical category.

Not only can a focus on urbanity open up new avenues of research into the last moments, but the deathbed can also tell us much about urbanity. The ways in which features of urbanity were on display around the deathbed, how

---

55 Ibidem 36.

rituals and ideas had to be negotiated constantly and the inherent ambiguities in their discussions around the deathbed shows that urbanity in spaces like the early modern bedchamber can enhance our understanding of what it meant to live and die in the city.

Bibliography

Primary Printed Sources

Becon Thomas, *The sycke mans salue VVherin the faithfull christians may learne both how to behaue them selues paciently and thankefully, in the tyme of sickenes, and also vertuously to dispose their temporall goodes, and finally to prepare them selues gladly and godly to die. Made and newly recognised by Maister Tho. Becon* (London, no printer: 1561).

Browne Edward, *A Rare Paterne of Iustice and Mercy; Exemplified in the Many Notable, and Charitable Legacies of Sr. Iames Cambel, Knight, and Alderman of London, Deceased : Worthy Imitation. Whereunto Is Annexed a Meteor, and a Starre : Or, Briefe and Pleasant Meditations of Gods Providence to His Chosen, of the Education of Children and of the Vertue of Love; with Other Poems. / by Edw: Browne.* (London, William Ley: 1642).

Doolittle Samuel, *The righteous man's hope at death consider'd and improv'd for the comfort of dying Christians, and the support of surviving relations : to which is added Death-bed reflections, &c. proper for a righteous man in his last sickness* (London, Printed for Thomas Cockerill: 1693).

Dunton John, *The pilgrims guide from the cradle to his death-bed with his glorious passage from thence to the New-Jerusalem, represented to the life in a delightful new allegory, wherein the Christian traveller is more fully and plainly directed than yet he hath been by any, in the right and nearest way to the celestial paradice : to which is added The sick-mans passing-bell : with no less than fifty several pleasant treatises ... : to these are annext, The sighs and groans of a dying man* (London, Printed for John Dunton: 1684).

Gyford P. (ed.), *The Diary of Samuel Pepys. Daily entries from the 17th century London diary* (https://www.pepysdiary.com/about/) (last accessed 03 January 2023).

Kettlewell John, *Death made comfortable, or, The way to dye well consisting of directions for an holy and an happy death : together with an office for the sick and for certain kinds of bodily illness, and for dying persons, and proper prayers upon the death of friends* (London, Printed for Robert Kettlewell: 1695).

Lorrain Paul, *The Dying man's assistant, or, Short instructions for those who are concern'd in the preparing of sick persons for death being also no less worthy the consideration of all good Christians in time of health, as shewing the importance of an early preparation for their latter end, with regard as well to their temporal, as eternal state* (London, Printed for John Lawrence: 1697).

Perneby William, *A direction to death: teaching man the way to die well, that being dead, he may liue euer. Made in the forme of a dialogue, for the ease and benefite of him that shall reade it. The speakers therein are Quirinus and Regulus* (London: Imprinted for Thomas Man, 1599).

Purchas Samuel, *Purchas his pilgrimage. Or Relations of the vvorld and the religions obserued in all ages and places discouered, from the Creation vnto this present In foure partes. This first containeth a theologicall and geographicall historie of Asia, Africa, and America, with the ilands adiacent. Declaring the ancient religions before the Floud … With briefe descriptions of the countries, nations, states, discoueries, priuate and publike customes, and the most remarkable rarities of nature, or humane industrie, in the same. By Samuel Purchas, minister at Estwood in Essex* (London, Printed by William Stansby for Henrie Fetherstone: 1613).

Robinson Ralph, *Christ All and in All. Or, Several Significant Similitudes by Which the Lord Jesus Christ Is Described in the Holy Scriptures Being the Substance of Many Sermons Preached by That Faithful and Useful Servant of Christ Mr. Ralph Robinson, Late Pastor at Mary Wolnoth London. Which Were Appointed by the Reverend Author on His Death-Bed (If His Brethren Should Think Fit) to Be Published* (London, printed for John Rothwel: 1656).

Taylor Jeremy, *The rule and exercises of holy dying in which are described the means and instruments of preparing our selves and others respectively, for a blessed death, and the remedies against the evils and temptations proper to the state of sicknesse : together with prayers and acts of vertue to be used by sick and dying persons, or by others standing in their attendance : to which are added rules for the visitation of the sick and offices proper for that ministery* (London, Printed for R.R. and are to be sold by Edward Martin, bookseller: 1651).

Secondary Literature

Bard R., *Graveyard London: Lost and Forgotten Burial Grounds* (London: 2008).

Boehrer B.T., "Early Modern Syphilis", *Journal of the History of Sexuality* 1/2 (1990), 197–214.

Bowden C., Vine E., Whitehouse E. (eds.), *Religion and Lifecycles in Early Modern England* (Manchester: 2021).

Brunner B., Die gedruckte Leichenpredigt als Erbauungsbuch – eine Erfolgsgeschichte des 17. Jahrhunderts?, *Medium Buch. Wolfenbütteler interdisziplinäre Forschungen* 1 (2019) 87–105.

Champion J.A.I. (ed.), *Epidemic Disease in London* (London: 1993).

Christ M. – González Gutiérrez C., "Introduction: Death and the City in Premodern Europe", *Mortality* 27/2 (2022) 129–143.

Christ M., "Co-Spatiality in the Early Modern European Bedchamber", *Religion and Urbanity Online* (Berlin – Boston, 2020), online database.

Christ M., "Preaching during Plague Epidemics in Early Modern Germany, c.1520–1618" Studies in Church History 58 (2022) 91–111.

Clark O., "The Ancient Office of Parish Clerk and the Parish Clerks Company of London", *Ecclesiastical Law Journal* 8/38 (2006) 307–322.

Cole L., "Of Mice and Moisture: Rats, Witches, Miasma, and Early Modern Theories of Contagion", *Journal for Early Modern Cultural Studies* 10/2 (2010) 65–84.

Cressy D., *Birth, Marriage and Death: Ritual, Religion and the Life-Cycle in Tudor and Stuart England* (Oxford: 1997).

Gittings C., *Death, Burial and the Individual in Early Modern England* (London: 1984).

Griffiths P. – Jenner M.S.R. (eds.), *Londinopolis. Essays in the Cultural and Social History of Early Modern London* (Manchester – New York: 2000).

Harding V., *The Dead and the Living in Paris and London, 1500–1670* (Cambridge: 2002).

Harris J., "The Grecian Coffee House and Political Debate in London 1688–1714", *The London Journal* 25/1 (2000), 1–13.

Henry W.S., "Women Searchers of the Dead in Eighteenth- and Nineteenth-Century London", *Social History of Medicine* 29/3 (2015) 445–466.

Holmes B., *The London Burial Grounds* (London: 1897).

Houlbrooke R., *Death, Religion and the Family in England 1480–1750* (Oxford: 2000).

Lang R.G., "Social Origins and Social Aspirations of Jacobean London Merchants", *The Economic History Review* 27/1 (1974).

Lenz R. "Leichenpredigten – eine Quellengattung", *Blätter für deutsche Landesgeschichte* 111 (1975) 15–30.

Litten J., *The English Way of Death: The Common Funeral since 1450* (London: 2002).

Marshall P. – Walsham A. (eds.), *Angels in the Early Modern World* (Cambridge, 2006).

Marshall P., *Beliefs and the Dead in Reformation England* (Oxford: 2004).

Mauelshagen F., "Pestepidemien im Europa der Frühen Neuzeit", in Meier M. (ed.), *Pest. Die Geschichte eines Menschheitstraumas* (Stuttgart, 2005) 237–266.

Meller H. – Parsons B., *London Cemeteries. An Illustrated Guide and Gazetteer* (London: 2008).

Munkhoff R., "Poor Women and Parish Public Health in Sixteenth-Century London", *Renaissance Studies* 28/4 (2014) 579–596.

Munkhoff R., "Reckoning Death: Women Searchers and the Bills of Mortality in Early Modern London" in Vaught J.C. (ed.), *Rhetorics of Bodily Disease and Health in Medieval and Early Modern England* (Surrey: 2010).

Munkhoff R., "Searchers of the Dead: Authority, Marginality, and the Interpretation of Plague in England, 1574–1665", *Gender & History* 11/1 (1999) 1–29.

Murel J., "Print, Authority, and the Bills of Mortality in Seventeenth-Century London", *The Seventeenth Century* 36/6 (2021), 935–959.

Newton G. – Smith R., "Convergence or divergence? Mortality in London, its suburbs and its hinterland between 1550 and 1700", *Annales de démographie historique* 126/2 (2013), 17–49.

Oldland J., "The Wealth of the Trades in Early Tudor London" *London Journal* 31/2 (2006) 127–155.

Rau S. – Rüpke J., "Religion und Urbanität: Wechselseitige Formierungen als Forschungsproblem", *Historische Zeitschrift* 310/3 (2020) 654–680.

Ross S., *The Plague and the Fire of London* (London: 1965).

Rüpke J. – Rau S., "Religion and Urbanity: Reciprocal Formations", *Religion and Urbanity Online* (Berlin – Boston, 2020), online database.

Slack P., "Counting People in Early Modern England: Registers, Registrars, and Political Arithmetic Get access Arrow", *The English Historical Review* 137/587 (2022) 1118–1143.

Spence C., *Accidents and Violent Death in Early Modern London, 1650–1750* (Cambridge: 2016).

Thorpe L.E., *'In Middest of Death': Medical Responses to the Great Plague of 1665 with Special Reference to John Allin* (Ph.D. dissertation, Royal Holloway, University of London: 2017).

Vine E., "'Those Enemies of Christ, If They Are Suffered to Live among Us': Locating Religious Minority Homes and Private Space in Early Modern London", *The London Journal* 43/3 (2018) 197–214.

Walsham A., *Catholic Reformation in Protestant Britain* (London: 2014).

Walsham A., *Charitable Hatred: Tolerance and Intolerance in England, 1500–1700* (Manchester – New York: 2006).

Weinreich S.J., "Sums Theological: Doing Theology with the London Bills of Mortality, 1603–1666", *Church History. Studies in Christianity and Culture* 90/4 (2022) 799–823.

Wirth L., "Urbanism as a Way of Life", *American Journal of Sociology* 44 (1938) 1–24.

PART 2

Ideal Deathbeds

∴

CHAPTER 5

Deathbed Scenes in the Early Modern Atlantic World: Cross-Cultural Perspectives

Erik R. Seeman

European historians pioneered the academic field of death studies. Starting in the 1970s with field-defining works by Philippe Ariès and Pierre Chaunu, and continuing in the 1980s with important books by John McManners, Michel Vovelle, and Clare Gittings, European historians set the agenda for scholars on both sides of the Atlantic who sought to put death in historical perspective.[1] This groundbreaking work demonstrated how much could be learned about religion, society, and *mentalité* through the study of deathways, that is, the beliefs and practices surrounding dying and death, from deathbed scenes and corpse preparation to funerals and memorialization.[2] In no historical era was this more relevant than in the early modern period, when mortality rates remained extraordinarily high and both Catholics and Protestants placed preparation for a good death at the center of their religious practices. In the last decade or so, European historians have continued to play a leading role in the study of death, particularly in analyses of deathbed scenes.

This chapter offers a bridge between recent work on deathbed scenes in early modern Europe and scholarship on the broader Atlantic world. To understand colonialism, the rise of slavery and the slave trade, and the emergence of hybrid cultures in the Americas, one must understand Europe and Europeans. Likewise, to understand the cross-cultural and transatlantic dimensions of deathbed narratives in the early modern Atlantic world, one must understand European deathbed narratives. This chapter builds on the scholarship on early modern European deathbed scenes by showing how its analytical frameworks can be applied to deathbed scenes in the Americas. Thus this chapter operates

---

1 Ariés P., *L'homme devant la mort* (Paris: 1977); Chaunu P., *La mort à Paris: 16e, 17e, 18e siècles* (Paris: 1978); McManners J., *Death and the Enlightenment: Changing Attitudes to Death in Eighteenth-Century France* (New York: 1981); Vovelle M., *La mort et l'Occident: de 1300 à nos jours* (Paris: 1983); Gittings C., *Death, Burial, and the Individual in Early Modern England* (London: 1984). On the North American side, see Stannard D., *The Puritan Way of Death: A Study in Religion, Culture, and Social Change* (New York: 1977).
2 Seeman E.R., *Death in the New World: Cross-Cultural Encounters, 1492–1800* (Philadelphia: 2010) 1.

on two levels simultaneously: analyzing deathbed scenes that took place in the early modern Atlantic world, and analyzing the interpretations formulated by historians of early modern Europe. I conclude by briefly arguing that while European scholars have continued to develop important models for understanding deathbed scenes, their work would be enhanced by greater attention to scholarship on the Americas.

∴

One of the most useful analytical concepts developed by European deathbed scholars in the past decade is Hillard von Thiessen's category of *Normenkonkurrenz*, or the competition of norms.[3] Von Thiessen argues that in the early modern period, religious, political, and community norms were in competition with social norms. He points out that such competition was not unique to the early modern period; moderns experience it too. But these norms were changing in the early modern period, diverging from their late medieval manifestations, and therefore the competition among the normative categories was especially intense and noteworthy.[4] And a key difference between the early modern period and today was the perceived moral authority of the dying person, because he or she was in a normative threshold situation [*in einer normativen Schwellensituation*], or what van Gennep would call a liminal state between two states of being, between life and the afterlife.[5]

Von Thiessen's competition of norms occurs when different norms apply to the same situation. He offers the hypothetical case of a man in early modern Europe who is insulted by another man of the same rank. The discourse of honour calls for physical retaliation – violence – in response to the insult. But the discourse of religion calls for Christian forgiveness. What approach should the

---

3   Von Thiessen H., "Das Sterbebett als normative Schwelle: Der Mensch in der Frühen Neuzeit zwischen irdischer Normenkonkurrenz und göttlichem Gericht", *Historische Zeitschrift* 295 (2012) 625–659. Some of the best recent work on early modern deathbeds focuses on German-speaking regions. See also Reinis A., *Reforming the Art of Dying: The* ars moriendi *in the German Reformation (1519–1528)* (Aldershot, Eng.: 2007); Aikin J.P., "'Ich sterbe': The Construction of the Dying Self in the Advance Preparations for Death of Lutheran Women in Early Modern Germany", in Bielby C. – Richards A. (eds.), *Women and Death 3: Women's Representations of Death in German Culture since 1500* (Rochester, N.Y.: 2010) 31–50; Bepler J., "Practicing Piety: Representations of Women's Dying in German Funeral Sermons of the Early Modern Period", in Bielby C. – Richards A. (eds.), *Women and Death 3*, 12–30.
4   On early modern norms more broadly, see Von Thiessen H., *Das Zeitalter der Ambiguität: Vom Umgang mit Werten und Normen in der Frühen Neuzeit* (Köln, 2021).
5   Van Gennep A., *Les rites de passage* (Paris: 1909).

insulted man take? Which normative system takes precedence?[6] This dynamic could also play out on the deathbed. Even though many of our sources about deathbed scenes are religious in nature – written by ministers or missionaries, meant to demonstrate for pious readers what a good Christian death looked like – there were numerous other competing norms that swirled around the room where a person lay dying. There were the inevitable economic questions of inheritance and estate transference, the social dynamics of neighbors and friends and family, and political ramifications in the deaths of powerful people.[7] Which norms would take precedence, not only in how people experienced the deathbed scene but in how it was narrativized and remembered?

This concept of the competition of norms can be applied to deathbed scenes in the slaveholding societies of the Americas, both in the deaths of slaveowners and of enslaved persons themselves. Consider the dying scene of an enslaved woman named Rose, who served as the nurse and body servant of Sarah Haynsworth Gayle in the U.S. state of Alabama in the early nineteenth century. When Rose fell ill from lockjaw the two women's roles were reversed, with Sarah Gayle tending to the enslaved woman. According to her diary, Gayle did not leave Rose's side for three weeks. 'Indeed, she would not suffer me to do so', Gayle wrote, 'but called to me whenever I left the door'. The plantation mistress placed Rose into a 'neat and every way comfortable room' and prayed by the sick woman's side. As Rose's illness went from bad to worse, Gayle called her children and husband to the deathbed. When the enslaved woman finally died, Gayle closed Rose's eyes and prayed in 'tears and fervor' that eventually she would be united with Rose 'in happiness in another world'. Gayle insisted that 'color made no difference, but [...] [Rose's] life would have been as precious, if I could have saved it, as if she had been white as snow'.[8]

The competition of norms is clearly evident in this deathbed scene. On the one hand, Sarah Gayle felt compelled to enact a scene of Christian benevolence infused with bourgeois sentimentality. Even though she never formally affiliated with a particular denomination, she regularly attended Protestant services. She had imbibed a vision of the good Protestant death that was allegedly colour-blind; whites and blacks could adhere to the scripts of both the dying person and the bereaved observer. On the other hand, this claim of a

---

6 Von Thiessen, "Das Sterbebett als normative Schwelle", 635.
7 On social dynamics in European deathbed scenes, see Düselder H., "'Wer so stirbt, der stirbt wohl!' Der Umgang mit der Sterbestunde im Spiegel von Leichenpredigten", in von Hülsen-Esch A. – Westermann-Angerhausen H. (eds.), *Zum Sterben Schön: Alter, Totentanz, und Sterbekunst von 1500 bis Heute* (Regensburg: 2006) 238–249.
8 Wiggins S.W. – Truss R.S. (eds.), *The Journal of Sarah Haynsworth Gayle, 1827–1835: A Substitute for Social Intercourse* (Tuscaloosa, Ala.: 2013) 285–287.

colour-blind Christian community ran smack into the race-based norms of slavery. One is not surprised to learn that Sarah Gayle did not manumit any of her slaves after this intense experience at Rose's deathbed.

A similar dynamic played out in the death of Joseph Jones, but in this case the dying person was a wealthy white man and the observers were his enslaved laborers. Jones was badly wounded in an accident when his horse bolted and threw him from a carriage. The head injuries he sustained caused him to lose all power of speech; it quickly became evident that he was going to die. In his final hours his son called the enslaved laborers from the fields to say goodbye to their owner. The son held up his father's wrist so each slave could shake the dying man's hand. 'I told them to come in one by one', his son wrote, 'and bid him farewell forever'. According to the son, the enslaved men and women wept and said, 'God bless you master'.[9] As with the death of Rose, this scene demonstrates the competing norms by which the Jones family enacted the death of their patriarch. Members of the 'family, black and white', as southern slave owners liked to call it, were brought together to enact the grief demanded by the good Protestant death.[10] And yet these enslaved workers were not at the bedside of their own free will: 'I told them to come in one by one' was the command that came naturally to the mouth of the son, who was steeped in the competing norm of race-based slavery.

Catholic slaveowners' deaths throughout Latin America were likewise marked by a competition of norms. Take, for example, the 1682 dying scene of Micaela de Torres, a slaveowner in Lima, Peru. As she approached death, her enslaved woman, Margarita de Torres, asked for a 'letter of freedom' (*carta de libertad*) for herself and her two enslaved sons. Declaring herself of sound mind and judgement, Micaela signed a notarized document indicating that the family was free. The letter of freedom stated, 'In order to do right by the boys, so that they can secure their freedom together with the said Margarita, their mother, who has been a good slave to me, and because of the love and goodwill that I have for her, I want to do this'.[11] On the very next day after

---

9 Jones C.C., "Some Account of My Dear and Honored Father's Death" (1846), quoted in Warren J., *Masters of the Dead: Slavery, Death, and Ideology in the Antebellum South* (Ph.D. dissertation, Indiana University: 2014) 60–62.

10 On the 'family, black and white', see Winter K.J., *The American Dreams of John B. Prentis, Slave Trader* (Athens, Ga.: 2011) ch. 5.

11 McKinley M.A., "Till Death Do Us Part: Testamentary Manumission in Seventeenth-Century Lima, Peru", *Slavery & Abolition* 33 (2012) 381–401, quotation at 382. Other important works on death in Latin America include Lomnitz C., *Death and the Idea of Mexico* (Cambridge, Mass.: 2005); Ramos G., *Death and Conversion in the Andes: Lima and Cuzco, 1532–1670* (Notre Dame, Ind.: 2010).

signing this document, Micaela died. Margarita and her sons gained their freedom, but their struggle was not over. Micaela's four adult daughters soon filed a lawsuit against Margarita, saying that the letter of freedom was invalid because it had been 'extracted under duress on Micaela's deathbed'.[12] The case worked its way through the courts for nine years, ultimately generating five hundred pages of testimony before the court ruled in favour of the daughters. The point here is not the case's outcome but rather its origin: a deathbed scene in which competing norms were clearly in evidence. Whereas the dying mother enacted norms of Christian benevolence, the daughters drew on legal discourses of property transfer to assert their rights to Margarita and her sons. As a highly charged ritual space, the deathbed illuminated these competing norms as if by a flash of light.

Or consider the even more tangled case of Polonia de Ribas, a wealthy *mulata* woman in Veracruz, Mexico. In March 1679, as de Ribas lay dying, she, like Micaela de Torres, notarized a document freeing one of her slaves. The document states, 'I declare that among my belongings is Gerónimo de Yrala, *negro criollo* [that is, a man of African descent born in the Americas], my slave. […] It is my will, given that he provides 40 pesos as he has promised, that when the time comes […] my executors provide him with a *carta de libertad*'. The remarkable thing about this deathbed manumission was that the freed man was the dying woman's brother. As a result, the scene illuminates several competing norms. The Christian deathbed benevolence demonstrated by de Ribas is tempered by the fact that she kept her own brother as a slave for many years, and by the complete lack of sentimental language in the manumission document. Contrast this with the language she used in freeing another slave, this one of no relation, who 'has served me with so much purpose and loyalty' and 'has always aided and supported me with much love'.[13] Here, the deathbed scene sheds light on competing norms of family, property, and Christian generosity. In fact, were it not for the rituals surrounding the deathbed, these norms would not have come into such direct competition.

Other European scholars provide additional valuable analytical concepts, such as Radmila Pavlíčková in a thought-provoking 2016 article.[14] Pavlíčková focuses on several Catholic *Sterbebücher* (books of dying) from sixteenth-century

---

12 McKinley, "'Till Death Do Us Part'" 385.
13 Williams D.T., "'My Conscience Is Free and Clear': African-Descended Women, Status, and Slave Owning in Mid-Colonial Mexico", *The Americas* 75 (2018) 525–554, quotations at 545–546.
14 Pavlíčková R.P., "'Unter den Ketzern zu leben und zu sterben ist gar schwerlich und geferlich': Das Sterbebuch des Johann Leisentritt im Kontext der Katholischen Sterbebücher des 16. Jahrhunderts", *Archiv für Reformationsgeschichte* 107 (2016) 193–216.

Oberlausitz, also known as Lusatia, on today's Germany-Poland border just north of the Czech Republic. When the Reformation began, this region quickly became majority-Protestant. Pavlíčková convincingly shows that as early as the 1530s – and not later, as previous historians have assumed – Catholic writers in this region used deathbed scenes as part of their polemics against Lutheran concepts of salvation. According to the Catholic authors, dying was not confessionally neutral. One dies as either a Catholic or a Lutheran, the latter group denigrated as *Ketzern* or heretics. A good Catholic could have his or her dying scene compromised – with salvation endangered – by the presence of these "heretics". Writers thus weaponized deathbed scenes in their confessional struggles.[15]

We can see similar dynamics playing out in many parts of colonial North America where missionaries to American Indians found themselves surrounded by indifferent or actively hostile residents. In those contexts, missionaries likewise weaponized deathbed scenes, using them against the Indigenous "heretics" in their midst and in their continuing confessional struggles with other Europeans. Among the Wendats of present-day Ontario, Canada, in the land the Natives called Wendake, seventeenth-century Jesuit missionaries described deathbeds as a key battleground in their war against Indigenous "heretics". Because the Jesuit descriptions of "good" deaths drew so much from the European *ars moriendi* literature, these sources must be used carefully.[16] They tell us more about the polemic messages the Jesuits were trying to convey than what actually happened on the deathbed. They are, nonetheless, revealing.

In the 1640s a Christian Wendat woman, five months pregnant and in fine health, went to visit her relatives some thirty miles from her village. While staying with her relatives, she fell ill. She surprised her family members by saying that she needed to head to the Jesuit mission at Sainte-Marie. 'I leave you', she reportedly said, 'because I wish to die among the faithful, and near my brothers who bring the words of eternal life. They will assist me at death, and I desire that they attend to my burial'. Her wish was not merely for the Jesuits to care for her on earth. 'I shall rise again with them, and I do not wish my bones to

---

15   For a different perspective, one that emphasizes Catholic adoptions of and adaptations to Lutheran practices, see Christ M., "Catholic Cultures of Lutheranism? Confessional Ambiguity and Syncretism in Sixteenth-Century Upper Lusatia", *Past and Present* 234 (2017) 165–188; Christ M., *Biographies of a Reformation: Religious Change and Confessional Coexistence in Upper Lusatia, 1520–1635* (Oxford: 2021), esp. ch. 5 on Johann Leisentrit.

16   On the European *ars moriendi* tradition, see O'Connor M.C., *The Art of Dying Well: The Development of the* Ars moriendi (New York: 1942); Beaty N.L., *The Craft of Dying: A Study in the Literary Tradition of the* Ars moriendi *in England* (New Haven: 1970); Ariés, *L'homme devant la mort*, ch.6; Reinis, *Reforming the Art of Dying*.

be mingled with those of my deceased relatives, who will be nothing to me in eternity'.[17] So the woman paddled back to her village and then walked the nine miles to Sainte-Marie, where she was able to receive communion before dying. Like the minority Catholics in the sixteenth-century Lausitz, the Jesuits represented Christian Wendats as surrounded by heretics who could undermine their hopes for salvation. Thus they eagerly recounted this story of a woman who wanted to 'die among the faithful'.

Deathbeds were indeed supercharged sites where the battle between Catholicism and heresy played out. During a 1636–1637 epidemic of what may have been a strep infection, a Native shaman named Tonnerawanont challenged the Jesuits in Wendake. This renowned healer directly opposed the Jesuit attempts to baptize the dying, urging the sick instead to participate in dances and feasts and to purify themselves in sweat lodges. But then in early 1637 Tonnerawanont slipped on the ice in front of his longhouse and broke his leg. It seems that an infection set in, for over the next three weeks the shaman weakened and died. The death of the Jesuits' rival immediately improved their fortunes. In one longhouse the missionaries found the atmosphere dramatically changed. 'While the little sorcerer Tonnerawanont was there', the Jesuits recalled, 'we had always been badly received, especially upon the subject of baptism. We had been loaded with insults there'. When they tried to baptize a dying woman, her father said they did not need the Jesuits' help: 'We have a certain road that our souls take after death'. The implication was they did not want to follow the Jesuits' path. But after Tonnerawanont died, the family no longer resisted the Jesuits' attempts to baptize the woman. 'God had (it seems) changed their hearts'.[18] They performed the ritual and the woman soon died. Once again a deathbed scene was a site of religious combat: when the equivalent of an Indigenous field marshal died, it cleared the way for what Jesuits described as a triumph. They narrated this story for a European audience because it represented the deathbed as a place where God would demonstrate his power over "heretics", to return to Pavlíčková's keyword.

Whereas this was a "good" or "model" death, according to Catholic standards, Jesuits also recounted numerous "bad" or what I prefer to call "unorthodox" deaths. Elsewhere I have argued that these unorthodox deaths are more likely to offer evidence of how people actually died, because they contain unique, idiosyncratic elements and have not been forced into the *ars moriendi*

---

17   Thwaites R.G. (ed.), *The Jesuit Relations and Allied Documents*, 73 vols. (Cleveland: 1896–1901) 26:207–209. Hereafter cited as JR. See also Seeman E.R., *The Huron-Wendat Feast of the Dead: Indian-European Encounters in Early North America* (Baltimore: 2011).
18   JR 13:251.

framework.[19] Such deaths likewise show the weaponization of deathbeds in the battle between Christians and so-called heretics. Take the case of a Wendat man named Joutaya, who was dangerously ill during an epidemic. Jesuits used his deathbed scene to demonstrate what they considered in this case to be the victory of Catholicism over heretical beliefs. Joutaya was interested in receiving baptism, which made him distinctive during the early years of the Jesuit mission in Wendake. But as he lay dying, Joutaya experienced a supernatural vision that the head missionary, Jean de Brébeuf, found troubling. As Brébeuf put it, 'the Devil appeared to [Joutaya] in the form of one of his deceased brothers'. This is almost certainly a revision of the man's words. It is much more likely that Joutaya simply stated that his dead brother's spirit had visited him; dying Wendats frequently reported similar supernatural interventions.[20]

The brother entered Joutaya's longhouse without greeting the dying man – a clear breach of Wendat social protocol. He then sat on the side of the fire opposite the dying man for a long time without saying anything. If Joutaya wondered why the spirit was angry with him, he soon found out. The spirit asked, 'How now, my brother, do you wish to leave us'? This must have been a reference to Joutaya's flirtation with Christianity. By accepting baptism, Joutaya threatened to leave the religious world of his ancestors. Unnerved, Joutaya tried to win back the favour of the spirit world. 'No, my brother', he replied, 'I don't wish to leave you; I won't leave you'. The spirit was mollified. He moved closer to the dying man and tenderly caressed him. Soon Joutaya was dead.[21] From Brébeuf's perspective this was a "bad" death; it certainly did not adhere to the *ars moriendi* model. But from the perspective of Pavlíčková's analytical framework, this is a clear example of the deathbed as a battleground between different faiths: not only in Wendake between Catholic and Wendat beliefs, but also in Europe between Catholics and Protestants. For the European audience of the *Jesuit Relations*, in which these examples were published, Indian deathbed scenes were evidence of the expansion of Catholicism, implicitly at the expense of Protestantism. Indeed, deathbed scenes provided some of the best evidence of Jesuit conversions in North America; they appear over and over again in the *Relations*.

Catholics, of course, were not the only confessional group to use deathbed scenes as evidence of their overseas success. The Church of England in 1701

---

19 Seeman E.R., "Reading Indians' Deathbed Scenes: Ethnohistorical and Representational Approaches", *Journal of American History* 88 (2001) 17–47.
20 On supernatural aspects of English deathbeds, see Marshall P., "Angels around the Deathbed: Variations on a Theme in the English Art of Dying," in Marshall P. – Walsham A. (eds.), *Angels in the Early Modern World* (New York: 2006) 83–103.
21 JR 8:137–139.

created the Society for the Propagation of the Gospel (SPG) to promote missionary activity around the British Atlantic. Anglicans saw the SPG as a counterweight to aggressive Catholic, and especially Jesuit, missionary efforts. In its first decade of existence the SPG employed a New England missionary named Experience Mayhew to produce a book of Psalms and the Gospel of John in the Wampanoag language, which he had learned in infancy growing up in a missionary family on Martha's Vineyard, an island off the coast of Massachusetts.[22] With alternating columns of Wampanoag and English text, his translation was published in 1709.[23] His most famous book, however, appeared in 1727: *Indian Converts; or, Some Accounts of the Lives and Dying Speeches of a Considerable Number of the Christianized Indians of Martha's Vineyard*. This book was dedicated to the SPG, which had long supported Mayhew's work on the island.

Even more to the point, the book's opening 'Attestation', signed by eleven Boston ministers, contrasted Mayhew's propagation of Protestantism, 'a Faith, which emancipates Mankind from the worst of Slaveries and Miseries', with the expansion of Catholicism. 'The Missionaries of Antichrist are more than can be numbred, and the Bigots are at prodigious Pains to propagate the Romish Idolatries'.[24] After the 'Attestation' the book is less explicit in its confessional polemics, but each deathbed scene – all seventy-seven of them – shows an Indian dying well, according to the Protestant model of the good death.

Paradoxically, even though deathbeds were weapons in confessional warfare, as Pavlíčková asserts, such narratives shared a great deal across the confessional divide. This is a point made with great subtlety in a recent chapter by Charles Green. Green's aim is to investigate the 'discursive and polemical contexts' that catalyzed the publication of deathbed narratives in England from 1592 to 1646. At the same time he sees the deathbed narrative as 'an emergent devotional subgenre that combined many features across the confessional divide that gave rise to it'.[25] In other words, confessional competition helped

---

22 The classic treatment of the SPG in New England is Kellaway W., *The New England Company, 1649–1776: Missionary Society to the American Indians* (New York: 1961). On Mayhew, see Leibman L.A. (ed.), *Experience Mayhew's* Indian Converts: *A Cultural Edition* (Amherst, Mass.: 2008).
23 Mayhew E., *The Massachusett Psalter; or, Psalms of David, with the Gospel According to John* (Boston: 1709).
24 Mayhew E., *Indian Converts; or, Some Accounts of the Lives and Dying Speeches of a Considerable Number of the Christianized Indians of Martha's Vineyard* (London: 1727) xiv.
25 Green C., "'Now the Lord hath made me a spectacle': Deathbed Narratives and Devotional Identities in the Early Seventeenth Century", in Clarke E. – Daniel R.W. (eds.), *People and Piety: Protestant Devotional Identities in Early Modern England* (Manchester, Eng.: 2020) 259–274, quotations at 261.

promote the publication of deathbed scenes even as Protestant and Catholic narratives contained much that was similar.

This was strikingly evident in the model Indian deathbed scenes that missionaries to North America described in the seventeenth and eighteenth centuries. These narratives were of course shaped by European precedents: the Catholic *ars moriendi* tradition and the Protestant version that evolved from it. But it would be an oversimplification to see the Indian model death as simply the European model transplanted to North America. Granted, missionaries described Indian model deaths in familiar European terms to make the scenes palatable to European and Euro-American readers. Yet Indian actions on the deathbed forced missionaries to adapt the European templates they brought with them to the Americas. In the European templates the question of whether the dying person wanted to receive a Christian burial were almost never addressed. Simply not an issue in European and Euro-American deathbed narratives, Christian burial cut to the heart of the missionary endeavour in North America. Whereas missionaries could occasionally overlook some Indian traditions that crept into deathbed scenes, burial was non-negotiable. This was a characteristic that united both Protestant and Catholic narratives.[26]

Likewise, the importance of the dying person exhorting friends and family crossed the confessional divide.[27] In European and Euro-American scripts, such speeches served a very different purpose, namely, to urge the survivors to live upright lives and to prepare for death. In the Indian model, by contrast, the dying person most commonly urged the observers to maintain their adherence to Christianity. This new element in the script was not apparent until the missionaries achieved a critical mass of converts and wished to represent their charges as exemplary and not just nominal Christians. In 1648, for example, the Jesuit Gabriel Lalemant described the good death of a Christian Wendat man. After receiving extreme unction, this highly respected individual gave a lengthy speech to 'his people' in which he urged them to 'drive the wicked away from amid your cabins, lest they should pervert you'.[28] By 'pervert' the dying man did not mean simply that his fellow Christian Indians might be led into sin but that they might be led to abandon Christianity altogether. Protestants included similar speeches in their model deathbed scenes. In 1685, for example,

---

26   Wyss H.E. "'Things That Do Accompany Salvation': Colonialism, Conversion, and Cultural Exchange in Experience Mayhew's *Indian Converts*", *Early American Literature* 33 (1998) 39–61; Seeman E.R., "Reading Indians' Deathbed Scenes"; Rivett S., *The Science of the Soul in Colonial New England* (Chapel Hill, N.C.: 2011) ch. 4.

27   Brunner B., "Die gedruckte Leichenpredigt als Erbauungsbuch – eine Erfolgsgeschichte des 17. Jahrhunderts?", *Medium Buch* 1 (2019) 87–105.

28   JR 32:237.

the Massachusetts missionary John Eliot reported that 'Old Jacob' began his deathbed speech as follows: 'My Brethren: now hear me a few words, stand fast all you people in your praying to God'.[29] The context had changed from European scripts, but in the Americas both Catholic and Protestant clergymen represented model Indian deathbed scenes as including exhortative speeches to family and friends. What was new compared to Europe was that these dying exhortations urged loved ones to remain Christians.

Another aspect of model Indian deathbed scenes that crossed the confessional divide was representing the dying as being resigned to God's will. Again this carried different valences among Indians than in Europe. This element of the script was absolutely standard in European models; dying people were almost always represented as indicating they were willing to die, and their willingness was linked to their hope they were going to heaven. This likewise became a frequent element in Indian deathbed scenes, as missionaries were eager to show that their converts could serve as models even for European and Euro-American audiences. It should be emphasized that this discussion has focused mostly on *model* Indian deathbed scenes, where Indian agency can be hard to identify because of missionary efforts to fit the experiences of dying Indians into pre-existing templates. The situation was rather different with unorthodox deathbed scenes – such as Joutaya's, above – that did not adhere to the European model, where one may discern Indians working to shape their deaths according to their own cultural priorities. In model Indian scenes, however, elements such as resignation to God's will were present whether the missionary crafting the narrative was Protestant or Catholic.

Thus, because of the deep roots of the *ars moriendi* tradition that both Catholics and Protestants inherited, there were aspects of deathbed scenes that crossed the confessional divide. But of course there were confessional and denominational distinctions that people considered important. Here we can combine insights from Green and Pavlíčková to shed light on deathbed scenes in the Americas. Green observes that it has long been a tendency in Reformation history 'to describe deathbeds in the terminology of theatre'.[30] Even when historians are not making explicitly performative arguments they talk about 'roles' and 'performances' in the 'staging' of deathbed scenes. At the same time, Pavlíčková insists that because these performances were semi-public, enacted before an audience of friends and family and neighbors, they were an important means of what she calls 'collective confessional self-disciplining'.[31] Using

29 Eliot J., *The Dying Speeches of Several Indians* (Cambridge, Mass.: 1685?) 6.
30 Green, "'Now the Lord hath made me a spectacle'" 269.
31 Pavlíčková, "'Unter den Ketzern zu leben'" 215.

both Pavlíčková's insight about how people learned the deathbed conventions of their confession and Green's performative analysis allows us to see how deathbeds were important sites of learning how to die 'correctly', as defined by one's co-religionists. In other words, members of the two confessions – and I would add members of the various Protestant denominations – used deathbed scenes to teach and to learn what was distinctive about their faith.

Indeed the more distinctive the faith the more distinctive its deathbed scenes, and therefore Moravian deaths provide a good opportunity to witness this dynamic. In the middle of the eighteenth century the Moravians, a German Pietist denomination, were notable for their intense focus on Christ's wounds – especially what they called the side hole – and his bodily fluids.[32] In addition, Moravians were nearly alone among Protestant missionaries in systematically collecting deathbed scenes of the enslaved. Christian Oldendorp included forty-seven of these brief descriptions in his *History of the Mission of the Evangelical Brethren* (1777). The scenes took place between 1741 and 1768 on the Caribbean island of St. Thomas. They include descriptions of the deaths of thirty-one women and sixteen men, a nearly 2:1 female-to-male ratio that was even more lopsided than the 57-to-43 ratio that obtained for the 1,800 Moravian converts on St. Thomas in 1768. They are almost all model deathbed scenes, so again they are not the best sources for understanding what actually happened on the deathbeds of the enslaved. But as model scenes they are valuable for understanding what the Moravians considered to be their success stories in the Caribbean.

A distinctive aspect of Moravian deathbed scenes was the importance of singing as the person lay dying.[33] More than in other Protestant denominations, dying Moravians used deathbed songs to express love for Christ and demonstrate a willingness to die. Singing also allowed observers to console the dying with reminders of Christ's love. When an enslaved woman named Antoinette was dying in 1766, her husband Jonathan anxiously kept a vigil by her bedside. As her dying hour approached, he 'entertained her with the singing of consoling songs'. This pleased her so much that she 'asked him to continue singing until her last breath'.[34]

In this case we do not know what Antoinette's husband sang, but it is clear from other deathbed scenes that baptized slaves responded to the Moravian

32   Fogleman A.S., *Jesus is Female: Moravians and the Challenge of Radical Religion in Early America* (Philadelphia: 2007).
33   Wheeler R. – Eyerly S., "Songs of the Spirit: Hymnody in the Moravian Mohican Missions", *Journal of Moravian History* 17 (2017) 1–26, esp. 20–22.
34   Highfield A.R. – Barac V. (eds.), *C.G.A. Oldendorp's History of the Mission of the Evangelical Brethren* (Ann Arbor: 1987) 418. See also Seeman, *Death in the New World* ch.6.

focus on Christ's bodily fluids, an emphasis that struck many Europeans and Euro-Americans as peculiar. As an enslaved man named Johannes was dying of consumption in 1767, he gathered his last few breaths and 'tried to join in singing the verse of the song about "the sweat of Jesus' face saves you from coming to the tribunal"'. Likewise, when an enslaved woman named Christina drew close to death in 1756 her fellow slave Cornelius was said to have sung to her, 'The blood of Christ and His righteousness, that is your embellishment and your cloak of honor'.[35] For people of African descent, whose death practices always incorporated music, the Moravian practice of singing with the dying was powerfully attractive. It is also a good example of Pavlíčková's concept of collective self-disciplining. The dying and their observers acted out the distinctive elements of Moravian belief and practice, including its focus on singing and on Christ's bodily fluids. They learned not only from books and from ministers how they should behave, but also from one another.

As the stories of Antoinette and Christina make clear, Moravian missionaries paid careful attention to the dying words and actions of enslaved women. This connects with another analytical framework that has been important in the European scholarship, not just in recent years but going back a couple of decades: namely, that the deathbed offered women real – albeit temporary – power to speak and be heard. Denied the right to a formal religious voice by Paul's injunction to 'keep silence in the churches' (1 Cor. 14:34 KJV) and other cross-confessional norms, women found themselves in an unfamiliar position at the center of religious attention on their deathbeds. Because the dying were believed to straddle this world and the next, and to be privy to rare glimpses of the afterlife, their words were granted a weight that ordinary words did not carry. Women took advantage of this power, even though it was only fleeting.

Ralph Houlbrooke makes these points in a 1996 chapter on English Puritan deathbed scenes. He writes that Puritan women 'had certain exceptional opportunities on the death-bed'. They could 'utter prayers, exhortations, and statements of faith which were heard with a special respect'. And whereas the dying of all denominations were expected to show resignation to God's will, Houlbrooke argues that the Puritan way of death, which 'particularly encouraged the outward manifestation of individual faith, allowed women a prominent role in the drama of their own death-beds'.[36]

I would argue that Houlbrooke exaggerates the distinctiveness of the *Puritan* emphasis on the 'outward manifestations of individual faith', but his

---

35 Highfield – Barac (eds.), *C.G.A. Oldendorp's History* 418, 547.
36 Houlbrooke R., "The Puritan Death-bed, c.1560–c.1660", in Durston C. – Eales J. (eds.), *The Culture of English Puritanism, 1560–1700* (New York: 1996) 122–44, quotations at 140.

larger point stands: women's dying words were indeed received with special respect.[37] This dynamic likewise marked cross-cultural deathbed scenes in the Americas. Returning to the Moravians, Christian Oldendorp recorded numerous women delivering forceful messages as they died. In some scenes, women urged their friends and family to hold true to the new faith. Such was the case with an enslaved woman named Eunica as she grew weaker and weaker in December 1762. According to Oldendorp, 'She summoned her friends and acquaintances to her deathbed and exhorted them with the following words: "I implore you, stay with the Savior and hold firm to him"'. Note Oldendorp's word to describe Eunica's action: she 'exhorted' her loved ones. Moravians were more open to female exhorters than most other Protestants; the formerly enslaved Rebecca Protten, for example, was a preacher of some renown in the Caribbean.[38] Still, it is notable that Oldendorp attributed such agency to a woman like Eunica who was held in bondage. Likewise, Oldendorp used active language to describe the dying scene of an enslaved woman named Regina. First she 'exhorted' her unbaptized children, then she 'urged' her baptized daughter to stay true to the faith, and finally she 'addressed' the assembled sisters with her parting words.[39] Although Eunica and Regina were soon dead, they left memories of active and forceful speech among their families, their fellow enslaved Christians, and – through Oldendorp's celebratory writings – a transatlantic audience of readers.

Even when the words were not so forceful they were afforded attention. This is evident in the letters that the Methodist missionary William Fish sent from Jamaica to London in the years around 1800. In one he described a Methodist convert in Kingston, 'an old black woman, for many years infirm in body but lively in spirit', who died without warning. One Sunday she went to church, attended the Lord's Table, and 'attended her Class' in the evening. That night she was suddenly seized with difficulty breathing and died before friends could be called. 'Our hope of her', Fish wrote, 'is therefore founded on her conduct and experience in *life*, and not on her *dying* testimony'.[40]

37 Similar points are made in Beier L.M., "The Good Death in Seventeenth-Century England", in Houlbrooke R. (ed.), *Death, Ritual, and Bereavement* (New York: 1989) 43–61; Hallam E.A., "Turning the Hourglass: Gender Relations at the Deathbed in Early Modern Canterbury", *Mortality* 1 (1996) 61–82; Seeman E.R., *Pious Persuasions: Laity and Clergy in Eighteenth-Century New England* (Baltimore: 1999) 73–77; Becker L.M., *Death and the Early Modern Englishwoman* (Farnham, Eng.: 2003) ch.5.
38 Sensbach J.F., *Rebecca's Revival: Creating Black Christianity in the Atlantic World* (Cambridge, Mass.: 2005).
39 Highfield – Barac (eds.), *C.G.A. Oldendorp's History* 548, 576–77.
40 Rev. William Fish, Kingston, to Joseph Butterworth, London, 11 May 1804, in the Wesleyan Methodist Missionary Society Archive, West Indies General Correspondence, box 111,

One can hear in Fish's tone his longing for the more complete information dying words would have offered. This he received in several other cases that he reported, including that of Elizabeth Poynter, a 'black woman' who lived thirty miles from Kingston yet still made the trek there once a month to receive communion. Fish did not witness Poynter's death but rather learned about it from her friends and fellow communicants. 'I am inform'd her last days were her best', Fish wrote. 'She grew more fervent than ever; and enjoy'd a great increase of the love of God as was evident by the fruits thereof to all who were with her'. Fish portrayed a scene in which observers paid close attention to the dying woman as her words grew more 'fervent' and provided evidence of her 'love of God'. The careful observations continued to the very end: 'Her indisposition of body was so gentle, that no one thought her in danger 'till almost the very moment when she cheerfully resign'd her soul to Him who had bought it with His own blood'.[41] Even though Fish did not report Poynter's exact words, it is clear that the observers paid careful attention to her deathbed speech. Fish was so impressed by the proceedings that he sent this and several other deathbed accounts to Joseph Benson, the London-based editor of the widely circulated *Methodist Magazine*. Thus did readers on both sides of the Atlantic encounter cross-cultural deathbed scenes that took place in the Americas.

...

In this chapter I have identified four especially helpful analytical contributions by Europeanists: 1) the competition of norms, which shows how deathbed scenes illuminate the tensions and slippages between social, political, and religious discourses; 2) the polemics of deathbeds, which demonstrate how people mobilized deathbeds in cross-confessional and cross-cultural conflicts; 3) the cross-denominational and even cross-confessional similarities of deathbed scenes, which persisted even as the discursive use of deathbeds arose from those very divides; and 4) the power that women could gain on the deathbed, even if that power was temporary.

It is clear that historians of early modern European deathbeds have a lot to offer scholars studying cross-cultural deathbed scenes in the Americas. This makes sense: virtually all of the examples that survive in the historical

FBN 1, no. 4, Special Collections, SOAS National Research Library. Emphasis in original. See also Brown V., *The Reaper's Garden: Death and Power in the World of Atlantic Slavery* (Cambridge, Mass.: 2008) 206.

41 Rev. William Fish, Kingston, to Rev. [Joseph] Benson, London, 26 April 1804, in the Wesleyan Methodist Missionary Society Archive, box 111, FBN 1, no. 2. I have not been able to confirm whether this scene appeared in the *Methodist Magazine*.

record were written by people of European descent (even when details were first gathered by Indigenous or African observers). Deathbed scenes are unlike other mortuary practices in that they leave almost no trace in the material record, except for a few paintings and drawings. Whereas archaeologists have unearthed abundant evidence of Indigenous and African burial and memorial practices in the Americas,[42] scholars must rely almost exclusively on European and Euro-American observers to learn about deathbed scenes. It is therefore logical that European analytical categories are useful in the Americas.

But the impressive European literature is open to critique because of its relative insularity. Many historians are content to work within a single European national context, without much reference to scholarship on areas outside that nation, except perhaps for a nod to Ariès. To this general rule there are, of course, important exceptions, including some excellent comparative work.[43] Yet even the European authors who look beyond the borders of their own studies only rarely consult the scholarship on deathbed scenes in the Americas. Examples of relevant work include that by scholars such as Kristina Bross on dying Indian speeches in colonial New England literature, or Sarah Rivett on the science of dying in Puritan deathbed testimonies, or Michelle McKinley on testamentary manumission in seventeenth-century Peru.[44]

There are two costs associated with overlooking these and other scholars. The first is historical. By the middle of the seventeenth century, American travel and missionary writings were increasingly available to literate European audiences. In France people read the *Jesuit Relations*, in England the accounts of colonization boosters such as Richard Hakluyt circulated widely, and everywhere readers encountered the reports of Hernán Cortéz, Samuel de Champlain, John Smith, and other colonizers who wrote about interactions with American Indians and Africans. Thus, literate Europeans learned about cross-cultural deathbed scenes, and future research should investigate the impacts this had on European ways of dying.

---

42   A very small sample would include Handler J.S. – Lange F.W., *Plantation Slavery in Barbados: An Archaeological and Historical Investigation* (Cambridge, Mass.: 1978); Rubertone P.E., *Grave Undertakings: An Archaeology of Roger Williams and the Narragansett Indians* (Washington, D.C.: 2001); Frohne A.E., *The African Burial Ground in New York City: Memory, Spirituality, and Space* (Syracuse, N.Y.: 2015).

43   See, for example, Harding V., *The Dead and the Living in Paris and London, 1500–1670* (Cambridge, Eng.: 2002); Laqueur T.W., *The Work of the Dead: A Cultural History of Mortal Remains* (Princeton: 2015).

44   Bross K., "Dying Saints, Vanishing Savages: 'Dying Indian Speeches' in Colonial New England Literature", *Early American Literature* 36 (2001) 325–352; Rivett S., "Tokenography: Narration and the Science of Dying in Puritan Deathbed Testimonies", *Early American Literature* 42 (2007) 471–494; McKinley M.A., "Till Death Do Us Part".

The second cost associated with inattention to American deathbed scenes is analytical. Historians of deathbed scenes in the Americas have offered analytical models that could be fruitfully employed in European contexts, perhaps in places where different deathways came into contact, as in multi-confessional communities, or even just within specific denominational or confessional contexts. These analytical models from the Americas offer several insights that could be useful for Europeanists. For example, they have shown that new, syncretic deathways were formed in the encounters between people of different cultures. Participants observed the dying scenes of those around them and sometimes incorporated aspects into their own practices. Moreover, historians of the Americas have demonstrated that people sometimes recognized similarities in other cultures' deathbed scenes when confronted with unfamiliar ways of dying. These perceived similarities allowed for communication across cultural lines, even when such communication facilitated, ironically enough, conflictual encounters.[45]

Much work remains to be done before scholarship on deathbed scenes in the Americas and in Europe is integrated into a field that is truly transatlantic. Given that the history of death has been a lively and important field of study for nearly fifty years, it is time to strengthen those connections.

Bibliography

Primary Printed Sources

Eliot J., *The Dying Speeches of Several Indians* (Cambridge, Mass.: 1685?).
Mayhew E., *The Massachusett Psalter; or, Psalms of David, with the Gospel According to John* (Boston: 1709).
Mayhew E., *Indian Converts; or, Some Accounts of the Lives and Dying Speeches of a Considerable Number of the Christianized Indians of Martha's Vineyard* (London: 1727).

Primary Manuscript Sources

Rev. William Fish, Kingston, to Rev. [Joseph] Benson, London, 26 April 1804, in the Wesleyan Methodist Missionary Society Archive, box 111, FBN 1, no. 2.
Rev. William Fish, Kingston, to Joseph Butterworth, London, 11 May 1804, in the Wesleyan Methodist Missionary Society Archive, West Indies General Correspondence, box 111, FBN 1, no. 4, Special Collections, SOAS National Research Library.

---

45 Seeman, *Death in the New World*.

Secondary Literature

Aikin J.P., "'Ich sterbe': The Construction of the Dying Self in the Advance Preparations for Death of Lutheran Women in Early Modern Germany", in Bielby C. – Richards A. (eds.), *Women and Death 3: Women's Representations of Death in German Culture since 1500* (Rochester, N.Y.: 2010) 31–50.

Ariés P., *L'homme devant la mort* (Paris: 1977).

Beaty N.L., *The Craft of Dying: A Study in the Literary Tradition of the* Ars moriendi *in England* (New Haven: 1970).

Becker L.M., *Death and the Early Modern Englishwoman* (Farnham, Eng.: 2003).

Beier L.M., "The Good Death in Seventeenth-Century England", in Houlbrooke R. (ed.), *Death, Ritual, and Bereavement* (New York: 1989) 43–61.

Bepler J., "Practicing Piety: Representations of Women's Dying in German Funeral Sermons of the Early Modern Period", in Bielby C. – Richards A. (eds.), *Women and Death 3: Women's Representations of Death in German Culture since 1500* (Rochester, N.Y.: 2010) 12–30.

Bross K., "Dying Saints, Vanishing Savages: 'Dying Indian Speeches' in Colonial New England Literature", *Early American Literature* 36 (2001) 325–352.

Brown V., *The Reaper's Garden: Death and Power in the World of Atlantic Slavery* (Cambridge, Mass.: 2008).

Brunner B., "Die gedruckte Leichenpredigt als Erbauungsbuch – eine Erfolgsgeschichte des 17. Jahrhunderts?", *Medium Buch* 1 (2019) 87–105.

Chaunu P., *La mort à Paris: 16e, 17e, 18e siècles* (Paris: 1978).

Christ M., "Catholic Cultures of Lutheranism? Confessional Ambiguity and Syncretism in Sixteenth-Century Upper Lusatia", *Past and Present* 234 (2017) 165–188.

Christ M., *Biographies of a Reformation: Religious Change and Confessional Coexistence in Upper Lusatia, 1520–1635* (Oxford: 2021).

Düselder H., "'Wer so stirbt, der stirbt wohl!' Der Umgang mit der Sterbestunde im Spiegel von Leichenpredigten", in von Hülsen-Esch A. – Westermann-Angerhausen H. (eds.), *Zum Sterben Schön: Alter, Totentanz, und Sterbekunst von 1500 bis Heute* (Regensburg: 2006) 238–249.

Fogleman A.S., *Jesus is Female: Moravians and the Challenge of Radical Religion in Early America* (Philadelphia: 2007).

Frohne A.E., *The African Burial Ground in New York City: Memory, Spirituality, and Space* (Syracuse, N.Y.: 2015).

Gittings C., *Death, Burial, and the Individual in Early Modern England* (London: 1984).

Green C., "'Now the Lord hath made me a spectacle': Deathbed Narratives and Devotional Identities in the Early Seventeenth Century", in Clarke E. – Daniel R.W. (eds.), *People and Piety: Protestant Devotional Identities in Early Modern England* (Manchester, Eng.: 2020) 259–274.

Hallam E.A., "Turning the Hourglass: Gender Relations at the Deathbed in Early Modern Canterbury", *Mortality* 1 (1996) 61–82.

Handler J.S. – Lange F.W., *Plantation Slavery in Barbados: An Archaeological and Historical Investigation* (Cambridge, Mass.: 1978).

Harding V., *The Dead and the Living in Paris and London, 1500–1670* (Cambridge: 2002).

Highfield A.R. – Barac V. (eds.), *C.G.A. Oldendorp's History of the Mission of the Evangelical Brethren* (Ann Arbor: 1987).

Houlbrooke R., "The Puritan Death-bed, c.1560–c.1660", in Durston C. – Eales J. (eds.), *The Culture of English Puritanism, 1560–1700* (New York: 1996) 122–44.

Kellaway W., *The New England Company, 1649–1776: Missionary Society to the American Indians* (New York: 1961).

Laqueur T.W., *The Work of the Dead: A Cultural History of Mortal Remains* (Princeton: 2015).

Leibman L.A. (ed.), *Experience Mayhew's* Indian Converts: *A Cultural Edition* (Amherst, Mass.: 2008).

Lomnitz C., *Death and the Idea of Mexico* (Cambridge, Mass.: 2005).

Marshall P., "Angels around the Deathbed: Variations on a Theme in the English Art of Dying," in Marshall P. – Walsham A. (eds.), *Angels in the Early Modern World* (New York: 2006) 83–103.

McKinley M.A., "Till Death Do Us Part: Testamentary Manumission in Seventeenth-Century Lima, Peru", *Slavery & Abolition* 33 (2012) 381–401.

McManners J., *Death and the Enlightenment: Changing Attitudes to Death in Eighteenth-Century France* (New York: 1981).

O'Connor M.C., *The Art of Dying Well: The Development of the* Ars moriendi (New York: 1942).

Pavlíčková R.P., "'Unter den Ketzern zu leben und zu sterben ist gar schwerlich und geferlich': Das Sterbebuch des Johann Leisentritt im Kontext der Katholischen Sterbebücher des 16. Jahrhunderts", *Archiv für Reformationsgeschichte* 107 (2016) 193–216.

Ramos G., *Death and Conversion in the Andes: Lima and Cuzco, 1532–1670* (Notre Dame, Ind.: 2010).

Reinis A., *Reforming the Art of Dying: The* ars moriendi *in the German Reformation (1519–1528)* (Aldershot, Eng.: 2007).

Rivett S., "Tokenography: Narration and the Science of Dying in Puritan Deathbed Testimonies", *Early American Literature* 42 (2007) 471–494.

Rivett S., *The Science of the Soul in Colonial New England* (Chapel Hill, N.C.: 2011).

Rubertone P.E., *Grave Undertakings: An Archaeology of Roger Williams and the Narragansett Indians* (Washington, D.C.: 2001).

Seeman E.R., *Pious Persuasions: Laity and Clergy in Eighteenth-Century New England* (Baltimore: 1999).

Seeman E.R., "Reading Indians' Deathbed Scenes: Ethnohistorical and Representational Approaches", *Journal of American History* 88 (2001) 17–47.

Seeman E.R., *Death in the New World: Cross-Cultural Encounters, 1492–1800* (Philadelphia: 2010).

Seeman E.R., *The Huron-Wendat Feast of the Dead: Indian-European Encounters in Early North America* (Baltimore: 2011).

Sensbach J.F., *Rebecca's Revival: Creating Black Christianity in the Atlantic World* (Cambridge, Mass.: 2005).

Stannard D., *The Puritan Way of Death: A Study in Religion, Culture, and Social Change* (New York: 1977).

Thwaites R.G. (ed.), *The Jesuit Relations and Allied Documents*, 73 vols. (Cleveland: 1896–1901).

Van Gennep A., *Les rites de passage* (Paris: 1909).

Von Thiessen H., "Das Sterbebett als normative Schwelle: Der Mensch in der Frühen Neuzeit zwischen irdischer Normenkonkurrenz und göttlichem Gericht", *Historische Zeitschrift* 295 (2012) 625–659.

Von Thiessen H., *Das Zeitalter der Ambiguität: Vom Umgang mit Werten und Normen in der Frühen Neuzeit* (Cologne: 2021).

Vovelle M., *La mort et l'Occident: de 1300 à nos jours* (Paris: 1983).

Warren J., *Masters of the Dead: Slavery, Death, and Ideology in the Antebellum South* (Ph.D. dissertation, Indiana University: 2014).

Wheeler R. – Eyerly S., "Songs of the Spirit: Hymnody in the Moravian Mohican Missions", *Journal of Moravian History* 17 (2017) 1–26.

Wiggins S.W. – Truss R.S. (eds.), *The Journal of Sarah Haynesworth Gayle, 1827–1835: A Substitute for Social Intercourse* (Tuscaloosa, Ala.: 2013).

Williams D.T., "'My Conscience Is Free and Clear': African-Descended Women, Status, and Slave Owning in Mid-Colonial Mexico", *The Americas* 75 (2018) 525–554.

Winter K.J., *The American Dreams of John B. Prentis, Slave Trader* (Athens, Ga.: 2011).

Wyss H.E. "'Things That Do Accompany Salvation": Colonialism, Conversion, and Cultural Exchange in Experience Mayhew's *Indian Converts*", *Early American Literature* 33 (1998) 39–61.

CHAPTER 6

Confessing in the Contexts of Dying and Narratives of Death

Irene Dingel

1   Introduction

The question of the role of "confessing" in the context of dying or in narratives of death in the early modern period is, on the one hand, an obvious topic, because for the people of that time, the hour of death was an exemplary evocation of man's existence before God. But, on the other hand, it is a somewhat nebulous or vague and therefore difficult question. First, what we mean by the concept "confessing" must be clarified. Does it refer to the confession of sin or the confession of faith? Does it mean a commitment to the unique features of the teaching of a specific confessional document or a confessional community? Before analyzing specific source documents, a rough overview of different texts will demonstrate that in narratives of dying, readers encounter a multitude of statements relevant to the concept of "confessing" that are difficult to classify. In fact, only seldom did the commitment to a specific confessional group play a role. That is due first and foremost to the fact that narratives of dying in the early modern period are found largely in Lutheran funeral sermons.[1] As the final point or culmination of the biographies they contain, these narratives present an important element in published funeral writings. Indeed, the practice of funeral sermons was adapted also in the sphere of Reformed churches, but there it never experienced a comparable flowering to prominence as in Lutheran circles. A comparison of Lutheran and Reformed narratives of dying in funeral sermons makes it clear that the dying person's affiliation with one confessional group or the other appears less in his "confession" or in a specific form or content of the act of "confessing his or her faith,"

---

1   On the definition and development of the funeral sermon, which is eminently a Lutheran literary genre, cf. Lenz R., "Leichenpredigt", in Müller G. (ed.), *Theologische Realenzyklopädie*, vol. 20 (Berlin – New York: 1990), 665–669, as well as Düselder H. – Winkler E., "Leichenpredigt", in Jaeger F. (ed.), *Enzyklopädie der Neuzeit*, vol. 7 (Stuttgart – Weimar: 2008), 821–825. Cf. also Dingel I., "'Recht glauben, christlich leben und seliglich sterben'. Leichenpredigt als evangelische Verkündigung im 16. Jahrhundert", in Lenz R. (ed.), *Leichenpredigten als Quelle historischer Wissenschaften*, vol. 4 (Stuttgart: 2004), 9–36.

but much more in contexts referring to the typical Reformed understanding of the Lord's Supper or in contexts related to the doctrine of predestination. In this paper "confessing" therefore includes a broad understanding of the concept: confession of sin, confession of faith, and formulations determined by confessional documents.

That "confessing" plays any role at all in narratives of dying relates to the reformational reshaping of the *ars moriendi* literature and – as a result of that – with a new conception of an "ars bene vivendi". For the Wittenberg reformer Martin Luther, the entire existence of the human being in God's presence is comprehended in consummate fashion in the hour of death.[2] At the moment of death the relationship between God and the individual is all that matters. This relationship, according to Luther, consisted no longer primarily in the tension of guilt and punishment, but in the light of the fundamental articles of the faith that define the Christian. That is what the dying person had to know and remember. The *ars moriendi* that emerged from a long medieval tradition was accordingly transformed by Luther into an art of dying in which the reformational doctrine of justification stood at the center. The admonition to repent and to perform good works was no longer prominent in the preparation for a good death; instead the crossing of the threshold between life and death came to be emphasised. Pronouncement of the forgiveness of sins and assurance of justification through faith in Christ, mediated by the sacraments of baptism and the Lord's Supper, set the tone. Luther's "Sermon on the Preparation for Dying" from 1519 pioneered and exemplified this approach.[3] This sermon offered a model for such reformational *ars moriendi*. It shaped narratives of dying that arose in the early modern period in the evangelical world. This is the context into which "confessing" at the time of death must be placed. It aims at the comfort that provides the focal point for life and death in the hour of dying, the assurance of justification.

Indeed, to formulate reliable appraisals of the concept of "confessing in the contexts of dying" requires the most extensive evaluation of sources possible, and it is most obvious, that means turning to funeral sermons as the basis.

---

2 Cf. Mohr, R., "Ars moriendi II. 16.–18. Jahrhundert", in Müller G. (ed.), *Theologische Realenzyklopädie*, vol. 4 (Berlin – New York: 1979), 149–154, at 149, and Martin Luther's first Invocavit sermon, 9.3.1522, in WA 10/III, 1–13. Here the urgency of his formulation is clear: 'WJr seindt allsampt zu(o) dem tod gefodert und wirt keyner für den andern sterben, Sonder ein yglicher in eygner person für sich mit dem todt kempffen. Jn die oren künden wir woll schreyen, Aber ein yglicher mu(o)ß für sich selber geschickt sein in der zeyt des todts: ich würd denn nit bey dir sein noch du bey mir. Hierjnn so muß ein yederman selber die hauptstück so einen Christen belangen, wol wissen und gerüst sein, [...]': WA 10/III, 1,7–2,2.

3 Cf. Luther M., Ein Sermon von der Bereitung zum Sterben, 1519, in: WA 2, 680–697.

To accomplish that *in extenso*, however, is not possible in view of the entirety of the countless publications of funeral material since the Reformation.[4] In view of the immense amount of extant material, no more than a sampling is possible. What is attempted here is the selection of sources from the broadest possible spectrum in order to construct a picture of the various narrative contexts during a period from the late sixteenth century, when the literary genre of funeral sermon emerged, to the eighteenth century, as the time of the publication of funeral materials was coming to its end. By the very nature of the phenomenon, the overwhelming number of these publications focus on the context of Lutheran preaching, but narratives of dying that are clearly from the Reformed sphere will also be cited. Sermons on both men and women are taken into consideration. The report "On the Christian Departure from this mortal Life of the beloved, highly-respected Man, Matthaeus Ratzenberger"[5] presents a narrative of dying that is not part of the rich culture of funeral publications, but dovetails nicely with it. The results of this chapter, which arises out of this sort of scattered microstudies, must be viewed with the premise that no hasty generalizations are possible. Nevertheless, these studies convey an impression of how confessing "in the context of dying" took place, or of how it was reported. This analysis was guided by the question of the function of the act of "confessing" in narratives of dying, that is, of the function that the authors of the narrative, the theologians and pastors, attribute to it.

---

4 "Funeralschriften" are a literary genre that arises for the first time at the end of the sixteenth century. Families that could afford it – in addition to the burial and memorials to the deceased – had texts printed that documented the departure of the deceased from life on this earth and the expressions of sympathy from the grieving. In the center stood the funeral sermon. Other elements, above all the biography of the deceased (*Personalia*), a brief word of thanks to the participants in the burial (*Abdankung*) along with poems mourning the departed (*Epicedien*). In the "Funeralschriften" that were published in the context of burials of nobles and rulers, depictions of the funeral procession were sometimes included. This memorial literature, designed for public distribution, was commissioned by the family and served not only to preserve the memory of the departed in the long run but also to demonstrate the importance of the person (this was especially true in the context of ruling dynasties). This definition expands on that given by Werner Hupe in his article "August Buchner (1591–1661)", in Leben in Leichenpredigten (10/2011), http://www.personalschriften.de/leichenpredigten/artikelserien/artikelansicht/details/august-buchner-1591-1661.html [25.07.2021]

5 Cf. Poach Andreas, *Vom(m) Christlichen Abschied aus diesem sterblichen Leben des lieben thewren Mannes Matthei Ratzenbergers der Artzney Doctors Bericht durch Andream Poach Pfarherrn zun Augustinern in Erffurdt / vnd andere / So dabey gewesen / kurtz zusamen gezogen. Anno Domini M.D.LIX. Mense Ianuario.* (Jena, Thomas Rebart: [1559]).

2 A Blessed Death and the Function of Confessing as Consolation: Consolatio et Aedificatio

The report of Erfurt pastor Andreas Poach from 1559 on the course of dying of Erfurt municipal physician Matthäus Ratzenberger, a process which extended over four months, is a most informative testimony to the value of confessing in the context of the process of dying. Poach belonged to Ratzenberger's closest circle of friends. Ratzenberger had served as court physician at several princely courts before he found his last employment in the city of Erfurt.[6] As an eye-witness to the unfolding of the Reformation – he had come at age sixteen, probably in April 1517, to Wittenberg[7] – and a dedicated adherent of the reformational teaching of Martin Luther, he took on a special significance as an example of a dying person. The Erfurt pastor described the various stages of his gradual demise, in that he not only traced in detail the medical development of his physical state but also the spiritual interaction as he was giving pastoral care to Ratzenberger. Poach began to accompany him on the path toward death as Ratzenberger felt that death was near, on September 4, 1558, with confession and absolution and the reception of the Lord's Supper. On December 24, 1558, Ratzenberger made his confession of sins again; he did not – in good reformational fashion – enumerate individual sins. Instead, he wove his confession of sins and his confession of faith together to reinforce his evangelical faith by receiving the Lord's Supper one more time.[8] Poach regarded it as very important to make it clear that Ratzenberger was conscious of his leaving behind the traditional Roman faith for the faith of the Reformation,[9] and he reported that on his death bed Ratzenberger had expressly regretted not having made his confession of the Reformation faith

---

6   He was the personal physician of Electress Elisabeth von Brandenburg, then personal physician of Count Albrecht VII of Mansfeld and finally served from 1538 to 1546 as personal physician and confidant of Elector Johann Friedrich of Saxony. When Johann Friedrich returned from his imperial imprisonment, sentenced in connection with the Schmalkaldic War, Ratzenberger moved first to Nordhausen and then became municipal physician in Erfurt. Cf. Siebert S., "Matthäus Ratzenberger", in Bautz T. (ed.), Biographisch-Bibliographisches Kirchenlexikon vol. 7 (Herzberg: 1994), 1394–1395; Kolb R., "Ars moriendi lutherana. Andreas Poachs Schrift 'Vom Christlichen Abschied aus diesem sterblichen Leben ... Matthei Ratzenbergers' (1559)", in Graf G. – Hasse H.-P. et al. (eds.), Vestigia pietatis. Studien zur Geschichte der Frömmigkeit in Thüringen und Sachsen. Ernst Koch gewidmet. Herbergen der Christenheit. Sonderband 5 (Leipzig: 2000), 95–112.

7   Cf. Poach A., Vom christlichen Abschied, fols. A3v–A4r.

8   Cf. Ibidem, fols. B4r–v.

9   'Das ich aber in der Lere vnd im Glauben mit allen Menschen nicht eins bin / da kan ich nicht fu(e)r / Gott wird mir das auch nicht zur Su(e)nde rechnen', Ibidem, fols. B4r–v.

public during his lifetime (which he in fact had done quite clearly), and that for this reason he had asked Poach to make this testimony public in his place.[10] The Erfurt pastor said as Ratzenberger's stand-in,

> Jch bin auch willens gewesen mein Bekentnis von allen Artikeln zu fassen / vnd die Jrrthum dieser zeit anzuzeigen / Vnd solche Artikel hinter mir zu lassen / damit zubezeugen offentlich fu(e)r aller welt / das ichs mit der Jrrthum keinem gehalten hab / noch heutigs tags halte / die neben vnd nach der Augspurgischen Confession (so Anno Domini M.D.XXX. dem Keiser vnd gantzem Reich von den Euangelischen Chur vnd Fu(e)rsten vberantwort ist) auffkomen sind / Aber ich bin bisher daran verhindert worden / durch meine vielfaltige gescheffte. [...] vnd bin nu zu schwach solchs zuthun / Darumb will ichs jtzt bey diesem Bekentnis bleiben lassen / vnd bitte euch als meinen Beichtuater / wollet mir meines Glaubens vnd Bekentnis zeugnis geben fu(e)r Gott vnd aller welt.

> I have been wanting to formulate my confession on all the articles of faith and to identify the errors of this time, and to leave behind me these statements, in order to give witness publicly before the entire world that I have not held to any single one of these errors, nor do I accept any of them to this very day, errors that emerged at the time of the Augsburg Confession (that was presented to the emperor and the entire empire by the evangelical electors and princes in 1530) or since that time. I have been prevented from doing so by my many and varied duties [...] and am now too weak to do so. Therefore, I wish to remain by this confession and ask you as my confessor to bear witness of my faith and confession before God and the entire world.[11]

Ratzenberger's commitment to the Confessio Augustana, the foundational confession of the Wittenberg Reformation, also proved to be true in his understanding of the Lord's Supper, which Poach – reporting on another communion of the dying man on December 29 – unmistakably distinguished from the Zwinglian interpretation.[12] Ratzenberger's confession thus performed the function of distinguishing him from both the Old Faith and the position of the Zurich theologians. But it was not limited to that. Much more, in the process

---

10   Poach also gave such testimony in the publication of his report on Ratzenberger's death.
11   Ibidem, fol. B4v.
12   Cf. his specific rejection of a "figürliches Verständnis" (symbolic understanding), Ibidem, fol. C2v.

of dying described here, the confession also served to provide pastoral comfort and to convey spiritual encouragement. Poach reported that Ratzenberger asked him to remind him repeatedly of his confession of faith in order to comfort him.[13] Ratzenberger himself succeeded, according to the report of his pastor Poach, in attaining complete calm and certainty since the reminder of his baptism and his reception of the Lord's Supper gave him a sacramental assurance and the guarantee of the content of his confession of the reformational faith. In this context the following statement of Ratzenberger in his last hours gives resonance to his confession of faith:

> Jch hab mich vnd alles dem gnedigen willen Gottes langst ergeben / vnd heimgestelt / der wird mich auch in einer ku(e)rtz erlo(e)sen / vnd von diesem Jamertal zu sich in sein Schos nemen / daran hab ich keinen zweiuel. Denn ich bin daran durch Gottes wort versichert / bin darauff getaufft / vn(d) hab den Leib vnd das Blut des HErrn Christi darauff gessen vnd getruncken.

> I have surrendered myself to the gracious will of God and placed myself in his hands. He will deliver me soon and take me out of this vale of tears and into his embrace. I have no doubt about that. For I have been assured of this by the word of God; I am baptized and have eaten and drunk the body and blood of the Lord Christ.[14]

On the one hand, Poach goes into detail to describe the departure of Ratzenberger, but on the other hand, the process of dying proves itself to be cast into ritual form. His farewell to family and friends, the reading of verses of the Bible, the singing of hymns, and the speaking of prayers shaped his last hours. In the course of this process his confessing took on great significance, also in the recitation of the traditional form of the Apostles Creed, in which the dying man was led by Poach. The pastor reported,

> Vnd als ich den Glauben ausgebetet hatte / vnd merckte / das der kranck etwas vnd sonderlich den letzten Artikel geho(e)rt hatte [gemeint sind die Aussagen über Auferstehung und ewiges Leben] / sprach ich / Herr Geuatter / Das ist ja noch ewer Glaube vnd Bekentnis? Da neiget er das heubt gegen mir / vnd antwortet deutlich / Ja.

---

13 Cf. Ibidem, fol. C4v, also fol. E1v.
14 Ibidem, fol. E1r.

And as I prayed the Creed aloud and noted that despite his illness he listened particularly to the last articles [i.e. "resurrection of the dead" and "life of the world to come"], I said, 'my dear father, is that indeed still your faith and confession? He nodded to me and answered clearly, 'yes'.[15]

The process of dying, described as exemplary, had been permeated by such statements and actions of confessing.

This result, which appears to demonstrate that confessing played a central role in the context of dying, can be confirmed through the analysis of a limited number of sermons in published accounts of funerals. In 1589 the Lutheran theologian Nikolaus Selnecker published two volumes that brought together funeral sermons that he had preached.[16] The collection was conceived as a book for meditation and edification. He dedicated it to Duchess Hedwig, the wife of Duke Julius of Braunschweig-Wolfenbüttel, who at the time that the volume appeared had recently become a widow, on May 3, 1589.[17] In his preface Selnecker dwelt on the "ungodly death" that was caused ever more frequently by false teaching, as it was being spread by sects and not least by the "sacrament Schwärmer". He was referring to all those who had set themselves apart from the Lutheran Formula of Concord (1577) that had been published in the Book of Concord (1580).[18] Duke Julius had initially promoted the production of the Formula but finally had refused to subscribe to this unifying document with its Lutheran colouring, for reasons not related to its theology so much as to matters of Julius's public policies.[19] Very subtly Selnecker criticized govern-

---

15 Ibidem, fol. G2r.
16 Cf. Selnecker Nicolaus, *Christliche Leÿchpredigten So vom Jar 1576. bis fast an das 1590. Jar zu Leipzig / Durch D. Nicolaum Selneccerum der zeit Superintendenten vnd Professorem alda / geschehen vnd auffgezeichnet worden sind* [...] *Erster Theil Von Anno 1576 bis auff das Jar 1584.* [...], (Magdeburg, Paul Donat Jn verlegung Ambrosij Kirchners: 1590). – *Ander theil Christlicher Leÿchpredigten Zu Leipzig gehalten von Anno 1584. bis auff das 189, Jar.* [...], (Magdeburg, Paul Donat Jn verlegung Ambrosij Kirchners: [1590]).
17 The dedicatory preface dated on 17.10.1589, cf. Ibidem, fol. 4v.
18 The Formula of Concord appears in a critical edition in Dingel Irene (ed.), *Die Bekenntnisschriften der Evangelisch-Lutherischen Kirche* [= BSELK]. Vollständige Neuedition (Göttingen: 2014).
19 In 1578 Julius had his eldest son, Heinrich Julius, consecrated as bishop of Halberstadt. In the same year his two younger sons, Philipp Sigismund and Joachim Karl, received the 'prima tonsura' to make it possible for them – against the advance of the Wittelsbach family – to counter their influence in the Roman Catholic foundations. As a result, Julius withdrew his subscription to the Book of Concord, and this led to fierce confrontations with his theologians. Cf. Mager I., *Die Konkordienformel im Fürstentum Braunschweig-Wolfenbüttel. Entstehungsbeitrag – Rezeption – Geltung.* Studien zur Kirchengeschichte Niedersachsens 33 (Göttingen: 1993), 325–339 and 367–370.

mental authority, but in such a way that it was clear only to the reader steeped in the confessional politics of the time.[20] In detail he made clear the fateful connection between false teaching and a falsely-directed "epicurean" life or uncertainty in the faith and inconsistency in confessing. God does not let such things go unpunished.[21] Even worse, however, he stated, is that loss of the 'true Christian art of dying' that takes place because of this.[22] For Selnecker, the triad of true faith, a Christian life, and a blessed death was essential.[23] For this reason his collection of funeral sermons was to serve as a guide on the path to a blessed hour of death. Confession functioned in this process as a witness for the "*certitudo fidei*" and as comfort both for the dying person in the last hour of life and for the bereaved in their mourning.[24]

Looking at Selnecker's funeral sermons from this point of view, a focus on confessional differences or polemic against sects can hardly be found. To be sure, at the end of a funeral sermon at the burial of a deceased wife, in an address to God that was at the same time aimed at the bereaved, Selnecker admonished,

> Wer dein Wort fahren lesset / vnd aus den Augen und Hertzen setzt / der kennet dich schon nicht mehr / sondern hat dich verloren / vnd fellet dahin in Jrrthumb vnd Sicherheit / wie wir an vnsern stoltzen Schwermern und Sacramentfeinden sehen. Dafu(e)r behu(e)te vns gnediglich / vnd erhalte vns in deiner waren Erkentnis biß an vnser letzten Seufftzen / wie du diese Matron in deiner Erkentnis / Bekentnis / vnd Anruffung erhalten / vnd zu dir seliglich abgefordert hast.

---

20 In his 'preface to the Christian reader' it becomes immediately clear that Selnecker himself – at sixty years of age – saw himself at the end of his life. He said that he had published these sermons on the Festival of Saint Michael and All Angels with the admission 'stehet den mehren theil meine Christliche Confession auch in diesen kurtzen predigten ...' (fol. A1r). He pledged himself to the Book of Concord, of which he was a co-author, and expressed the assurance, that he wished to remain Lutheran his entire life. Cf. Selnecker, *Christliche Leichpredigten* 1, fols. A1r–v.

21 Ibidem, fol. 3v and fols. 4r–v.

22 'Den(n) was thun vnsere Geistliche vnd Weltliche newe schwermer vnd gifftige Geister jetzt anders / die gern Lutherum vnd seine Geistreiche heilsame schrifften / sonderlich aber seine streitschrifften wider die Zwinglische Gottslesterung wolten vnter die banck stossen / denn das sie damit alle gnad / Geist / vnd segen Gottes verjagen / vnd der Epicurischen Weltweisheit thor und thu(e)r auffthun / vnd glauben / gewissen / bekentnis / redligkeit / richtigkeit / gewisheit / trost / vnd die rechte Christliche sterbkunst verlieren?', Ibidem, fol. v.

23 Selnecker in his preface Ibidem, fol. 3r.

24 Cf. Ibidem, fol. A2r.

Whoever lets go of your word, and places it outside the purview of his eyes and heart, such a person does not recognize you any longer but has lost you and fallen into error and presumption, as we see in our proud Schwärmer and the foes of the sacraments. Graciously protect us from this and preserve us in true knowledge of you to our last breath, as you preserved this lady in knowing you, confessing and praying, whom you called blessedly to you.[25]

But normally, whenever Selnecker mentioned confessing in the process of dying, it did not concern confessional difference but statements of trust in the forgiveness of sins, justification, and redemption. These were theological teachings that were likewise taught by the dissenters, the so-called sects, or the Reformed. Nevertheless, a typical Lutheran tone did resonate through Selnecker's sermons echoing the deeply pastoral thrust of Luther's *Sermon on Preparation for Dying*.[26] Even though Selnecker did not cite any passage from this work or paraphrase it, he presented the battle of the dying against death and devil in a similar manner, holding fast to God's word without wavering so that the dying were able 'to fall asleep in a blessed, peaceful, gentle manner, with peace and joy' and thus 'having life in the midst of death.'[27]

3   Confessing as Reminder, Admonition for Proper Teaching, and Assurance: Memoria, Admonitio et Recognitio

In close connection with the function of finding comfort in the act of confessing is the reminder of the content of the faith conveyed both to the dying

---

25   Funeral sermon 14, in Ibidem, fol. 53v.
26   Cf. e.g., WA 2, esp. 694,7–16.
27   Cf. the admonition of Selnecker at the end of the eighth funeral sermon for the burial of Hieronymus Rauscher, Selnecker, *Christliche Leichpredigten* 1, fol. 29r: 'Wenn wir vns aber darzu schicken vnd sagen / HErr Christe / du bist mein Bruder worden / der du zugleich mit dem Vater vnd heiligem Geist Ewiger / Allmechtiger GOTT bist / vnd hast dich also tieff gedemu(e)tiget / das du deinen Leib fu(e)r mich auffgeoffert [!] / vnd dein Blut fu(e)r meine Su(e)nde vergossen hast / Jch bitte dich / du wollest durch seinen heiligen Geist den rechten Glauben in mir vermehren / auff das wenn der Teufel ko(e)mpt / vnd mir solches aus meinem Hertzen nehmen will / vnd der Tod zu mir einstu(e)rmet / nimmet mir meine Sinne / Jch jnen durch dein heiliges Wort ko(e)nne Widerstand thun / vnd an dir hangen bleibe / wie eine Klette am Rock klebet / vnd dich nicht von mir lasse / biß du mich segenest vnd auffnehmest / wie der Patriarch Jacob saget / etc. Als denn so ko(e)nnen wir seliglich / wol vnd sanfft / mit Fried vnd Freud / einschlaffen / vnd mitten im Tode leben.'

and also to the bereaved, along with the admonition to keep the faith without wavering despite all attacks on it. Such reminders, admonitions, and assurances, however, are difficult to distinguish from the comforting function of confession. Basically, all these components work together. A powerful example for the function of remembering and admonishing in the act of confessing is found in the funeral sermon published in 1653 by Matthaeus Girbigius, pastor in Wischitz, for the Silesian nobleman Hans Christoph von Dyhrn.[28] On the basis of the sermon text from Revelation 2,[29] 'Be faithful unto death and I will give you the crown of life' Girbigius emphasized that a Christian under the threat of death, as he lies dying, should hold fast to Jesus Christ as his hope and comfort.[30] He assured the bereaved that the deceased had really done this: 'the pious lord, Lord Hans Christoph von Dyhrn, remained faithful to his God with his confession of the faith.'[31] In view of the constant hostility between the true church and false teachers and heretics, he accentuated this particularly. For the toleration guaranteed in the Religious Peace of Augsburg of 1555 did not apply to the followers of the Reformation in Silesia, to whom the deceased Hans Christoph von Dyhrn belonged. Therefore, those committed to the Reformation continued to see themselves surrounded with false doctrine and suppressed by false teachers. All the more clearly the preacher expressed

---

28 Girbigius Matthaeus, *Trewer und Besta(e)ndiger Christ=Ritter* PRIVILEGIUM *Und Gnaden=Brieff / Auß dem Spru(e)chlein Apoc. 2. v. 9. & 11. Bey Christ=Adelicher Hochansehlicher Volck= und Thra(e)nenreicher Leichbega(e)ngnu(e)ß Deß Weyland Hoch und Wohl Edelgebohrnen Gestrengen Hochbenambten Herren Hansz Christoph von Dyhren von und auff Gleinitz/ Wischitz/ Schlaup und Krischitz/ Deß Hochlo(e)blichen Ko(e)nigl. Gurauischen Mannrechts Wohlverordneten vornehmen Assessoris:* [...] *welcher im* [?]*ligsten Jahr seines alters/ deß Jahres Christi 1653. den 20 Januar. zu Wischitz sanft und seelig auff Christi teures Verdienst/ und in und mit dem Su(e)ssen Nahmen JEsu im HErren entschlaffen/ und den 1. Julij desselbten Jahres/ Christ=Adelichem Brauche nach/ in die Adeliche Grufft gebracht worden* (Liegnitz, Zacharias Schneider: [1653]). On this sermon cf. also Dingel I., "Spuren reformierter Konfessionalität in Leichenpredigten auf Angehörige des schlesischen Adels", in Bahlcke J. – Dingel I. (eds.), *Die Reformierten in Schlesien. Vom 16. Jahrhundert bis zur Altpreußischen Union von 1817*, Veröffentlichungen des Instituts für Europäische Geschichte Mainz Beihefte 106 (Göttingen: 2016), 15–30, especially 20.

29 Apoc. 2 v. 8–9 & 10–11. 'DAS saget der Erste und der Letzte / der Todt war und ist Lebendig worden / Jch weiß deine Werck / und deine Tru(o)bsal / sey getreu biß in den Todt / so wil Jch dir die Crone deß Lebens geben. Wer Ohren hat zu ho(e)ren der Ho(e)re / waß der Geist den Gemeinen saget / wer überwindet dem sol kein Leidt geschehen vom andern Tode ', Girbigius, *Privilegium*, fol. B3r.

30 'Ein Christ sol auch Trew sein in Todes noth / das Er im Sterbe=Stu(e)ndlein / mit der Christlichen Kirchen Singe: Allein zu dir HERR JESU Christ / Mein Hoffnung steht auff Erden: Jch weiß daß du mein Tro(e)ster bist / Kein Trost mag Mir sonst werden', Ibidem, fol. F2r.

31 Ibidem, fol. F4r.

his certainty that the deceased had not only believed in the forgiveness of sin, life, and salvation in Christ, but also had confessed it, in line with the Pauline rule in Romans 10:20, 'if you confess with your mouth that Jesus is the Lord and believe in your heart that God has raised him from the dead, you will be saved. For a person believes with the heart and is justified, and confesses with the mouth and is saved.' Not least to be mentioned, Christoph von Dyhrn thereby followed the example of the evangelical princes and estates, who in 1530 had confessed their faith with the Confessio Augustana before the emperor and the empire.[32] According to the report of the pastor on the death at the end of the biography, this confessing in the hour of his death was expressed only in the simple affirmation given to the question 'whether he still had the Lord Jesus in his heart and intended to die a blessed death in him' and through the folding of his hands.[33]

A similar exemplary case is described in the trust-filled confessing of Ursula Magdalena, Lady of Dyhrn and Schönau by Johann Georg Kleiner, pastor in Reesewitz.[34] Ursula Magdalena died on November 26, 1721, after severe, protracted suffering over a nearly four-month period. In this long process of dying, which the preacher interpreted as the temptation of the devil to foster fear and faint-heartedness, she nevertheless displayed an amazing steadfastness of faith and assurance. Kleiner reported,

> Aber auch allhier ließ sich Jhr treuer GOtt als ein ma(e)chtiger Vertheidiger mit seinem starcken Arm sehen. Er legte sich gleichsam durch seine Macht und Sta(e)rcke / wie ein Schild an Sie / und offenbarete

---

32 Cf. Ibidem, fols. F4v–G1r. Here is stated: 'So du mit deinem Munde bekennest JHESUM / das ER der HERR sey / vnd gla(e)ubest in deinem Hertzen das Jhn GOTT von den Todten auferwecket hat / so wirstu Seelig / denn so man von Hertzen gla(e)ubet so wird man gerecht / und so man mit dem Munde bekennet so wird man Seelig.'

33 '[...] ob Er auch noch den HERREN JESUM in seinem Hetzen hette / und auff Jhn geda(e)chte Seelig zusterben [...]', Ibidem, fols. L4r–v.

34 Vgl. Kleiner Johann George, *Die doppelte Glu(e)ckseligkeit der Gerechten, Wurde Aus dem V. Cap. v. 16.17. des Buches der Weißheit Bey denen Der weyland Hoch=und Wohlgebohrnen Frauen / Frauen Ursula Magdalena, Freyin von Dyhrn und Scho(e)nau / [....] Die Den 26. Tag des Monats Novembr. des 1721sten Jahres, nach einer 15. Wochen lang u(e)berstandenen harten Niederlage, dieses Zeitliche mit dem Ewigen durch ein ho(e)chst seligst genommenes Ende 3. Viertel auf 7. Uhr des Abends verwechselt / Und Dero entseelter Co(e)rper / Den 29. Tag bemeldten Monaths und Jahres darauf, Mit Christ=Freyherrlichen Ceremonien [...] beygesetzet worden, Den 26. Tag des Monaths Febr. itztlauffenden 1722sten Jahres Jn dem Reesewitzer Gottes=Hause Vollzogenen letzten Ehr= und Geda(e)chtniß=Solennita(e)ten / Der Wohl=Seligen zu im(m)erwa(e)hrendem Ruhm, Denen sa(e)mmtlichen Hoch=Leydtragenden zu einiger Gemu(e)ths=Befriedigung, und zu aller unserer Seelen=Erbauung vorgestellet und betrachtet [...]* (Brieg, Gottfried Tramp: [1722]).

sich Jhr nach seinem kra(e)fftigen Worte / als ein ma(e)chtiger Helffer, Beschu(e)tzer und Vertheidiger.

But throughout this suffering, her faithful God caused her to see him as her mighty defender with his strong arm. He placed himself, as it were, as a shield for her through his might and strength, and revealed himself to her according to his powerful word as a mighty helper, protector, and defender.[35]

Kleiner's question regarding her continuing trust in God in her last hour she answered with a simple, 'Ach ja. Ja!'[36] This confession was in fact the last words of the dying woman.

Also among the Reformed, Calvinist nobility of Silesia, who were a minority in comparison to the Lutherans, confessing played a role in the hour of death, although more as a verification of election. This is clear in the funeral sermon published in 1602 by Martin Füssel at the burial of Joachim von Berge.[37] Von Berge had been an imperial court counselor for three emperors of the Holy Roman Empire, namely for Ferdinand I, Maximilian II, and Rudolph II. He had chosen the biblical text for the sermon himself, from John 10:27, 'my sheep hear my voice, and I know them and they follow me; and I give them eternal life …' In his application of the text to the deceased, in which Füssel at the same time described scenes from the course of his dying, Füssel forcefully emphasized that in the hour of death, just as previously throughout his entire life, the Holy Spirit had given witness in the heart of the deceased that he indeed was God's child. This election by God took center stage in the hour of von Berge's death. The preacher saw his task as giving assurance both to the dying man in his mortal distress and to the bereaved by bringing this to mind again and again through the formulations of his confession. Many times, Füssel stated, Joachim von Berge had been asked about the inner testimony of the Holy Spirit and had repeatedly confirmed it steadfastly. So it was also on the day on which he died:

---

35   Ibidem, 27–28.
36   Ibidem, 28.
37   Cf. Füssel Martin, *Christliche Leichpredigt / Bey dem Begra(e)bnu(e)ß deß Edelen Gestrengen / Ehrenvesten / Hoch vnd Wolbenambten / Herren Joachim von Berge / auff Herndorff vnd Clade / Weiland Ferdinands deß I. Maximilians deß II. Rudolffs des II. aller dreyer Ro(e)m: Kayser Reichshoffrath / etc. Welcher den 5. Martij am Abend nahe nach 9. Vhr / in diesem 1602. Jahr / seines alters im 76. Jahr / weniger ein Monat / zu Herndorff in Christo Seeliglich entschlaffen ist. Bey grosser Adelicher versamlung in der Kirchen zu Herndorff den 1. April gehalten* […] (s.l. s.n.: 1602). On this sermon, see also Dingel I., "Spuren reformierter Konfessionalität", 15–30, especially 22–25.

> Da wart mit fleiß stille gehalten / vnd nach dem Zeugnuß deß heiligen Geistes / in seinem Hertzen gefraget / ob er auch ein solch Zeugnus in seinem Hertzen fu(e)lete. Er aber hat wol vnd verstendlich drauff geantwortet / Also vnd nicht anders.
>
> All was peace and quiet, and he was asked about the testimony of the Holy Spirit in his heart, whether he felt such a testimony in his heart. And he answered clearly and understandably, indeed, and nothing else.[38]

Also in this context the act of confessing was reduced to a simple affirmation, the chief function of which consisted of assuring the dying person and also the mourners of the blessedness of the death that depended on God's gracious election. Until the end Joachim von Berge had persevered in prayer. Füssel reported,

> Darnach hat der Erzhirte Jesus Christus / diesen Edelen Herren / als sein Scha(e)flin fu(e)hlen lassen / das er von jhm erkant sey / das ist / erwehlet / durch den glauben auff die gnade Gottes. [...] Solchen seinen glauben / hat er nicht nur mit worten bekennet / sondern es hat jhn auch bezeuget der scho(e)ne Friede mit Gott / der in seinem Hertzen regieret hat.
>
> After this the chief shepherd Jesus Christ, caused this noble lord to feel that he was his lamb, that he was known by him, that is, elect, through faith in God's grace [...] He had not only confessed that this was his faith with words, but he had also the testimony of his wonderful peace with God, who had ruled in his heart.[39]

In the course of his departure the dying man had repeatedly been asked about his inner disposition, and in this way had been invited to confess with words or gestures.[40] That the preacher in his funeral biography and report of the

---

38   Füssel, *Christliche Leichpredigt*, 27.
39   Ibidem, 31.
40   Cf. Ibidem, especially 32 and 42–43. Here it is reported: 'Denn Dinstags fru(e)e / wir den fromen Herren voriges eingehaltenes trostes erinnerten / neben etlichen vorgesprochenen Psalmen / vnd anderen gebeten / vmb endliche bestendigkeit / vnd ein seeliges stu(e)ndlein. Welches biß nahe an 11. vhr gewa(e)hret / vnd der fromme Herr alles wol angenommen vnd verstanden. Letztesmahls / als er befraget ward vmb denn friede deß gewissens / vnd vmb das feste vertrawen / auff das verdienst Christi / obs noch vnbeweglich bey jhm were / Antwortet er / Ja / vnd weil er mit dem Munde nicht

death dwelt on the *feeling* of being elect and the subsequent confessing of the faith, appears to be characteristic of Reformed funeral culture. Occasionally one has the impression that it was most important to provide assurance to the bereaved that, without any doubt, the death of Joachim von Berge had taken place under divine election. At the same time, the manner of self-examination on the deathbed was held up as an example for the bereaved.

That the doctrine of election or predestination, which since the end of the sixteenth century had become a marker of confessional identity, gained a firm place in funeral sermons and narratives of dying is shown by the sermon that Adam Samuel Hartmann preached at the burial of Maria von Canitz.[41] He used this funeral sermon to summarize the significance of election in six points that laid out the doctrine in confessional form, and he used the solemnity of the hour to exhort his hearers forcefully:

> Das ist die Lehre unserer Kirchen / von der Gnaden=Wahl. Auff diese gründen wir unsere Vermanungen und Straff=Reden an alle / die nebenst der a(e)ußerlichen Beka(e)ntnu(e)ß des Glaubens einen gottlosen Wandel fu(e)hren. Ho(e)ret / ihr Sorg=lose Christen. Wie schadet jhr eurer Seeligkeit mit un=Christlichem Leben.

> That is the teaching of our church on election. On this we ground our admonition and call to repentance to those who along with their outward confession of the faith lead a godless life. Listen, you untroubled

---

kondte / hat er mit der hand die frewdigkeit seines hertzens / vnd das starcke vertrawen auff Christum ferner bezeuget / vnd zuverstehen geben mit dem schnippen der finger / er were der seeligkeit in seinem Hertzen so gewiß / das er dem teuffel / helle / vnd todt wol mo(e)ge trotz bieten / vnd wie feste er auff dem halte / darauff er gefragt ward' (42–43).

41 Hartman Adam Samuel, I[n] N[omine] D[omini] N[ostri] J[esu] C[hristi]. Der letzte Wille des Sohnes Gottes / Belangend Seine Gla(e)ubigen / Wie Derselbe/ Jn seinem Allerheiligsten / Allerbeweglichsten / Aller=tro(e)stlichsten Letzten Geba(e)the / Durch Seinen Eigenen Go(e)ttlichen Mund / Seinem Himmlischen Vater ist vorgetragen worden: Johann. am XXII. v. 24. Bey Hoch=Adelicher Leich=Bega(e)ngnu(e)sse/ und Bestattung zur Erden Der numehr Sa(e)ligst= in GOtt=Ruhenden Hoch= Wohl= Edel= Gebornen/ Hoch= Ehren= und Hoch= Tugend= begabten Frawen/ Frawen MARIA Canitzin / Gebornen von SENJTZJN / etc. etc. Auff Urßka/ Wandritsch / Groß= und Klein-Gaffron / etc. etc. Jn einer Christlichen Leichen=Predigt/ und sehr Volck=reicher Hoch= Frey= Herrlichen/ Hoch=Adelichen etc. etc. Versammlung/ Jn der Evangelischen Kirchen zu klein Gaffron / Anno 1677. den Schrifftma(e)ßig erkla(e)ret. Auff Gna(e)diges Begehren aber nu in den Druck gegeben Von ADAM-SAMUEL HARTMAN, SS. Theol. D. der Evangelischen nach dem Worte GOttes Reformirten Gemeinen in Groß=Pohlen und Preussen Superintendente. (Lissa, Michael Bukke: [1677]).

Christians. How you do damage to your salvation with your unchristian life.[42]

It was different with the deceased, Maria von Canitz, who at age of 65 died as a widow as the result of a stroke.[43] The preacher stylized her as a flawless model for the "ars bene vivendi." For in her faith, hope, and love, in repentance, patience and good works, she had not only found her election by God confirmed, but had also individually experienced in her innermost parts the assurance that she was a "child of salvation."[44] She appealed to that also in the hour of her death.[45]

4 Conclusion

From the analysis of examples from different times and contexts, it becomes clear that confession in narratives of dying is discussed as a presupposition and sign of a blessed death. On the confession of the dying person – whether it is a longer, formulaic statement or a simple affirmation in response to a question posed by the pastor – it became clear what was important in the hour of death: an individual's relationship to God. Indeed, Lutherans and Reformed addressed this situation in different ways. Lutherans, for example, emphasized the certainty of salvation conveyed in on-going fashion by absolution and the sacraments of baptism and the Lord's Supper; among the Reformed, the dying person was led to an intensive examination of self to demonstrate divine election as exhibited in looking back on a good life and in the inner disposition of the heart. Both confessional groups held that the confession should have a comforting, strengthening, or edifying impact. This function of comfort and edification applied to the dying person and also to the bereaved in mourning.

Closely connected is the function of admonition and reassurance that took place in the act of confession. Confessing was a reminder that, especially in the last hour, it was important to have a faith that was built upon proper doctrine. Mentioning such a confession reminded readers not to let their faith be undermined by spiritual attacks of all kinds, to which the dying person had been exposed in great distress. At the same time confessing served as verification of faith amidst doubts about whether the person was elect or not. It served

---

42   Ibidem, 32.
43   This can be gathered from the *Personalia*, cf. Ibidem, 47–48.
44   Ibidem, 33.
45   Ibidem, 38–39.

as confirmation that in this particular case the dying person had been preserved in God's predestination as one of the elect. This could be of great significance in the Reformed context, especially when the process of dying had been extended and hard, which was most likely difficult to harmonize with what was understood to be "a blessed death."

Even if such confessionally oriented nuances in narratives of dying became evident, there was no confessional polemic to be found in these funeral accounts. Confessing was an essential element of the *ars moriendi* constructed by the Reformation, which was designed to have a comforting and edifying impact upon the bereaved, reminding and admonishing them, and thus was aimed at an "ars bene vivendi."

Bibliography

Primary Printed Sources

Dingel Irene (ed.), *Die Bekenntnisschriften der Evangelisch-Lutherischen Kirche* [= BSELK]. Vollständige Neuedition (Göttingen: 2014).

Füssel Martin, *Christliche Leichpredigt / Bey dem Begra(e)bnu(e)ß deß Edelen Gestrengen / Ehrenvesten / Hoch vnd Wolbenambten / Herren Joachim von Berge / auff Herndorff vnd Clade / Weiland Ferdinands deß I. Maximilians deß II. Rudolffs des II. aller dreyer Ro(e)m: Kayser Reichshoffrath / etc. Welcher den 5. Martij am Abend nahe nach 9. Vhr / in diesem 1602. Jahr / seines alters im 76. Jahr / weniger ein Monat / zu Herndorff in Christo Seeliglich entschlaffen ist. Bey grosser Adelicher versamlung in der Kirchen zu Herndorff den 1. April gehalten […]* (s.l. s.n.: 1602).

Girbigius Matthaeus, *Trewer und Besta(e)ndiger Christ=Ritter* PRIVILEGIUM *Und Gnaden=Brieff / Auß dem Spru(e)chlein Apoc. 2. v. 9. & 11. Bey Christ=Adelicher Hochansehlicher Volck= und Thra(e)nenreicher Leichbega(e)ngnu(e)ß Deß Weyland Hoch und Wohl Edelgebohrnen Gestrengen Hochbenambten Herren Hansz Christoph von Dyhren von und auff Gleinitz/ Wischitz/ Schlaup und Krischitz/ Deß Hochlo(e)blichen Ko(e)nigl. Gurauischen Mannrechts Wohlverordneten vornehmen Assessoris: […] welcher im [?]ligsten Jahr seines alters/ deß Jahres Christi 1653. den 20 Januar. zu Wischitz sanft und seelig auff Christi teures Verdienst/ und in und mit dem Su(e)ssen Nahmen JEsu im HErren entschlaffen/ und den 1. Julij desselbten Jahres/ Christ=Adelichem Brauche nach/ in die Adeliche Grufft gebracht worden* (Liegnitz, Zacharias Schneider: [1653]).

Hartman Adam Samuel, *I[n] N[omine] D[omini] N[ostri] J[esu] C[hristi]. Der letzte Wille des Sohnes Gottes / Belangend Seine Gla(e)ubigen / Wie Derselbe/ Jn seinem Allerheiligsten / Allerbeweglichsten / Aller=tro(e)stlichsten Letzten Geba(e)the / Durch Seinen Eigenen Go(e)ttlichen Mund / Seinem Himmlischen Vater ist vorgetragen worden: Johann. am XXII. v. 24. Bey Hoch=Adelicher Leich=Bega(e)ngnu(e)sse/ und Bestattung zur Erden Der numehr Sa(e)ligst= in GOtt=Ruhenden Hoch= Wohl= Edel= Gebornen/ Hoch= Ehren= und Hoch= Tugend= begabten Frawen/ Frawen* MARIA *Canitzin / Gebornen von* SENJTZJN */ etc. etc. Auff Urßka/ Wandritsch / Groß= und Klein=Gaffron / etc. etc. Jn einer Christlichen Leichen=Predigt/ und sehr Volck=reicher Hoch= Frey= Herrlichen/ Hoch=Adelichen etc. etc. Versammlung/ Jn der Evangelischen Kirchen zu klein Gaffron / Anno 1677. den Schrifftma(e)ßig erkla(e)ret. Auff Gna(e)diges Begehren aber nu in den Druck gegeben Von* ADAM-SAMUEL HARTMAN, SS. *Theol. D. der Evangelischen nach dem Worte GOttes Reformirten Gemeinen in Groß=Pohlen und Preussen Superintendente.* (Lissa, Michael Bukke: [1677]).

Kleiner Johann George, *Die doppelte Glu(e)ckseligkeit der Gerechten, Wurde Aus dem V. Cap. v. 16.17. des Buches der Weißheit Bey denen Der weyland Hoch=und Wohlgebohrnen Frauen / Frauen Ursula Magdalena, Freyin von Dyhrn und Scho(e)nau / [....] Die Den 26. Tag des Monats Novembr. des 1721sten Jahres, nach einer 15. Wochen lang u(e)berstandenen harten Niederlage, dieses Zeitliche mit dem Ewigen durch ein ho(e)chst seligst genommenes Ende 3. Viertel auf 7. Uhr des Abends verwechselt / Und Dero entseelter Co(e)rper / Den 29. Tag bemeldten Monaths und Jahres darauf, Mit Christ=Freyherrlichen Ceremonien [...] beygesetzet worden, Den 26. Tag des Monaths Febr. itztlauffenden 1722sten Jahres Jn dem Reesewitzer Gottes=Hause Vollzogenen letzten Ehr= und Geda(e)chtniß=Solennita(e)ten / Der Wohl=Seligen zu im(m)erwa(e)hrendem Ruhm, Denen sa(e)mmtlichen Hoch=Leydtragenden zu einiger Gemu(e)ths=Befriedigung, und zu aller unserer Seelen=Erbauung vorgestellet und betrachtet [...]* (Brieg, Gottfried Tramp: [1722]).

Luther Martin, *Ein Sermon von der Bereitung zum Sterben*, 1519, in Knaake J.K.F., Kawerau G., Thiele E. et al. (ed.), D. Martin Luthers Werke. Kritische Gesamtausgabe [= WA], vol. 2 (Weimar: 1884), 680–697.

Luther Martin, *Invokavitpredigt*, 9.3.1522, in WA 10/III, 1905, 1–13.

Poach Andreas, *Vom(m) Christlichen Abschied aus diesem sterblichen Leben des lieben thewren Mannes Matthei Ratzenbergers der Artzney Doctors Bericht durch Andream Poach Pfarherrn zun Augustinern in Erffurdt / vnd andere / So dabey gewesen / kurtz zusamen gezogen. Anno Domini* M.D.LIX. *Mense Ianuario.* (Jena, Thomas Rebart: [1559]).

Selnecker Nicolaus, *Christliche Leÿchpredigten So vom Jar 1576. bis fast an das 1590. Jar zu Leipzig / Durch D. Nicolaum Selneccerum der zeit Superintendenten vnd Professorem alda / geschehen vnd auffgezeichnet worden sind* [...] *Erster Theil Von Anno 1576 bis auff das Jar 1584.* [...], (Magdeburg, Paul Donat Jn verlegung Ambrosij Kirchners: 1590). – *Ander theil Christlicher Leÿchpredigten Zu Leipzig gehalten von Anno 1584. bis auff das 189, Jar.* [...], (Magdeburg, Paul Donat Jn verlegung Ambrosij Kirchners: [1590]).

Secondary Literature

Dingel I., "'Recht glauben, christlich leben und seliglich sterben'. Leichenpredigt als evangelische Verkündigung im 16. Jahrhundert", in Lenz R. (ed.), *Leichenpredigten als Quelle historischer Wissenschaften*, vol. 4 (Stuttgart: 2004), 9–36.

Dingel I., "Spuren reformierter Konfessionalität in Leichenpredigten auf Angehörige des schlesischen Adels", in Bahlcke J. – Dingel I. (eds.), *Die Reformierten in Schlesien. Vom 16. Jahrhundert bis zur Altpreußischen Union von 1817*, Veröffentlichungen des Instituts für Europäische Geschichte Mainz Beihefte 106 (Göttingen: 2016), 15–30.

Düselder H. – Winkler E., *"Leichenpredigt"*, in Jaeger F. (ed.), *Enzyklopädie der Neuzeit*, vol. 7 (Stuttgart – Weimar: 2008), 821–825.

Hupe W., "*August Buchner (1591–1661)*", in *Leben in Leichenpredigten* (10/2011) http://www.personalschriften.de/leichenpredigten/artikelserien/artikelansicht/details/august-buchner-1591-1661.html [25.07.2021].

Kolb R., "Ars moriendi lutherana. Andreas Poachs Schrift 'Vom Christlichen Abschied aus diesem sterblichen Leben … Matthei Ratzenbergers' (1559)", in Graf G. – Hasse H.-P. et al. (ed.), *Vestigia pietatis. Studien zur Geschichte der Frömmigkeit in Thüringen und Sachsen. Ernst Koch gewidmet.* Herbergen der Christenheit. Sonderband 5 (Leipzig: 2000), 95–112.

Lenz R., "Leichenpredigt", in Müller G. (ed.), *Theologische Realenzyklopädie*, vol. 20 (Berlin – New York: 1990), 665–669.

Mager I., *Die Konkordienformel im Fürstentum Braunschweig-Wolfenbüttel. Entstehungsbeitrag – Rezeption – Geltung.* Studien zur Kirchengeschichte Niedersachsens 33 (Göttingen: 1993).

Mohr R., "Ars moriendi II. 16.–18. Jahrhundert", in Müller G. (ed.), *Theologische Realenzyklopädie*, vol. 4 (Berlin – New York: 1979), 149–154.

Siebert S., "Matthäus Ratzenberger", in Bautz T. (ed.), *Biographisch-Bibliographisches Kirchenlexikon* vol. 7 (Herzberg: 1994), 1394–1395.

CHAPTER 7

The Catholic Reformation and the Dying: Confraternities and Preparations for Death in France 1550–1700

Elizabeth Tingle

1   Introduction

For early modern Catholics, mutual aid, to support each other in the quest for heaven, was important in life and death. Affluent individuals and families seeking to prepare their souls for eternity could invest in the luxury of perpetual masses to ease their anxieties about dying and to ensure their ultimate entry into paradise. But the less well-off had to seek cheaper solutions. The majority turned therefore to communal assistance and collaboration, in their search for spiritual support and salvation.[1] It would be wrong, however, to differentiate between 'popular' communal and elite 'personal' strategies, for wealthy and poorer individuals alike relied on group representation for their souls. Preparation of the soul during life and transition from the earthly to the heavenly realm, required the support of family, friends, and community for all social groups. A contemporary painting of the deathbed of King Henry II of France who died in 1559, shows the gathered crowds of family, clergy and retainers around him, assisting the king's passing, while the witness lists of last wills and testaments attest to priestly and lay companions for the middling sort.[2] One of the most important local institutions which helped in practical preparations for death and supported the dying, was the confraternity. The aim of this chapter is to examine the role of the confraternity in aiding Catholics of the early modern period to prepare for death, spiritually, through devotional activities and materially, by providing for mortuary rites and post-mortem intercession. Theologically and materially, their role was to give merit through lifetime actions, provide comfort, guidance and resolution in the final hours as

---

1   For a detailed study of post-mortem intercession strategies see Tingle E.C., *Purgatory and Piety in Brittany 1480 to 1720* (Farnham: 2012), especially chapter 6.
2   https://www.rct.uk/collection/402694/the-death-of-henry-ii-of-france Accessed 16 January 2023.

a final form of good work, and above all, to assure that after death, individuals would be catered for by the ongoing activities of their chosen community.[3]

Guilds and confraternities were widespread in the later Middle Ages, but the Reformation attack on saintly and collective intercession led to a decline in membership. From the later part of the sixteenth century, however, with the reaffirmation of intercession by the Council of Trent and papal sponsoring of high-profile Roman confraternities as agents of Counter Reform, the confraternity once again became a prominent institution of local religious life.[4] These groups all provided funerary assistance from the moment of death and commemoration in the longer term. In addition, associations created specifically to assist the dying were introduced in the post-Tridentine period. Confraternities were also major consumers of another post-Reformation revival, the indulgence. Pardons, especially papal plenary pardons, were widely sought as a means of preparing for death, to ensure the avoidance of purgatory and a passport straight to heaven.[5] To illustrate how these activities worked in practice, focus will be on a case study of the confraternities of Brittany in western France, although comparisons will be drawn with other regions as well. Brittany is a region considered to have had a particularly potent culture of the dead, so consideration of the dying offers an interesting commentary on that historiography.[6]

2   Before the Reformation: Confraternities and Preparation for Death in the Later Middle Ages

Nicolas Terpstra defines the confraternity as 'a self-governing congregation of lay Christians adapting and adjusting traditional clerical forms of group

---

3   There are numerous studies of the mortuary role of confraternities. A concise study for Spain that has analogies with France is Flynn M., "Baroque Piety and Spanish Confraternities", in Donnelly J.P. – Maher M.W. (eds.), *Confraternities and Catholic Reform in Italy, France and Spain* (Kirkville MO: 1999) 233–246, at 233–35. For Brittany, Restif B., *La Révolution des paroisses: culture paroissiale et Réforme catholique en Haute-Bretagne aux XVIe et XVIIe siècles* (Rennes: 2006), chapters 5 and 9.

4   The introduction of Donnelly and Maher (eds.), *Confraternities and Catholic* and the works of Nicolas Terpstra and Stefano Simiz are useful here. Terpstra N., *Lay Confraternities and Civic Religion in Renaissance Bologna* (Cambridge: 1995) and Simiz S., *Confréries urbaines et dévotion en Champagne (1450–1830)* (Villeneuve-d'Ascq: 2002).

5   Tingle E., *Indulgences after Luther. Pardons in Counter Reformation France, 1520–1720* (London: 2015).

6   See the work of Alain Croix and Ellen Badone: Croix A., *La Bretagne aux XVIe et XVIIe siècles. La vie – la mort – la foi*, 2 vols. (Paris: 1981); Badone E., *The Appointed Hour: Death, Worldview, and Social Change in Brittany* (Berkeley: 1989).

worship to their own situation and times.'[7] They were relatively independent organisations, raising and administering their own funds under limited supervision from clergy. Confraternities began to appear in numbers in northern and western Europe from the twelfth century, but really took off after 1300. In the area around Avignon, Jacques Chiffoleau found that 10 per cent of wills mentioned confraternities in the fourteenth century but in the fifteenth century, 37 per cent of testators left them money or goods.[8] In Lyon, the city council summoned 30 local confraternities to a meeting in 1496, but in the sixteenth century there were at least 60.[9] There were different types of confraternity and individuals could be members of more than one association. The craft fraternity was an association of artisans of a particular trade dedicated to the veneration of a particular saint. Parish associations, for the local community, may have been the commonest form of guild, in both town and countryside. A third type was formed for a specific charitable or devotional purpose, such as the running of a hospital, maintaining a chapel or shrine, or for a special social group. Some individuals never joined confraternities; others joined several, such as Gilles Jumel, choir priest of Notre Dame of Nantes, whose will of 1559 stated that he was a member of the Holy Sacrament confraternity in Sainte-Croix and of Saints Anthony and Sebastian in Saint-Saturnin parish churches.[10]

The diversity of association is exemplified in Nantes, the largest city of Brittany. The earliest associations were guilds for nobles and wealthy bourgeois, the confraternities of the Passion founded in 1364 and the Veronica founded in 1413, the latter established by Duke Jean V in the Dominican church. Several crafts and trades founded religious associations, such as the joiners with their guild of St Anne.[11] The religious orders founded city-wide confraternities at altars in their churches, of which the most important was Notre-Dame-des-Carmes in the Carmelite church. In 1532, this had 435 members; 229 men, of whom 15 were Carmelites and 18 secular priests, 216 women including 60 widows, 79 wives with their husbands, 69 wives without their spouses and one nun. Membership was relatively accessible; entry cost 12 *sous* (the daily wage of a building artisan was eight *sous* in this period).[12]

7   Terpstra, *Lay Confraternities* 49.
8   Chiffoleau J., *La comptabilité de l'au-delà. Les hommes, la mort et la religion dans la région d'Avignon à la fin du Moyen Age (c.1320–c.1480)* (Rome: 1980) 267, 273.
9   Hoffman P.T., *Church, and Community in the Diocese of Lyon 1500–1789* (New Haven: 1984) 26.
10 Archives Départementales de la Loire-Atlantique (ADLA) G 325. Notre Dame de Nantes. Fondations.
11 Bois P. (ed.), *Histoire de Nantes* (Toulouse: 1977) 219.
12 Durand Y., *Un couvent dans la ville. Grands Carmes de Nantes* (Rome: 1997) 92–93; wage data from Musgrave E.C., *The Building Industries of Eastern Brittany 1600–1790* (PhD Dissertation, University of Oxford: 1988), chapter 5.

There were also parish-based confraternities such as Notre-Dame-de-la-Cité of Saint-Saturnin and Notre-Dame-de-Chandeleur of Saint-Nicolas. In the latter parish church, two other late medieval confraternities are known, St Catherine and St Nicolas the parish patron.[13] Finally, confraternities devoted to charitable work existed, principally that of Toussaints, which ran a hospital. Nantes therefore had an extensive and varied network of religious confraternities, like other French cities. In the countryside, confraternities seem rarer, but this is a result of a lack of documentary evidence. The parish association of Saint-Grégoire, near to Rennes, may have been typical. Membership cost 3 *sous* 4 *deniers* to join and the revenues were spent largely on masses for the members. About 15 members died each year and around the same number enrolled.[14] Confraternities were a regular part of the religious landscape of the later Middle Ages, across France and western Europe.

Historians have given different emphases to the functions of late medieval confraternities, from public piety to charity to local neighbourhood solidarity. Above all, they have stressed the role of confraternities in burial provision and perpetual intercession for dead members, which augmented in scope as belief in purgatory became ever more prominent after 1300.[15] Joining a confraternity was central to many people's preparation for death and the afterlife, because they provided for decent funerals and ongoing post-mortem masses, even when heirs died out. Medieval and Renaissance confraternities were not so much involved in consoling the dying, as providing security for the living that once deceased, their body and soul would be well provided for. This gave reassurance to individuals that the community would take responsibility for their salvation when they were no longer able to do so themselves. The statutes of medieval confraternities specify in detail the obligations which members owed to deceased brothers and sisters. Confraternities organised funeral processions and masses with mortuary sheets, charitable doles and other works, lights, and prayers, and they organised perpetual intercessions. Many guilds accepted the registration of members already deceased to benefit from these activities. As John Bossy states, 'the fraternity practiced the rituals of togetherness in this world and procured the salvation of its members in the next'.[16] Confraternities prepared the living for death, therefore, by providing reassurance that their time in purgatory would be shortened.

13 Bourdeaut A., Le culte et les arts à Saint-Nicolas de Nantes avant le Concile de Trente', *Bulletin de la Société Archéologique et Historique de Nantes et la Loire-Inférieure* 62 (1922) 101–144, 120.
14 Restif, *La Révolution des paroisses* 88.
15 See Chiffoleau, *La comptabilité de l'au-delà* 267 for discussion.
16 Bossy J., "Holiness and Society", *Past and Present* 75 (1977) 119–137, at 121.

Again, we can see these practices in late medieval Nantes. The locksmiths' guild founded in 1492 had a confraternity dedicated to St Eloi with an altar in Notre Dame church. When masters, mistresses or their children died, all the masters were obliged to accompany the body to church on pain of a fine of ½ pound of wax, and they were bound to attend the feast day of their patron saint, part of which was dedicated to requiem masses for the souls of deceased members.[17] In the tailors' guild founded around 1471 and dedicated to the Holy Trinity, masters paid two *deniers* a week as fees for themselves and their wives while journeymen and servants paid one *denier* each week. The day after the annual feast a requiem mass was held for deceased brothers and sisters. When a master, journeyman or their wives died, the guild held ten masses, including one sung requiem mass, with four torches, four large candles around the bier and the guild would accompany the body to the church.[18] Other confraternities had similar provisions.

3 Renewal and Revival: the Catholic Reformation, Confraternities, and Preparation for Death

The Reformation of the sixteenth century saw changes in these traditions. Protestantism's attack on saintly and collective intercession for the living and the dead led to a decline in confraternity membership, even in Catholic regions.[19] There was also royal criticism of some associations, particularly those linked with crafts. In 1539, Francis I reformed artisanal guilds, including religious associations, fearing they served as a basis for labour agitation.[20] Further, there were criticisms of confraternities at the Council of Trent. Their independence was disliked by clerical elites. In the XXIII session of the Council in 1562, canons VIII and IX ruled for episcopal control over confraternities to bring them under greater clerical supervision.[21] In all, the traditional religious confraternity came under pressure on several fronts. Yet, from the mid-century, two processes worked to revive confraternal associations. First, the sectarian

---

17 Pied E., *Les anciens corps d'arts et métiers de Nantes*, 3 vols (Nantes: 1903) I, 128.
18 Archives Municipales de Nantes (AMN) HH 168. Corporations. Tailleurs.
19 Galpern A.N. *The Religions of the People in Sixteenth Century Champagne* (Cambridge MA: 1976) 103, 188, 190.
20 Diefendorf B., *Beneath the Cross. Catholics and Huguenots in Sixteenth Century Paris* (Oxford: 1991) 34.
21 Black C., "Confraternities and the Parish in the Context of the Italian Catholic Reform", in Donnelly J.P. – Maher M.W. (eds.), *Confraternities and Catholic Reform in Italy, France and Spain* (Kirkville MO: 1999) 1–26, 8.

and military conflicts of the French religious wars after 1560 saw a revival and reshaping of confraternities. The chief features of the new and revived fraternities were greater emphasis on the performance of charitable work, rejection of convivial festivities, new devotional emphases on frequent confession and communion and above all overt statements or demonstrations of Catholic faith.[22] The new confraternities played an important role in the mobilization of Catholics against heresy and in the shaping of confessional identity. Devotional confraternities, encouraged particularly by the mendicant orders, also expanded.[23] Another type of confraternity which came to characterise Catholic piety in the south of France and in the larger cities of the north, was that of the Penitents, based on Italian and Spanish models.[24] A second influence on the revival of confraternities was Tridentine reform and the restatement of the validity of good works and intercession at the Council of Trent. A key development here was the creation of archconfraternities, whereby local groups throughout Catholic Europe affiliated with Roman confraternities to share their structures, devotions and particularly their indulgences. After 1600, the confraternity once again became a prominent institution of religious life for clergy and laity alike, in town and countryside, and there was a major expansion of devotional and philanthropic associations across France and Catholic Europe. With this came new opportunities to prepare for one's end.

Historians have identified new departures in the nature and functions of Counter Reformation confraternities. Tridentine reformers sought to impose greater clerical authority over these voluntary associations.[25] Following on from the rulings of Trent, the Bull *Quacumque* of Pope Clement VIII of 1604 gave powers to parish priests to curb the autonomy of confraternities, to elect or at least to veto their officials, to scrutinise their accounts and to control when they celebrated offices in order to avoid clashes with parish celebrations.[26] Further, the separation of the sacred from the profane was a preoccupation of reformers. In confraternities, they stressed the sanctifying aspects of fellowship but played down sociability.[27] Fraternity feasts and secular activities were therefore discouraged and not allowed to take place in guild chapels or in connection with masses. Processions with the sacrament needed permission from

---

22 Bossy J., "Leagues and Associations in Sixteenth-Century French Catholicism", *Studies in Church History* 23 (1986) 171–189, at 175 and 177.
23 Armstrong M., *The Politics of Piety. Franciscan Preachers during the Wars of Religion* (Woodbridge, 2004) 99–101.
24 Bossy, "Leagues and Associations" 176.
25 Ibidem, 183.
26 "Introduction" in Donnelly – Maher (eds.), *Confraternities* 8.
27 Po-Hsia R., *The World of Catholic Renewal 1540–1770* (Cambridge: 1998) 202.

the bishop and any money collected above the needs of fraternity masses was to be used for pious works.[28]

But the most frequently observed change is the increase in new devotional confraternities. Their hallmarks were sombre exercises of piety, with masses and sermons instead of feasts. Two in particular were highly successful. Holy Sacrament confraternities were founded to promote the cult of the Eucharist through more frequent administration of the sacraments of confession, penance and communion and confraternities of the rosary encouraged Marian devotions. Rosary associations originated before Trent, sponsored by the Dominicans of northern Europe, and with the revival of Marian devotions after Trent, they mushroomed.[29] Trevor Johnson observed that many of these were members of archconfraternities, satellites of a larger group and 'thereby linked ... to a universal project' in the wider church.[30] Historians such as Bruno Restif argue that they marked a departure from the past. Rather than a concern with intercession, as in previous centuries, they were devotional fraternities where multiple exercises of collective piety were practised and individual pious behaviour was formed and encouraged.[31] In Maixent near Saint-Malo, the priest Noël Georges recorded that the new confraternity of the Holy Sacrament 'seemed already by the splendour of its light ... to obscure the lustre of ancient devotions hitherto given to other confraternities', notably those dedicated to Saints Maxent and John the Baptist.[32] But many older confraternities simply adopted new invocations, especially Marian confraternities which changed into those of the Rosary. Hoffman shows this for the Lyonnais where old parish guilds such as Holy Spirit fraternities declined, to be replaced by Holy Sacrament and Rosary confraternities; these had not existed in 1610, but by the mid-eighteenth century there were forty-two Holy Sacrament and twenty-eight Rosary confraternities in the 108 parishes of the north-east of the diocese.[33]

The innovations of the Counter Reformation can be overstated, however. Many traditional confraternities continued to operate. Hospital guilds, parish groups, crafts and trades, ancient associations with their own chapels, were resuscitated and strengthened after 1600. Most regions operated a mixed economy. In Rennes diocese in the seventeenth and eighteenth centuries,

---

28 Bossy, "Leagues and Associations" 183.
29 Hsia, *Catholic Renewal* 202.
30 Johnson T., *Magistrates, Madonnas, and Miracles. The Counter Reformation in the Upper Palatinate* (Farnham: 2009) 170.
31 Restif, *La Révolution des paroisses* 179–180.
32 Restif, *La Révolution des paroisses* 181.
33 Hoffman, *Church and Community* 110–111.

Catherine Jamet has located 302 confraternities, an average of 1.2 per parish. Almost 50 per cent were Marian dominated by rosary groups; one-third were Christological, mostly Holy Sacrament and the rest were dedicated to a variety of saints.[34] There were, however, changes in emphasis in their spirituality across the seventeenth century. David Gentilcore characterised this as a vocation to internal missionism.[35] As well as evoking the aid of a saintly protector, these associations expected their members to engage personally in repeated acts of piety or asceticism. By these means, Tridentine spiritual mores passed into most communities in France.

The new and revived confraternities provided more support for the dying than had previous groups. Pierre Chaunu argues that most confraternities in Paris continued to be mutual associations to assure their members aid to assist the living, comfort the dying and provide solidarity between both worlds through intercession for the repose of departed souls.[36] Matters were similar in Brittany. There was a return to the late medieval concern for the soul in purgatory and a resurgence of collective activity to help the dying navigate judgement and reduce his or her sojourn in the third place. In particular, confraternities continued to reassure the living membership that 'decent' funerals, prayers for the dead and perpetual intercession would be provided for, as in earlier decades, which was proposed as a comfort to the dying. In Nantes, the barber-surgeons' statutes of 1692 show they had an ancient confraternity dedicated to Saints Cosme and Damien, to which newly-received masters paid a fee of 100 *sous* and all masters had to accompany confreres and their wives to their funerals, on pain on thirty *sous*' fine.[37] The nail makers were incorporated around 1683 and their statutes ruled that each master had to pay an annual fee of five *sous* to the fraternity for the costs of services for the souls of dead masters.[38] But confraternity statutes of some groups of this period also show that deathbed assistance – even at a distance – was part of their work. Holy Sacrament confraternities played an important role in supporting the dying. Members were asked to assist sick confreres, notably by accompanying the viaticum from the parish church to their house, and by praying for the sick and the recently deceased. Statutes of the Holy Sacrament confraternity founded in the chapel of Notre-Dame-des-Lices of Vannes in 1610 stated that members

---

34 Jamet C., "Les confréries de dévotion dans le diocèse de Rennes aux XVIIe et XVIIIe siècles", *Annales de Bretagne* 87 (1980) 481–491, 482–483.
35 Gentilcore D., *From Bishop to Witch. The System of the Sacred in Early Modern Terra d'Otranto* (Manchester: 1999) 78.
36 Chaunu P., *La mort à Paris: XVIe, XVIIe, XVIIIe siècles* (Paris: 1978) 215.
37 Pied, *Les anciens corps* I, 90.
38 Ibidem, 323.

would accompany the host to the house of sick members with torches and candles and that members should pray for the dying.[39] The Agonisants based at La Trinité church of Machecoul had a bell rung for each confrere who was dying, so that prayers could be said for him or her.[40] Confraternities were also keen to acquire indulgences for their members, discussed below, which were seen as a great comfort to the dying, by assuring their salvation through the accrued merits of the whole Catholic Church.

The membership of a confraternity was thus an important part of preparation for departure from this life, with prayers offered for the sick and dying. Yet for most groups, their post-mortem provision remained the main preparation for death and their chief comfort for the dying. That it was a pastoral work needs to be stated strongly. All confraternities, new and old, continued to hold funeral services for their members and at least an annual requiem mass on the day after their principal feast. The confraternity of the Holy Sacrament of Plouay, founded in 1683, organised Thursday services, where the sacrament would be displayed and taken in procession around the church and cemetery; a high mass would follow, followed by a benediction of the Holy Sacrament and a *Libera* for the souls of deceased confreres.[41] Rosary confraternities also incorporated the dead. The 1661 statutes of the Rosary confraternity of Arradon stated that there would be four anniversaries held a year for deceased confreres; following the death of a member, the others undertook to say a rosary or, if wealthy enough, to have a mass said for them at the rosary altar, within 40 days of the death.[42] There were special prayer cycles using the rosary that could be said for the dead; the Jesuit Marc de Bonnyers recommended a cycle where the large beads could be used for an Ave or a Pater Noster and the small beads, to pray 'Pie Jesus, sweet Jesus, give them eternal rest' or 'Requescant in pace, amen' and he gave other rosary prayers for souls as well.[43]

Confraternity membership was a guarantee of having a good death, with prayers and sacraments, but also a fine death with a decent and well-attended funeral, where participants would offer prayers for the departed soul. The collectivity guaranteed post-mortem intercession, with its annual services and regular prayers with an assured congregation. Indeed, confraternities and

---

39 ADM 57 G 1. Cathédrale de Vannes. Confréries.
40 Ghenassia J., "Les 'chevauchées' d'un archidiacre à la fin du 17e siècle: la visite d'Antoine Binet dans le diocèse de Nantes (1682–1698)", *Revue d'Histoire de l'Eglise de France* 57 (1971) 83–95, 93.
41 ADM G 954.
42 ADM G 1143. Arradon. Fondations.
43 de Bonnyers Marc, *L'advocat des âmes de purgatoire ou moyens faciles pour les aider* (Lille: 1640) 83.

religious orders continued to attract donors by offering distinctive cycles of masses for the deceased. For example, the confraternities of the Carmelites of Nantes offered a high requiem service and 10 low masses for deceased members.[44] In the 1680s, in the church of Le Palais on Belle-Isle, the Holy Sacrament confraternity organised anniversaries comprising the exhibition of the sacrament, high mass, first and second vespers.[45] Also, most confraternities continued to accept deceased members, enrolled by their relatives or executors. For example, the Agonisants of Saint-Léonard of Fougères received 17 new members from 1689–91, of whom eight were already dead and one was dying.[46]

The security of knowing that a good send-off was secure, was comforting to many individuals. We might ask how widespread membership was – whether it was the prerogative of certain social groups or a popular way of preparing for death. What is notable about Counter Reformation confraternities is their wide membership. For example, in Rennes diocese, the confraternities of the Holy Sacrament charged low fees, to encourage widespread participation; at Boistruden, there was no entry fee or annual charge, to encourage the participation of the poor.[47] In the archdeaconry of Retz, south of Nantes, by the 1680s total membership of confraternities varied between 5 and 40 per cent of adults in many parishes. The entry fee for the All-Saints' confraternity at Saint-Jean de Montfaucon was 40 *sous* but that at Saint-Hilaire-du-Bois was only 2 *sous* and Saint-Fiacre's confraternity charged 15 *deniers*, in addition to yearly subscriptions. These are not large sums when the daily wage of a mason was around 15 *sous* at this time.[48]

4   New Departures: Specialist Confraternities for the Dying and Deceased

A new feature of the Catholic Reformation period was the growth of more specialist confraternities for the dying and the departed.[49] We see emerging

---

44   Durand, *Un couvent dans la ville* 176.
45   ADM G 945. Le Pallais Belle-Isle. Fondations.
46   Jamet, "Les confréries" 490.
47   Restif, *La Révolution des paroisses* 187.
48   Ghenassia, "Les 'chevauchées' d'un archidiacre" 93.
49   The terms Catholic and Counter Reformation are largely used interchangeably here, as in much Anglo-American historiography. However, Catholic Reformation tends to be used when reform and innovation is examined; Counter Reformation when practices are introduced which have an anti-Protestant dimension.

a concern with supporting the dying with prayers and the sacraments – a confraternal development of late medieval *ars moriendi* practice – and with focusing on intercession for souls in purgatory as the primary good work of the group. The origins of these groups in Brittany lay in the transition period of the mid-sixteenth century. We know most about two associations founded specifically to intercede for departed souls, confraternities of the Trépassés founded in the cathedral cities of Saint-Pol in 1533 and Vannes in 1543. The preamble of the statutes of Vannes' confraternity clearly describes the beliefs of the founders about the best means of preparing for and managing their experiences after death:

> Considering the universal resurrection on the terrible, dreadful great day of judgement and firmly believing that it is possible to help and assist the souls of the departed tormented by the burning fire of Purgatory, through prayer, alms, and the offering of the holy and precious body of our saviour and redeemer Jesus Christ made by the priest in the holy sacrifice of the mass.

the confreres sought,

> to change their transitory temporal goods into spiritual goods ... to the honour and glory of God the all-powerful, of the Blessed Virgin advocate of poor humanity before God, and of the archangel St Michael, protector and defender of poor sinners while alive and also of miserable souls in the face of cruel and horrible death [when] passing from this mortal life to the immortal, against the enemy and infernal dragon the Devil who searches for poor souls to ruin them completely.[50]

The primary activity of the confraternity was to hold a weekly Monday mass for departed souls in the chapel of Saint-Michel in the suburbs of Vannes. The choice of patron was important, for the archangel weighed souls and helped them in their passage to their next destination in the afterlife. The mass was a sung requiem at the chapel's high altar preceded by vespers and vigils of the dead and a procession around the cemetery. The immediate objective was a civic and collective one, to pray for those buried in the precinct of Saint-Michel who no longer had living friends and relatives to intercede for them, to 'relieve and diminish the pains their souls suffer in the fire of purgatory'. Before the service, the officers of the confraternity would pass through Vannes ringing a

---

50   ADM 57 G 3. Confrérie des Trépassés Vannes.

hand bell, to alert the members to the mass. Other forms of intercession were provided as well. The officers were to pass through the city at Midnight on Sundays, Wednesdays, and Fridays, ringing a hand bell at each street corner, calling upon the inhabitants to pray for the departed. The confreres also undertook to toll the large bell of Saint-Michel to mark All Souls' Day, from Vespers on the eve to the morning following the feast, in remembrance of the dead. The theology of good works and intercession lay behind these activities.

As for its own members, the Vannes confraternity provided lights for their funeral services and the confreres would accompany the corpse of the deceased to the church and attend the mass. Each member would also contribute 1 *denier* towards a requiem service, which all would attend, to pray for his/her soul and for the souls of all the departed.[51] The statutes of the slightly earlier confraternity of the Trépassés of Saint-Pol founded in 1533 are similar, with a primary concern to arrange Monday services and cemetery processions in and around Saint-Pierre parish church. Also, members who died would have a solemn service of vigils for the dead, a sung mass, prayers for the deceased, a *De profundis* and other orations, followed by a low mass of the Name of Jesus within fifteen days of burial. The funerary and intercessory provisions for members of the associations were important and members no doubt joined to benefit from these arrangements.

These were not common confraternities in the later Middle Ages, however. Fewer than five are known from Brittany in this period. Also, membership was relatively small, probably because they had a specialist and localised function rather than being generalist or craft groups. In Vannes, the first membership list of 1543 comprised four priests and 64 named laymen. In 1552, listed members comprised seven priests, six men accorded 'sieur' titles, twenty-three named men 'and several others.'[52] Membership costs were not particularly high, however. In 1543, the Vannes statutes ruled that each confrere and consoeur should pay 20 *deniers* a year, 10 *deniers* at Easter and 10 *deniers* at All Souls; deceased family members could be enrolled for 20 *deniers* a year. Members were also expected to give alms to the confraternity at All Souls.[53] In the confraternity of Saint-Pol, the entry fee was 100 *sous* for couples, 50 *sous* for widows, priests, and other unmarried people. There was also an annual fee of 5 *sous* cash and 4 *sous* of wax, or 2 *sous* for single people.[54] A register of new receptions exists for Saint-Pol for 1538–42 and 1549–64. In most years, there were only one or

---

51   ADM 57 G 3.
52   ADM 57 G 3.
53   ADM 57 G 3.
54   Archives Départementales de Finistère (ADF) 9 G 2. Statutes copy of 1543, articles 9–11.

two new entrants.[55] Both of the Breton confraternities of the Trépassés were therefore relatively small and specialised in function, influenced by the clerical culture of the episcopal cities of Vannes and Saint-Pol.

The first half of the seventeenth century also saw new groups for the solace of the dying with the emergence of Agonisant and *Bonne Mort* associations. These were not found before 1600. Some of the Agonisant confraternities were affiliated formally with the archconfraternity of the same name at Rome, created in 1616. In Brittany, Agonisant confraternities developed in the second half of the century. In Rennes, one confraternity and in the diocese, eight associations of Notre Dame des Agonisants were created after 1659 and particularly after 1680.[56] Their objectives were to give spiritual aid to those who were in their last agonies and to aid them in the final combat with the devil, through the last rites, final communion, and prayers. The statutes of the Rennes association stated they existed for mutual charity, to comfort each other in their last moment, which was the most important time of all.[57] The statutes of the association of Nancy in eastern France give more detail of their work. The family of a dying member was to alert the parish priest, who would organise the association to ring the great bell thirty-two times while he or another priest put out the holy sacrament onto the church's altar for adoration. The membership would assemble there and say prayers for the dying; if they were detailed elsewhere, they should say prayers at that place.[58]

The Bonne Mort associations had a different focus, to help individuals prepare for their own death. They were linked to a confraternity established by the Jesuits of Rome in their church of the Gesù in 1648. Two thirds of the known associations in Europe were housed in a Jesuit church.[59] Membership was linked to regular exercises of prayer and meditation, for which meetings were held monthly or at other regular intervals, where there would be devotions, reflections, and a sermon. Members were encouraged to imagine their own illness, dying and death. The Bonne Mort groups were not nearly as popular as the Agonisants, which turned outwards to sustain the dying in their final 'agonies'; at the end of the seventeenth century there were three times as many Agonisant groups as Bonne Mort confraternities.[60] Agonisants were

---

55 ADF 9 G 4. Saint-Pol. Confrérie des Trépassés. Lettres de réception.
56 Restif, *La Révolution des paroisses* 183.
57 Froeschlé-Chopard, *Dieu pour tous*, 247.
58 Froeschlé-Chopard, *Dieu pour tous*, 248.
59 Hernandez F., "Les confréries des diocèses d'Orange et de Saint-Paul-Trois-Châteaux à la fin du XVIIe siècle", in Froeschlé-Chopard M.-H – Devos R., (eds.), *Les confréries, l'Eglise et la cité. Cartographie des confréries du Sud-Est* (Grenoble: 1988) 97–112, 313.
60 Froeschlé-Chopard, *Dieu pour tous* 249.

also strongly planted in the parishes as well as the mendicant churches.[61] The emphasis of the new groups on the dying reflects evolving views on the best time for intercession – during the lifetime of a sinner – that was eventually to reduce investment in perpetual post-mortem intercession. Indeed, collective intercession expanded at the time that individual foundations declined in the early eighteenth century.

The Ames du Purgatoire, with the objective of providing prayer for departed, suffering souls, were mostly found in the southern part of France. Their equivalent in Brittany was the Trépassés, which as a devotion was resurrected in the seventeenth century in some of the western Breton cities. The confraternity of the Trépassés in Vannes grew in strength over the first two thirds of the century. It continued its membership among the middling sort of the city; its provosts were notaries, merchants, surgeons, and other master craftsmen. The period between 1600 and 1626 witnessed 12 foundations of masses for the confraternity, so that there was a sung requiem mass and procession in the confraternity's chapel every day as well as on feast days including All Souls and St Michael.[62] Revenues increased, from 400 *livres* in 1635 to 880 *livres* in 1663.[63] In the 1630s, the confraternity organised between forty-five and fifty funerals a year.[64] Similarly in Saint-Pol, the confraternity was also the recipient of new foundations across the first two-thirds of the seventeenth century, with a peak in the period 1630–1660.[65] The confraternity also received smaller donations, such as a *rente* of forty-five *sous* per year on land in Ploudiry by a group of parishioners in 1626, to participate in the prayers and indulgences of the confraternity, and a *rente* of sixteen *sous* per year given by François Kerdelant for himself and his late wife in 1637, on land in the same parish, for remembrance.[66] By the later seventeenth century, both the Vannes and the Saint-Pol confraternities became sufficiently important in their cities to be transferred into the cathedrals. In the later seventeenth century, there was a Trépassés fraternity in Quimper Cathedral, for it was granted a four *livre rente* on a house in the city by Jean Le Bac shoemaker and his wife Marguerite, to be remembered in its masses and public prayers.[67] There are altars with retables dedicated to the Trépassés in the present-day churches of Brélévenez and Plounéour-Menez, the latter of which came from the Dominican church

---

61 Hernandez, "Les confréries" 313.
62 ADM 57 G 3.
63 ADM 72 G 3. Vannes. Confrérie des Trépassés. Comptes.
64 ADM 72 G 3.
65 ADF 9 G 1.
66 ADF 9 G 2.
67 ADF 2 G 121. Chapitre de Cornouaille. Confrérie des Trépassés.

in Morlaix, evidence for past confraternities.[68] Concerned with souls as they were, these associations were 'societies of mutual spiritual assistance; they assured a vast exchange of prayers of the living for the sufferings of souls which created a powerful solidarity of the mystical body and the cohabitation of the dead and the living, united by grace.'[69]

5   Preparation for Death through Good Works

Confraternities provided a framework in which members could undertake good works and build up their own store of treasure in heaven as an essential part of preparing for the afterlife. For post-mortem intercession to be effective, wider good works for the living and the dead were vital: specific charitable work, prayer for the craft or parish community, all contributed to the wider spiritual merit of the individual. To separate out charity, devotion and mortuary intercession makes no sense: a fraternity's purpose was veneration and worship, and the support of the living by charity, understood widely, and the dead through prayers.[70] Terpstra comments that they activated a faith meant as much to protect the body from evil as to console and save the soul.[71] But their main good work was prayer and masses, for the saint or devotion to which their group was dedicated. As Claude de la Barre wrote in 1628 'charity must be the first spiritual food of our souls … one day we will appear before the tribunal of Jesus Christ to receive the reward for our works, good and bad'.[72] Each act was an essential preparation for dying and death, as it accrued merit against which the soul would ultimately be judged.

A second important reason for confraternity membership after 1600 was the access it gave to indulgences, the acquisition of which was a popular form of good work and one of the most important means of preparing for dying and death in the Catholic Reformation. After a dip in popularity across the mid-sixteenth century, following scathing Protestant attacks, indulgences again emerged as a lively part of the economy of salvation. For Andéol de Lodève, writing in 1638, indulgences were the fourth means of escaping purgatory, after the Eucharist, charity, and 'satisfactory works' which included

---

68   Croix A., *La Bretagne aux XVI*ᵉᵐᵉ *et XVII*ᵉᵐᵉ *siècles*, 2 vols (Paris: 1981) II, 1049.
69   Bee M., "La société traditionnelle et la mort", *XVII*ᵉ *siècle* 106–107 (1975) 81–111, at 84–85.
70   Brigden S., "Religion and Social Obligation in Early Sixteenth-Century London", *Past & Present* 103 (1984) 67–112, 96.
71   Terpstra, *Lay Confraternities* 66.
72   Barre, Claude de la, *Resolution à scavoir si l'on doit apprehender et craindre ou bien aymer et souhaiter la mort* (Paris: 1628) 54, 60.

prayer, vigils, and fasts.[73] Most surviving indulgences from the seventeenth century were papal plenary pardons, evidence of shifts in authority over power to lose and bind towards Rome. Across the post-Tridentine period indulgences became more powerful as they were closely associated with the highest good work of all, the sacrifice of the mass, because to obtain a plenary indulgence necessitated confession, contrition, and communion.[74]

Confraternities vied with each other to provide an attractive portfolio of pardons for their members.[75] Philippe Desmette argues that it appears to have become normal practice in the late-sixteenth and seventeenth centuries for newly-founded confraternities – and those already in place – to solicit the Holy See for indulgences, as a matter of course.[76] This had not always been the case. Early sixteenth-century confraternities did not endow their members with lavish pardons and indeed, not all seventeenth-century associations did so. Indulgenced confraternities seem to have originated in Italy and spread into France from the later sixteenth century; they were particularly associated with new devotional forms and were widespread enough, by the end of the period, to make pardons accessible to many people. Plenary indulgences were granted on condition that on the day of their entry, members would confess and receive the holy sacrament. Plenary remission was also granted to the dying if they confessed and received the sacrament, if they were able to, or at least had contrition. A plenary indulgence was also granted for visiting the chapel or altar of the confraternity on its principal feast day. In addition, seven years of pardon were granted for assisting at the four annual feasts celebrated by the confraternity, if communion was also taken.[77] For those contemplating mortality, the indulgence was a powerful and sure way of circumventing purgatory and achieving heaven, a strong consolation for the dying person.

It was the plenary indulgence offered on the death bed that was one of the great attractions of confraternities, especially the new devotional groups. From the later sixteenth century, the form this took was standardised across the Catholic Church, part of the wider Romanisation of practice. The indulgence briefs issued describe the deathbed rituals associated with the pardon. The dying person should make confession and take communion if they were

---

73 Andéol de Lodève, *Defense du purgatoire et de l'honneur des ecclésiastiques et des religieux mesprizez et calumnies sans raison par les ministres de la religion pretendue reformée* (Tournon, Antoine Pichou: 1638) 108–109.
74 See Tingle, *Indulgences after Luther*.
75 Johnson, *Magistrates, Madonnas and Miracles* 192.
76 Desmette P., *Les brefs d'indulgences pour les confréries des diocèses de Cambrai et Tournai aux XVIIe et XVIIIe siècles* (Brussels: 2002) 27.
77 ADF 9 G 2. Chapitre de la cathédrale de Saint-Pol-de-Léon.

able, or at least repent and be contrite for their sins; as death approached, they should invoke the holy name of Jesus and recommend their souls to God, or say these things in their hearts if they could not speak.[78] Holy Sacrament members might also be counselled to look at an image of the Eucharist and say the words 'honour to the holy sacrament of the altar'. These rituals would action the plenary indulgence they were promised on entry to their confraternity. Confraternity membership also offered indulgences to members who assisted the dying; Holy Sacrament groups, members who accompanied the priest carrying the viaticum to a sick person, was granted 100 days of pardon. Sixty days were frequently available to members who knelt to pray for the dying person, while the procession passed by.[79]

As one specific example shows, the Rosary confraternity was extremely well-endowed with indulgences. Pius V in 1569 offered a plenary indulgence to members joining the confraternity who said one third of the rosary and recited another on their deathbed, as well as partial indulgences of ten years and ten quarantines to those who recited part-rosaries on three main Marian feast days. Pius attributed the victory of Lepanto of 1571 to the intercession of the Virgin Mary through the rosary, so he created a feast day on 7 October and accorded a plenary indulgence to all churches with rosary confraternities for that day. These pardons were extended by Sixtus V and Paul V.[80] In 1600, a confraternity of the Rosary was erected in the church of Locminé in Vannes diocese. It received members of both sexes 'to participate in all the graces, privileges, and indulgences which the other confreres enjoyed in the other churches of [the] order'.[81] Thus, Locminé's confraternity had access to general indulgences granted to all Dominican Rosary confraternities. In 1657, it obtained its own papal indulgence for saying rosaries in private and, in 1666, another indulgence for visitors to its altar. Membership of an indulged confraternity was thus a powerful form of preparation for dying. It was possible

---

78   Examples of this item is widespread in indulgence briefs and common to many confraternities, such as Cord of St Francis confraternities, for which see Basset, F.B., *Petit traicté des indulgences, divise en trois parties pour estre lie au livret de la confrérie du Cordon benist de S. François* (Paris: 1601) and in confraternities of the Holy Name of Jesus as in *Sommaire des indulgences, graces, privileges, statuts et reigles de la confrerie du sainct nom de Jesus establie par les RR PP Freres de l'Ordre Saint Dominique* (Fribourg: 1641).

79   A good example of statutes for Holy Sacrament confraternities is *Indulgences et Statutes de l'Archiconfrérie du tres-sainct Sacrement de l'Autel érigée dans le diocèse de Montauban* (Montauban: 1646).

80   Forestier Pierre, *Histoire des indulgences et des jubilez, avec des instructions pour en expliquer le dogme et où il est encore traité de l'origine des confréries* (Paris, Charles Robustel: 1702) 156–58.

81   ADM G1061. Locminé. Confrérie du Rosaire.

to avoid purgatory by dying in possession of a plenary indulgence, with the words 'Jesus Maria' on the lips and in the heart, so long as contrition was felt. Salvation could be assured, with foresight; although contingent on dying in the right state of mind and faith, indulgences were the ultimate form of collective intercession, drawing on the merits of the whole church. The importance of pardons to such confraternities is shown in every booklet and printed image distributed by these groups, which detail the indulgences available for members and advertise the spiritual benefits to be gained by adherence.

Traditional confraternities also sought pardons for their members. In the second half of the seventeenth century, numerous urban churches undertook serious indulgence-acquisition programmes. Through its confraternities, Saint-Patern parish church in the suburbs of Vannes undertook such a campaign. In 1676, the confraternity of the Agonisants obtained a plenary indulgence for members and for visitors to their chapel on the feast of the Annunciation; the chapel of the fraternity of Saint Marie-Madeleine followed in 1685 with a pardon for its feast day and in 1695 the confraternity of Saint-Barbe also gained an indulgence, for members and for its feast.[82] But local confraternities with plenary indulgences were only ever a minority of all associations. Most groups did not acquire such privileges. The main reason was the high cost of acquiring a papal pardon. Episcopal indulgences were obtained instead. For example, the statutes of the confraternity of the pilots, captains, and sailors of Bordeaux, printed in 1669, advertised indulgences granted by Archbishop Henri de Sourdis. At their request, he granted forty days' pardon to confrères each time they received the holy sacrament, thirty days to those who accompanied viaticum processions and another forty days for the dying.[83] The form of the indulgences, mirroring those of papal plenary indulgences, suggests that in the absence of this privilege, bishops' pardons were sought as a substitute. While not a plenary indulgence, it was hoped that the offer of some pardon would be attractive to members.[84] Local and traditional confraternities brought different privileges, those of intercession and mutual aid, as they had in the past, reliant as they were on more limited and local resources.

Finally, gauging how far confraternity membership led to the acquisition of pardons is difficult. Urban centres were better provided with pardons than rural communities. For example, in the parish church of Saint-Vivien in Rouen, a survey of 1724 listed thirteen confraternities, of which seven had indulgences,

---

82   ADM G 1053. Saint-Patern de Vannes. Indulgences.
83   Archives Départementales de Gironde (ADG) G 670. Confréries.
84   Archives Départementales de la Seine-Maritime (ADSM) G 1576. Confréries du doyenné d'Aumale, diocèse de Rouen.

spread equally over old and new devotions.[85] The countryside also had parish pardons and confraternities. It seems likely that the aggregative or archconfraternities were the most frequent means of indulgence access, for these groups had the best links to Rome and could deploy the benefits of their mutual spiritual aid.[86] As a minimum guide, therefore, the geographical extent and membership of the archconfraternities can be used as a rough indicator of popular access to pardons. In Saint-Malo diocese, in 171 parishes and chapelries, Restif has counted eighty-two confraternities of the Rosary, forty-six dedicated to the Holy Sacrament and thirty-two parishes where other confraternities, to saints or the guardian angel, were organised. Thus, two thirds of parishes had easy access to indulgences through such groups.[87] In the south of France, indulgenced confraternities were even more widespread. In the diocese of Senez, 79 per cent of parishes had rosary confraternities in the late seventeenth century.[88] In Provence, there were at least four confraternities in each parish and often more, although only one in the parishes of Dauphiné and eastern Languedoc.[89] The great confraternities promoted by Catholic reformers meant that indulgences reached all levels of Christian people in towns and in the countryside, either as association members or as visitors to their altars on feast days.[90] Thus the Catholic church catered for the needs of the dying and the deceased, of most social groups.

6 Conclusions

When she made her will in 1646, the widow Barbe Le Febvre of Saint-Saturnin parish of Nantes, was a member of the confraternities of Saints Anthony and Sebastien and Notre-Dame-de-la-Cité in the parish church, of Jesus Maria in the Minimes convent and of Notre-Dame-de-Pitié in the Carmelites, where she was buried. She asked for the 'usual' services provided by each confraternity.[91]

---

85 ADSM G 1246. Saint-Vivien de Rouen.
86 Froeschlé-Chopard, *Dieu pour tous* 164.
87 Restif, *La Révolution des paroisses* 187.
88 Bertrand R., "Dévotions et confréries dans le diocèse de Senez au temps de Mgr Soanen", in Froeschlé-Chopard – Devos (eds.), *Les confréries* 121.
89 Froeschlé-Chopard M.-H., "Les confréries dans le temps et dans l'espace. Pénitents et Saint-Sacrement", in Froeschlé-Chopard – Devos (eds.), *Les confréries*, 15.
90 Simiz S., "Les confréries face à l'indulgence. Tradition, quête, accueil et effets dans la France de l'est (XV–XVIIIeme siècles)", in Dompnier B. – Vismara P. (eds.), *Confréries et dévotions dans la catholicité moderne (mi-XVe–début XIXe siècle)* (Rome: 2008) 103–124, 117.
91 ADLA H 228. Carmes de Nantes. Fondations.

Confraternity membership was one of the most important means of preparation for death. Across the later Middle Ages and early modern period, membership gave access to spiritual succour for the living, through prayers and intercession of the collective group, and was a form of insurance that decent burial and post-mortem intercession would be carried out. For most groups, active involvement in the death bed and dying itself was limited; rather, it was lifetime preparation through good works and assurance of continued remembrance after death that were important.

The Catholic Reform saw two important shifts, a result of the slow refocusing of the main site of salvation from the deathbed to the active life of the living. The first was the creation of a small number of confraternities which gave active support to the dying member, usually through prayer. The Agonisants were the main group here, although they were never an organisation on the scale of the Rosary or the Carmelite groups. A second was the active procurement of plenary indulgences for and by living members of confraternities, giving them an insurance policy of a good death and eternal salvation. Again, advance preparation rather than deathbed support, was the main function of membership.

Confraternities were therefore important institutions for the support of the dying in early modern Europe. While membership varied – the poor may not have been members, and not all middling and upper sorts joined them – the majority of Catholic Europeans seem to have been a member of at least one group. Through prayer and sacraments while alive and the acquisition of indulgences, they guaranteed their place in heaven and gave security of salvation. When private chantries and obits declined rapidly after 1680 confraternities and indulgences continued to be active and even to expand. By the end of the seventeenth century, collective associations overtook private foundations in the volume of intercession they offered for the dead. In the priority given historiographically to the 'rise of the individual', the continuing popularity of group intercession, to support the dying has been overlooked.

Bibliography

Primary Printed Sources

[no author] *Sommaire des indulgences, graces, privileges, statuts et reigles de la confrerie du sainct nom de Jesus establie par les* RR PP *Freres de l'Ordre Sainct Dominique* (Fribourg: 1641).

[no author] *Indulgences et Statutes de l'Archiconfrérie du tres-sainct Sacrement de l'Autel érigée dans le diocèse de Montauban* (Montauban: 1646).

Barre Claude de la, *Resolution à scavoir si l'on doit apprehender et craindre ou bien aymer et souhaiter la mort* (Paris: 1628).

Basset F.B., *Petit traicté des indulgences, divise en trois parties pour estre lie au livret de la confrérie du Cordon benist de S. François* (Paris: 1601).

de Bonnyers Marc, *L'advocat des âmes de purgatoire ou moyens faciles pour les aider* (Lille: 1640).

de Lodève Andéol, *Defense du purgatoire et de l'honneur des ecclésiastiques et des religieux mesprizez et calumnies sans raison par les ministres de la religion pretendue reformée* (Tournon: 1638).

Forestier Pierre, *Histoire des indulgences et des jubilez, avec des instructions pour en expliquer le dogme et où il est encore traité de l'origine des confréries* (Paris: 1702).

Primary Manuscript Sources

Archives Départementales de Finistère (ADF)
9 G 2. Statutes copy of 1543.
9 G 4. Saint-Pol. Confrérie des Trépassés. Lettres de réception.
2 G 121. Chapitre de Cornouaille. Confrérie des Trépassés.
9 G 2. Chapitre de la cathédrale de Saint-Pol-de-Léon.

Archives Départementales de Gironde (ADG)
G 670. Confréries.

Archives Départementales du Morbihan (ADM)
57 G 1. Cathédrale de Vannes. Confréries.
G 945. Le Pallais Belle-Isle. Fondations.
G 954. Plouay. Confréries.
G 1143. Arradon. Fondations.
57 G 3. Confrérie des Trépassés Vannes.
ADM 72 G 3. Vannes. Confrérie des Trépassés. Comptes.
ADM G1061. Locminé. Confrérie du Rosaire.
ADM G 1053. Saint-Patern de Vannes. Indulgences.

Archives Municipales de Nantes (AMN)
HH 168. Corporations. Tailleurs.

Archives Départementales de la Seine-Maritime (ADSM)
G 1576. Confréries du doyenné d'Aumale, diocèse de Rouen.
G 1246. Saint-Vivien de Rouen.

Archives Départementales de la Loire-Atlantique (ADLA)
G 325. Notre Dame de Nantes. Fondations.
H 228. Carmes de Nantes. Fondations.

Secondary Literature

Armstrong M., *The Politics of Piety. Franciscan Preachers during the Wars of Religion* (Woodbridge: 2004).
Badone E., *The Appointed Hour. Death, Worldview and Social Change in Brittany* (Berkeley: 1989).
Bee M., "La société traditionnelle et la mort", *XVIIe siècle* 106–107 (1975) 81–111.
Black C., "Confraternities and the Parish in the Context of the Italian Catholic Reform", in Donnelly J.P. – Maher M.W. (eds.), *Confraternities and Catholic Reform in Italy, France and Spain* (Kirkville MO: 1999).
Bois P. (ed.), *Histoire de Nantes* (Toulouse: 1977), 1–26.
Bossy J., "Holiness and Society", *Past and Present* 75 (1977) 119–137.
Bossy J., "Leagues and Associations in Sixteenth-Century French Catholicism", *Studies in Church History* 23 (1986) 171–189.
Bourdeaut A., "Le culte et les arts à Saint-Nicolas de Nantes avant le Concile de Trente", *Bulletin de la Société Archéologique et Historique de Nantes et la Loire-Inférieure* 62 (1922) 101–144.
Brigden S., "Religion and Social Obligation in Early Sixteenth-Century London", *Past & Present* 103 (1984) 67–112.
Chaunu P., *La mort à Paris: XVIe, XVIIe, XVIIIe siècles* (Paris: 1978).
Chiffoleau J., *La comptabilité de l'au-delà. Les hommes, la mort et la religion dans la région d'Avignon à la fin du Moyen Age (c.1320–c.1480)* (Rome: 1980).
Croix A., *La Bretagne aux XVIe et XVIIe siècles. La vie- la mort – la foi*, 2 vols. (Paris: 1981).
Desmette P., *Les brefs d'indulgences pour les confréries des diocèses de Cambrai et Tournai aux XVIIe et XVIIIe siècles* (Brussels: 2002).
Diefendorf B., *Beneath the Cross. Catholics and Huguenots in Sixteenth Century Paris* (Oxford: 1991).
Durand Y., *Un couvent dans la ville. Grands Carmes de Nantes* (Rome: 1997).
Flynn M., "Baroque Piety and Spanish Confraternities", in Donnelly J.P. – Maher M.W. (eds.), *Confraternities and Catholic Reform in Italy, France and Spain* (Kirkville MO: 1999) 233–246.
Galpern A.N. *The Religions of the People in Sixteenth Century Champagne* (Cambridge, MA: 1976).
Gentilcore D., *From Bishop to Witch. The System of the Sacred in Early Modern Terra d'Otranto* (Manchester: 1999).

Ghenassia J., "Les 'chevauchées' d'un archidiacre à la fin du 17e siècle: la visite d'Antoine Binet dans le diocèse de Nantes (1682–1698)", *Revue d'Histoire de l'Eglise de France* 57 (1971) 83–95.

Hernandez F., "Les confréries des diocèses d'Orange et de Saint-Paul-Trois-Châteaux à la fin du XVIIe siècle", in Froeschlé-Chopard M.-H – Devos R., (eds.), *Les confréries, l'Eglise et la cité. Cartographie des confréries du Sud-Est* (Grenoble: 1988) 97–112.

Hoffman P.T., *Church, and Community in the Diocese of Lyon 1500–1789* (New Haven: 1984).

Jamet C., "Les confréries de dévotion dans le diocèse de Rennes aux XVIIe et XVIIIe siècles", *Annales de Bretagne* 87 (1980) 481–491.

Johnson T., *Magistrates, Madonnas, and Miracles. The Counter Reformation in the Upper Palatinate* (Farnham: 2009).

Musgrave E.C., *The Building Industries of Eastern Brittany 1600–1790* (PhD Dissertation, University of Oxford: 1988).

Pied E., *Les anciens corps d'arts et métiers de Nantes*, 3 vols. (Nantes: 1903).

Po-Hsia R., *The World of Catholic Renewal 1540–1770* (Cambridge: 1998).

Restif B., *La Révolution des paroisses: culture paroissiale et Réforme catholique en Haute-Bretagne aux XVIe et XVIIe siècles* (Rennes: 2006).

Simiz S., "Les confréries face à l'indulgence. Tradition, quête, accueil et effets dans la France de l'est (XV–XVIIIeme siècles)", in Dompnier B. – Vismara P. (eds.), *Confréries et dévotions dans la catholicité moderne (mi-XVe–début XIXe siècle)* (Rome: 2008) 103–124.

Simiz S., *Confréries urbaines et dévotion en Champagne (1450–1830)* (Villeneuve-d'Ascq: 2002).

Terpstra N., *Lay Confraternities and Civic Religion in Renaissance Bologna* (Cambridge: 1995).

Tingle E.C., *Purgatory and Piety in Brittany 1480 to 1720* (Farnham: 2012).

Tingle E., *Indulgences after Luther. Pardons in Counter Reformation France, 1520–1720* (London: 2015).

CHAPTER 8

Dying in Communities: the Ideal Death between Individual and Communal Requirements in Early Modern Protestantism

Benedikt Brunner

1   Introduction

In early modern European Protestantism, norms of dying and grief were closely connected to ethical norms of life.[1] Death and the ways to cope with it, however, were always part of a specific Christian and perhaps confessional identity. Research has repeatedly stated that the Reformation led to fundamentally new interpretations of death and the circumstances surrounding it.[2] Protestant funeral writings offer a large variety and number of sources regarding questions on how one dealt with death and the use of different coping strategies, which, as will be shown, have by no means been exhaustively tapped for these questions.[3]

In the early modern period they tend to combine consolation with certain ethical exhortations. The reason for this seems to be that according to the mainstream Protestant opinion that evolved over the course of the Reformation, the fate of the deceased was already decided at the moment of their death. Accordingly, rather than praying for them, the sermons focus on the surviving and most often grieving community which assembled, for instance, during the burial. Thus, funeral sermons seem to have been regarded as a suitable opportunity for theological and ethical instruction along the lines of the

---

1 Cf. Brunner B., "To exhort, to edify and to commemorate. Funeral Sermons as Instruments to convey 'Lifestyles' and Deathways in 17th and early 18th Century Protestantism", in Christ M. – Hrachovec P. – Zdychinec J. (eds.), *Early Modern Cultures of Death. Graveyards, Burials and Commemoration in Central Europe, c. 1500–1800* [In print].
2 Cf. Marshall P., "After Purgatory: Death and Remembrance in the Reformation World", in Rasmussen T. – Flæten J.O. (eds.), *Preparing for Death, Remembering the Dead* (Göttingen: 2015) 25–43; Ibid., "Was there a Protestant Death?", in Angel S. et al. (eds.), *Were we ever Protestants? Essays in Honor of Tarald Rasmussen* (Berlin – Boston: 2019) 143–160; Wollgast S., *Zum Tod im späten Mittelalter und in der Frühen Neuzeit* (Berlin: 1992).
3 Cf. Brunner B., "Was passiert mit dem 'stinkenden Madensack'? Der Umgang mit dem Tod als Lackmustest der reformatorischen Bestimmung von Leib und Seele", *Theologische Zeitschrift* 76/2 (2020) 164–190.

often quoted saying that the right way of life leads to a blissful and peaceful death.[4]

This contribution will examine the significance of community at the moment of death from different angles. It asks which individual and community-related requirements were formulated in the funeral writings. I intend to show that dying in community was of great importance.[5]

2   The Role of "Communion" as a Means for Preparation

One of the most important symbols of the Christian community was the Lord's Supper. It is no coincidence that most of the fiercest and polemically charged theological struggles of the sixteenth century were fought about its proper interpretation.[6] Funeral sermons regularly report on the consumption of the Lord's Supper in the context of the preparation for death as well as in the context of the deathbed, even if, as will be seen in the following, usually only briefly. Participation in the Lord's Supper was not least regarded as a visible sign that someone not only joined the community of believers, but also outwardly carried his or her belonging to this community that was founded and established by Jesus Christ.[7]

In the biography of James Houblon, who died at the age of 90, Gilbert Burnet, who was chaplain in London at this time, points out this aspect. An eventful life such as Houblon led, with periods on the run and in exile, was not a sign that God had withdrawn his favour or would not honour his perseverance. Houblon was originally from Flanders, his parents having fled to England in the sixteenth century. Burnet took this as an opportunity to give a historical outline of the Duke of Alba's reign of terror, to which many faithful Christians

---

4   Cf. for instance Dingel I., "'Recht glauben, christlich leben und seliglich sterben'. Leichenpredigt als evangelische Verkündigung im 16. Jahrhundert", in Lenz R. (ed.), *Leichenpredigten als Quelle historischer Wissenschaften*, vol. 4 (Stuttgart: 2004), 9–36 and also her chapter in this volume.

5   This chapter is based on studies for my *Habilitation* project about Protestant coping practices in Nuremberg, Basel, London and Boston between 1580 and 1750. I analysed around 700 funeral sermons, which I also consulted for this piece.

6   Cf. for instance Ehlers C., *Konfessionsbildung im Zweiten Abendmahlsstreit (1552–1558/59)* (Tübingen: 2021).

7   Cf. Pasewark K.A., "The Body in Ecstasy: Love, Difference, and the Social Organism in Luther's Theory of the Lord's Supper", *Journal of Religion* 77 (1997) 511–540; Hunt A., "The Lord's Supper in Early Modern England", *Past & Present* 161 (1998) 39–83; Burnett A.N., "The Social History of Communion and the Reformation of the Eucharist", *Past & Present* 211 (2011) 77–119.

had fallen victim. He then moved on to outline the deceased's services to the city of London and its urban community as well as to his congregation.[8] He had been one of the pillars of the French congregation in London, which he had also served as an elder. He went to communion regularly and observed the holidays. 'He was known to be a very devout Man and frequent in Prayers, both in publick and private; he was always breathing out that deep Sense he had of Religion to those about him'.[9] The service to the congregation and the urban community deliberately overlaps, and the reference to the Lord's Supper is certainly not accidental in the middle of this narrative.

Occasionally, however, funeral writings also report problems with taking communion that had to do with the illness of the dying. Martin Beer, a clergyman from Nuremberg, reported in 1649 on the preparations of the patrician Lucas Friedrich Behaim. Behaim had already suffered for a good 12 years, during which time he had been held down by a great weariness that hardly allowed him to carry out his official duties.[10] An important keyword that led to the description of the actual preparations was the patience with which Behaim had endured all adversities and difficulties and his great trust in God. The first step Beer had observed could be described as a spiritual orientation towards Christian dying. This included the preparation of his burial place, which he had eagerly awaited to be completed.[11] In funeral sermons, the timely, spiritually prepared participation in the Lord's Supper was repeatedly pointed out. In this context, however, Behaim suffered a violent coughing fit with large quantities of phlegm; from then on, he could hardly leave his sickbed. Behaim had to spit out the bread he had eaten. The preacher mentions this fact but does not evaluate it. Whether it is to be interpreted as a bad sign or rather to emphasise the patrician's great suffering is left open by him. However, this episode shows the importance of the Lord's Supper and how closely the taking of it on the deathbed was observed.

---

8   Burnet Gilbert, *A Sermon Preached at the Funeral of Mr. James Houblon* [...], (London, Richard Chiswell: 1682), 26: 'You see what the Nation and this City has gained by the Reception of the Strangers that fled hither for refuge in the last Age: You see how great a Citizen you had in him that is now dead, and into how many he is now divided, who by their Interest could almost make a City alone: and you do not know how many such may be in the Loins of those that now come among you, who may produce many to be as great Blessings to the next Age, as this Family is to the present.'

9   Ibidem, 28.

10 Cf. Beer Martin, *Davids Liebe zu dem Hause des HERRN/ Bey Christlicher Leichbegängniß deß Weil. Edlen/ Ehrnvesten/ Fürsichtigen vnd Hochweisen Herrn Lucas=Friederich Behaims/ deß ältern geheimen Rahts/ vördersten Scholarchen vnd Kirchenpflegers* [...] (Nürnberg, Endter: 1649) 23.

11 Cf. ibidem, 23–24.

This is also evident in the deathbed events of the young patrician's son Christoph Jacob Pömer, of whom a whole series of contemplative statements have been handed down. Among other things, there was an exchange between him and his father, which is described in detail by the preacher Kornelius Marci. Through comments in the margins, the Nuremberg clergyman identified two of these statements as "visions". On the one hand, Pömer had seen a group of angels reaching for him. Secondly, he had seen a Latin letter in which it was written 'Quod dictum, dictu. What has been said/ has been said.'[12] At first, the meaning of these signs was not clear to the young Pömer himself. One day later, he had become weaker and weaker and was approaching death. This led to a dialogue with his father.

> Da jhn dann sein Herr Vatter gefragt: Ob er auch/ nach GOTTES Schickung/ gern von Hinnen scheiden wollte: Antwortete er: Ja/ hertzlich gern/ wann es GOtt haben will. Bat darbey den Allmächtigen jnniglich/ daß er jhm seine Schmertzen lindern/ vnnd es nach seinem gnädigen Willen zur Enderung schicken wollte. Auff ferners Fragen/ Ob er nach dem heiligen Abendmahl kein Verlangen trüge? Sagte er: Ja/ ein vberauß sehnliches. Wann ich nur so selig werden/ es empfangen/ vnd aber auch behalten könte: Dann das Erbrechen sich noch nicht wollen stillen vnd halten lassen.[13]

The father's questions were similar to ones that could also be asked by a clergyman in the context of the deathbed. The willingness to die was stated, should this correspond to God's plan. The statements all have the character of a confession of faith.[14] The young Pömer saw this as the end of his suffering. Typical of Lutheran funeral writings was the significance of the Lord's Supper. In this case, in Augustine's sense, the willingness and desire to partake was

---

12 Marci Kornelius, *Emblema Idumaei, Oder Hiobs Sinn=Bild/ Von der auffgehenden vnd Abfallenden Menschen=Blum:* [...] *Bey trawriger Leichbegängnus Deß Edlen vnd Vesten/ Christoph=Jacob Pömers* [...] ([Nürnberg], n.p.: 1643) 32.

13 Ibidem, 33: 'His father then asked him if he also wanted to leave home according to God's will: He answered: Yes/ with all my heart/ if God wants it. He then asked the Almighty that he would alleviate his pain and send him to his end according to his gracious will. On further questioning/ Whether he had no desire for Holy Communion, He said: Yes, an exceedingly eager desire. If only I could be so blessed/ receive it/ and keep it: The vomiting had not yet been stopped and held.'

14 Cf. Dilherr Johann Michael. *Sichere Seelen=Verwahrung eines glaubigen Christen/ gezeiget in Erklärun des sechsten Versiculs/ aus dem 31. Psalm/ bei trauriger und Volckreicher Leichbestattung Des Edlen/ Ehrnvesten/ Fürsichtigen und Wohlweisen Herrn Johann Christoph Schlüsselfelders/ des Jnnern Raths* [...] (Nürnberg, Endter: [1654]) [21].

taken for the act, because the son himself was prevented from taking communion by persistent vomiting. What was most important to him, however, was to become blessed and to surrender to the fate imposed by God and thus also to the Lutheran community of faithful Christians.

He did not perceive his exemplary behaviour as his own achievement, but he referred to the work of the Holy Spirit and thus appeared both humble and pious in accordance with the Lutheran doctrine of justification. This was also evident when he succeeded in administering the Last Supper the following day. After the vomiting had stopped for a short time

> ist er/ auff sein inständiges Begehren mit dem H. Abendmahl/ alsmit dem rechten Zehrpfennig zum ewigen Leben/ versehen worden. Welches er mit höchstem Eifer empfangen/ vnd zuvorher/ auff geschehene gnugsame Ermahnung/ seine Sünde hertzlich berewet/ dieselbigen hernach zuvorderst GOtt im Himmel/ dann auch seinen lieben Eltern/ vnd letzlich allen vnnd jeden Vmbstehenden/ mit dermassen kläglichen vnnd hertzbeweglichen Worten abgebetten/ daß sich niemands darbey deß Weinens enthalten können.[15]

The sacrament of the Lord's Supper had a double function in the context of the Lutheran deathbed. On the one hand, it sacramentally connected the earthly community with the transcendental God. On the other hand, the administration of the Lord's Supper served to strengthen the dying person spiritually for the upcoming final act. The emotionality with which this passage was embellished in language may be surprising, but it also makes clear how much the preacher himself was involved in this event. On the same day that he had enjoyed communion, the young Pömer died 'nach vielen vorangeschickten Hertzens=Seufftzerlein/ mit beyden gen Himmel auffgehabenen Armen'.[16]

In the observations described here, it becomes comprehensible how intensively the dying individual and the community around him interacted during the moments of death and what spiritual topics they discussed in the process. Spiritual, pious behaviour, such as the desire for the Lord's Supper, are not values in themselves, but supported the dying person on his or her way to heaven and can thus also be seen as aspects of resilient behaviour, as will be shown in

---

15 Marci, *Emblema* 34: 'At his earnest request, he was provided with Holy Communion as the right pledge of eternal life. Which he received with the utmost zeal, and beforehand, after having been exhorted, heartily repented of his sin, and afterwards offered it first of all to God in heaven, then also to his dear parents, and finally to all those present, with such lamentable and heartfelt words that no one could refrain from weeping.'

16 Ibidem, 35: 'after many heartfelt sighs with both arms raised towards heaven'.

more detail below.[17] The aforementioned double function is common. Johann Leonhard Frisch referred to the painful illnesses of the patrician Eustachius Carl Holzschuher of Neuenbürg in a funeral sermon. The sacrament played an important role as a pivot between the sickbed and the deathbed.

> Da nun Jhr Herligkeit gesehen/ daß es mit Jhm nicht gut thun/ und GOtt ein anders mit Jhm machen möchte/ haben Sie sich dem Willen GOttes willig ergeben/ die Absolution und das H. Abendmahl verschienenen Sontag mit grosser devotion empfangen/ vnnd darauff von stund zu stund schwächer/ vnnd mit grössern Schmertzen überfallen worden/ welche Er aber als ein rechter Geistlicher Ritter mit Gedult ertragen/ vnd wider sein Fleisch vnd Blut/ welches in solchen Fällen offt schwach/ Luc.22 / tapffer gekämpffet [...].[18]

At this point, participation in the Lord's Supper aimed at strengthening the individual for the suffering that lay ahead. The sacrament symbolised the internalised community with God, which was supposed to protect against loneliness and make the dying person aware that he or she was not alone in the physical and spiritual struggles that dying brings with it. Strength, patience and stamina were provided through the Lord's Supper.[19] However, these references are not specified. It is above all about the community of the godly, which finds a visible sign in the Lord's Supper.

In none of the Reformed cities considered here (Basel, London and Boston) was the Lord's Supper as important for coping with death and dying as it was in Nuremberg, at least not according to the funeral writings on the basis of which

---

17 Cf. Myhldorf Andreas, *Nürnbergischer Josia! Bey Allgemeiner Traur/ und höchstkläglicher hochansehlicher Leich=Begängnuß Des Wol=Edlen/ Gestrengen/ Fürsichtig und Hochweisen Herrn Georg Christof Behaim!* [...] (Nürnberg, Felsecker: [1676]) 40–41.

18 Frisch Johann Leonhard, *Leich=Sermon bey Adel= vnd Ansehlicher Bestattung/ Deß weyland Edlen/ Ehrenvesten/ Fürsichtigen vnd Wolweisen Herrn Eustachii Carl Holtzschuhern/ von Neuenbürg* [...] (Nürnberg, Endter: 1639) [22]: 'Since Your Glory saw that it was not good with Him and that God wanted to do something different with Him, you willingly surrendered to God's will, received absolution and Holy Communion with great devotion on Sunday of last year, and were thereupon weakened from hour to hour and assailed with greater pains, which He, however, as a true spiritual knight, endured with patience and fought against His flesh and blood, which is often weak in such cases [...]'.

19 Cf. furthermore Heering Justus Daniel, *Justa Justa Tetzeliana. Das ist/ Rechtmäsiges Ehrengedächtnis Lobwürdigen Lebens vns Seligen Sterbens Deß weiland Edlen/ Gestreng= Fürsichtig= vnd Hochweisen Herrn/ Johann Jacob Tetzels/ von vnd zu Kirchensittenbach* [...] (Nürnberg, n.p.: 1646) [38].

this chapter attempts to make conclusions. Here, other community aspects seem to have been more significant.

3   The Dying Person as a Role Model for Communities

Since the moment of death was so important in Protestantism, dying people were observed very closely. The condition at the moment of death was the final determinant of a person's salvation. The situation could be precarious because of the challenges involved in the process. It was therefore even more important to highlight exemplary behaviour worthy of imitation, conveyed through funeral writings.

Theodor Zwinger, one of Basel's key church figures in the mid-seventeenth century, picked up on these tendencies and linked them in turn to the idea of the *vanitas* of man's worldly aspirations. 'Selig ist der Mensch/ welcher diese zweyfache Kunst, nammlich/ gottselig zu leben/ vnd selig zu sterben/ recht ergriffen vnd erlernett hat.'[20] Since he had to preach on the occasion of the death of a councillor, Zwinger chose Joseph of Arimathea as an example of a lifestyle worthy of imitation, since he had 'shone' through his moral, political and spiritual virtues.[21] The uncertainty of the time of death was understood as an appeal to 'take care of the remaining [days, BB] all the more diligently', as Augustine had said.[22] Lucas Gernler, later the leading clergyman of the city, made the connection between the inner-worldly visibility of salvation and the question of the certainty of salvation explicit. In 1671 he admonished his listeners and readers: 'Lernet alhier/ daß der gläubige Mensch des ewigen Lebens gewiß sey. Er weißt nicht nur/ daß sein Seel in dem Tod auß dem jrdischen Hause außziehen/ sonderen auch/ daß sie in das himlische einziehen werde.'[23]

---

20 Zwinger Theodor, *Christliche Leich-predigt/ Von Der rechten Lebens vnd Sterbens-Kunst. Gehalten zu Basel […] Bey Christlicher vnd Ansehenlicher Bestattung/ Des Ehrenvesten/ Frommen/ Fürsichtigen vnd Weisen Herren Niclaus Bischoffs […]* ([Basel], Georg Decker: [1650]) 6: 'Blessed is the man who has rightly grasped and learned this twofold art, namely, to live godly and to die blissfully.'

21 Ibidem, 12.

22 Hertenstein Melchior, *Christliche Leich-predigt/ Von Den vngewissen Vmbständen deß Todes/ vnd wie wir vns dabey erzeigen sollen. Gehalten […] Bey Christlicher vnd Ansehenlicher Leich-begängnuß/ Der Ehren= vnd Tugendreichen Frawen Anna Fäschin […]* ([Basel], Georg Decker: [1657]) 7.

23 Gernler Lucas, *Christliche Leichpredigt/ Von gläubiger Seele Jrdischen vnd Himmlischem Hauß. Gehalten […] Bey Christlicher Bestattung/ der Ehren= vnd Tugendreichen Frawen/ Anna-Maria Gemusaein […]* ([Basel], Jacob Bertsche [1671]) 6: 'Learn here that the

As evidence, he then cited a whole series of biblical authors who had spoken of this certainty, as well as the holy martyrs who had known about it. His argumentation in a rather typical way combined the Holy Bible and the authorities of the early Church.[24] The exemplary character of such Christians therefore did not begin on their deathbeds, but was preceded by a corresponding way of life, which was also part of the *"praeparatio ad mortem"*. The preacher tried to establish connections to previous generations of Christians through such references.

Regarding such descriptions, there seems to be a certain Reformed preponderance. Cotton Mather in Boston authored numerous funeral writings that contain extensive descriptions of this kind. The communal character of the deathbed event and the exchange between the dying and the bereaved were particularly important to him. His brother Nathanael Mather, for example, had spiritual texts read to him to encourage him the night before his death.[25] In the funeral writings for which he was responsible, there are always detailed descriptions of what happened on and around the deathbed. Mather was very interested in what was discussed there if the person was still able to do so. The Boston preacher Joshua Moodey had mainly uttered expressions of self-condemnation on his deathbed.[26] This was accompanied by a likewise explicitly expressed deep trust in God's grace. This exchange had taken place between him and a clergyman, who had then told Mather about it.

Sudden death was of course a veritable theological and pastoral problem also in Boston if one did not want to see it as a sweeping judgment of God. Rather, it was important to ensure that people who died unplanned should also understand this as part of God's plan.

> Is not a Sudden Death a Frequent Sight? There are very many so suddenly Snatched away, by the Whirlwind of the Vengeance of the Almighty, that they have not opportunity, so much as to say, Lord have mercy upon me!

---

believer is certain of eternal life. He not only knows that his soul will leave the earthly home in death, but also that it will enter the heavenly one.'

24 Cf. Brunner B., "'… wie Chrysostomus schreibet.' Kirchenväterzitate als normative Referenzen für den Umgang mit Trauer in frühneuzeitlichen Funeralschriften. Herausforderungen und Potenziale der Digital Humanities für ihre Erforschung", *Journal of Ethics in Antiquity and Christianity* 4 (2022), 77–99.

25 Cf. Mather Cotton, *Early Piety, Exemplified in the Life and Death of Mr. Nathanael Mather* […] (London, J. Astwood: 1689) 58–59.

26 Cf. Mather Cotton, *The Way to Excel. Meditations, Awakened by the DEATH of the Reverend Mr. Joshua Moodey*; […] (Boston, B. Green: 1697) 30: 'His Discourses were generally full of Self Condemnation; and indeed, that man knows not how to Dy, who thinks to Dy otherweise, than Condemning of himself, Exceedingly.'

> And, Let me tell you, That a Sudden Death is most likely to be the portion of those who most presumptuously put off to a Death bed, the work of Committing their Spirits, into the Hand, that can alone befriend them.[27]

In Boston, both can be found: There is a great deal of interest in the actions on the deathbed as well as the necessary pastoral flexibility in the case of sudden deaths, if the previously maintained way of life allowed for it.[28] Cotton Mather freely confessed that not all Christians were privileged 'to Dy with Triumphant Joyes.'[29] However, this is not to be understood as an indicator for the soteriological evaluation of the dying person, because God in his infinite wisdom supplies each person with what is right, especially regarding death.[30]

Due to his closeness to the events, Mather frequently also passed on statements by the dying person to which he attributed special significance. After she was sure that she was going to die, his sister Jerusha spoke the following words to him:

> Here it is a Strange Thing! when I was in Health, Death was a Terror to me. But now I know, I shall Dy. I am not at all afraid of it. She said, This is a Wonderful Work of GOd! I know, that I am going to Christ: That I shall shortly be in the Heavenly Jerusalem, with an Innumerable Company of Angels, and among the Spirits of Just Men made Perfect. Said she; I see things that are Unutterable! Then she Sang for Joy.[31]

Normatively, Mather conveys two aspects. On the one hand, what was usually called "resignation", that is the acceptance of death as subordination to the divine will. On the other hand, the joy for what was to come, which was to take the terror out of the current situation and bring the individual into joyful expectation. The intended effect was to be intensified by coming from

---

[27] Mather Cotton, *A Good Man making a Good End. The Life and Death, of the Reverend Mr. John Baily, Comprised and Expressed in a Sermon, On the Day of his Funeral* [...] (Boston, B. Green: 1698) 20.

[28] Cf. Barnard John, *The Peaceful End of the Perfect and Upright Man. A Sermon Occasioned by the Death of Mr. John Atwood* [...] (Boston, B. Green: 1714) 17–19.

[29] Mather Cotton, *Memorials of Early Piety. Occurring in the Holy Life and Joyful Death of Mrs. Jerusha Oliver* [...] (Boston, T. Green: 1711) 48.

[30] Cf. Wadsworth Benjamin, *Early Seeking of GOD, Earnestly Recommended* [...]. DEATH *by Sudden Accidents, Consider'd & Improv'd from Deut. 19.5. Two Sermons* (Boston, B. Green: 1715) 29–34.

[31] Mather, *Memorials* 49–50.

the mouth of a person who had handed down these words with a high degree of authenticity.[32]

About the deathbed of his daughter Katherine, however, Cotton Mather could also report that there were doubts and that the path to resignation was not always straightforward. Katherine had repeatedly asked him whether her soul was safe and whether her Saviour Jesus Christ would accept her.[33] He himself stayed with her continuously and gave her pastoral support. At the same time, she had repeatedly spoken to her brothers and sisters and asked them to orient themselves completely towards God's will and to accompany her on this path.[34] Obedience was central in these contexts; a keyword that was of fundamental importance for the Boston approach to death. Thus, communal dying was normatively encouraged, insofar as it was possible. Mather recommended and personally exemplified close pastoral care for dying parishioners. The ultimate goal, which the listener and reader should also embrace through descriptions of specific procedures, consisted in a willing submission to the will of God in joyful hope for better times.

4 The Resilience-Enhancing Power of Community

According to the relevant reports in European funeral writings, the function of the community was not to leave the dying person alone on his or her last journey and to support him or her both spiritually and physically. Resilience is a modern concept that cannot be directly applied to historical contexts. However, many early modern preachers were aware of the importance of the phenomenon. Considering the great importance of dying the "right" way, it was necessary to think about the factors that could make this process more likely to succeed.[35]

---

32 Cf. also Mather Cotton, *A Soul Well-Anchored. A Little Manual for Self-Examination; To assist a Christian In Examining his Hopes of a Future Blessedness.* [...] (Boston, B. Green: 1712) 22. For this way to communicate cf. Brunner B., "Heilige Stimmen. Die kommunikative Funktion der Toten in protestantischen Funeralschriften der Frühen Neuzeit", *Jahrbuch für Kommunikationsgeschichte* 24 (2022) 29–55.
33 Cf. Mather Cotton, *Victorina. A Sermon Preach'd On the Decease and At the Desire, of Mrs. Katharin Mather* [...] (Boston, B. Green: 1717) 73.
34 Cf. ibidem, 74–75.
35 Cf. for instance Wabel T., "Weisen von Verkörperung in der christlichen Schmerztradition und die Frage nach Resilienz", in Richter C. (ed.), *Ohnmacht und Angst aushalten. Kritik der Resilienz in Theologie und Philosophie* (Stuttgart: 2017), 91–106; Bröckling U., "Resilienz: Belastbar, flexibel, widerstandsfähig", in ibid, *Gute Hirten führen sanft. Über Menschenregierungskünstler* (Frankfurt am Main: 2017) 113–139.

The funeral writings, which also described the lives of the deceased, spoke frequently about how to deal with sickness. As an example, we can refer to Thomas Taylor's writing The Pilgrims Profession from 1622. In the detailed biography, Taylor first explained that the agony had not caught the dying woman unprepared. Yet she had to struggle with the pain and temptations of death.[36] Her perseverance was promoted by the fact that she saw the whole process as a spiritual battle that could and should be shaped through prayer. She asked God for patience and that he would give her the strength to endure her pain. Taylor confirms that this prayer was answered because no impatient word was heard from her.[37] She had also addressed the deathbed community with a request not to mourn for her, but for themselves, because she would shortly be happier than they could imagine, 'and therefore cease your mourning, and help me thither by your Prayers as fast as you can.'[38] Therefore, there is also something like a false, misguided mourning that does not recognise that for the dying Christian the day of death is a day of joy. Especially for the sad people at the deathbed it is important to keep this in mind and to say with Psalm 116:15: 'Precious in the sight of the Lord is the death of his Saints.'[39]

Another example is the Nuremberg pastor's wife Margareta Welhammer. Before her death, she had to struggle with severe symptoms of illness that deprived her of sleep for a long period of time. However, she was not alone in her illness, but was visited by many ministers and friends. She drew strength from praying and singing spiritual songs together.[40] It was of utmost importance to the preachers that sickness and the approaching death were not confronted alone, but that they were faced in community.

Interestingly, the remarks intended to help individuals cope with such contingent events should also help them cope with grief. For death could cause severe grief to the bereaved. The widower's heart was torn in two by the death of his wife, as Kornelius Marci, another Nuremberg pastor, reported empathically. The loss must also have weighed heavily on the children left behind. Marci then brought himself into the mourning process and also called on others to do the same:

---

[36] Taylor Thomas, *The Pilgrims Profession. Or A Sermon Preached at the Funerall of Mris Mary Gvnter* (London, Printed by I.D[awson] for Io: Bartlet 1622) 180–184.
[37] Cf. ibidem, 184–185.
[38] Ibidem, 188.
[39] Quoted after Cannon Nathaniel, *A Casket Of Ievvels and precious Pearles. Set forth in a Fvnerall Sermon, Preached [...] at the Buriall of a Religious young Gentleman, Mr. Barnabas Creswell [...]* (London, T. S[nodham] for Nathanael Newbery 1625) 1.
[40] Marci, Trostpredigt [20]

> vnd wer wolte ob diesem thewre Verlust nicht mitleyden mit euch tragen? sonderlich wer da höret ewer seufftzen vnd sihet ewre Threnen über die Wangen fliessen. Wolan! seydt gestrost! der Vatter aller Wittben vnd Wäysen/ wie sich Gott nennet im 68. Psalm/ wird euch nicht verlassen/ ja ewrer weniger vergessen/ als ein Mutter jhres Kindes/ ist gewiß vnd waar [...].[41]

The call to compassion originally had its place in the service, since we may assume that this passage also belonged to the sermon preached there. The grief of the bereaved is not criticised or belittled; rather it is important not to leave them alone in this difficult time. The presence of God, who would especially turn to the widowed and orphaned, was also acknowledged. In many cases, the *Epicedia* included in the printed funeral writing are much more than mere poems of friendship. Johann Gerhard, at that time rector at the University of Jena and one of the most famous theologians of his time, wrote the following poem for his friend Welhammer, the widower of Margareta:

> Wellhammere sacri Praeco fidissime verbi, Theiologos inter gloria prima viros,
> Cur vitae sociam mortis ficilice peremptam Lugendo, lachrymis ora genasque; rigas?
> Illa Dei faciem laetissima cernit, & omnis Expers lachrymulae gaudia mente capit.
> Cur pulla indutus tastaris veste dolorem? Candidula in coelis Sindon amicit eam.
> Quod dederat DEUS, hoc repetens de jure reposcit, Quot repetit, largo foenore reddet idem.[42]

Epicedia also had a pastoral function and cannot be regarded as mere exercises for the authors. Both the surviving relatives who knew Latin and the readers who later consulted the printed funeral writing could find comfort and edification in them and thus support in difficult phases of life.[43] The fact that accord-

---

41 Ibidem, [21]: 'And who would not bear with you in this great loss? Especially he who hears your sighs and sees your tears flowing down your cheeks. Well on! Be comforted! The Father of all widows and wives/ as God calls Himself in the 68th Psalm/ will not leave you/ yes, He will forget you less/ than a mother of her child/ is certain and certain [...].'
42 Johann Gerhard, I., in Marci, *Trostpredigt* [23].
43 Cf. Till Dietmar, "Poetik der Trauer. Zwei Spielarten des Epicediums um 1700", in Plotke S. – Ziem A. (eds.), *Sprache der Trauer. Verbalisierungen einer Emotion in historischer Perspektive* (Heidelberg: 2014) 175–200.

ing to Rom 8:28 all things are for the good of the Christian is not invalidated by serious temptations, illnesses or sudden, unexpected deaths, but rather confirmed by such events.[44]

Cotton Mather dealt particularly intensively with the aspect of resilient behaviour in his funeral writings. This may certainly have been evoked by the fact that he had to deal personally with numerous deaths in his close family environment. On almost 200 pages, he collected funeral sermons that he had delivered for various close relatives, which, as he admits at various points, was not always easy for him.[45] He had preached the second sermon on the occasion of the death of his daughter Mary. It has the programmatic title 'The Fear of God, Under Tryals from The Hand of God.'[46] In it, Mather tried to show how such trials of God could be overcome. He was able to acknowledge that such a death was indeed a severe ordeal. At the same time, the right behaviour in such situations was immensely important and could be seen as a sign of whether someone had truly lived in the fear of God.[47] But it was also clear that it is God who puts temptations in people's way. And it is up to man to deal with them adequately. Mather also referred to them as probations, as tests that God wants to give to people.[48] Especially in such situations, a person can learn something about God's grace, more precisely about the covenant that was made between him or her and God through his or her conversion. An individual also learns a lot about himself and the priorities he or she has set in his or her life so far.[49] Someone who is tested by God in this way must ask: 'Do our Tryals drive us more Heartily, Fervently, Constantly, to seek the Face of God who sends the Tryal?'[50] Everyone should ask themselves this question for self-examination in order to change their actions if necessary. It should also be examined whether each person, when tempted by God, humbly acknowledges and honours God's righteousness, regardless of how they feel at the moment. All of this ultimately boiled down to humble obedience, coming from the heart, by which could be discerned whether someone was in the state of grace and behaving in a

---

44 Cf. Werenfels Johann Jakob, *Christliche Leich-predigt: Von Gott=liebender Christen Glückseligkeit/ auch in dem Vbelstand. Gehalten* [...] *Bey bestattung der Ehren= vnd Tugendreichen Frauwen Salome Sattlerin* [...] (Basel, Johann Schröters Erben: [1634]).
45 Cf. Mather Cotton, *Meat out of the Eater. Or, Funeral Discourses, Occasioned By the Death of several Relatives.* [...] (Boston, Printed [by B. Green & J. Allen] for Benjamin Eliot: 1703) 9, 37–38.
46 Ibidem, 32.
47 Cf. his 'Doctrine' ibidem, 38.
48 Cf. ibidem, 41.
49 Cf. ibidem, 43.
50 Ibidem, 47.

Christian manner in the face of challenges. Mather wanted to draw attention to the fact that no one must go through these times without support.

> Quest. VII. In our Tryals what are our Supports, and where do we go to make up that we have lost in our Tryals? [...] If we are visited with Death after Death, how do we Support our selves? Is it by thinking, The Lord lives, and blessed be my Reck! [...] Suppose God will not let our Houles grow, Is this the Consolation of our Soul, that God hath made a New Covenant with us? Do we comfort our selves with this, We have Christ in the New Covenant, where there is Grace and Glory, and every good Thing? Are the Promises of God our Consolation at our Funerals? can we say, I had perished in mine affliction, unless I had had the Word of God. Now I know that thou Fearest God.[51]

Mather found it particularly helpful to remember the new covenant made between God and man. Christ could comfort and strengthen based on this covenant, because he had given his life for humanity. The tasks were, so to speak, divided according to the Trinity. While God the Father placed temptations in man's path, at the same time a reservoir of strength was made available through Jesus Christ and the Holy Spirit, which was necessary to get through them. This was the right perspective because there was always something good that God wanted to bring forth through such situations.[52] It is all the more important, however, to examine oneself again and again to see whether one is living in accordance with God's will, so that one does not deviate from God's will in such challenging situations.[53] However, it is clear from such statements that in Mather's work a great deal is required of the individual. Although no one must go through these things alone, God himself comes to the help, the focus is clearly on the individual and his or her actions.

It can thus be stated that a life that is as exemplary and "perfect" as possible was seen as promoting resilience, and not only by Mather. The more intense the piety of the individual, the stronger his or her connection to Jesus Christ established in good times, the more present the power of the Holy Spirit, the greater his resilience was considered to be.[54] This view became even more

---

51 Ibidem, 53–54.
52 Cf. ibidem, 55. Cf. also Mather Cotton, *Maternal Consolations. An Essay On, The Consolations of God;* [...] *Made on the Death of Mrs. Maria Mather* [...] (Boston, T. Fleet: 1714) 21–25.
53 Cf. Mather, *Meat* 57–61.
54 Cf. Colman Benjamin, *The peaceful End of a perfect and upright Life, remark'd and contemplated In a Sermon After the Death of the Universally Esteemed Thomas Steel, Esq* [...] (Boston, S. Kneeland and T. Green: 1735) 35.

pronounced during the Great Awakening, which is directly related to the changes in the image of God conveyed in funeral writings.[55] However, it is astonishing how little attention the community in which all this is taking place receives, i.e. the congregation. In Puritanism, and something similar is also found in certain currents of Pietism, the thesis of this chapter is turned on its head. The individual and his or her piety are attributed resilience-promoting power, while the community fades into the background to a certain extent. The Enlightenment then took this development to the extreme.

5 Conclusion: the Dangers of Bad Company

Prepared, accompanied, conscious dying in community was an ideal in the early modern period, which certainly was not met by all deaths and dying processes. Rarely do we get insights into "unsuccessful" dying. For not every form of community in life as well as in dying was evaluated positively by preachers. Rather, sinful relations with other people could fundamentally endanger salvation. An English vicar named Robert Abbot (c.1588–1662) published a funeral writing in London in 1636, which appeared under the title 'The Yovng-Man's VVarning-peece'. In this case, the subtitle in particular made it clear in what way this sermon, which was quite obviously not written according to the motto "De mortuis nil nisi bene", intended to argue: 'A Sermon preached at the buriall of William Rogers, Apothecary. Together with an Historie of his sinfull Life, and woefull Death. Dedicated to the Young-men of the parish, especially to his Companions.'[56]

In this rather extensive text, there is a general reckoning with the lifestyle of the deceased, who was even named in this case. Abbot detailed the numerous misdeeds of the deceased. In the dedicatory letter, he directly addressed his friends to warn and admonish them. All too often, they would prefer 'an ale-house' to the house of God.[57] He tried to make them realise:

---

55 Cf. furthermore Townsend Jonathan, *God's terrible Doings are to be observed. A Sermon* [...] *Occasion'd By the sudden and awful Death of Mr. Thomas Gardner, jun.* [...] (Boston, S. Kneeland and T. Green: 1746); Prince Thomas, *The Pious cry to the Lord for Help when the Godly and Faithful fail among them. A Sermon Occasion'd By the great and publick Loss In the Death of the honourable Thomas Cushing* [...] (Boston, T. Rand: 1746).

56 Abbot Robert, *The Yovng-Man's VVarning-peece: or A Sermon preached at the buriall of William Rogers, Apothecary. Together with an Historie of his sinfull Life, and woefull Death. Dedicated to the Young-men of the parish, especially to his Companions* (London, n.p.: 1636), unpaginated cover. For London cf. also the chapter by Martin Christ in this volume.

57 Ibidem, A3r.

> You have had (in your daies) many examples, teaching, that there is no bargain to be had in a wicked way; it is folly to lay out your silver, and not for bread. But to have two in one yeere, laies the axe to the root of the trees of the Wood, and preacheth, that except ye amend, ye shall likewise perish.[58]

Normally, it was not good manners to speak negatively about the deceased. He had usually adhered to this, but the present occasion was different.

> I have something to say to the person, before I speake to the Text. I am intreated, earnestly intreated, by the miserable yong [!] man who lies dead at our feet, to preach to all the young men of the parish, especially to his wicked companions (as he called them) something at his buriall to warne them, by his example, to take a better course, that they be not burned in hell with him for ever and ever.[59]

He then retracted his condemnation of him a little because God's judgement of him could not be anticipated and was God's alone. According to the preacher, his actions, and not least the community in which he had lived his life, made it possible to draw conclusions about his salvation.[60]

Dying in communities was thus a multifaceted theme in European funeral writing. In this context, the sacrament of the Lord's Supper as a central group identity-forming ritual was given the role, especially in Lutheran examples, that one might have expected from Reformed sources as well.[61] This does not, however, diminish the fact that the community was given a central role in the context of dying, perhaps to a greater extent than in the late medieval *ars moriendi*. During the early eighteenth century, however, the focus then seems to have increasingly shifted to the individual and his or her behaviour, without the community, the good community of believing Christians above all, losing its value in the process. An examination of these sources may reveal a whole range of different communities. A relationship between God and the dying person was necessary and crucial for salvation. Mediated through Jesus Christ,

---

58   Ibidem, A4r–A4v.
59   Ibidem, 3.
60   Cf. ibidem, 4: 'What are wee that wee should sit in Gods chaire? He did rise and fall to his owne Master, whose judgements are alwayes just, often secret: and to Him wee leave him, withe feare & trembling, though not without some hope.'
61   Cf. Kaufmann T., "Abendmahl und Gruppenidentität in der frühen Reformation", in Ebner M. (ed.), *Herrenmahl und Gruppenidentität* (Freiburg – Basel – Vienna: 2007) 194–210.

the salvation of the human being depended on this relationship. However, the constellations between the believer and the Christian community as well as his relationships with friends and family members were made visible.[62]

In funeral writings, at any rate, fundamental principles about how communities should conduct themselves at the moment of death were articulated and, through the printing of the funeral writings, also passed on to the following generations with normative intent.

Bibliography

Primary Printed Sources

Abbot Robert, *The Yovng-Man's VVarning-peece: or A Sermon preached at the buriall of William Rogers, Apothecary. Together with an Historie of his sinfull Life, and woefull Death. Dedicated to the Young-men of the parish, especially to his Companions* (London, n.p.: 1636).

Barnard John, *The Peaceful End of the Perfect and Upright Man. A Sermon Occasioned by the Death of Mr. John Atwood* […] (Boston, B. Green: 1714).

Beer Martin, *Davids Liebe zu dem Hause des HERRN/ Bey Christlicher Leichbegängniß deß Weil. Edlen/ Ehrnvesten/ Fürsichtigen vnd Hochweisen Herrn Lucas=Friederich Behaims/ deß ältern geheimen Rahts/ vördersten Scholarchen vnd Kirchenpflegers* […] (Nürnberg, Endter: 1649).

Burnet Gilbert, *A Sermon Preached at the Funeral of Mr. James Houblon* […] (London, Richard Chiswell: 1682).

Cannon Nathaniel, *A Casket Of Ievvels and precious Pearles. Set forth in a Fvnerall Sermon, Preached* […] *at the Buriall of a Religious young Gentleman, Mr. Barnabas Creswell* […] (London, T. S[nodham] for Nathanael Newbery: 1625).

Colman Benjamin, *The peaceful End of a perfect and upright Life, remark'd and contemplated In a Sermon After the Death of the Universally Esteemed Thomas Steel, Esq* […] (Boston, S. Kneeland and T. Green: 1735).

Dilherr Johann Michael, *Sichere Seelen=Verwahrung eines glaubigen Christen/ gezeiget in Erklärun des sechsten Versiculs/ aus dem 31. Psalm/ bei trauriger und Volckreicher Leichbestattung Des Edlen/ Ehrnvesten/ Fürsichtigen und Wohlweisen Herrn Johann Christoph Schlüsselfelders/ des Jnnern Raths* […] (Nürnberg, Endter: [1654]).

Frisch Johann Leonhard, *Leich=Sermon bey Adel= vnd Ansehlicher Bestattung/ Deß weyland Edlen/ Ehrenvesten/ Fürsichtigen vnd Wolweisen Herrn Eustachii Carl Holtzschuhern/ von Neuenbürg* […] (Nürnberg, Endter: 1639).

---

62 Cf. also Lenz R., "Ehestand, Wehestand, Süßbitter Standt? Betrachtungen zur Familie der Frühen Neuzeit", *Archiv für Kulturgeschichte* 68 (1986) 371–405.

Gernler Lucas, *Christliche Leichpredigt/ Von gläubiger Seele Jrdischen vnd Himmlischem Hauß. Gehalten* [...] *Bey Christlicher Bestattung/ der Ehren= vnd Tugendreichen Frawen/ Anna-Maria Gemusaein* [...] ([Basel], Jacob Bertsche [1671]).

Heering Justus Daniel, *Justa Justa Tetzeliana. Das ist/ Rechtmäsiges Ehrengedächtnis Lobwürdigen Lebens vns Seligen Sterbens Deß weiland Edlen/ Gestreng= Fürsichtig= vnd Hochweisen Herrn/ Johann Jacob Tetzels/ von vnd zu Kirchensittenbach* [...] (Nürnberg, n.p.: 1646).

Hertenstein Melchior, *Christliche Leich-predigt/ Von Den vngewissen Vmbständen deß Todes/ vnd wie wir vns dabey erzeigen sollen. Gehalten* [...] *Bey Christlicher vnd Ansehenlicher Leich-begängnuß/ Der Ehren= vnd Tugendreichen Frawen Anna Fäschin* [...] ([Basel], Georg Decker: [1657)].

Marci Kornelius, *Emblema Idumaei, Oder Hiobs Sinn=Bild/ Von der auffgehenden vnd Abfallenden Menschen=Blum:* [...] *Bey trawriger Leichbegängnus Deß Edlen vnd Vesten/ Christoph=Jacob Pömers* [...] ([Nürnberg], n.p.: 1643).

Mather Cotton, *Early Piety, Exemplified in the Life and Death of Mr. Nathanael Mather* [...] (London, J. Astwood 1689).

Mather Cotton, *The Way to Excel. Meditations, Awakened by the* DEATH *of the Reverend Mr. Joshua Moodey*; [...] (Boston, B. Green: 1697).

Mather Cotton, *A Good Man making a Good End. The Life and Death, of the Reverend Mr. John Baily, Comprised and Expressed in a Sermon, On the Day of his Funeral* [...] (Boston, B. Green: 1698).

Mather Cotton, *Meat out of the Eater. Or, Funeral Discourses, Occasioned By the Death of several Relatives.* [...] (Boston, Printed [by B. Green & J. Allen] for Benjamin Eliot: 1703).

Mather Cotton, *Memorials of Early Piety. Occurring in the Holy Life and Joyful Death of Mrs. Jerusha Oliver* [...] (Boston, T. Green: 1711).

Mather Cotton, *A Soul Well-Anchored. A Little Manual for Self-Examination; To assist a Christian In Examining his Hopes of a Future Blessedness.* [...] (Boston, B. Green: 1712).

Mather Cotton, *Maternal Consolations. An Essay On, The Consolations of God;* [...] *Made on the Death of Mrs. Maria Mather* [...] (Boston, T. Fleet: 1714).

Mather Cotton, *Victorina. A Sermon Preach'd On the Decease and At the Desire, of Mrs. Katharin Mather* [...] (Boston, B. Green: 1717).

Myhldorf Andreas, *Nürnbergischer Josia! Bey Allgemeiner Traur/ und höchstkläglicher hochansehlicher Leich=Begängnuß Des Wol=Edlen/ Gestrengen/ Fürsichtig und Hochweisen Herrn Georg Christof Behaim!* [...] (Nürnberg, Felsecker: [1676]).

Prince Thomas, *The Pious cry to the Lord for Help when the Godly and Faithful fail among them. A Sermon Occasion'd By the great and publick Loss In the Death of the honourable Thomas Cushing* [...] (Boston, T. Rand: 1746).

Taylor Thomas, *The Pilgrims Profession. Or A Sermon Preached at the Funerall of Mris Mary Gvnter* (London, Printed by I.D[awson] for Io: Bartlet 1622).

Townsend Jonathan, *God's terrible Doings are to be observed. A Sermon* [...] *Occasion'd By the sudden and awful Death of Mr. Thomas Gardner, jun.* [...] (Boston, S. Kneeland and T. Green: 1746).

Wadsworth Benjamin, *Early Seeking of GOD, Earnestly Recommended* [...]. *DEATH by Sudden Accidents, Consider'd & Improv'd from Deut. 19.5. Two Sermons* (Boston, B. Green: 1715).

Werenfels Johann Jakob, *Christliche Leich-predigt: Von Gott=liebender Christen Glückseligkeit/ auch in dem Vbelstand. Gehalten* [...] *Bey bestattung der Ehren= vnd Tugendreichen Frauwen Salome Sattlerin* [...] (Basel, Johann Schröters Erben: [1634].

Zwinger Theodor, *Christliche Leich-predigt/ Von Der rechten Lebens vnd Sterbens-Kunst. Gehalten zu Basel* [...] *Bey Christlicher vnd Ansehenlicher Bestattung/ Des Ehrenvesten/ Frommen/ Fürsichtigen vnd Weisen Herren Niclaus Bischoffs* [...] ([Basel], Georg Decker: [1650]).

Secondary Literature

Bröckling U., "Resilienz: Belastbar, flexibel, widerstandsfähig", in ibid, *Gute Hirten führen sanft. Über Menschenregierungskünstler* (Frankfurt am Main: 2017) 113–139.

Brunner B., "Was passiert mit dem 'stinkenden Madensack'? Der Umgang mit dem Tod als Lackmustest der reformatorischen Bestimmung von Leib und Seele", *Theologische Zeitschrift* 76/2 (2020) 164–190.

Brunner B., "Heilige Stimmen. Die kommunikative Funktion der Toten in protestantischen Funeralschriften der Frühen Neuzeit", *Jahrbuch für Kommunikationsgeschichte* 24 (2022) 29–55.

Brunner B., "'... wie Chrysostomus schreibet.' Kirchenväterzitate als normative Referenzen für den Umgang mit Trauer in frühneuzeitlichen Funeralschriften. Herausforderungen und Potenziale der Digital Humanities für ihre Erforschung", *Journal of Ethics in Antiquity and Christianity* 4 (2022) 77–99.

Brunner B., "To exhort, to edify and to commemorate. Funeral Sermons as Instruments to convey 'Lifestyles' and Deathways in 17th and early 18th Century Protestantism", in Christ M. – Hrachovec P. – Zdychinec J. (eds.), *Early Modern Cultures of Death. Graveyards, Burials and Commemoration in Central Europe, c. 1500–1800* [In Print].

Burnett A.N., "The Social History of Communion and the Reformation of the Eucharist", *Past & Present* 211 (2011) 77–119.

Dingel I., "'Recht glauben, christlich leben und seliglich sterben'. Leichenpredigt als evangelische Verkündigung im 16. Jahrhundert", in Lenz R. (ed.), *Leichenpredigten als Quelle historischer Wissenschaften*, Volume 4 (Stuttgart: 2004) 9–36.

Ehlers C., *Konfessionsbildung im Zweiten Abendmahlsstreit (1552–1558/59)* (Tübingen: 2021).

Hunt A., "The Lord's Supper in Early Modern England", *Past & Present* 161 (1998) 39–83.

Kaufmann T., "Abendmahl und Gruppenidentität in der frühen Reformation", in Ebner M. (ed.), *Herrenmahl und Gruppenidentität* (Freiburg – Basel – Vienna: 2007) 194–210.

Lenz R., "Ehestand, Wehestand, Süßbitter Standt? Betrachtungen zur Familie der Frühen Neuzeit", *Archiv für Kulturgeschichte* 68 (1986) 371–405.

Marshall P., "After Purgatory: Death and Remembrance in the Reformation World", in Rasmussen T. – Flæten J.O. (eds.), *Preparing for Death, Remembering the Dead* (Göttingen: 2015) 25–43.

Marshall, P., "Was there a Protestant Death?", in Angel S. et al. (eds.), *Were we ever Protestants? Essays in Honor of Tarald Rasmussen* (Berlin – Boston: 2019) 143–160.

Pasewark K.A., "The Body in Ecstasy: Love, Difference, and the Social Organism in Luther's Theory of the Lord's Supper", *Journal of Religion* 77 (1997) 511–540.

Till D., "Poetik der Trauer. Zwei Spielarten des Epicediums um 1700", in Plotke S. – Ziem A. (eds.), *Sprache der Trauer. Verbalisierungen einer Emotion in historischer Perspektive* (Heidelberg: 2014) 175–200.

Wabel T., "Weisen von Verkörperung in der christlichen Schmerztradition und die Frage nach Resilienz", in Richter C. (ed.), *Ohnmacht und Angst aushalten. Kritik der Resilienz in Theologie und Philosophie* (Stuttgart: 2017) 91–106.

Wollgast S., *Zum Tod im späten Mittelalter und in der Frühen Neuzeit* (Berlin: 1992).

PART 3

Objects and the Moments of Death

∴

CHAPTER 9

Candles of Death and the Death of the Virgin Mary as a Model of the Ideal Death on the Threshold of the Early Modern Era

Vera Henkelmann

1   Introduction

The chapter examines the meaning and function of so-called candles of death, which were given to a person on his or her deathbed, in late medieval depictions of the death of the Virgin Mary as a central element of the moment of dying and the rituals accompanying it.[1] It becomes clear that they were intended to provide the viewer with a model for an appropriate preparation for his or her own personal death, in which rituals played a central role. The death candle was of eminent importance at this moment of transition from earthly to otherworldly life – as a threshold experience for the dying and his or her companions,[2] since it was in principle available to any believer, but also as a means of strengthening the social bonds between the survivors. By focusing explicitly on this element, the chapter aims to make a further contribution to previous research on representations of the death of the Virgin Mary in the context of preparations for death.[3]

Death candles are depicted in numerous late medieval representations of the deaths of other saints and in *ars moriendi* depictions of the deaths of ordinary

---

1 The completion of the text was funded by the Deutsche Forschungsgemeinschaft (DFG, German Research Foundation) – FOR 2779.
2 On the liminality of the moment of death, see von Thiessen H., "Das Sterbebett als normative Schwelle. Der Mensch in der Frühen Neuzeit zwischen irdischer Normenkonkurrenz und göttlichem Gericht", *Historische Zeitschrift* 295 (2012) 625–659.
3 Cf. for example Kretzenbacher L., *Sterbekerze und Palmzweig-Ritual beim "Marientod". Zum Apokryphen in Wort und Bild bei der koimesis, dormitio, assumptio der Gottesmutter zwischen Byzanz und dem mittelalterlichen Westen*, Sitzungsberichte der Österreichischen Akademie der Wissenschaften. Philosophisch-historische Klasse 667 (Vienna: 1999); Schreiner K., "Der Tod Marias als Inbegriff christlichen Sterbens. Sterbekunst im Spiegel mittelalterlicher Legendenbildung", in Borst A. – Gravenitz G. von – Patschovsky A. (eds.), *Tod im Mittelalter*, Konstanzer Bibliothek 20 (Constance: 1993) 261–312; Holzherr G., *Die Darstellung des Marientodes im Spätmittelalter* (Tübingen: 1971); Nissen R., "Die Münze in der Sterbekerze. Ein Beitrag zu Conrad von Soest", *Westfalen* 21 (1936) 68–72.

lay people.[4] This chapter rather focuses on representations of the death of the Virgin as the object of study because in the late Middle Ages, the death of Mary had an explicit exemplary character for all dying people – whether saints or lay people. It is precisely the difference between the deaths of the viewers, i.e. ordinary mortals, on the one hand and the death of the Mother of God on the other hand, that underlines the relevance of such candles for ideas and behaviour in the context of the inescapable moment of death. They were a means, accessible to all, for an exemplary and ideal way of dying. Among the numerous late medieval depictions of the death of the Virgin, Dutch/German works, both expressive and well-known, have been selected for this chapter because they frequently depict the death candle, whereas this motif seems to have been less common in southern Europe, for example.[5]

2   Candles of Death and Their History and Meaning

In a narrower sense, the term "candle of death" or "death candle" means the single candle that was given to the dying person lying on his or her deathbed. It does not refer to the light placed in a lantern when the priest took the Blessed Sacrament to the dying person. Candles placed around the deathbed and serving to venerate the Blessed Sacrament for the *viaticum* or for general lighting of the death room must also be distinguished from the death candle. The same applies to candles placed around the deathbed later when the deceased was laid out in the house of the deceased, candles carried in the funeral procession from the house of the dead to the church, candles placed around the corpse during the exequies in the church as well as to candles placed on the anniversaries or memorial days at the catafalque or grave of the memorialized dead. Obviously, then, the use of death candles was not isolated, but part of an explicit and differentiated use of light in the context of dying, death, burial, and commemoration of the dead.[6]

---

4   Cf. with further literature for representations of the *ars moriendi* Preising D. – Rief M. – Vogt C. (ed.), *Der gute Weg zum Himmel: Spätmittelalterliche Bilder zum richtigen Sterben. Das Gemälde „ars bene moriendi" aus der Sammlung Peter und Irene Ludwig*, exh. cat., Ludwiggalerie Schloss Oberhausen – Suermondt-Ludwig-Museum Aachen (Bielefeld: 2016); for the death of saints cf. von der Nahmer D., *Der Heilige und sein Tod. Sterben im Mittelalter* (Darmstadt: 2013).

5   Cf. on the fact that the death candle is found mainly in German and Dutch representations of the death of Mary, while it does not seem to have been very widespread in France, Italy and Spain: Holzherr, *Die Darstellung des Marientodes* 61–99.

6   For definitions of death candles see Seidel K., *Die Kerze: Motivgeschichte und Ikonologie*, Studien zur Kunstgeschichte 103 (Hildesheim – Zurich – New York: 1996) 115–116; Büll R.,

One of the earliest references to the custom of the death candle can be found in Ephrem the Syrian (306–373).[7] While it was not part of the Carolingian *Ordo visitationis infirmorum*,[8] from the late Middle Ages it was part of collections of rites (obsequials, manuals or agendas) but also *Libri ordinarii*.[9] According to the Liège *Liber ordinarius* of the thirteenth century the death candle was put into the dying person's right hand.[10] A placement of candles in the folded hands of the dying person was also possible; for example in an account about St. Ferdinand (d. 1252).[11] As late as 1497, Johann Geiler von Kaysersberg (1445–1510) in his *ars moriendi* emphasizes the need for the dying person to hold the death candle him- or herself.[12] Partly twisted candles are depicted, sometimes with a strong flame, which would suggest a special wick. The practice after death varied. The death candle could be extinguished and kept for use in other deaths or be deliberately burned down.[13] In any case, numerous pictorial sources suggest relatively thin, tall candles which the dying person could hold in his or her own hand.

The use of the candle of death served by no means purely practical purposes, rather, it served to stage the dying, the performative actions and rituals,

---

Vom Wachs. Hoechster Beiträge zur Kenntnis der Wachse (Frankfurt: 1959–1977) 914. Franz A., *Die kirchlichen Benediktionen im Mittelalter*, 2 vols. (Freiburg: 1909), vol. 2, 457. Mühlbauer W., *Geschichte und Bedeutung der (Wachs-)Lichter bei den kirchlichen Funktionen* (Augsburg: 1874) 74–75. For further use of light in the context of burial and commemoration of the dead, see Henkelmann V., "Künstliches Licht im mittelalterlichen Sakralraum – eine erste Annäherung", *Liturgisches Jahrbuch* 68/3 (2018) 173–196, at 193–195.

7   Pfistermeister U., *Wachs. Volkskunst und Brauch*, 2 vols. (Nuremberg: 1982–1983), vol. 2, 62; Mühlbauer, *(Wachs-)Lichter* 74.
8   Cf. on the *ordo visitationis infirmorum* Angenendt A., *Geschichte der Religiosität im Mittelalter* (Darmstadt: 2009) 664. Cf. on the early medieval *Roman Ordo* Kaczynski R., "Sterbeliturgie", *Lexikon für Theologie und Kirche* (Freiburg: 2009) 981–982, at 981.
9   For an overview of the sources see Berger P., *Religiöses Brauchtum im Umkreis der Sterbeliturgie in Deutschland* (Münster: 1966) 14–16, 141–146. On the death candle custom in the late Middle Ages in general, see Angenendt, *Geschichte Religiosität* 665; Daxelmüller C., "Totenbräuche. III. Frömmigkeitsgeschichtlich", *Lexikon für Theologie und Kirche* (Freiburg: 2009) 123–125, 124. Schreiner K., *Maria. Jungfrau, Mutter, Herrscherin* (Munich: 1994) 483; Berger, *Religiöses Brauchtum* 44.
10 Cf. Berger, *Religiöses Brauchtum* 46. For holding in the right hand, see also Schreiner, "Der Tod Marias" 294–295.
11 Cf. Mühlbauer, *(Wachs-)Lichter* 77.
12 Cf. Hoch A. (ed.), *Geilers von Kaysersberg „Ars moriendi" aus dem Jahre 1497*, Straßburger theologische Studien 4/2 (Freiburg: 1901) (Johann Geiler von Kaysersberg, Ars moriendi, 23. Frucht).
13 Cf. Pfistermeister, *Wachs*, vol. 2, 64. Seidel, *Die Kerze* 116. On the special case of candles with coins cf. Nissen, "Münze"; Schreiber G., "Liturgie und Abgabe. Bußpraxis und Beichtgeld an französischen Niederkirchen des Hochmittelalters", *Historisches Jahrbuch* 76 (1957) 1–14.

the actors associated with it, and the place where this took place. Even more, it clarified the ideas of official church doctrine as well as popular belief associated with dying and death in equal measure.[14]

Like the holy water also used at the deathbed, the death candle was first connected to baptism. Its light reminded everybody of the fact that, according to the divine origin of all life and light, at birth man did not only see the light of life, but through baptism became a 'light in the Lord' (Eph 5:8), a child of light.[15] Thus, the death candle also recalled the baptismal candle.[16] Whether this candle was kept for the hour of death and used as a candle of death in the late Middle Ages – as was customary in some cases later on – is uncertain.[17] Reminiscent of baptism, the burning, self-consuming candle of death was also a symbol of the light of life diminishing and finally extinguishing,[18] which was closely linked to the idea of the soul as a light.[19] It was imagined that at the moment of death, the light present in the good soul would emerge from the body, rise to the afterlife and continue to burn there.[20]

---

14   Cf. Büll, *Vom Wachs* 1001–1002; Seidel, *Die Kerze* 110.
15   Cf. Bärsch J., "Suscipe pro anima famuli tui episcopi precis nostras ... Grundzüge der Liturgie des Bischofsbegräbnisses im Spätmittelalter", in Lutz G. – Müller R. (eds.), *Die Bronze, der Tod und die Erinnerung. Das Grabmal des Wolfhard von Roth im Augsburger Dom*, Veröffentlichungen des Zentralinstituts für Kunstgeschichte 53 (Passau: 2020) 15–28; Seidel, *Die Kerze* 114; Schiller G., *Ikonographie der christlichen Kunst*, vol. 4.2: Maria (Gütersloh: 1980) 134; Berger, *Religiöses Brauchtum* 49.
16   Cf. on the baptismal candle Pfistermeister, *Wachs* vol. 2, 54–57; Seidel, *Die Kerze* 114.
17   Cf. Vincent C., "Lumiere dans les pratiques funéraires au prisme des sources liturgiques", in Bocquet-Liénard A. – Chapelain de Séréville-Niel C. – Dervin S. (eds.), *Des pots dans la tombe (IXe–XVIIIe siècle). Regards croisés sur une pratique funéraire en Europe de l'Ouest*, Publications du CRAHAM, Série antique et médiévale (Caen: 2017) 441–452, at 443; Seidel, *Die Kerze* 115. Pfistermeister, *Wachs*, vol. 2, 62; Holzherr, *Die Darstellung des Marientodes* 39; Berger, *Religiöses Brauchtum* 45; Mühlbauer, *(Wachs-)Kerzen* 74. On the idea of *dies natalis*, i.e. the day of death as a day of birth in a life beyond, and death as a second baptism to remember see Vincent, "Lumiere" 443.
18   On the connection between the light of lights and a candlelight see Seidel, *Die Kerze* 108–113; Pfistermeister, *Wachs*, vol. 2, 53–54; Berger, *Religiöses Brauchtum* 43–44.
19   Cf. Bärsch J., *Allerseelen. Studien zu Liturgie und Brauchtum eines Totengedenktages in der abendländischen Kirche*, Liturgiewissenschaftliche Quellen und Forschungen 90 (Münster: 2004) 430; Sartori P., "Feuer und Licht im Totenbrauch" *ZVK* 17 (1907), 372–373.
20   Cf. Bärsch J., "Sinngehalt und Feiergestalt der liturgischen Totenmemoria im Mittelalter. Eine liturgiewissenschaftliche Vergewisserung als Beitrag zum interdisziplinären Gespräch", in Schilp T. (ed.), *Pro remedio et salute anime peragemus: Totengedenken am Frauenstift Essen im Mittelalter*, Essener Forschungen zum Frauenstift 6 (Göttingen: 2008) 37–58, at 57; Angenendt A., "Der Leib ist klar, klar wie Kristall", in Schreiner K. (ed.), *Frömmigkeit im Mittelalter: politisch-soziale Kontexte, visuelle Praxis, körperliche Ausdrucksformen* (Munich: 2002) 387–398, at 389–390; Angenendt A., *Heilige und Reliquien. Die*

The light of the candle of death thus characterized the moment of death as a phase of transition, from this life to the life in the next world. Like the death blessing formula spoken at the burial, "May he rest in peace and may the eternal light shine on him", already at the moment of dying the light of the death candle referred to the Eternal Light, towards which the dying person was going. This light – so it was believed – illuminated paradise and was so enormous that no mortal could bear to see it. The light of the death candle was therefore a visualization, an image of that light which is actually not visible to man. Moreover it symbolized the hope of the dying to rise during the Last Judgement into the fullness of this eternal light of paradise.[21] The death candle thus also had an eschatological character.[22] By equating the Eternal Light with Christ – the Lamb illuminates the Celestial City according to John's Revelation (Rev 21:23) – the light of such a candle was a reference to the expectation of Christ, who called himself the Light of the World, preceded the dying person in life as a light and will show him the way to paradise in the afterlife. Therefore, sometimes the death candle is also interpreted as a kind of light illuminating the path into the afterlife.[23]

Moreover, the candle of death, available at the moment of dying and lit in time, was an expression of a person's preparation for his or her own death. It was a sign of dying well and an element of the *ars moriendi* that set the tone for the end of the Middle Ages.[24] By holding the candle in his hands, the dying person demonstrated impressively that he or she was prepared for his or her death, and for the coming of the Lord. In this respect, the candle also referred to the Wise Virgins (Mt 25:1–13). Like these, the dying person, with the candle as the light of his faith in hand, should go to meet Christ.[25] As a light

---

Geschichte ihres Kultes vom frühen Christentum bis zur Gegenwart (Munich: 1997) 117; Büll, *Vom Wachs* 914, 1000.

21   Cf. Bärsch J., "Kirchenraum und Kirchenschatz im Horizont des mittelalterlichen Gottesdienstes. Die Liturgie als Sinnträger für Gebrauch und Funktion gottesdienstlicher Räume und Kunstwerke", in Wendland U. (ed.), *Das Heilige sichtbar machen. Domschätze in Vergangenheit, Gegenwart und Zukunft* (Regensburg: 2010) 31–58, ar 37, 46; Vincent C., *Fiat Lux. Lumière et luminaires dans la vie religieuse en Occident du XIIIᵉ siècle au début du XVIᵉ siècle*, Histoire Réligieuse de la France 24 (Paris: 2004) 293–295.
22   Cf. Schreiner, Maria 483; Schreiner, "Der Tod Marias" 296.
23   Cf. Angenendt, *Geschichte Religiosität* 670; Berger, *Religiöses Brauchtum* 44.
24   Cf. Bates S., "Preparations for a Christian Death. The Later Middle Ages", in Booth P. – Tingle E. (eds.), *A Companion to Death, Burial, and Remembrance in Late Medieval and Early Modern Europe, c. 1300–1700*, Brill's Companions to the Christian Tradition 94 (Leiden: 2021) 72–105.
25   Cf. Seidel, *Die Kerze* 116; Schreiner, Maria 483; Schreiner, "Der Tod Marias" 296; Mühlbauer, *(Wachs-)Kerzen* 77.

of faith, the death candle in turn referred to the most important element of the preparation for death: repentance in the sense of a timely return to faith, which was necessary in order not to die in sin and thus be excluded from the promise of paradise.

But even with the best preparation – so the faithful were convinced – the soul was endangered, especially in the hour of death, by the devil and demons who tried to get hold of it. By bravely holding the burning death candle in his or her hand, on the contrary, the dying person held on to his or her faith.[26] Here he or she was supported by the light of the candle, as light was generally said to have a purifying and apotropaic power: to keep demons away, to banish the danger of revenants and to prevent the dying person from taking another soul with him or her.[27] It is uncertain whether a consecrated candle was used as candle of death – as has sometimes been the case up to the present day.[28] However, this is an obvious assumption, because consecrated candles were said to have a special apotropaic effect.[29] In particular the Candles of Candlemas might have played a role in this context.[30] After consecration, these were handed out on Candlemas to the participants of the procession taking place on that day and carried along there. Some of these Candles of Candlemas were kept beyond the feast and used for special apotropaic purposes. However, for the Middle Ages, at least in the monastic context, there is isolated evidence of the use of other candles, too. In St. Blasien in Germany's Black Forest region, for example, the large candle of the Blasius Blessing was kept and placed next to the bed of dying friars as a death candle.[31]

Finally, the light of the candle of death was directed not only at the dying person but also at the people around him or her. It contributed to an atmosphere that characterized the moment of death as removed from the everyday. Moreover, just as the light space of the candle was shared by all, the use of the

---

26 Cf. Schmitz-Esser R., "Aufbahren, Verwesen, Auferstehen. Zeitkonzepte beim Umgang mit dem Leichnam im Mittelalter", in Weitbrecht J. – Bihrer A. – Felber T. (eds.), *Die Zeit der letzten Dinge. Deutungsmuster und Erzählformen des Umgangs mit Vergänglichkeit in Mittelalter und Früher Neuzeit*, Encomia Deutsch 6 (Göttingen: 2020) 61–80; 62–64.
27 Cf. Preising, *Der gute Weg zum Himmel* 36; Bärsch, *Allerseelen* 430; Vincent, *Fiat Lux* 503; Berger, *Religiöses Brauchtum* 131; Rühl E., "Stabkerzen, Leichenkerzen, Kerzenstangen. Ein Beitrag zur ostfränkischen Volkskunde", *Jahrbuch für fränkische Landesforschung* 11–12 (1953) 397–406, at 399.
28 Cf. Seidel, *Die Kerze* 166; Pfistermeister, *Wachs*, vol. 2, 63; Berger, *Religiöses Brauchtum* 46; Sartori, "Feuer und Licht" 361–362; Mühlbauer, *(Wachs-)Kerzen* 75, 361.
29 Cf. Schreiber, "Liturgie und Abgabe" 4; Berger, *Religiöses Brauchtum* 43.
30 Cf. Vincent, "Lumiere" 443; Franz, *Die kirchlichen Benediktionen*, vol. 1, 456–457.
31 Cf. Franz, *Die kirchlichen Benediktionen*, vol. 1, 457.

candle brought together the dying and those who live on.[32] The light of the death candle inspired a sense of community. First, by handing it to the dying person from the circle of attendants, the importance as well as the duty of those who continued to live was underlined and the handing of the candle was characterized as an act of active charity and help in dying.[33] Second, the light of the death candle united the dying person with the attendants in the hope of the Eternal Light of Paradise – in case of their own passing. Consequently, the candle of death reminded the attendants of their own death – not only as a *meditatio mortis*, the imaginative anticipation of one's own death,[34] but in the sense of a concrete and necessary preparation.

3 Representations of the Death of the Virgin Mary at the End of the Middle Ages

Depictions of the Death of the Virgin Mary (*dormitio*) showing the Mother of God dying in the circle of the apostles were widespread in the late Middle Ages. The popularity of this theme may be explained above all by the fact that Mary was considered a special intercessor in general and in the hour of death in particular. In this context, reference can be made to the phrase 'pray for us sinners, now and at the hour of our death', which was added to the Hail Mary in the late Middle Ages.[35] Mary's motherhood played a role in this, as people were convinced that Jesus would not reject his mother's requests on behalf of the faithful. Decisive, moreover, was the special holiness of Mary, the Mother of God and Virgin. This was proven firstly by her knowledge about her own death three days prior, secondly by her dying without suffering and hostility

---

32 On the importance of community at the moment of death, see. Baumgartner K., "Christliches Brauchtum um Sterben, Tod und Trauer", in Becker H. – Einig B. – Ullrich P.-O. (eds.), *Im Angesicht des Todes. Ein interdisziplinäres Kompendium* (St. Otilien: 1987), 91–134, 102; Ariès P., *Bilder zur Geschichte des Todes* (Berlin: 1984) 100; and the contribution by Benedikt Brunner in this volume.

33 In every household there should be a set of necessary death utensils, including candles: Baumgartner, "Christliches Brauchtum" 96.

34 Cf. Pawlak A., "Ars bene moriendi: der "Transitus Mariae" in der niederländischen Kunst der Frühen Neuzeit", in Dürr R. – Gerok-Reiter A. – Holzem A. – Patzold S. (eds.), *Religiöses Wissen im vormodernen Europa. Schöpfung – Mutterschaft – Passion* (Paderborn: 2019) 431–462, at 431, 435.

35 Cf. Welzel B., "Bilder – Kontexte – Identitäten. Die Marienbilder des Conrad von Soest im spätmittelalterlichen Dortmund", in Schilp T. – Welzel B. (eds.), *Dortmund und Conrad von Soest im spätmittelalterlichen Europa*, Dortmunder Mittelalter-Forschungen 3 (Bielefeld: 2004) 309–328, at 316.

from the devil, and finally and above all by her bodily Assumption into heaven (*assumptio corporis*).[36] This special holiness of Mary was to be emphasized in the depictions, which is why there was often a simultaneous depiction of Mary's death, burial and, above all, Assumption. In Israhel van Meckenem's work [Fig. 9.1],[37] the funeral procession depicted in the upper left is particularly striking. But conspicuously, candles are not shown here, although it was customary to carry burning candles with the funeral procession.[38] In contrast, the main scene shows in addition to the dying candle in the hands of the Blessed Mother another lighted candle on a large candelabrum placed at the foot of the bed. In Hugo van der Goes' work in Bruges [Fig. 9.2][39] and the Pacher altar in Sankt Wolfgang [Fig. 9.3],[40] the focus is on the events of dying and the imminent Assumption – indicated by Christ turning from heaven, accompanied by angels.[41] In addition, Mary was depicted clothed and not naked like a normal mortal or even in agony on her deathbed.[42] She seems to be sleeping peacefully lying in bed, is depicted sitting in bed – as it is the case with Israhel van Meckenem – or enthroned in front of the bed. In the latter case, the deathbed could also be omitted entirely. Finally, in the depictions of the death of the Virgin Mary, there are no demons that seek Mary's soul. Even where – as in Bruges – the scenery is clearly marked as a nocturnal event,[43] Mary herself is wrapped in a light of special quality to which we will return later.

36 Cf. Schreiner, *Maria* 465–471.
37 The Death of the Virgin, Israhel van Meckenem after Hans Holbein the Elder, 1490/1500, National Gallery of Art (Rosenwald Collection), Washington: Max Lehrs M., *Geschichte und kritischer Katalog des deutschen, niederländischen und französischen Kupferstichs im XV. Jahrhundert*, vol. 9 (Vienna: 1934) 51–76 cat. no. 50–61, at 69–71 cat. no. 60. https://www.nga.gov/collection/art-object-page.39892.html.
38 Cf. Henkelmann, "Künstliches Licht" 193–195.
39 The Death of the Virgin, Hugo van der Goes, 1475–1482, Groeningemuseum, Bruges: Kemperdick S. – Eising E. (eds.), *Hugo van der Goes. Zwischen Schmerz und Seligkeit*, exh. cat., Gemäldegalerie Berlin (Munich: 2023) 226–233 cat. no. 28 (Till-Holger Borchert); Depoorter M. – De Visch L. –Everaarts M. – Steyaert G. – van Oosterwijk A. (eds.), *Face to Face with Hugo van der Goes: Old Master, New Interpretation* (Veurne: 2022); Pawlak, "Ars bene moriendi" 436–444.
40 The Death of the Virgin, right inner wing of Pacher-Altar, Michael Pacher, 1471–1481, parish church of Sankt Wolfgang (Austria): Kahsnitz R., *Die großen Schnitzaltäre: Spätgotik in Süddeutschland, Österreich, Südtirol* (Munich: 2005) 76–105; Schiller, *Ikonographie der christlichen Kunst* 136.
41 Although in Bruges the Assumption is not explicitly depicted, the concrete representation of Mary's soul ascending to Christ is missing, Pawlak, "Ars bene moriendi" 442.
42 Cf. Holzherr, *Die Darstellung des Marientodes* 50, 142.
43 On night and darkness as demonically understood time/space in the Middle Ages and the early modern era see Koslofsky C., *Evening's Empire: A History of the Night in Early Modern*

CANDLES OF DEATH AND THE DEATH OF THE VIRGIN MARY AS A MODEL 173

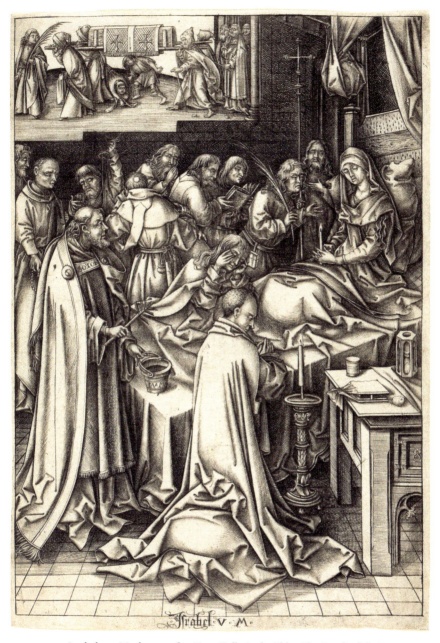

FIGURE 9.1   Israhel van Meckenem after Hans Holbein the Elder, The Death of the Virgin, 1490/1500, engraving
WASHINGTON, NATIONAL GALLERY OF ART (ROSENWALD COLLECTION)

FIGURE 9.2 Hugo van der Goes, The Death of the Virgin, 1475–1482, oil on panel, 147.8 × 122.5 cm
BRUGES, GROENINGEMUSEUM

CANDLES OF DEATH AND THE DEATH OF THE VIRGIN MARY AS A MODEL 175

FIGURE 9.3 Michael Pacher, The Death of the Virgin, right inner wing of Pacher-Altar, 1471–1481, oil on panel, Sankt Wolfgang (Austria), parish church
IMAGE KINDLY PROVIDED BY PETER BÖTTCHER, INSTITUT FÜR REALIENKUNDE, UNIVERSITÄT SALZBURG

These positive, explicitly presented circumstances of Mary's death turned it into a model of the good death, especially in the late Middle Ages, and this less in the sense of an admonition than a consolation of the faithful.[44] Pictures of the death of Mary visualized this exemplariness of the death of the Virgin and handed down normative expectations to the viewer.[45] Whoever follows Mary's example can die 'knowing' like her. This means recognizing one's own impending death in time to make appropriate preparations for dying well, thus having the opportunity for timely repentance and conversion before death, and having the chance to rise at the end of time. Therefore, the Assumption of Mary, implicitly or even explicitly depicted in the picture, strengthened the viewer in his hope for resurrection at the end of time.

As Mary, the sinless one, did not need any repentance and was taken up bodily into heaven immediately after her death, a tension arose between the presuppositions of the sinfulness of mere mortals and the special holiness of the Virgin Mary. A possible irritation and uncertainty for the faithful was resolved by giving him or her in text and picture real, for him or her attainable offers of action for a good way of dying, amongst them especially the candle of death.[46] This was accompanied by a higher degree of reality in representations of the death of the Virgin Mary in general, and an appreciation of the death rituals in particular.[47] On the one hand, such late medieval depictions offered a glimpse of a real interior, which occupied an increasingly large pictorial space.[48] On the other hand, the apostles were given (liturgical) tasks, with Saint Peter often acting as liturgist, while the other apostles assist him and are entrusted with incense and holy water.

Europe, New Studies in European History (Cambridge: 2011) 19–45; Youngs D. – Harris S., "Demonizing the Night in Medieval Europe: A Temporal Monstrosity?", in Bildhauer B. – Mills R. (eds.), *The monstrous Middle Ages* (Cardiff: 2003) 134–154; Verdon J., *Night in the Middle Ages* (South Bend: 2002), 6–68; Boiadjiev T., "Loca nocturna – Orte der Nacht", in Aertsen J.A. – Speer A. (eds.), *Raum und Raumvorstellungen im Mittelalter*, Miscellanea mediaevalia 25 (Berlin: 1998) 439–451.

44 Cf. Preising, *Der gute Weg zum Himmel*, 35; Myslivec J., "Tod Mariens", Lexikon der christlichen Ikonographie (Freiburg: 1972) 333–338, at 336–337; Schreiner, *Maria* 474–477; Schiller, *Ikonographie der christlichen Kunst* 133; Holzherr, *Die Darstellung des Marientodes* 50.

45 Cf. Preising, *Der Gute Weg zum Himmel* 15, 25, 35–36; Welzel, "Marienbilder" 316; Schreiner, *Maria* 474.

46 Cf. Schreiner, *Maria* 474–475.

47 Cf. Schreiner, *Maria* 474; Schreiner, "Der Tod Marias" 271, 297 (the emphasis on the death rituals in the death of Mary leads to an ecclesiasticalization of the scene); Schiller, *Ikonographie der christlichen Kunst* 135; Holzherr, *Die Darstellung des Marientodes* 25 (the higher degree of reality of the representation is accompanied by a certain secularization of the death of Mary).

48 Holzherr, *Die Darstellung des Marientodes* 45–46, 50, 106.

4 Meaning and Function of the Candle of Death in Late Medieval Representations of the Death of the Virgin Mary

Special significance of the candle of death in late medieval representations of the death of the Virgin Mary[49] is evident from the fact that it was often visually emphasized by being placed in the centre of the picture or by a dark background. On the Pacher altar (Sankt Wolfgang; Fig. 9.3) the candle is not only in the centre of the picture but forms a direct axis with Christ – a clear reference to the Christological interpretation of the light of the death candle. Furthermore, it is given in the signal colour red. The red of its wax is also found in a cloth hanging over the edge of the bed, which in turn leads to the red mantle of Christ in heaven. Therefore, the candle's red could also be a reference to the Passion of Christ. Scriptural sources are silent on the colour of the medieval death candles. Perhaps the red one depicted in Sankt Wolfgang goes back to the fact that red candles were said to have apotropaic power.[50]

In contrast to his Cologne version of the Death of the Virgin [Fig. 9.4],[51] in Munich Joos van Cleve not only places the candle's flame in front of the dark background of the picture [Fig. 9.5],[52] but also calls attention to the candle in the centre of the picture by having John the Apostle point at it with his index finger. As if to assure Our Lady that the candle he is placing in her hands with his left hand is indeed burning. Here as elsewhere, the death candle is highlighted when it is embedded in actions, specifically the apostles' service, in which presenting lighting and/or supporting such a candle in the folded hands of the Virgin played a central role. The relevance of the apostles in the context of the dying candle goes back, among other things, to the Sermon on the Mount. There, Jesus himself refers to the apostles as the light of the world, which should shine for all people (Mt 5, 14–16). Just as they carried the light and teachings of Jesus Christ into the world and proclaimed them among the people, at the moment of the Blessed Mother's death they provided that light referring to the Eternal Light and the Lord and Saviour in equal measure.

---

49 Cf. Schiller, *Ikonographie der christlichen Kunst* 135.
50 Cf. Sartori, "Feuer und Licht" 307.
51 The Death of the Virgin, Joos van Cleve, 1515, Wallraf-Richartz-Museum, Cologne: Teplitzky T., "Joos van Cleve. Zwei Triptychen mit dem Tod Mariae. Überlegungen zu den Altären aus der Hackeneyschen Hauskapelle und St. Maria im Kapitol und zu ihrer Beziehung zum Haus Habsburg", Colonia Romanica 24 (2009), 303–315; Eikemeier P., "Cleve, Joos van. Flügelaltar", in *Alte Pinakothek München. Erläuterungen zu den ausgestellten Werken* (Munich: 1999) 140–141, at 141.
52 The Death of the Virgin, Joos van Cleve, after 1515, Alte Pinakothek Munich: Teplitzky, "Joos van Cleve"; Eikemeier, "Cleve, Joos van", 140–141.

FIGURE 9.4 Joos van Cleve, The Death of the Virgin, 1515, oil on panel, 65 × 125.5 cm
COLOGNE, WALLRAF-RICHARTZ-MUSEUM

FIGURE 9.5 Joos van Cleve, The Death of the Virgin, after 1515, oil on panel, 130 × 154 cm
MUNICH, ALTE PINAKOTHEK

Often, it was John – the favourite disciple to whom Jesus dying had entrusted his mother – who was assigned the death candle and handed it to the Blessed Mother.[53] However, this was not always the case. Hugo van der Goes (Bruges; Fig. 9.2) found an individual solution by combining Peter and another apostle in their candle service. Its relevance was increased further by the unusual abandonment of holy water and incense in the picture. Moreover, the second apostle is presumably not John, whom we may rather assume in the beardless apostle squatting at Mary's right. Here, possibly Jacob lights the candle,[54] while Peter receives it to hand it to the Blessed Mother. More often, however, the death candle was depicted held in Mary's hands or supported in her hands by one of the apostles – usually John; while on the Pacher altar in Sankt Wolfgang [Fig. 9.3] Peter supports the candle in Mary's hands.

One reason for the special role of the candle of death in representations of the death of the Virgin Mary may have been the fact that, in contrast to the blessing of incense and holy water also depicted, the death candle corresponded to a more or less active part of Mary, which should result in the same behaviour of the viewer. So, the Virgin held the candle in her hands or was about to hold it. In fact, however, the death candle in representations of the death of the Virgin as well as in the cult of relics from the Virgin's death candle was ahistorical,[55] since there is no evidence of such a custom during Mary's lifetime or in the first century. Also, neither Biblical apocrypha nor (German) legends about the death of Mary report the death candle.[56] The fact that this detail of the representation was nevertheless given special attention finds its explanation in the fact that it was the death candle that enabled the faithful to express their faith as well as their adequate preparation for a good death. The Virgin Mary with the death candle served as a role model to mark this behaviour as exemplary for the faithful. In this respect, it is not surprising that candle relics also existed. In inventory lists of the relic treasure of Holy Roman Emperor Charles IV (1316–1378) at Karlstein Castle wax from the Virgin Mary's candle of death is mentioned.[57]

The Apocrypha and legends only mention that lamps or additional lights lit by the apostles were burning at the moment of the Virgin Mary's death,[58]

53   Holzherr, *Die Darstellung des Marientodes* 141.
54   Cf. Pawlak, "Ars bene moriendi" 438.
55   Cf. Schreiner, "Der Tod Marias" 296; Kretzenbacher, *Sterbekerze* ann. 49.
56   Cf. Kretzenbacher, *Sterbekerze* 44; Schreiner, *Maria* 483; Holzherr, *Die Darstellung des Marientodes* 3–5.
57   Cf. Kretzenbacher, *Sterbekerze* ann. 49.
58   Cf. Kretzenbacher, *Sterbekerze* 20; Schreiner, *Maria* 466, 483; Benz R. (transl.), *Die Legenda aurea des Jacobus de Voragine* (Darmstadt: 1997) 585.

which is depicted in some pictures.[59] In Joos van Cleve's Munich version of the death of Mary [Fig. 9.5], the death candle is joined by both a candle from a low candlestick on a small table at the foot of the deathbed and candles on two candlesticks flanking a closed so-called "Hausaltärchen" (a small altar piece in a private context). The clearly burnt candle on the table, with the rosary and an opened book – probably a Book of Hours – next to it, refers to Mary's actively practiced piety just before her death, while the burning candles in front of the house altar could well have just been lit, possibly by the apostles. In Joos van Cleve's Cologne version [Fig. 9.4], on the other hand, there is only one other burning candle, placed on a so-called "Blaker" above the entrance, whose metal back plate reflects the light.[60] Hugo van der Goes (Bruges; Fig. 9.2) found an individual solution by depicting a lamp in the upper right corner, its shadow appearing on a curtain in the picture's background. The oil lamp with its weak light, designed as an eternal light, refers to medieval ideas according to which Christ himself instructed John not to extinguish the lights until Mary's death, whereupon Peter chose three virgins – surely a reference to the Wise Virgins – to take care that the lamps did not go out.[61] Just as the apostles were responsible for the candles' and lamps' light and were prepared for their duty, the believer should be prepared for his or her own death.

Furthermore, a miracle of light is said to have occurred at the Assumption of Mary, in that it is said to have taken place in unearthly splendour.[62] This light, especially in the texts, referred to the luminous soul of Mary[63] and was deliberately staged in some depictions of the death of the Virgin Mary:[64] Unlike in the texts, in Bruges [Fig. 9.2] the main source of light emanates from Christ illustrating the entrance of the heavenly sphere into the earthly one as well as

---

59   Cf. Seidel, *Die Kerze* 183–184, 183 ann. 46.
60   In contrast to the Death of Mary by Joos van Cleve in Munich, this is not solely a reference to the virtue and piety of the Mother of God (cf. for Munich Eikemeier, "Cleve, Joos van", 140), since motifs depicted in Munich, such as the book and the rosary, are not associated with the candlestick here and the candle is not burned far here.
61   Cf. sermons of Cosmas Vestitor (ca. 750–830): Kretzenbacher, *Sterbekerze* 20. The lamp depicted by Hugo van der Goes is clearly burning; its flame has not been extinguished (cf. Depoorter, *Face* 40).
62   Cf. Kretzenbacher, *Sterbekerze* 10. Cf. also Holzherr, *Die Darstellung des Marientodes* 3.
63   Cf. Kretzenbacher, *Sterbekerze* 11, 13, 17 (according to the Pseudo-Melito, "her righteous soul shone white as a light" and Christ said to Peter: "The souls of all men are white from the beginning like Mary's, but through sin they become dark"); Holzherr, "Darstellung des Marientods" 1–2, 6 (according to John of Thessalonica (d. 649), at the Ascension the apostles observe the soul of Mary "in human form with all limbs, but sexless, seven times more luminous than the sun"); Voragine, *Legenda aurea* 586 ("But the apostles saw their soul so light that no tongue can utter it").
64   Cf. Holzherr, *Die Darstellung des Marientodes* 105–108.

the Eternal Light of Paradise, which was equated with Christ, the Redeemer, himself. But his appearance remains apparently unnoticed by the apostles despite the enormous gleam of light[65] – as no mortal could bear to see this enormous, other-worldly Eternal Light. In Sankt Wolfgang [Fig. 9.3], it was the gold in the picture's background that not only represented the Eternal Light shining behind the gate of Paradise depicted as a church portal, but also connected Mary's dying room in the picture's foreground and Christ's appearance still before the gate of Paradise, i.e. in the here and now of the apostles – without them noticing. The light of this gold background could be effectively activated, even brought to life, by the glow of the real candles illuminated at this altar. So that it seemed as if the viewer could catch a glimpse of this light actually not visible to mere mortals. In the picture, the light of the death candle is subordinated to this miracle of light,[66] but this does not have to be seen as a contradiction, since the light of the death candle referred to Christ and to the light of Mary's soul in equal measure. In addition, it visualized the idea of Mary as a light bearer or light bringer because through Mary, Jesus Christ had entered the world, calling himself the light of the world.[67] Here, one should make a reference to Martin Schongauer's death of Mary (Berlin; Fig. 9.6),[68] which refrains from an explicit depiction of Christ, but placed prominently at the end of the Virgin's death bed a large candelabrum with an equally large burning candle. We find just such a candlestick with a burning candle in Israhel van Meckenem's illustration [Fig. 9.1], albeit not presented quite as prominently. In size and design, these candlesticks are reminiscent of large altar candelabra, whose candlelight visualized the presence of Christ in the liturgy.[69] The candlesticks depicted in these pictures, and their candlelight, may therefore have served as a reference to Christ and Mary as well.[70]

65 Cf. Pawlak, "Ars bene moriendi" 441–442.
66 Cf. Kretzenbacher, *Sterbekerze* 41.
67 Cosmas Vestitor praises Mary as a *trifidum triadici luminis candelabrum*, that is, as a three-flame candelabrum of the lights of the Trinity: Kretzenbacher, *Sterbekerze* 20. In the sermons of John Damascene, in the Hymn of Praise to the Virgin Mary, he also refers to her as the source of true light: Holzherr, *Die Darstellung des Marientodes* 7.
68 The Death of the Virgin, Martin Schongauer, before 1475, Kupferstichkabinett SMPK, Berlin: Holzherr, *Die Darstellung des Marientodes* 58–59.
69 Cf. with further literature Henkelmann V., "Leuchterinschriften im Kontext mittelalterlicher Messliturgie. Suggestion und Präsenz von Sakralität im Kirchenraum und ihre memorialen Implikationen", in Frese T. – Horstmann L. – Wenig F. (eds.), *Sakrale Schriftbilder. Zur ikonischen Präsenz des Geschriebenen im mittelalterlichen Kirchenraum*, Materiale Textkulturen (Berlin: forthcoming)..
70 On the interpretation of candles (not only the Easter candle) towards Christ cf. Seidel, *Die Kerze* 65–67.

FIGURE 9.6 Martin Schongauer, The Death of the Virgin, before 1475, engraving, 27 × 17.8 cm
BERLIN, KUPFERSTICHKABINETT (SMPK)

The use of candles and light at the moment of death, the Marian veneration and the *ars moriendi* thus obviously went hand in hand in the depictions of the death of the Virgin Mary. And it is clear that this in sum should appeal to the viewer and encourage him or her to behave accordingly, both by making provisions for his or her own death and by assisting others in the hour of their death.

The central element and motif here is the candle of death. The Cologne death of the Virgin by Joos van Cleve [Fig. 9.4], discussed above, can be cited in conclusion as a particularly striking example. It forms the central panel of an altar retable [Fig. 9.7] created for the private chapel of the very wealthy Hacqueney/Hackeney family of goldsmiths, bankers and merchants in Cologne.[71] The scene of the death of the Virgin with the death candle in the centre is flanked on the outer wings by the praying Hackeney family; two brothers who donated the altar and their wives and each of them accompanied by a saint. During services in their chapel, the Hackeney family entrusted themselves to the intercession of the Blessed Mother, as in the painting, praying and – as they hoped – recommended by saints standing behind them as intercessors. One of the two women is shown with St. Gudula. Her attribute is a lantern, which the devil tried in vain to extinguish when she was going to church at night. In the given context, the burning light of the lantern guarded by Gudula also refers to the burning lamps of the Wise Virgins, who go prepared to meet the Lord. An ideal that was especially exemplary for the family's women, reminding them in a special way of the need for a dying candle as part of a good death. In attending services, by the depiction of the Virgin's exemplary death all the members of the Hackeney family were reminded of their own death and the necessary preparation for it. Thus, in reality as well as in the pictorial space they intensely contemplated the dying of the Blessed Mother. Cleverly emphasised by the arrangement of the central panel with the death of the Virgin indoors and the altar wings with the Hackeney family praying outdoors but facing the central scene, they became, as it were, part of the surrounding group of apostles – although respectfully and appropriately separated from the central scene by the picture's frame and rendered in an outdoor space rather than in the Virgin's dying room. The family thus demonstratively underlined that they were prepared for their own death and that of all family members. This may also be related to the fact that the chapel was part of the Hackeney court at the Neumarkt in Cologne. The court served not only as the family's home, but also as Holy Roman Emperor Maximilian's residence when he was in Cologne. In this respect, too, the family certainly wanted to stage

---

71   Teplitzky, "Joos van Cleve" 303–304.

FIGURE 9.7 Joos van Cleve, Altar retable with the death of the Virgin, 1515, oil on panel, 65 × 243.5 cm
COLOGNE, WALLRAF-RICHARTZ-MUSEUM

themselves as planning ahead and being prepared for the visit as well as the passing of the ruler as well – especially since the emperor was already preoccupied with his own demise at the time.[72] The second version of the Death of the Virgin by Joos van Cleve in Munich [Fig. 9.5] shows two almost identical outer wings, while the scene of the death of the Virgin differs slightly from the Cologne version. But here, too, the dying candle is the focus, certainly not by chance in the centre of the whole retable as well as highlighted against a dark background and by gestures of the apostles. The Hackeney family had donated this retable for the altar of the cross in the church of St. Maria im Kapitol Cologne, which stood in front of the rood screen and was also financed by the family.[73] In the private circle of their house chapel as well as at the crucifix altar accessible to all parishioners, i.e. to the public, both retables thus recalled and perpetuate not only the Hackeney family's intercession addressed to the Mother of God but also their appropriate preparation for their own dying. And we may be sure that they all took care that a candle of death was available at the critical and decisive moment of their death.

5   Conclusion

The candle of death was an essential element of the late medieval preparation for dying, the experience of that moment, and of the equipment of the deathbed and the bedchamber. By reminding the viewer of the light of

[72] Other details of the painting can also be related to its close relationship with Holy Roman Emperor Maximilian I, who, by the way, himself commissioned a painting of the death of the Virgin Mary in Vienna, depicting himself among the apostles gathered at Mary's side. After the completion of the altar, however, Maximilian no longer seems to have stayed in Cologne, where he had last resided in 1512: Teplitzky, "Joos van Cleve" 305–307, 310–313.

[73] Cf. Teplitzky, "Joos van Cleve" 304, 312; Eikemeier, "Cleve, Joos van" 141.

baptism and the light of life as well as the Eternal Light, the death candle was presented as an appropriate means of dying prepared and in hope of salvation through Christ the Saviour at the moment of death and protection from demons by this sign of faith. Furthermore, the death candle is characterized as a community-building element at the moment of death, reminding the viewer of his or her duty to assist the dying during their last moments and, in this act of charity, to remember his or her own imminent death.

Realia such as the candle of death were integrated – albeit ahistorical – into the moment of the Virgin Mary's death in the sense of a central element of the ideal death of all mortals. Just as the apostles assisted the Blessed Mother, so should the faithful, and when the moment of his or her own death has come, he or she should – like the Virgin Mary – be prepared and accompanied by a community meet the Lord.

While depictions of the death of the Virgin Mary became less common in the Renaissance, and during the Counter-Reformation depictions of the glorification of Mary were the focus of considerable interest,[74] the custom of the death candle nevertheless survived on the Catholic side through the Reformation.[75] In Pieter Bruegel's 1564 death of Mary the shades of grey are differentiated by the effective use of various types of light from different light sources.[76] The light of the dying candle in the hands of the Mother of God is subordinated to the light emanating from herself. By the way, the use of the candle of death could be even more intensified by perfumed candles and aromatized lamp oil, as can be seen in isolated cases of that time.[77] The reformers generally sought to curb the use of fire and light, which were considered ineffective, pagan or even idolatrous.[78] Rembrandt's etching of the death of the Virgin Mary [Fig. 9.8],

---

74   Cf. Pawlak, "Ars bene moriendi" 456; Schiller, *Ikonographie der christlichen Kunst* 133, 140.
75   Cf. Christ M., "Between Domestic and Public: Johann Leisentrit's (1527–1586) Instructions for the Sick and Dying of Upper Lusatia", in Faini M. – Meneghin A. (eds.), Domestic Devotions in the Early Modern World, Intersections 59/2 (Leiden: 2018) 82–106, at 88, 91; Berger, *Religiöses Brauchtum* 46–49; Mühlbauer, *(Wachs-)Kerzen* 74. On the continuing importance of preparation for death in the early modern period in general cf. Ramakers B. – Wouk, E.H, "Art and Death in the Netherlands: An Introduction", in Ramakers B. – Wouk E.H. (eds.), *Art & Death in The Netherlands, 1400–1800*, Netherlands Yearbook for History of Art/Nederlands Kunsthistorisch Jaarboek 72 (Leiden: 2022) 7–21), 11–13; Thiessen, "Sterbebett" 642–643, 649–650, 656, 658–659.
76   The Death of the Virgin Mary, Pieter Bruegel the Elder, around 1564, Upton House, Warwickshire: Pawlak, "Ars bene moriendi" 444–457.
77   Cf. Deschryver L., "You Only Die Once: Calvinist Dying and the Senses in Lille and Tournai During the Dutch Revolt", *Early Modern Low Countries* 4/1(2020), 35–57, at 51.
78   Cf. ibidem 37; Christ, "Between Domestic and Public" 86; Arnulf A., "Repräsentative Inanspruchnahme und funktionale Umnutzung altgläubiger Kirchenräume in protestantischen Territorien", in Helmut-Eberhard P. – Rott S. (eds.), *Schlosskirchen und*

FIGURE 9.8 Rembrandt (Harmenszoon van Rijn), The Death of the Virgin Mary [one of three states of the etching], 1639, etching, 41 × 31.5 cm
AMSTERDAM, RIJKSPRENTENKABINET (RIJKSMUSEUM)

FIGURE 9.9 The Grace of the Sacrament of Death, 1734, oil painting, 150 × 175 cm. Vreden, parish church St George (possession of the brotherhood of the Fear of the Death)

dated 1639, dispenses with both the death candle and a death ritual according to the Roman rite. The etching probably belonged to the Catholic community of Amsterdam, who were forced to practise their faith in secret.[79] But there was

---

Protestantismus. Die protestantische Schlosskirche und ihr Verhältnis zum Schlossbau (Regensburg: 2017) 104–118, 107. On the (continuing) use of the candle as a pictorial symbol of faith cf. Walsham A., "Domesticating Reformation. Material Culture, Memory, and Confessional Identity in Early Modern England", *Renaissance Quarterly* 69/2 (2016) 566–616, at 594.

79   The Death of the Virgin Mary, Rembrandt (Harmenszoon van Rijn), 1639, Rijksmuseum (Rijksprentenkabinet), Amsterdam [one of three states of the etching]: Pawlak, "Ars bene moriendi" 457–462 (with further literature). A reception of the etching outside of the Catholic community also seems conceivable in view of the representation seemingly

also open resistance to the reformers' views. This was particularly true of the use of light in funeral customs.[80] Perhaps this was due to deep-rooted ideas such as that of a light of life or the community-building aspect of the candle given to the dying or lit for him or her and the light emanating from such a candle of death. In Catholic circles, the death candle remained an essential,[81] albeit not a dominant part of a good death, as illustrated by a 1734 painting of the "Todesangstbruderschaft" (Brotherhood of the Fear of Death) in the parish church of St George in Vreden [Fig. 9.9]. It shows the priest passing the burning candle to a dying man. Here, however, the central motif is the cross, to which Our Lady of Sorrows explicitly points the dying man in the face of the struggle between the forces of good and evil for his soul.[82]

Thus, the candle of death remained an essential element of the preparation for the moment of death in the early modern period. On the Catholic side at least, the enduring example of the Virgin's death had a lasting effect. The faithful entrusted themselves in the hope that, following the Virgin's example and holding a burning candle of death in their hands, they could hope for salvation on the Last Day and enter into the eternal light of Paradise.

Bibliography

Secondary Literature

Angenendt A., "Der Leib ist klar, klar wie Kristall", in Schreiner K. (ed.), *Frömmigkeit im Mittelalter: politisch-soziale Kontexte, visuelle Praxis, körperliche Ausdrucksformen* (Munich: 2002) 387–398.

Angenendt A., *Geschichte der Religiosität im Mittelalter* (Darmstadt: 2009).

Angenendt A., *Heilige und Reliquien. Die Geschichte ihres Kultes vom frühen Christentum bis zur Gegenwart* (Munich: 1997).

---

  adapted to the political and confessional circumstances: Pawlak, "Ars bene moriendi" 459, 461–462.

80 Cf. Christ "Between Domestic and Public" 86; Berger, *Religiöses Brauchtum* 44–46.

81 Cf. Tingle E., "The Counter Reformation and Preparations for Death in the European Roman Catholic Church, 1550–1700", in Booth P. – Tingle E. (eds.), *A Companion to Death, Burial, and Remembrance in Late Medieval and Early Modern Europe, c. 1300–1700*, Brill's Companions to the Christian Tradition 94 (Leiden: 2021) 175–198, at 194.

82 The Grace of the Sacrament of Death, 1734, parish church St Georg (possession of the brotherhood of the Fear of the Death), Vreden: Kranemann B., *Sakramentliche Liturgie im Bistum Münster. Eine Untersuchung handschriftlicher und gedruckter Ritualien und der liturgischen Formulare vom 16. bis zum 20. Jahrhundert*, Liturgiewissenschaftliche Quellen und Forschungen 83 (Münster: 1998), 289; Tschuschke V., "Der Maler Franz Joseph Menninghausen von Vreden. Nachträge zu seinem Leben und Werk", *Studien zur Geschichte des Westmünsterlandes* 48 (1996), 129–134, 131–133.

Ariès P., *Bilder zur Geschichte des Todes* (Berlin: 1984).
Arnulf A., "Repräsentative Inanspruchnahme und funktionale Umnutzung altgläubiger Kirchenräume in protestantischen Territorien", in Helmut-Eberhard P. – Rott S. (eds.), *Schlosskirchen und Protestantismus. Die protestantische Schlosskirche und ihr Verhältnis zum Schlossbau* (Regensburg: 2017) 104–118.
Bärsch J., "Kirchenraum und Kirchenschatz im Horizont des mittelalterlichen Gottesdienstes. Die Liturgie als Sinnträger für Gebrauch und Funktion gottesdienstlicher Räume und Kunstwerke", in Wendland U. (ed.), *Das Heilige sichtbar machen. Domschätze in Vergangenheit, Gegenwart und Zukunft* (Regensburg: 2010) 31–58.
Bärsch J., "Sinngehalt und Feiergestalt der liturgischen Totenmemoria im Mittelalter. Eine liturgiewissenschaftliche Vergewisserung als Beitrag zum interdisziplinären Gespräch", in Schilp T. (ed.), *Pro remedio et salute anime peragemus: Totengedenken am Frauenstift Essen im Mittelalter*, Essener Forschungen zum Frauenstift 6 (Göttingen: 2008) 37–58.
Bärsch J., "Suscipe pro anima famuli tui episcopi precis nostras … Grundzüge der Liturgie des Bischofsbegräbnisses im Spätmittelalter", in Lutz G. – Müller R. (eds.), *Die Bronze, der Tod und die Erinnerung. Das Grabmal des Wolfhard von Roth im Augsburger Dom*, Veröffentlichungen des Zentralinstituts für Kunstgeschichte 53 (Passau: 2020) 15–28.
Bärsch J., *Allerseelen. Studien zu Liturgie und Brauchtum eines Totengedenktages in der abendländischen Kirche*, Liturgiewissenschaftliche Quellen und Forschungen 90 (Münster: 2004).
Bates S., "Preparations for a Christian Death. The Later Middle Ages", in Booth P. – Tingle E. (eds.), *A Companion to Death, Burial, and Remembrance in Late Medieval and Early Modern Europe, c. 1300–1700*, Brill's Companions to the Christian Tradition 94 (Leiden: 2021) 72–105.
Baumgartner K., "Christliches Brauchtum um Sterben, Tod und Trauer", in Becker H. – Einig B. – Ullrich P.-O. (eds.), *Im Angesicht des Todes. Ein interdisziplinäres Kompendium* (St. Otilien: 1987) 91–134.
Benz R. (transl.), *Die Legenda aurea des Jacobus de Voragine* (Darmstadt: 1997).
Berger P., *Religiöses Brauchtum im Umkreis der Sterbeliturgie in Deutschland* (Münster: 1966).
Boiadjiev T., "Loca nocturna – Orte der Nacht", in Aertsen J.A. – Speer A. (eds.), *Raum und Raumvorstellungen im Mittelalter*, Miscellanea mediaevalia 25 (Berlin: 1998) 439–451.
Büll R., *Vom Wachs. Hoechster Beiträge zur Kenntnis der Wachse* (Frankfurt: 1959–1977).
Christ M., "Between Domestic and Public: Johann Leisentrit's (1527–1586) Instructions for the Sick and Dying of Upper Lusatia", in Faini M. – Meneghin A. (eds.), *Domestic Devotions in the Early Modern World*, Intersections 59/2 (Leiden: 2018) 82–106.
Daxelmüller C., "Totenbräuche. III. Frömmigkeitsgeschichtlich", *Lexikon für Theologie und Kirche* (Freiburg: 2009) 123–125.

Deschryver L., "You Only Die Once: Calvinist Dying and the Senses in Lille and Tournai During the Dutch Revolt", *Early Modern Low Countries* 4/1 (2020) 35–57.

Eikemeier P., "Cleve, Joos van. Flügelaltar", in *Alte Pinakothek München. Erläuterungen zu den ausgestellten Gemälden* (Munich: 1999) 140–141.

Franz A., *Die kirchlichen Benediktionen im Mittelalter*, 2 vols. (Freiburg: 1909).

Henkelmann V., "Künstliches Licht im mittelalterlichen Sakralraum – eine erste Annäherung", *Liturgisches Jahrbuch* 68/3 (2018) 173–196.

Henkelmann V., "Leuchterinschriften im Kontext mittelalterlicher Messliturgie. Suggestion und Präsenz von Sakralität im Kirchenraum und ihre memorialen Implikationen", in Frese T. – Horstmann L. – Wenig F. (eds.), *Sakrale Schriftbilder. Zur ikonischen Präsenz des Geschriebenen im mittelalterlichen Kirchenraum*, Materiale Textkulturen (Berlin: forthcoming).

Hoch A. (ed.), *Geilers von Kaysersberg „Ars moriendi" aus dem Jahre 1497*, Straßburger theologische Studien 4/2 (Freiburg: 1901).

Holzherr G., *Die Darstellung des Marientodes im Spätmittelalter* (Tübingen: 1971).

Kaczynski R., "Sterbeliturgie", *Lexikon für Theologie und Kirche* (Freiburg: 2009) 981–982.

Kahsnitz R., *Die großen Schnitzaltäre: Spätgotik in Süddeutschland, Österreich, Südtirol* (Munich: 2005).

Kemperdick S. – Eising E. (eds.), *Hugo van der Goes. Zwischen Schmerz und Seligkeit*, exh. cat., Gemäldegalerie Berlin (Munich: 2023).

Koslofsky C., *Evening's Empire: A History of the Night in Early Modern Europe*, New Studies in European History (Cambridge: 2011).

Kranemann B., *Sakramentliche Liturgie im Bistum Münster. Eine Untersuchung handschriftlicher und gedruckter Ritualien und der liturgischen Formulare vom 16. bis zum 20. Jahrhundert*, Liturgiewissenschaftliche Quellen und Forschungen 83 (Münster: 1998).

Kretzenbacher L., *Sterbekerze und Palmzweig-Ritual beim "Marientod". Zum Apokryphen in Wort und Bild bei der koimesis, dormitio, assumptio der Gottesmutter zwischen Byzanz und dem mittelalterlichen Westen*, Sitzungsberichte der Österreichischen Akademie der Wissenschaften. Philosophisch-historische Klasse 667 (Vienna: 1999).

Lehrs M., *Geschichte und kritischer Katalog des deutschen, niederländischen und französischen Kupferstichs im XV. Jahrhundert*, vol. 9 (Vienna: 1934).

Mühlbauer W., *Geschichte und Bedeutung der (Wachs-)Lichter bei den kirchlichen Funktionen* (Augsburg: 1874).

Myslivec J., "Tod Mariens", *Lexikon der christlichen Ikonographie* (Freiburg: 1972) 333–338.

Nahmer D. von der, *Der Heilige und sein Tod. Sterben im Mittelalter* (Darmstadt 2013).

Nissen R., "Die Münze in der Sterbekerze. Ein Beitrag zu Conrad von Soest", *Westfalen* 21 (1936) 68–72.

Pawlak A., "Ars bene moriendi: der 'Transitus Mariae' in der niederländischen Kunst der Frühen Neuzeit", in Dürr R. – Gerok-Reiter A. – Holzem A. – Patzold S. (eds.), *Religiöses Wissen im vormodernen Europa. Schöpfung – Mutterschaft – Passion* (Paderborn: 2019), 431–462.

Pfistermeister U., *Wachs. Volkskunst und Brauch*, 2 vols. (Nuremberg: 1982–1983).

Preising D. – Rief M. – Vogt C. (ed.), *Der gute Weg zum Himmel: Spätmittelalterliche Bilder zum richtigen Sterben. Das Gemälde „ars bene moriendi" aus der Sammlung Peter und Irene Ludwig*, exh. cat., Ludwiggalerie Schloss Oberhausen – Suermondt-Ludwig-Museum Aachen (Bielefeld: 2016).

Ramakers B. – Wouk, E.H., "Art and death in the Netherlands: An introduction", in Ramakers B. – Wouk E.H. (eds.), *Art & Death in The Netherlands, 1400–1800*, Netherlands Yearbook for History of Art/Nederlands Kunsthistorisch Jaarboek 72 (Leiden: 2022) 7–21.

Rühl E., "Stabkerzen, Leichenkerzen, Kerzenstangen. Ein Beitrag zur ostfränkischen Volkskunde", *Jahrbuch für fränkische Landesforschung* 11–12 (1953) 397–406.

Sartori P., "Feuer und Licht im Totenbrauch", *ZVK* 17 (1907) 372–373.

Schiller G., *Ikonographie der christlichen Kunst*, vol. 4.2: Maria (Gütersloh: 1980).

Schmitz-Esser R., "Aufbahren, Verwesen, Auferstehen. Zeitkonzepte beim Umgang mit dem Leichnam im Mittelalter", in Weitbrecht J. – Bihrer A. – Felber T. (eds.), *Die Zeit der letzten Dinge. Deutungsmuster und Erzählformen des Umgangs mit Vergänglichkeit in Mittelalter und Früher Neuzeit*, Encomia Deutsch 6 (Göttingen: 2020) 61–80.

Schreiber G., "Liturgie und Abgabe. Bußpraxis und Beichtgeld an französischen Niederkirchen des Hochmittelalters", *Historisches Jahrbuch* 76 (1957) 1–14.

Schreiner K., *Maria. Jungfrau, Mutter, Herrscherin* (Munich: 1994).

Schreiner K., "Der Tod Marias als Inbegriff christlichen Sterbens. Sterbekunst im Spiegel mittelalterlicher Legendenbildung", in Borst A. – Gravenitz G. von – Patschovsky A. (eds.), *Tod im Mittelalter*, Konstanzer Bibliothek 20 (Constance: 1993) 261–312.

Seidel K., *Die Kerze: Motivgeschichte und Ikonologie*, Studien zur Kunstgeschichte 103 (Hildesheim – Zurich – New York: 1996).

Depoorter M. – De Visch L. – Everaarts M. – Steyaert G. – van Oosterwijk A. (eds.), *Face to Face with Hugo van der Goes: Old Master, New Interpretation* (Veurne: 2022).

Teplitzky T., "Joos van Cleve. Zwei Triptychen mit dem Tod Mariae. Überlegungen zu den Altären aus der Hackeneyschen Hauskapelle und St. Maria im Kapitol und zu ihrer Beziehung zum Haus Habsburg", *Colonia Romanica* 24 (2009), 303–315.

Thiessen H. von, "Das Sterbebett als normative Schwelle. Der Mensch in der Frühen Neuzeit zwischen irdischer Normenkonkurrenz und göttlichem Gericht", *Historische Zeitschrift* 295 (2012) 625–659.

Tingle E., "The Counter Reformation and Preparations for Death in the European Roman Catholic Church, 1550–1700", in Booth P. – Tingle E. (eds.), *A Companion* to *Death, Burial, and Remembrance in Late Medieval and Early Modern Europe, c. 1300–1700*, Brill's Companions to the Christian Tradition 94 (Leiden: 2021) 175–198.

Tschuschke V., "Der Maler Franz Joseph Menninghausen von Vreden. Nachträge zu seinem Leben und Werk", *Studien zur Geschichte des Westmünsterlandes* 48 (1996), 129–134.

Verdon J., *Night in the Middle Ages* (Notre Dame: 2002).

Vincent C., *Fiat Lux. Lumière et luminaires dans la vie religieuse en Occident du XIIIe siècle au début du XVIe siècle*, Histoire Réligieuse de la France 24 (Paris: 2004).

Vincent C., "Lumiere dans les pratiques funéraires au prisme des sources liturgiques", in Bocquet-Liénard A. – Chapelain de Seréville-Niel C. – Dervin S. (eds.), *Des pots dans la tombe (IXe–XVIIIe siècle). Regards croisés sur une pratique funéraire en Europe de l'Ouest*, Publications du CRAHAM, Série antique et médiévale (Caen: 2017) 441–452.

Walsham A., "Domesticating Reformation. Material Culture, Memory, and Confessional Identity in Early Modern England", *Renaissance Quarterly* 69/2 (2016) 566–616.

Welzel B., "Bilder – Kontexte – Identitäten. Die Marienbilder des Conrad von Soest im spätmittelalterlichen Dortmund", in Schilp T. – Welzel B. (eds.), *Dortmund und Conrad von Soest im spätmittelalterlichen Europa*, Dortmunder Mittelalter-Forschungen 3 (Bielefeld: 2004), 309–328.

Youngs D. – Harris S., "Demonizing the Night in Medieval Europe: A Temporal Monstrosity?", in Bildhauer B. – Mills R. (eds.), *The monstrous Middle Ages* (Cardiff: 2003) 134–154.

CHAPTER 10

Contested Kingship – Controversial Coronation: York's Paper Crown

Imke Lichterfeld

1   Introduction

Paper crowns are made to play a king. Children often cut them from sheets of paper as handicraft for their games. They have become a Christmas tradition worn as colourful and festive headgear after opening Christmas crackers: 'Traditionally, Christmas crackers contain a small toy, a corny joke or riddle, and a paper crown'.[1] The coloured crown is a flimsy piece of thin paper that will adorn guests and demand photographs. They are fun and make their wearers joyful and look silly.

This article will illuminate an incidence when there was mocking involved but no light-heartedness. It will delve into the symbolism of the paper crown in the third part of Shakespeare's trilogy on *King Henry VI* (*3 Henry VI*), where – like Christ's crown of thorns – a paper crown is meant to ridicule and subvert: The Duke of York suffers a mock coronation with a paper crown on a battlefield. This incident will be compared to the historical sources, a possible Christian reading, and then evaluated as a highly controversial situation combining unbearable emotion and comic relief.

Shakespeare's *3 Henry VI* (*c*.1591) contains one of the author's most fascinating moments of death: Richard of York, contender of the Plantagenet crown, is killed on the battlefield as he is fighting against the Lancastrian King Henry VI in the Wars of the Roses. Violent death might seem predictable in the History Plays when enemies are confronted.[2] Richard of York, however, is executed by the 'she-wolf of France' (1.4.111), Henry's Queen Margaret of Anjou, who

---

1   Covato E., 'What's the History Behind English Christmas Crackers and the Paper Crowns in Them?', *Country Living*, 25 August 2020. URL: https://www.countryliving.com/life/a46116/christmas-crowns/ Last Access 8 July 2021, n.p.
2   Shakespeare's 'History Plays' as well as those of his contemporaries deal with subject matter of the English medieval past. His two tetralogies concentrate on the English kings from Richard II to Richard III, i.e., the late fourteenth and fifteenth century. Cf. Chernaik, W., *The Cambridge Introduction to Shakespeare's History Plays* (Cambridge: 2007); Hattaway, M. (ed.), *The Cambridge Companion to Shakespeare's History Plays* (Cambridge: 2002).

places the caught opponent on a molehill, tortures him with the details of his youngest son's violent end, and in derision sets a paper crown upon his head. She mocks his pretentious claims to the throne and later orders his head to be displayed on York City walls. Indeed, the scene is of unbearable cruelty, as Margaret is intent on torturing her arch-enemy.

Richard, Duke of York (1411–1460) had claimed the kingship via the female line: he was a descendant of Edward III's third son Lionel, Duke of Clarence (and through the male line, Richard was a descendant of the fifth brother Edmund, Duke of York) while the Lancastrian kings asserted the throne via the fourth son John of Gaunt. 'It was this distinguished ancestry that provided the basis for his explosive participation in the troubled politics of the 1450s', Watts summarises.[3] Richard's father Richard of Conisburgh, Earl of Cambridge had led a treasonous rebellion against Henry VI's father Henry V and was executed for this – a scene Shakespeare stages in *Henry V*.[4] Henry VI, at first childless, had in the past accepted Richard of York as his heir; however, then Henry became father to a son with his wife Margaret: this clarified primogeniture for the descendant of Henry as the rightful heir. However, Richard had gathered so much force and political influence that, in October 1460, Henry, due to pressure and fear, was politically urged to accept Richard as his heir and successor to the throne again. This was the reason for Henry's wife Margaret to not only despise her weak husband but also target the re-established successor and thereby her determined opponent York. Indeed, in the play, too, Margaret is furious with Richard who had interfered in her son's right to his father's crown and deprived Henry's son of the inheritance. In addition, not sufficiently content with the settled achievement of their future acquisition of the crown, the Yorkist faction have declared war against the Lancastrian king and they proceed with this martial intervention to achieve a quicker procuration of the intended inheritance on the battlefield. Their enmity comes to a heat in the 1460 battle of Wakefield.

2   Shakespeare's Richard of York

Shakespeare orchestrates this conflict in *3 Henry VI*. Igor Djordjevic introduces the character of Richard with the following eclectic fascination: 'York brings

---

3   Watts J., "Richard of York, Third Duke of York (1411–1460)", URL: https://doi.org/10.1093/ref:odnb/23503 Last Access 14 March 2021.
4   Shakespeare William, *King Henry V*, ed. T.W. Craik (London: 1995) Scene 2.2. On the conspiracy, see Pugh T.B., *Henry V and the Southampton Plot of 1415* (Gloucester: 1988); Kerrigan, J., "Oaths, Threats and 'Henry V'", *The Review of English Studies* 63/262 (2012) 551–571, 558.

a mixed bag of dynastic "right", Machiavellian political savvy, bravery, English patriotic Gallophobia, seditious skulduggery, fierce family loyalty, vengefulness, and an unforgettable death scene'.[5] As becomes clear from the quote, Richard is an extremely compelling character desperate to promote Yorkist interests. In the battle scene 1.4 in *3 Henry VI*, York is captured by Clifford and Northumberland, both loyal to the Queen. Joining them, Margaret demands satisfaction against his political affront and draws out his death: 'Hold, valiant Clifford! for a thousand causes/ I would prolong awhile the traitor's life.' (1.4.51–52). In fact, once they have bound the pretender to the throne, Margaret protracts the scene and teases the captive.

> Come, make him stand upon this molehill here,
> That raught at mountains with outstretched arms,
> Yet parted but the shadow with his hand.
> What! was it you that would be England's king?
> Was't you that revell'd in our parliament,
> And made a preachment of your high descent? (1.4.67–72)[6]

To set him on a molehill of course stresses that Margaret deems Richard of low status, wrong, and ridiculous in claiming a position any higher than that of cousin to the king. However, apart from the fact that one of the sources mentions a molehill, this setting seems an odd but illuminating choice for an execution for another reason: in the ensuing act, King Henry also places himself upon a molehill – i.e. he lowers himself – and watches the action on the battlefield from afar, commenting on the passing of time, the ephemeral quality of life, and the inanity of human desire.[7] In that scene, the King highlights his own inaptitude and impotence. This parallel, while drawing on the idea of the crown's significance as a burden, then also underlines the vanity of the desire for the crown. In this earlier scene, the place is chosen for the vain, immodest, and unsuccessful Richard as deliberate demotion and humiliation. Margaret inquires after York's four sons and then smears Richard's face with a blood-stained handkerchief: 'Where are your mess of sons to back you now?/ [...] Or, with the rest, where is your darling Rutland?/ Look, York: I stain'd this napkin with the blood' (1.4.73–79). The blood is that of his son: Rutland is the

---

5 Djordjevic I., "'The breath of kings' and 'the pleasure of dying': Political 'Sin' and Theatrical Redemption in *Eikon Basilike*", in Partenza P. (ed.), *Sin's Multifaceted Aspects in Literary Texts* (Göttingen: 2018) 15–36, at 32.
6 Shakespeare William, *King Henry VI Part Three*, eds. Cox J.D.– Rasmussen E. (London: 2001). The line indication will be given in brackets after each quotation for convenience.
7 Shakespeare, *3 Henry VI* 2.5.1–54.

youngest and apparently dearest of Richard's four sons in the play.[8] The scene underscores the brutal rivalry between the Lancastrians and the Yorkists and their willingness to do anything for the protection of their own offspring and power. In the play, as Margaret indicates, Rutland is already dead: Clifford had killed him in the scene before. The tainted handkerchief Margaret holds in this scene becomes a prophetic mark of violent death on her opponent's face, as she vows to provoke him further:

> Why art thou patient, man? thou shouldst be mad;
> And I, to make thee mad, do mock thee thus.
> Stamp, rave, and fret, that I may sing and dance.
> Thou wouldst be fee'd, I see, to make me sport: (1.4.89–92)

Margaret longs to see him perform a scene of heartbreak as his last moment alive and seems enraged by his silence. Indeed, it appears clear that in fact, she wants to induce him to cry for her amusement. These are the sad polemics of execution. Because of Richard of York's pretention to be the rightful king, Margaret mocks him with a paper coronation:

> York cannot speak, unless he wear a crown.
> A crown for York! and, lords, bow low to him:
> Hold you his hands, whilst I do set it on.
> *Putting a paper crown on his head*
> Ay, marry, sir, now looks he like a king! (1.4.93–96)

Margaret arranges this coronation, demanding her Lords to bow before Richard and pronounce him 'like' a king. Paul Strohm comments that 'the point of the derision is an ironical inversion, in which the claimant is given something he sought, but not in the form in which he sought it': a crown, but of paper.[9] Margaret directs an ultimate performance of subversive, comic value. She gleefully scorns at Richard's downfall:

---

8 Rutland was historically born in 1443; this means he was actually seventeen years old at the time of his death in the battle of Wakefield. His brothers are, next to Edward (later Edward IV), George (Duke of Clarence), and Richard (later Duke of Gloucester and Richard III). The historical chronicles and likewise Shakespeare make him younger, in fact they portray him the youngest of the four brothers – which he was not. Edward was a year older, but Clarence and Richard were both much younger, born in 1449 and 1452 respectively. Cf. Genealogical Table in Shakespeare, *3 Henry VI* 426.

9 Strohm P., "York's Paper Crown: 'Bare Life' and Shakespeare's First Tragedy", *Journal of Medieval and Early Modern Studies* 36/1 (2006), 75–102, 80.

> And this is he was his adopted heir.
> But how is it that great Plantagenet
> Is crown'd so soon, and broke his solemn oath?
> As I bethink me, you should not be king
> Till our King Henry had shook hands with death.
> And will you pale your head in Henry's glory,
> And rob his temples of the diadem,
> Now in his life, against your holy oath? (1.4.98–105)

Indeed, by declaring war before the time of the promised inheritance, Richard breaks the deal he had with Henry – which Margaret had obviously already despised –, and therefore she now prolongs the mocking and decides about his fate for good: he shall not be a prisoner but will be executed: 'O, 'tis a fault too too unpardonable!/ Off with the crown, and with the crown his head' (1.4.106–107). After a long speech in which he in turn curses her, she finally utters the obliterative words of fame 'Off with his head' (1.4.179). Strohm underlines that, actually, from the moment of his capture, York 'is as good as dead'.[10] This might be his reason to stay silent, endure, and await his execution. Margaret's verdict closes thus: 'Off with his head and set it on York gates;/ So York may overlook the town of York' (1.4.179–180). Richard's head is to adorn the gates of York. This macabre spectacle will be the end of Richard, Duke of York. It is neither by far the end of the Wars of the Roses nor Shakespeare's description of it, as Richard's sons will indeed acquire the crown through battle, diplomacy, and deviance.

Later in the following play *Richard III*, Richard of Gloucester, almost King Richard III by that time, will remind the audience of what Margaret does in the previous play – 'The curse my noble father laid on thee,/ When thou didst crown his warlike brows with paper' – and thereby continues their expressed aversion.[11] She, historically in exile and dead in 1482, makes an appearance in the later play and haunts the stage like a ghostly old hag. She curses any Yorkist she comes across, thereby reminding the audience how much this civil strife cost. That is how Shakespeare presents the scene he read and learned about from historical chronicles.

---

10 Strohm, "York's Paper Crown" 88.
11 Shakespeare William, *King Richard III*, ed. A. Hammond (London: 1981) 1.3.174–175.

3   History and Historiography

Sylvia Morris claims that 'Shakespeare gets this wrong as Margaret wasn't even present at the Battle of Wakefield' as she apparently spent late December in Scotland, but sources differ here.[12] One of Shakespeare's main sources, Edward Hall's chronicle *The Union of the Two Noble and Illustre Families of Lancastre and Yorke* places Margaret on the battlefield. Hall's 1548 '*Union* [...] is a narrative history of England from the time of Henry IV to Henry VIII'.[13] It serves as a vital source for historical plays of Shakespeare's time:

> Hall's *Union* was also one of the most ideological and moralising of the 16th-century chronicles, searching for causation and seeing history as an object lesson from which to learn. Although Hall shows varying support for the houses of Lancaster and York in his account, he is consistent in his disapproval of rebels and his support for the reigning monarch.[14]

Apart from this verdict on the famous chronicle, Morris states that, in fact, 'Hall gave Shakespeare the cue from which he created one of the most memorable scenes in all his plays'.[15] So Hall inspired Shakespeare's cruel and entertaining display of Richard's moment of death.

As can be expected from most history plays, Shakespeare describes changes in politics taking place rather quickly from one scene to another, putting many years 'into an hourglass'.[16] Yet the historical proceedings of late 1460 might be judged accordingly, as the chronicles prove: a settlement of the contested crown had been reached, if not amicably then at least peaceably: Richard of York had (again) been accepted by Henry VI as his heir through a 'Royal Assent' in the 'Act of Accord'.[17] In Shakespeare, as described above, Margaret reminds the audience of his revelling in parliament.[18] Due to pressure, Richard was historically (re-)accepted by Henry VI as his heir – though the latter had a legitimate son – which Hall describes in the following terms: 'Richard Duke of

---

12   Morris S., "Rehabilitating Shakespeare's 'she-wolf of France', Margaret of Anjou", *The Shakespeare Blog*. 31 May 2018. URL: http://theshakespeareblog.com/2018/05/rehabilitating-shakespeares-she-wolf-of-france-margaret-of-anjou/ Last Access 8 July 2021, n.p.
13   British Library, "Edward Hall's account of Richard III", electronic article, https://www.bl.uk/collection-items/edward-halls-account-of-richard-iii Last Access 13 December 2021, n.p.
14   Ibidem.
15   Morris, "Rehabilitating Shakespeare's 'she-wolf of France'" n.p.
16   Cf. Shakespeare, *King Henry V*, 1.0.31.
17   Cf. Goodman, A., *The Wars of the Roses. Military Activity and English Society, 1452–97* (London – New York: 1981) 41.
18   See above: *3 Henry VI*, 1.4.71.

Yorke, was by the sounde of a trumpet, solempnely proclaimed heire apparãt to the Croune of England, and Protector of the realme.'[19] Of course, this did not fully appease the different factions and created dissent: 'the Quene would spurne and impugne the conclusions agreed and taken in this parliament'.[20] Gerald Harriss remarks that this was due to the nobility's fear of an infringement of their personal possessions and power: 'None of the nobility, at this point, were seeking to initiate a civil war or engineer a change of dynasty, with all the attendant risks to their lives and estates.'[21] Agitation or intervention from Richard disturbed the nobility's arrangements and caused a 'lasting bitterness'.[22] The settlement was thus a diplomatic solution. Harriss explains that the English nobility 'accepted York's contention' as legal to appease the country but thereby demoted Henry VI's son Edward and Queen Margaret to 'the status of rebels', which seemed to prove the longevity of York's royal intentions.[23] This therefore led to further resistance from Lancastrian allies as the queen rebuilt her army in Northern England.[24] The arrangement only created peace for a short period of time. The contention soon culminated on the battlefield and Queen Margaret would – for that moment – find success: Two months after the political agreement, the contender of the crown was executed in the Battle of Wakefield that took place on 30 December 1460 near Sandal Castle. The parties encountered each other in 'The battaill at Wakefeld' and Richard found his death, albeit not through Margaret's torture and tainting but in action:[25]

> when he was in the plain ground betwene his Castle and the toune of Wakefelde, he was enuironed on euery side, like a fish in a net, or a deere in a buckstall: so that he manfully fightying, was with halfe an houre slain and ded, and his whole army discomfited[26]

---

19 Hall Edward, *Hall's chronicle: containing the history of England, during the reign of Henry the Fourth, and the succeeding monarchs, to the end of the reign of Henry the Eighth, in which are particularly described the manners and customs of those periods. Carefully collated with the editions of 1548 and 1550.* London: Printed for J. Johnson et al., 1809, URL: https://archive.org/details/hallschroniccoohalluoft/page/250/mode/2up Last Access 1 July 2021, 249.
20 Hall, *Hall's chronicle* 249.
21 Harriss G., *Shaping the Nation. England 1360–1461* (Oxford: 2005) 639.
22 Goodman, *The Wars of the Roses* 41.
23 Harriss, *Shaping the Nation* 642.
24 Cf. ibidem.
25 Hall, *Hall's chronicle* 250.
26 Ibidem.

According to this account by Hall, Richard dies in action, surrounded by enemies. This would be a quick moment of death that is contrasted in Shakespeare by a prolonged moment of sadistic preparation and elongated dying. Margaret is not mentioned by Hall as being part of the scene; in comparison, Shakespeare imagines the queen confronting her enemy directly. So Shakespeare seems to not adhere to Hall. He mentions Clifford only a few lines later who then kills Rutland.[27] Afterwards, Clifford comes across the dead body of the Duke of York:

> Yet this cruell Clifforde, & deadly bloudsupper not content with this homocyde, or chyldkillyng, came to Ye place wher the dead corps of the duke of Yorke lay, and caused his head to be stryken of, and set on it a croune of paper, & so fixed it on a pole, & presented it to the Quene, not lying farre from the felde, in great respite, and much derision, saiying: Madame, your warre is done, here is your kings raunsome, at which present, was much ioy, and great reioysing.[28]

Shakespeare apparently changes the scene that the chronicle describes differently: Clifford finds the dead body and decapitates the corpse, and then mockingly crowns the severed head with the paper crown. Following the victory, Richard of York's head, together with those of his fallen followers, were placed on a spike. Shakespeare plays with the proceedings and alters the moment of death: he employs the handkerchief with Rutland's blood to taunt the living Richard and uses the paper crown before Richard's death to highlight the failed attempt to overturn the Lancastrian dynasty by adding the scene of teasing that includes Queen Margaret, the higher ranked enemy.

4   Paper Crowns

It might be difficult to envision how the 'spectacular object' of a paper crown can exist on a battlefield.[29] Yet historical sources highlight that a crown was procured for this carnivalesque situation.[30] The symbolic importance of a

---

27 Ibidem.
28 Ibidem.
29 Strohm, "York's Paper Crown" 81.
30 Likewise, it might be questionable how to produce the prop on stage. However, in an artificial surrounding, this seems more smoothly solvable as the flowing example underlines: The director 'Seale solved inherent problems like the paper crown for York in 1.4. "Paper Crowns are not usually part of the impedimenta of battlefields. Where and how was it obtained?" (Jackson B., 51). The solution was to create a ghost role, a boy jester wearing a

paper crown is elicited via a brief overview on its history. Paper crowns today seem an echo of this morbid historical scene. The subversive image of the coronation that feeds into this scene does not originate in the battle of Wakefield. The paper crown tradition can be traced back to the ancient Romans, who wore festive headgear – ivy or vine leaves – to celebrate the Saturnalia that celebrated fertility and abundance:[31] 'In ancient Rome, these celebrations merged with a Bacchanalian festival where the Romans would feast, gamble, exchange gifts, and drink themselves into a state of intoxicated revelry', echoing Greek Dionysian rites.[32] It almost seems as if this can be compared to Margaret; her actions in Shakespeare can be likened to a victory-intoxicated feast, celebrating her enemy's utter loss and her own clever strategy in the battle's preparation.

The tradition carries on via the celebration of winter solstice. In the early modern age, it was adopted by the Inns of Court in London. During the carnival season after Christmas– the Twelve Days of Christmas – similar customs turned hierarchies into an inverted topsy-turviness including the election of a Lord of Misrule.[33] Today, paper crowns are a traditional Christmas headgear – ill-fitting and often brightly coloured.[34] Revelry dominates the symbolism of the paper crown: 'In fact, anyone who dons a paper crown from a Christmas cracker is paying homage to this custom of the mock king.'[35] It almost seems as if Margaret grants Richard such a status of a carnival king, yet this also transgresses to another level, as Colaiacomo underscores:

> paper crown who entered and died with Rutland at Clifford's hand in 1.3. Leaving his body on stage for the next scene not only supplied the requisite prop in a seemingly impromptu manner but did so in a way that thematically reinforced Margaret's cruel taunting of York before she killed him', making Richard almost complicit with a jester. Cf. *3 Henry VI*, 19.

31 Cf. Gildenhard I. – Zissos A. (eds.), "The Bacchanalia and Roman Culture", in Ovid, *Metamorphoses* (Cambridge: 2016) 65–67.

32 Mandryk D., *Canadian Christmas Traditions: Festive Recipes and Stories From Coast to Coast* (Toronto: 2013) 22. Cf. Moffitt, J.F., *Inspiration: Bacchus and the Cultural History of a Creation Myth* (Leiden: 2005) 125; Froidevaux, M., *Eros Bacchus, L'amour et le vin* (Lausanne: 2014) 25, 33; Emmerling-Skala, A., *Bacchus in der Renaissance* (Hildesheim – Zürich – New York: 1994) 58 and 107, electronic version https://www.researchgate.net/publication/264697464_Bacchus_in_der_Renaissance Last Access 13 December 2022.

33 Humphrey, C., *The Politics of Carnival. Festive Misrule in Medieval England* (Manchester – New York: 2001), 47–51; Horner, O., "Christmas at the Inns of Court", in Twycross, M. (ed.), *Festive Drama: Papers from the Sixth Triennial Colloquium of the International Society for the Study of Medieval Theatre, Lancaster, 13–19 July, 1989* (Woodbridge: 1996), 41–53, 42–44.

34 Mandryk, *Canadian Christmas Traditions* 24.

35 Ibidem.

A festive paper crown is certainly not able to wound York more mortally than having to wipe his eyes with a cloth soaked in the blood of the adolescent Rutland. But the queen's cruelty now backfires. The mock-coronation of him who had haughtily, sacrilegiously declared himself king and is now less than nothing changes on her lips into a blasphemous parody of the Passion.[36]

Colaiacomo here stresses the similarity of this moment to Christ's mock coronation. The symbolism of the paper crown connected to Christ's crown of thorns, which is meant to ridicule and subvert, plays a role in the associations displayed in the scene, as this analysis will show below. Clearly the symbolism underlines the exceptional quality of this moment of death.

In his account, Hall also indicates the grand scheme of cyclical history: he prophesies later events and becomes rather moral in his judgement by indicating the later fates of the protagonists in the Wars of the Roses:

> but many laughed then, that sore lamented after, as the Quene her self, and her sonne: And many were glad then of other mens deaths, not knowing that their awne were nere at hande, as the lord Clifford, and other. But surely, mans nature is so frayle, that thinges passed be sone forgotten, and mischiefes to come, be not forsene.[37]

Hall inserts a prolepsis within his battle descriptions; it seems as if the chronicler cannot refrain from a judgement on the cyclical nature of history before turning back to the aftermath of Wakefield. The chronicle then continues to concentrate on the ensuing events and describes how Richard's decapitated head was fixed on a spike to preside over Micklegate Bar, one of York's city gates on the southwest wall, to warn others of rebellion against the Lancastrian faction. Shakespeare did not invent the display of York's head on York's city gates:

> After this victory by y[e] Quene and her parte obteyned, she caused the earl of Salisbury, with all the other prisoners, to bee sente to Pomfret, and there to bee behedded, and sent all their heddes, and the dukes head of Yorke, to be set vpon poles, ouer the gate of the citie of Yorke, an despite

---

36 Colaiacomo P., "Wearing a Crown", in Giorcelli C. – Rabinowitz P. (eds.), *Habits of Being 4* (Minneapolis – London: 2015) 27–55, 39–40.
37 Hall, *Hall's chronicle* 251.

of them, and their lineage: [...]. This ende had the valeant lord, Rychard Plantagenet, duke of Yorke, & this fine ensued of his to much hardines.[38]

In closing his description of the Duke of York's futile attempt to gather the crown for himself, Hall underlines the valiant and hardy nature of the departed York in the political troubles. Hall's sources, William of Worcester's *Annales* termed Wakefield an 'execrabile bellum', and John Whethamstede's *Register* places the scene on an anthill to create a diminished image of a calvary.[39]

Both these sources were adopted not only by Edward Hall but also by Raphael Holinshed, and thereby found their way to Shakespeare. We know 'undoubtably' that Hall and Holinshed are the chronicles Shakespeare consulted as sources for his English history plays.[40] In fact, it appears as if Holinshed might be the more intriguing source for Richard's moment of death: Holinshed's *Chronicles of England, Scotland, and Ireland* is an admirable piece of Tudor historiography and possibly the most important single source for early modern writers: 'Popularly known as Holinshed's *Chronicles*, the work was first printed in 1577. The second, revised and expanded, edition followed in 1587. [...] The importance of Holinshed's *Chronicles* for the understanding of Elizabethan literature, history, and politics cannot be overestimated'.[41] In fact, the sources Shakespeare uses are Tudor chronicles. Of course, historiography of that period might have tainted its explorative and illuminating character as far as objectivity is concerned: 'These Tudor histories made a strong link between the fate of the nation and the character of its ruler'.[42] Holinshed's source was the earlier Chronicle by John Whethamstede, that Shakespeare very likely did not consult but that adds a martyr-like quality to the play that is usually called the third part of *Henry VI* today but that Shakespeare had labelled *The true Tragedie of Richard Duke of Yorke* (*and the death of good King Henrie the Sixt*). Holinshed asserts the cruelty of Richard's death and the mocking aspect of the paper crown display on his head. Strohm underlines in how far this allows

---

38 Ibidem.
39 Goodman, *The Wars of the Roses* 43. Cf. Strohm, "York's Paper Crown" 83–84.
40 British Library, "Edward Hall's account of Richard III", n.p.
41 Holinshed Raphael, *Chronicles of England, Scotland and Ireland* [*The firste* [*laste*] *volume of the chronicles of England, Scotlande, and Irelande conteyning the description and chronicles of England, from the first inhabiting vnto the conquest: the description and chronicles of Scotland, from the first original of the Scottes nation till the yeare of our Lorde 1571: the description and chronicles of Yrelande, likewise from the first originall of that nation untill the yeare 1571 / faithfully gathered and set forth by Raphaell Holinshed*] London: Imprinted for John Hunne, 1577, *The Holinshed Project*, electronic version, Early English Books Online, http://english.nsms.ox.ac.uk/holinshed/ Last Access 1 July 2021.
42 British Library, "Edward Hall's account of Richard III", n.p.

Richard to see his own death as a sacrifice and 'political martyrdom' for his family.[43] Holinshed's 1577 version describes 'The battaile of Wakfielde' in a manner that mostly echoes Hall and uses verbatim phrases – thus demonstrating that he would have been copying the earlier chronicle. He, too, describes brutal Clifford's 'vnmerciful' murder of Rutland and then continues to explore Clifford's 'encounter' with Richard of York:

> Lorde Clifforde [...] came to the place where the dead corpſe of the Duke of Yorke lay, and cauſed his heade to be ſtriken off, and ſet on it a Crowne of Paper, and ſo fixed it on a Poil, and preſented it to the Queene, not lying farre from the fielde, in greate diſpite and muche dereſion, at which preſent muche ioy, and great reioyſing was ſhewed: but they laughed then, that ſhortly after lamented, and were glad then of other mennes deathes, that knewe not theyr owne to bee ſo neare at hande.[44]

The above sounds familiar and echoes Hall. However, his chronicle presents a second record of this scene that diverges from the first and adds the molehill setting to the story. In this deviant account, Richard's extraordinary moment of death echoes the coronation at the calvary:

> Some write that the Duke was taken aliue, and in deriſion cauſed to ſtande vpon a Molehill on whoſe heade they put a garlande in ſteade of a Crowne which they had faſhioned and ſhade of Segges, or Bulruſhes, and hauing ſo crowned him with that Garlande, they kneeled downe b-fore him as the Iewes did to Ch[.../ rist]e in ſcorns, ſaying to him, haile King withoute rule [1587], hayle King without heritage, hayle Duke and Prince without people or poſſeſſions. And at length hauing thus ſcorned him with theſe and dyuerſe o|ther the lyke deſpitefull wordes they ſtroke off his heade, whiche (as yee haue heard) they preſented to the Queene.
>
> [...] After this victorie obteyned thus by the Q. and hir part, the Earle of Saliſburie and all the priſoners were ſent to Pomfret, and there beheaded, whoſe heades togyther with the Duke of Yorkes head, were conueyed to Yorke, and their ſet on Polles ouer the gate of the Citie, in deſpite of them and their lynage.[45]

Holinshed includes the location on the tiny mount as a fascinating detail of this mock-coronation. The depiction strongly mirrors the calvary on Golgatha

---

43   Strohm, "York's Paper Crown" 97.
44   Holinshed, *Chronicles of England, Scotland and Ireland*, 1304.
45   Ibidem.

and equips York with an aura of sacrifice. This might be read as irony but can be interpreted as allowing a certain royalty, or redeeming 'Christological significance' to this instant, as Strohm grants.[46] Whereas the paper crown underlines the carnivalesque derision of politics, this alternative version of the events with Holinshed's second explanation of crowning sedges or bulrushes, possibly not unlike thorns, remind the reader even stronger of a religious association.[47] A symbolic reading of the types of reed could add further details about the scene as a performance – an emoted moment of death – inverting Christianity. As such, the mock-coronation becomes a mock-crucifixion that calls into consideration the Bible's lines:

> Then the soldiers of the governor [...] platted a crown of thorns, and put it upon his head, and a reed in his right hand, and bowed their knees before him, and mocked him, saying, God save thee, King of the Jews, And spitted upon him, and took a reed, and smote him on the head.[48]

In fact, the recent editors of *3 Henry VI* remind the reader of Matthew's lines: 'Holinshed compares the mocking of York to the mocking of Christ, [...] and Margaret's determination to make a game out of her cruelty to York, while not in the chronicles, has a precedent in the buffering and scourging of Christ in the mystery plays'.[49] Cox and Rasmussen here underline that the association with Christ cannot be denied when looking at this scene. In fact, they remark, Shakespeare is not the first to take this idea into medieval or late medieval drama: Similarly, V.A. Kolve highlights the English medieval tradition of a dramatic representation of a scene like this:

> In the thirteenth and fourteenth centuries, as we have already noted, this image changed greatly, in response to new meditational modes, new theological ideas, new fashions in sensibility: Christ is depicted suffering on the cross, His body broken and bleeding. This transformation of Christianity's central image affected all art forms, the drama not least among them.[50]

---

46 Strohm, "York's Paper Crown" 89.
47 It might also be fruitful to apply the Bakhtinian idea of the carnivalesque concept to this situation. Cf. Bakhtin M.M., *Rabelais and His World* (Bloomington: 1984) 5–8; Bakhtin, M.M., *Literatur und Karneval* (Frankfurt: 1990) 47.
48 *Geneva Bible* 1599, electronic version on *Biblegateway*, https://www.biblegateway.com/versions/1599-Geneva-Bible-GNV/ Last Access 28 February 2022, Matthew 27:27–31.
49 Shakespeare, *3 Henry VI*, 216fn.
50 Kolve V.A., *The Play called Corpus Christi* (Stanford: 1966) 175.

In his study, Kolve investigates medieval mystery plays, and in what way their tradition plays a role in the development of drama in the fifteenth century. The mystery plays hint at Christ's pain and display specific suffering.[51] To a certain extent, such is also the case with this moment of death in *Henry VI*: Richard does suffer enormous physical and psychological pain in his death scene, so the audience is prompted to draw a comparison of this mock-coronation with the crucifixion, even if it is aware of the different status and importance of the subjects concerned. Kolve mentions how – in the mystery play – the high priests 'are shown genuinely to hate Him [Christ], and in their brutal fashion to take pleasure in His pain'.[52] An equivalent, devious pleasure also applies to Margaret in *3 Henry VI*. Shakespeare takes up the scene's dramatic value and uses the 'absolutely theatrical', 'medieval culture' to demonstrate an absurd and morbid display.[53] The scene uses the 'sacrificial trope' of the crucifixion to make the mock-coronation spectacular: Margaret's game of torture is similar to that of Christ.[54] Kolve terms this form 'in some sense arbitrary and formal'.[55] Likewise does Margaret seem to follow an idea of formal procedure: an enthronement is a formal ritual – but here, it is full of despotic, subverting spitefulness.

5   Shakespeare's Mock Coronation

It has to be remembered that there is no true sacred status around Richard of York – he is not anointed with royal balm. The scene yet causes mixed emotions: not only a venomous atonement and haughty derision but also a pitiful compassion. Shakespeare deliberately chooses to keep the molehill as a setting for the executional arrangement, as well as the paper crown, albeit not a crown of reeds. If Shakespeare's paper crown is part of a symbolic Christian tradition, it must therefore be stated again that Richard of York is certainly not presented as a Christ-like figure by Shakespeare. Djordjevic confirms this when he states that 'Richard of York, historically and in Shakespeare's rendition, is very far from Christ's example – both spiritually and politically'.[56] He is no mild and meek politician; his ambition ends in failure and there will be neither canonisation nor adoration; he does not find redemption. 'The audience evidently

---

51   Cf. Kolve, *The Play called Corpus Christi* 177–178.
52   Kolve, *The Play called Corpus Christi* 179.
53   Strohm, "York's Paper Crown" 84.
54   Djordjevic, "The breath of kings" 32.
55   Kolve, *The Play called Corpus Christi* 180.
56   Djordjevic, "The breath of kings" 32.

recognizes the Christic tropes in York's death scene, but Shakespeare's figurative encodation of the tableau redirects its dominant emotional response, anger, from the victim to the executioners'.[57] Yet the mocking image of sacrifice grants him a slice of earnest authority and his contention lives on.

The heads of York and his supporters are displayed on the walls of the City of York because it should quench the rebellion at the place where it was officially initiated. Historically, this was not unusual as it demonstrates the victory of the Lancastrians in the face of their enemies. The sources state that the paper crown is added posthumously: 'The Queen additionally ordered that Richard's head be adorned with a paper crown to mock his royal ambitions. It was a sudden, tragic and humiliating end for the man who had tried everything he could before claiming the throne for himself'.[58] However, in Shakespeare, the paper crown is placed upon the living Richard's head. This is a significant choice and unmistakably part of Margaret's 'personal vindictiveness'.[59] Strohm terms this a moment of 'sheer theatricality'.[60]

Richard of York dies a glorious and memorable death; he is not just killed in battle – and it is not the moment of death itself but the process of approaching death and its aftermath that is remembered by spectators, much more than that of Henry V or Henry VI, possibly as much as that of Richard II, a weak king like Henry VI who in the hour of his death – arguably for the first time in his reign – puts up a fight against his executioner. Richard II, in contrast, is often likened to Christ in interpretations of Shakespeare's eponymous play. The Almeida Theatre in London in 2018 advertised their production of *Richard II*, starring Simon Russell Beale in the lead with a poster showing the actor king with a yellow cut-out paper crown. There is no glamourous fun in such paper crowns; there is no comedy but pure tragedy. In their *Falstaff* adaptation of *Henry IV* in 2022 in Cologne, the claimant to the throne Mortimer wears a paper crown while plotting a battle against the king. Here, there is almost pitiful ridicule towards a weak aspirant to the crown.

As the chronicle proves and Shakespeare intensifies, the last moment of York's life is full of disruptive energy and presents a macabre image of a perverted coronation. Richard's claim, of course, lives on to provide the basis for Edward IV's succession in March 1461. Then the dramatis personae in the history cycle move on. The ensuing question will only be whether Margaret's

---

57 Ibidem.
58 Andrews, J.F., *Lost Heirs of the Medieval Crown: The Kings and Queens Who Never Were* (Barnsley: 2019) n.p.
59 Andrews, *Lost Heirs* n.p.
60 Strohm, "York's Paper Crown" 84.

triumph will hold, or, rather, at what point in time the price for her mocking cruelty will be paid in this feud (and it will). That is a different story told in the remainder of this play and in the ensuing history play *Richard III*.

The scene at the beginning of Shakespeare's *3 Henry VI* certainly offers a performative spectacle, a highlight in the trilogy, and a striking moment of death. The scene is less religious and more political in all its pragmatic and theatrical respects. The audience is provoked to a threefold reaction: first, the scene of mocking derision can be read as comic relief in a cruel battle, secondly, putting the crown on a living person's head might evoke an unbearable shock and more sadness in the viewer and make the spectator feel pity for Richard, thirdly, the audience might experience a sort of gratification for the Queen's revenge. In fact, the paper crown may symbolise how easily alliances might change in *Henry VI*. Richard of York in *Henry VI* is 'determined never again to be treated as a political outcast and branded as a traitor'; he does not succeed in this endeavour.[61] Shakespeare places the contemptuous coronation before York's death to further mock the adversary of the Lancastrian and extend his torture with the cruel spectacle. The paper crown symbolises this performance adequately as it represents the game surrounding the throne. Shakespeare gives us a grand moment of death: a controversial coronation-execution to deride and subvert political strife.[62] His paper crown is made to ridicule the mock-king.

Bibliography

Primary Printed Sources

Hall Edward, *Hall's chronicle: containing the history of England, during the reign of Henry the Fourth, and the succeeding monarchs, to the end of the reign of Henry the Eighth, in which are particularly described the manners and customs of those periods. Carefully collated with the editions of 1548 and 1550*. London: Printed for J. Johnson et al., 1809, electronic version, https://archive.org/details/hallschroniclecooohalluoft/page/250/mode/2up Last Access 1 July 2021.

Holinshed Raphael, *Chronicles of England, Scotland and Ireland* [*The firste* [*laste*] *volume of the chronicles of England, Scotlande, and Irelande conteyning the description*

---

61 Goodman, *The Wars of the Roses* 41.
62 Cf. Bronfen's idea on 'the theatricality of the politics'; Bronfen E., "Queen Margaret's Haunting Revenge", in Bronfen E. – Neumeier B. (eds.), *Gothic Renaissance. A reassessment* (Manchester – New York: 2014) 75–91, 77.

and chronicles of England, from the first inhabiting vnto the conquest : the description and chronicles of Scotland, from the first original of the Scottes nation till the yeare of our Lorde 1571 : the description and chronicles of Yrelande, likewise from the first originall of that nation untill the yeare 1571 / faithfully gathered and set forth by Raphaell Holinshed] London: Imprinted for John Hunne, 1577, *The Holinshed Project*, electronic version, Early English Books Online, http://english.nsms.ox.ac.uk/holinshed/ Last Access 1 July 2021.

Geneva Bible 1599, electronic version on *Biblegateway*, https://www.biblegateway.com/versions/1599-Geneva-Bible-GNV/ Last Access 28 February 2022.

Secondary Literature

Andrews J.F., *Lost Heirs of the Medieval Crown: The Kings and Queens Who Never Were* (Barnsley: 2019).

Bakhtin M.M., *Literatur und Karneval* (Frankfurt: 1990).

Bakhtin M.M., *Rabelais and His World* (Bloomington: 1984).

British Library, "Edward Hall's account of Richard III", electronic article, https://www.bl.uk/collection-items/edward-halls-account-of-richard-iii Last Access 13 December 2021.

Bronfen E., "Queen Margaret's Haunting Revenge", in Bronfen E. – Neumeier B. (eds.), *Gothic Renaissance. A reassessment* (Manchester – New York: 2014) 75–91.

Chernaik W., *The Cambridge Introduction to Shakespeare's History Plays* (Cambridge: 2007).

Colaiacomo P., "Wearing a Crown", in Giorcelli C. – Rabinowitz P. (eds.), *Habits of Being 4* (Minneapolis – London: 2015) 27–55.

Covato E., "What's the History Behind English Christmas Crackers and the Paper Crowns in Them?", *Country Living*, 25 August 2020. electronic article, https://www.countryliving.com/life/a46116/christmas-crowns/ Last Access 8 July 2021.

Djordjevic I., "'The breath of kings' and 'the pleasure of dying': Political 'Sin' and Theatrical Redemption in *Eikon Basilike*", Paola Partenza (ed.), *Sin's Multifaceted Aspects in Literary Texts* (Göttingen: 2018) 15–36.

Emmerling-Skala A., *Bacchus in der Renaissance* (Hildesheim – Zürich – New York: 1994), electronic version on https://www.researchgate.net/publication/264697464_Bacchus_in_der_Renaissance Last Access 13 December 2022.

Froidevaux M., *Eros Bacchus, L'amour et le vin* (Lausanne: 2014).

Goodman A., *The Wars of the Roses. Military Activity and English Society, 1452–97* (London – New York: 1981).

Harriss G., *Shaping the Nation. England 1360–1461* (Oxford: 2005).

Hattaway M. (ed.), *The Cambridge Companion to Shakespeare's History Plays* (Cambridge: 2002).

Horner O., "Christmas at the Inns of Court", in Twycross, M. (ed.), *Festive Drama: Papers from the Sixth Triennial Colloquium of the International Society for the Study of Medieval Theatre, Lancaster, 13–19 July, 1989* (Woodbridge: 1996), 41–53.

Humphrey C., *The Politics of Carnival. Festive Misrule in Medieval England* (Manchester – New York: 2001), 47–51.

Jackson B., "On Producing Henry VI", *Shakespeare Survey* 6 (1953), 49–52.

Johnson P.A., *Duke Richard of York, 1411–1460* (Oxford: 1988).

Kerrigan, J., "Oaths, Threats and 'Henry V'", *The Review of English Studies* 63/262 (2012), 551–571.

Kolve V.A., *The Play called Corpus Christi* (Stanford: 1966).

Mandryk D., *Canadian Christmas Traditions: Festive Recipes and Stories From Coast to Coast* (Toronto: 2013).

Moffitt J.F., *Inspiration: Bacchus and the Cultural History of a Creation Myth* (Leiden: 2005).

Morris S., "Rehabilitating Shakespeare's 'she-wolf of France', Margaret of Anjou", *The Shakespeare Blog*. 31 May 2018, electronic article, http://theshakespeareblog.com/2018/05/rehabilitating-shakespeares-she-wolf-of-france-margaret-of-anjou/ Last Access 8 July 2021.

Ovid, *Metamorphoses*, eds. I. Gildenhard – A. Zissos (Cambridge: 2016).

Pugh T.B., *Henry V and the Southampton Plot of 1415* (Gloucester: 1988).

Rubin M., *The Hollow Crown. A History of Britain in the Late Middle Ages* (London: 2005).

Shakespeare William, *King Henry V*, ed. T.W. Craik (London: 1995).

Shakespeare William, *King Henry VI. Part Three*, eds. J.D. Cox – E. Rasmussen (London: 2001).

Shakespeare William, *King Richard III*, ed. A. Hammond (London: 1981).

Strohm P., "York's Paper Crown: 'Bare Life' and Shakespeare's First Tragedy", *Journal of Medieval and Early Modern Studies* 36/1 (2006) 75–102.

Watts J., "Richard of York, third duke of York (1411–1460)", *Oxford Dictionary of National Biography*, electronic article, https://doi.org/10.1093/ref:odnb/23503 Last Access 14 March 2021.

CHAPTER 11

Miseraciones eius super omnia opera eius: Lucas Cranach the Elder's 'Der Sterbende' on the Brink of Reformation?

Friedrich J. Becher

1   Introduction

A man dies. Accompanied by his sorrowful wife and a priest he turns to the cross, his face showing undeniable signs of age, sickness, and suffering. Meanwhile, a doctor on his left concludes a final exam and two men go through his personal belongings. In the corner, a notary signs the dying man's last will. Unbeknownst to all but the soon-to-be-deceased, his soul is leaving his body, opening the doors to other, invisible and immortal realms. A guardian angel has joined the priest in his effort to remind the man of his sins and his faith in God's grace. The soul, depicted as a visibly younger version of the man and crying for mercy, finds itself torn between heaven and hell. Three demons appear to be witnesses of the prosecution, showcasing exhibits of the man's sins. In contrast, merely one angel with one sign of good deeds tries to help the man's soul. Beneath the scenery, right next to the doctor, hell opens its gates and a grinning demon reminds the dying man of his wrongdoings as well as of his earthly luxuries. Seeing all that, it could be concluded that the soul of the man is in serious danger and the final judgment is yet to come. But above all this turmoil, God has come to a decision. Accompanied by the heavenly choir of angels and saints singing in praise, God the Father holds Jesus while the Holy Spirit, depicted as a dove, flies above them. Jesus raises his wounded hands. In doing that, he reminds the demons, the angels, the soul, and the viewers of his suffering: God died for mankind's sins, so they can rely on God's mercy. The soul can rejoice for it will live in eternal grace.

    Above this vivid scenery of grace and damnation, another scene depicts a family praying while the mother of God appears. This scene is framed by two medallions with portraits of both a male and a female. Two prominent inscriptions are included. The one separating the scene of judgment and the praying family refers to Psalm 144.5 of the Vulgata, 'MISERACIONES EIUS SUPER OMNIA OPERA EIUS' – 'His mercy is upon all his works' – and must therefore be understood as a theme for the whole painting. The other inscription is a clue to why the painting as a physical piece exists. The painting was intended as an epitaph for Valentin Schmitburg, the father of Heinrich Schmitburg, who donated it in 1518. The father himself stays without a name, he is only identified through his fathership.

The donation was to be installed in the Nikolaikirche in Leipzig. Heinrich Schmitburg thereby replaced an older epitaph for his father in the same church. While the old epitaph was said to mark the place of the fathers burial, the original placement of the Cranach painting seems unknown.[1] [Fig. 11.1]

This chapter will elaborate on the artwork as a painted creed. Though beginning with a close description of the scenery, a step back is needed to highlight time and circumstances. The chapter will question the artist and the patron in terms of relationship(s): How did artists and donors work at the time? Who decided on what would be created and which underlying reasons – other than the painting's iconographic clues – have to be considered? In the process, the chapter will highlight how definitions of "traditional" or "reformed" beliefs are merely retrospective distinctions. Instead, the painting depicts general and ambiguous religious values shared by all – or most – Christians of the time.

According to the second inscription, the painting was used as an epitaph from 1518 onwards. Whilst some evidence – such as overlaps and grubbily written letters – suggest the existence of an earlier version, which was merely adapted and re-used by adding the two inscriptions, the year 1518 shall be used as a date post quem.[2] The artist's signature can be found on one of the boxes on

---

1 In 1522, the painting was incorporated in a bigger epitaph for the whole (male) Schmitburg family. About the locations of both the old and the new epitaphs see Preising D., "'Brille des Todes'. Das Einzelbild als Anleitung zu gutem Sterben im Spätmittelalter", in Preising D. – Rief M. – Vogt C. (eds.), *Der gute Weg zum Himmel. Spätmittelalterliche Bilder zum richtigen Sterben: das Gemälde ars bene moriendi aus der Sammlung Peter und Irene Ludwig*, exh. cat., Ludwiggalerie Schloss Oberhausen, Suermondt-Ludwig-Museum (Bielefeld – Berlin: 2016) 15–42, here 35. Stepner S., *Inscriptiones Lipsienses locorum publicorum academicorum pariter ac senatoriorum memorabiles* (Leipzig: 1686) No. 488. Heiland S., "Der Sterbende", in Guratzsch H. (ed.), *Vergessene altdeutsche Gemälde. 1815 auf dem Dachboden der Leipziger Nikolaikirche gefunden – 1997 anläßlich des 27. Deutschen Evangelischen Kirchentages präsentiert*, exh. cat., Museum der bildenden Künste Leipzig (Heidelberg: 1997) 54–56, here 54. Wulf I., *Protestantische Gemäldeepitaphien im Raum Wittenberg und in angrenzenden Territorien. Zur Entwicklung und Funktion des Gemäldeepitaphs vom Beginn der lutherischen Reformation bis zur Veröffentlichung des Konkordienbuches. 1517–1580* (Ph.D. dissertation, Freie Universität Berlin: 2011) 94.

2 The option was first discussed by Vogel J., "Zur Cranachforschung", *Zeitschrift für bildende Kunst, Neue Folge* 18 (1907) 219–226; Friedländer M.J. – Rosenberg J., *Die Gemälde von Lucas Cranach* (Berlin: 1932) 46. Further changes can be seen in the infrared and X-Ray scans provided by the Cranach Digital Archive, entry DE_MdbKL_40, online via http://lucascranach.org/DE_MdbKL_40 (Last checked on 06/24/2022).

CRANACH THE ELDER'S 'DER STERBENDE' ON BRINK OF REFORMATION? 213

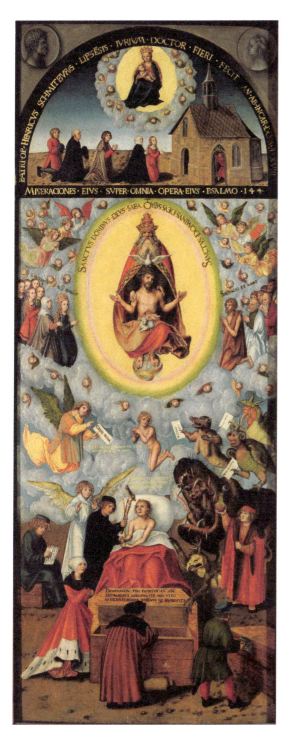

FIGURE 11.1
Lucas Cranach the Elder:
Der Sterbende, 1518, oil on
limewood, 93 × 36.2 cm, Leipzig,
Museum der bildenden Künste,
Inv.Nr. 40
IMAGE © WIKIMEDIA
COMMONS

the painting's lower part. Depicting a winged dragon, the artist is the famous Lucas Cranach the Elder (and/or his workshop). The patron and donor was Heinrich Schmitburg; the donation was made in Leipzig. Considering the time, the question about the religious background arises.

2 The Donor, the Craftsman and the Theologian: a Triangle of Influences

Just a year before, in 1517, a young Martin Luther published his ideas for a different approach to Christianity and structural changes within the church as a whole in Wittenberg.[3] Primarily, Luther criticized the sale of indulgences in his work. Not only did he consider it theologically wrong, but he also condemned the politically explosive monetary reason for the trade: The construction of the new St. Peter's Church in Rome was financed by the sale of indulgences. Luther, on the other hand, did not see God's grace as a commodity that could be bought; rather, good deeds should be performed for one's neighbours or to the local community. In addition to his 95 theses, Luther also prominently elaborated on this conviction in his "Sermon on indulgences and grace" from 1518. In the 95 theses, Luther attacked the structural and theological convictions of the Catholic Church, but he left other core elements of the faith untouched. He continued to regard Mary, the Mother of God, and the saints in general as necessary and important. Though the Reformation was less of a process but an accumulation of efforts happening for years in advance and all through society, the dramatic performance of Luther would later be known as a famous jump-start for what would ultimately result not only in a Reformation within the Roman-Catholic church itself but the birth of Protestantism – when in fact various actors from all over christianity were actively involved in changing the old church system. A confession that would become famous for abolishing the cult of the saints and the practice of indulgences, relying only on Scripture and faith in God's mercy. In 1518, however, Luther and other like-minded scholars were not trying to create a new doctrine, but were working on challenging the pope's authority. Why pay for indulgences, when the money would flow to the

---

3 As introductions to faith and beliefs in the region at the beginning of the sixteenth century see Bünz E. – Kühne, H. (ed.), *Alltag und Frömmigkeit am Vorabend der Reformation in Mitteldeutschland. Wissenschaftlicher Begleitband zur Ausstellung 'Umsonst ist der Tod'*, Schriften zur Sächsischen Geschichte und Volkskunde 50 (Leipzig: 2015). Bünz E., "Kirchliches Leben und Laienfrömmigkeit im spätmittelalterlichen Leipzig", in Bünz E. – Kohnle A. (eds.), *Das religiöse Leipzig. Stadt und Glauben vom Mittelalter bis zur Gegenwart*, Quellen und Forschungen zur Geschichte der Stadt Leipzig 6 (Leipzig: 2013) 27–61.

Vatican to build a new cathedral? In fact, he even opposed the idea of paying money for a shorter time in the eternal fires. To Luther, giving money to the poor and local parishes seemed the better option, resulting in him questioning the profane political impact of the pope in faraway Rome.[4] Therefore Luther may not have been a theological revolutionary (yet) but he already posed a danger to the church and ultimately to the German emperor and the political system in general.

By 1518, Cranach had already created a woodcut for Luther's "Eyn geystlich edles Bucheleynn" of 1516.[5] Some years later, the Luther and the Cranach families were friends. In retrospect this can be interpreted as a personal relationship in which both the theologian and the artist shared ideas and beliefs regarding how one should save one's soul.[6] This interpretation, while not wrong, cannot lead to the conclusion that Cranach used his creative powers to sneak subversive anti-Catholic (or at least anti-papal) ideas into his paintings. His workshop ran like a manufacture. Just like most artists of their time, Cranach and his employees produced what was requested – and paid for. The idea of an inspired artist, pouring soul and personal beliefs in the artworks, might be attractive in retrospect but Cranach and his collaborators worked for Catholic patrons years after getting in close contact to Luther.[7] Around 1518, Cranach

---

[4] Various of the ninety-five theses elaborate on the problem of indulgences versus giving money to the poor and local parishes. Most prominently, these 27 highlights the idea of souls leaving purgatory because of money (well) spent. Theses 28 and 42, 43 and 45 discuss this idea even further. In his "Sermon of indulgence and grace" he publishes the same arguments, pointing out that financing the new cathedral in Rome would be an acceptable donation, if both the poor and the local parish were helped before. He adds, that even then giving money to the Vatican must not be considered an indulgence! Luther also mentioned several saints and Mary in his 95 theses. In theses 29, 58, 59 and 77, he points out the positive aspects of different saints, see Dixon C., "Luther's Ninety-Five Theses and the Origins of the Reformation Narrative", *English Historical Review* 132 (2017), 533–569, here 556. Luther Martin, *Disputatio pro declaratione virtutis indulgentiarum*, ed. J.K.F. Knaacke et al., Vol. 1 (Weimar: 1883) 229–238. Luther Martin, *Ein Sermon von Ablaß und Gnade*, ed. J.K.F. Knaacke et al., Vol. 1 (Weimar: 1883) 239–246. Later on, Martin Luther's work on the "Magnificat" would highlight his adoration for the mother of Jesus. For further references on the idea of Mary in the work of Luther, see footnote 29.

[5] Luther Martin, *Vorrede zu der unvollständigen Ausgabe der "deutschen Theologie"*, ed. J.K.F. Knaacke et al., Vol. 1 (Weimar: 1883), 152–153, here 152. Schuchardt G., "Cranach und Luther – Aspekte einer Partnerschaft", in *Cranach, Luther und die Bildnisse. Thüringer Themenjahr "Bild und Botschaft"*, exh. cat. Wartburg (Regensburg: 2015) 10–23, here 12.

[6] Schuchard, "Cranach und Luther" 12–8. Jung M., *Die Reformation. Theologen, Politiker, Künstler* (Göttingen: 2008) 163.

[7] An introduction to the development from commissioned artist or artistic craftsman to autonomous and inspired artist is offered in Bätschmann O., *Ausstellungskünstler. Kult und Karriere im modernen Kunstsystem* (Cologne: 1997). See also Warnke M., *Hofkünstler. Zur*

not only created the painting in question with its (allegedly) ambivalent iconography, but also explicitly Catholic imagery: In his altar for the Nikolaikirche in Jütebog, two panels show the souls in purgatory. Even though the Panels were heavily damaged during the Reformation later on, the core elements are still recognisable. Below, the souls are suffering; above, a Maria lactans is about to intercede. An angel lifts up a soul. The destruction was mainly aimed at the faces of the figures; later, iconoclasts were active here.[8] The decisions on what kind of message should be delivered was the patrons' to make, thereby leaving merely the artistic choices such as composition and details to the painters.[9] For instance, the painting in question shows remarkable resemblances to Cranach's other works as well as to pieces by other artists of the time. While this chapter will discuss some of those resemblances in relation to their religious significance, others shall be excluded from our analysis for being mere aesthetic choices. Such is the case, for instance, of the demons, which seem to be taken right out of a work by Hieronymus Bosch – thereby indicating how Cranach was aware of artistic tendencies of his time and colleagues.[10]

Without naming the deceased father Valentin, the inscription gives insights into the mechanisms of patronage in the early sixteenth century. The patron Heinrich Schmitburg, a lawyer working as chancellor for the diocese of Naumburg from 1518 onwards, came from a family of medical experts and was

---

Vorgeschichte des modernen Künstlers (Cologne 1985); Krems E., "Vom Hofkünstler zum Ausstellungskünstler: Künstler und ihre Mäzene in der Frühen Neuzeit und der Moderne", in Strobel J. – Wolf J. (ed.), *Maecenas und seine Erben. Kunstförderung und künstlerische Freiheit – von der Antike bis zur Gegenwart* (Stuttgart: 2015) 198–216. Whereas Cranach was not dependent on a specific patron but worked for several commissioners, his workshop was still embedded in the idea of artistic craftsmen working on demand rather than autonomous inspiration.

8   Lucas Cranach the Elder: *Retabel der Nikolaikirche Jütebog*, 1515–1520, oil on limewood, 147.5 × 190.7 cm, Jütebog, Nikolaikirche. A Maria lactans is a iconographical type of depiction of Mary. She is depicted with bare breast(s), offering her breast milk as a relief, and in the Cranach piece, maybe as a way of soothing the burning torture. For a discussion on the painting, see Wegmann S., "Das nicht erloschene Fegefeuer. Zum Cranach-Retabel in der Nikolaikirche zu Jütebog", in *Johann Tetzel und der Ablass*, exh. cat. Jütebog (Berlin: 2017) 45–56.

9   Tacke A., "Mit Cranachs Hilfe. Antireformatorische Kunstwerke vor dem Tridentiner Konzil", in Brinkmann B. (ed.), *Cranach der Ältere*, exh. Cat., Städel Museum (Ostfildern: 2007) 81–89. Tacke A., "Lucas Cranach der Schnellste. Ein Künstler als Werkstattleiter", in Stamm R. (ed.), *Lucas Cranach der Schnellste*, exh. cat., Kunstsammlungen Böttcherstraße (Bremen: 2009), 12–28. Schuchardt "Cranach und Luther" 10–23.

10 Not only did Cranach travel to the Netherlands in 1508/09, he also copied Boschs painting of the Judgment day. Thereby it can be concluded that in 1518, Cranach was well aware of Boschs Oeuvre and his popular way of depicting hells minions. See Heiland "Der Sterbende" 50.

a respected member of his community. He never met Luther, but working for the local authorities Heinrich Schmitburg surely knew of Luther's ideas. He had even planned to meet Luther but died in 1520 before having the opportunity to do so. Allegedly, his motivation to meet Luther in person came from him sharing a similar set of beliefs. Unfortunately, the source for that information was Luther himself – bragging about this planned meeting and the bequest of 200 Gulden in a letter to his friend Spalatin.[11]

In purchasing a custom (or at least customized) work by the famous Lucas Cranach the Elder, Heinrich Schmitburg showcased his various capacities. Not only does this prove his wealth, but it also implies his need to exhibit his standing in society. He could afford to replace an epitaph where there was no need. His father, nameless to the visitor of the epitaph in the church in Leipzig, died in 1490. Barely anything is known about his faith. We only know that Valentin Schmitburg went on a pilgrimage to Jerusalem.[12] Almost thirty years after his death, his son Heinrich Schmitburg replaced the old epitaph with a new one, displaying his wealth and his Christian faith, and preparing a way of being remembered himself. By adding his name to the piece, the world would not only remember the father, but also – and even more so – the son.[13]

But why did he do this almost thirty years after his father's death? Why replace an existing epitaph with one displaying such an unnerving scenery? Every recorded contact of Luther and Schmitburg took place after the donation of the painting and there is no evidence suggesting that Schmitburg articulated any admiration for Luther before or in 1518. Still the coincidence seems odd. Could it be a hidden sign of sympathy for the new set of beliefs that was about to emerge, placed right in the centre of Leipzig – a city that would turn to Protestantism in 1539? In the past, various scholars argued for the painting to be either specifically influenced by the Reformation or, in contradiction, a statement of Catholicism. For instance, Bonnie-Jeanne Noble found proof for Catholic – and hence anti Reformation – iconography. In contrast, Jan

---

11   Schuchardt C., *Lucas Cranach des Aelteren Leben und Werke. Nach urkundlichen Quellen bearbeitet. Dritter Theil* (Leipzig: 1871) 170–171.
12   Buchwald G., *Reformationsgeschichte der Stadt Leipzig* (Leipzig; 1900) 17.
13   Preising "'Brille des Todes'" 35. Bünz E., "Rekonstruktion des Epitaphs der Familie Schmidburg-Pistoris", in Kühne H. – Bünz E. – Müller T. (eds.), *Alltag und Frömmigkeit am Vorabend der Reformation in Mitteldeutschland*, exh. cat., Museum am Lindenbühl, Stadtgeschichtliches Museum Leipzig, Kulturhistorisches Museum Magdeburg (Petersberg: 2013) 97–100, here 100. Heiland „Der Sterbende" 54. Wulf *Protestantische Gemäldeepitaphien* 93–94. Buchwald „Reformationsgeschichte" 17. Schuchardt C., *Lucas Cranach des Aelteren Leben und Werke. Nach urkundlichen Quellen bearbeitet. Zweiter Theil* (Leipzig: 1851) 170–171.

Nicolaisen and Dagmar Preising interpreted the same painting as an obvious depiction of lutheran ideas.[14]

In contrast, this chapter will show how Cranach's "Dying Man" is neither nor, but a typical example of the changing beliefs in early sixteenth century middle Germany.

To elaborate on that, the painting itself has to be examined to extract its iconographic details. By contrasting those with both traditional and contemporary texts, evidence will be procured if and how the epitaph reflects the changing situation of the time regarding ideas of faith and salvation.

It must already be emphasised that, apart from its mastery of staging, the work of art does not show any of Cranach's innovations in terms of the theology behind it, but rather compresses the *ars moriendi* sequence of images, which was widely known around 1500, into a simultaneous representation.

3 Death in Times of Pestilence: the Art of Dying (Well)

The *ars moriendi* – the art of dying (well) – was a series of scenes and texts from unknown origins that emerged in the fifteenth century during times of need. The *ars moriendi* arose as a reaction to the great waves of deaths since the middle of the fourteenth century. In 1346, the plague reached Europe. The disease quickly developed into a pan-European pandemic, which in its first and most extensive wave was rampant from 1347 to 1352. Its two manifestations, bubonic plague and pneumonic plague, the disease killed up to a third of the European population, sometimes within hours and at a rapid rate of spread in the well-connected Europe. In the following centuries, the plague was to flare up again and again. At the same time, from the beginning of the fourteenth century there were repeated major famines, and between 1337 and 1453 the Hundred Years' War, the first all-continental war, and its effects on everyday life were part of the reality of life for a large part of the population of "Europe". For the pastoral care of the people, this meant that they died more and more frequently without the assistance of a clergyman and the associated Catholic-Christian rituals of care for the afterlife, so that the possibility of

---

14   Preising "'Brille des Todes'" 34. Vogel "Zur Cranachforschung" 225. Noble B.-J., *The Lutheran Paintings of the Cranach Workshop. 1529–1555* (Ph.D. dissertation, Northwestern University: 1998) 79. Nicolaisen J., "Der Hofmaler in der Handelsstadt – Aufträge und Auftraggeber Lucas Cranachs in Leipzig", in Guratzsch H. (ed.), *Vergessene altdeutsche Gemälde. 1815 auf dem Dachboden der Leipziger Nikolaikirche gefunden – 1997 anläßlich des 27. Deutschen Evangelischen Kirchentages präsentiert*, exh. cat., Museum der bildenden Künste Leipzig (Heidelberg: 1997) 100–111.

saving the salvation of the soul was not guaranteed. Moreover, in the course of the epidemics there was an increasingly glaring lack of clergy who had either died themselves, were unable to cope with the increase in the number of dying people to be cared for or avoided the sick for fear of infection.[15]

The believers knew that their faith would be finally tested on their deathbed. If they resisted the temptations of the diabolical visitations, repented of their sins and thus proved their faithfulness, they would be assured of God's grace. The fear of hell would give way to heavenly bliss. This particular judgement – the arbitral judgement of individuals at the moment of their death on the basis of their selective behaviour – was only apparently in contradiction to the universal judgement at the end of days. This universal judgement at the bodily resurrection of all human beings was then rather to serve as a confirmation of the judgement that had already taken place, as a proclamation of damnation or redemption. In contrast to the older idea of the universal judgement with a weighing of human sins and good works, the possibility of significantly influencing the judgement through faithfulness and true repentance in the last moments of life was central in the particular judgement. In order to be able to pass and accompany this process of the last trial in extremis – especially as a person affected, but also as a caring relative as well as a responsible pastor – a ritualised form of guidance was needed, which was available in the form of the *ars moriendi*, the art of dying. This existed in a wide variety of forms, depending on the context of use and the recipient. For clergy and educated lay people, there were often theological texts written in Latin, which dealt with theological questions of dying, the spiritual preparation and the actual process on a spiritual level. More widespread among lay people, on the other hand, were text-picture compilations in book form, which explained the *ars moriendi* in practical terms with short, memorable passages of text and approximately corresponding sequences of pictures and thus served as a guide. These handouts did not merely offer practical instructions, but explored the necessity of

---

15   Roeck B., *Der Morgen der Welt. Geschichte der Renaissance* (Munich: 2017) 381–382 and 386. Vögele J. – Spanier L., "Stadt, Krankheit und Tod. Zur Entwicklung der Sterblichkeit in historischer Perspektive", in von Hülsen-Esch A. – Westermann-Angerhausen H., *Zum Sterben schön. Alter, Totentanz und Sterbekunst von 1500 bis heute. Band 1: Aufsätze*, exh. cat., Museum Schnütgen, Goethemuseum, Kunsthalle Recklinghausen (Regensburg: 2006) 211–226, here 212–213; Kühne H., "Frömmigkeit unterwegs", in Kühne H. – Bünz E. – Müller T. (eds.), *Alltag und Frömmigkeit am Vorabend der Reformation in Mitteldeutschland*, exh. cat., Museum am Lindenbühl, Stadtgeschichtliches Museum Leipzig, Kulturhistorisches Museum Magdeburg (Petersberg: 2013) 159–160; Fleck L., *Entstehung und Entwicklung einer wissenschaftlichen Tatsache. Einführung in die Lehre vom Denkstil und Denkkollektiv* (Frankfurt [Main]: 1980) 3–4; Smith J.C., *The Northern Renaissance* (London: 2004) 199; Ariès P., *Studien zur Geschichte des Todes im Abendland* (Munich: 1981) 34.

such help and the process. They were intended to serve both as help in the case of death and, beforehand, to offer possibilities for the theological realisation of one's own mortality. Some texts were particularly decisive and widespread in this regard; they all came from the circle of the councils in Basel and Constance. From these, texts for the laity developed which had the same message in terms of content, but a different conception than those previously thought for clerics. The versions for the laity dispensed with complex theological thought structures, were more concentrated on aspects of help for self-help, but also focused on piety and preparation before and accompaniment in dying. These texts for lay people were based on two texts in particular: The "Speculum artis bene moriendi", which presumably came from the circle of an order of preachers and was attributed to various authors such as Albertus Magnus, Thomas Aquinas, Heinrich Seuse or Hugo Ripelin, and the text "De arte moriendi" written by Johannes Gerson in 1408. The abridgement of the latter text was what became known as the *ars moriendi* text for laymen in combination with a sequence of images; the text was also attributed to Gerson, but written by an anonymous author and dated between 1408 and probably before 1414. The series of pictures – even if they became known in combination with the text – were not produced as direct illustrations of the text and were therefore independent. In the case of the series of images, too, it remains unclear who developed the images that would eventually become established and spread throughout "Europe" together with the texts. It is assumed that there was an original sequence of images, which is no longer preserved today, and which was copied or imitated several times. The best-known successor to this archetype, which is presumably from the northern Alps, is the sequence of pictures by Master E.S. – which can be dated to around 1445 – who, however, was very probably not the master of the archetype himself.[16]

---

16   Preising "'Brille des Todes'" 16. Lehrs M., "Der Künstler der Ars moriendi und die wahre erste Ausgabe derselben", *Jahrbuch der Königlich Preußischen Kunstsammlungen* 11 (1890) 161–168; Höfler J., *Der Meister E.S.. Ein Kapitel europäischer Kunst des 15. Jahrhunderts. Textband* (Regensburg: 2007); Plotzek J., "Ars moriendi, Neapel", in Plotzek J. et. al. (ed.), *Ars vivendi – Ars moriendi* (München: 2011) 546–571; Brückner W., "Der gute Tod", in Kühne H. – Bünz E. – Müller T. (eds.), *Alltag und Frömmigkeit am Vorabend der Reformation in Mitteldeutschland*, exh. cat., Museum am Lindenbühl, Stadtgeschichtliches Museum Leipzig, Kulturhistorisches Museum Magdeburg (Petersberg: 2013) 91–92, here 91; Scheffczyk L., "Himmel und Hölle: Kontinuität und Wandel in der Lehrentwicklung", in Greshake G. (ed.), *Ungewisses Jenseits? Himmel – Hölle – Fegefeuer*, Schriften der Katholischen Akademie in Bayern 121 (Düsseldorf: 1986) 41–42; Hesse J., "Ars moriendi. Die Kunst, zwischen den Versuchungen der Teufel und den Ermahnungen der Heiligen heilsam zu sterben", in Gesellschaft für das Schweizerische Landesmuseum (eds.), *Himmel – Hölle – Fegefeuer. Das Jenseits im Mittelalter*, exh. cat., Schweizerisches Landesmuseum (Zurich: 1994)

The *ars moriendi* – both in texts and pictures depending on the individuals' knowledge and capacities – showed people what would happen in their final moments. Eleven pictures constituted the standard *ars moriendi*. Five temptations were each followed by a scene of a helping angel. The eleventh picture concluded the series with a final scene after that process. Generally, the pictures had a similar composition: The focal point would be a bed with a dying man in it. Around the bed, demons and their illusions, angels and their good ideas as well as the patient's family and other worldly personnel – a priest, a maid and such – would make their entrance, all challenging or helping the dying man's final trial. The devil's spawns would try to seduce mortals in their faith, their desperation, impatience, vanity and greed by manifesting gruesome images of hell, by mirroring the patient's sins or by showing them earthly delights and heavenly pleasures. In contrast, Angels would try to secure the mortal's beliefs in God's unlimited mercy and grace which would save them from eternal damnation by reminding them of good examples like certain saints or by hiding temptations from the view. The *ars moriendi* was to be used as a guideline in case no priest was available as well as a handbook for timely preparations throughout life. With the help of the *ars moriendi* one would be able to navigate through those temptations and reach the goal of a merciful judgement.[17]

4   Reading Cranach: the Iconography of the "Sterbender"

In the "Sterbender" by Cranach, he not only depicted such a process of a final personal judgment with witnesses of both prosecution and defence and final temptations, but he also very visibly used scenes that people in his time would recognize from the *ars moriendi*. While shrinking an eleven piece series of images – five temptations, five helping angels, one final scene of the good death – into a single artwork, various persons seem to be right out of the series.

262–265, here 262; Wegmann S., *Auf dem Weg zum Himmel. Das Fegefeuer in der deutschen Kunst des Mittelalters* (Ph.D. dissertation, Universität Regensburg: 2000) 5.

17   Rudolf R., *Ars moriendi. Von der Kunst des heilsamen Lebens und Sterbens* (Cologne – Graz: 1957); Brückner "Der gute Tod" 91; Niederkorn-Bruck M., "Das Leben stirbt, wo es beginnt, und aufersteht, wo es zerrinnt. Der Tod und das Leben im Mittelalter", in Hameter W. – Niederkorn-Bruck M. – Scheutz M. (eds.), *Freund Hein? Tod und Ritual in der Geschichte*, Querschnitte Band 22 (Innsbruck – Vienna – Bozen: 2007) 60–81, here 67–68; Haas A., "Tod und Jenseits in der deutschen Literatur des Mittelalters", in Gesellschaft für das Schweizerische Landesmuseum (eds.), *Himmel – Hölle – Fegefeuer. Das Jenseits im Mittelalter*, exh. cat., Schweizerisches Landesmuseum (Zurich: 1994) 69–78, here 75; Olds C.C., *Ars Moriendi: A Study of the Form and Content of fifteenth-century Illustrations of the art of dying* (Ph.D. dissertation, Pennsylvania University: 1966) 47.

By showing the dying man's wife, the people going through his treasures and the doctor Cranach quotes the *ars moriendi*'s temptations through faith, desperation and greed. The boxes are symbols of earthly possessions, the man can not take those with him. The woman – symbolising the man's family – can be regarded as another personal belonging he will have to leave behind.[18]

All those things possessed a high risk for sin. Only when one can free oneself from mourning the loss of worldly luxuries, one will be able to go to heaven. Clinging onto them, even worrying too much about family means straying further from salvation. Therefore the notary in the left corner is of great help. Putting the dying man's last will into writing, he frees the man from earthly worries. He can focus on his own death.

The wife also poses another risk. As the man learns from the demon crawling out of hell's mouth, he sinned and fulfilled the devil's commands with his wife. Lust being a cardinal sin, the wife is shown as a temptress, which leads the man to sin. In pointing this out, the demon could lead the dying man right into despair from his sins. In the spirit of the *ars moriendi* it would be – from the devil's perspective – a good idea to just give up. Why even try to repent and belief?

Ultimately the doctor is both a sign of sin as much as he is a sign of positive help and patronage. In the figure of the doctor, ambivalently placed right next to the gates of hell, both positive and negative aspects can be found. Doctors can be a great risk by clouding people's belief in God's grace while highlighting worldly powers such as themselves and their knowledge. Not knowing their own shortcomings, they can offer false hope in a time where there is no hope for a cure and when a priest would be the better option to stand next to the bed.[19] In the painting, both are present. The priest is very close to the dying man, whereas the doctor – examining what seems to be a final urine sample – makes space for another kind of help. The doctor, generally a possible source of risk when its a severe diagnosis such as "death", is depicted as understanding professional who knows his own limits. Heinrich Schmitburg, the donor, came from a family of medical experts. His own father, the recipient of the epitaph, worked as a doctor and the family even endowed a full time medical position for

---

18   Ariès "Studien zur Geschichte" 39.
19   Laager J. (ed.), *Ars moriendi. Die Kunst, gut zu leben und gut zu sterben. Texte von Cicero bis Luther* (Zurich: 1996) 274; Seiler R., *Mittelalterliche Medizin und Probleme der Jenseitsvorsorge*, in Gesellschaft für das Schweizerische Landesmuseum (ed.), *Himmel – Hölle – Fegefeuer. Das Jenseits im Mittelalter*, exh. cat. Schweizerisches Landesmuseum Zürich (Zurich: 1994) 117–124, here 117–118 and 122.

the local university in Leipzig.[20] Knowing this, it is highly unlikely that a painting paid for by a patron of such a background would show a sinful doctor. More likely, the figure of the doctor was meant as a personal ode to the father and the capabilities of the profession. Where there was hope, a good doctor – like the father – could help. Where death was upon the patient, a good Christian – also like the father – stepped back to let spiritual healing commence.

It can be assumed that the dying man managed to resist all those final tests. Not only did he pay for a notary, he also managed to call for a priest. Preparation was key, being surprised by the own death meant not being prepared for what was to come.[21] Therefore the man in his bed, the priest with his cross and candle, the guardian angel and also the soul leaving the body are signs not only of timely preparations but also of a good death just like the *ars moriendi* suggested it. Cranach's version of the ascending soul is different from the traditional northern European iconography. Usually artists north of the Alps would depict the soul as an infant which may need some angelic assistance to rise up. Here, Cranach shows a more Italian type of soul: This soul is not only an adult person visibly stripped of age and sickness, it also manages to rise up on its own.[22] The soul finds itself in an in-between-state. Whereas the bed scene seemed to imply a good death, the soul is harassed by three demons confronting it with the sins of youth, adulthood and old age. As a witness of the defence one single angel suffices to bring attention to the good deeds. Unfortunately this does not mean that his good work was so impressive that it outweighs the three signs of sin. More accurately it has to be interpreted as defeat. The man who is dead and dying at the same time has sinned too much. His salvation will not come from his good works.[23]

Now only God's grace can help. While the actions surrounding his deathbed are ambivalent and while his soul has to beg, the merciful Trinity shows the signs of the suffering of Christ. He who has died for mankind wears a crown of thorns, his body heavily mutilated. On his lap, the lamb references the sacrifice of God. With his hands, Jesus does not judge, but bless.[24] Cranach's

---

20   Nicolaisen "Der Hofmaler" 102.
21   Niederkorn-Bruck "Das Leben stirbt" 67. Preising "'Brille des Todes'" 16.
22   The iconographic differences of the depiction of souls is discussed in Kemp W., *Seele*, in Kirschbaum E. (ed.), *Lexikon der christlichen Ikonographie. Band 4: Allgemeine Ikonographie. Saba, Königin von bis Zypresse. Nachträge* (Freiburg im Breisgau: 1972) 138–139.
23   Noble "Lutheran Paintings" 79.
24   Heiland "Der Sterbende" 56; Laukötter F., "Heilige Dreifaltigkeit", in Stamm R. (ed.), *Lucas Cranach der Schnellste*, exh. cat., Kunstsammlungen Böttcherstraße (Bremen: 2009) 88–89, here 88.

Trinity is not only a dominant depiction of God's mercy, but also an artistic self-reference. By using an arrangement of poses which he used before – and will use in later works – Cranach embeds this Trinity in his oeuvre. By using the papal crown for God-Father, Cranach uses the usual iconography of the time while determining the pope's authority. Still, this detail does not mean that the painting positions the patron on one or the other side. While Luther's ideas up to 1518 angered the pope, the theologian from Wittenberg did not plan to abolish the papal authority per se – not yet.[25]

Though in retrospect this imagery – a sinful human saved only by believing in the mercy of a loving God – sounds like a creed to the Lutheran idea of sola gratia – only grace –, it is in fact not. Luther articulated his principles – only grace, only faith, only the bible, only Jesus – in the years to come.[26] In 1518 no such idea was labelled Lutheran. This might sound curious in regards of indulgences which Luther so prominently opposed, but believing in God's mercy was a standard idea of that time, for traditional Catholics and admirers of that upcoming Reformation school of thinking alike. Therefore the inscription with Psalm 114:5 is also no indication of a specific set of beliefs. Claiming that God's mercy is upon all his creations it was one of the core beliefs for Christians of the time. For instance, Luther clarified that mercy upon all did not mean unconditional entrance to heaven. In fact, God would show mercy to everyone, but only those who accepted it into their hearts would be saved. To the sinners, unable to accept Jesus as their saviour, the same mercy and grace would become so unreachable, that the lack thereof would suffice as punishment.[27]

Other than this picture of dying, trying and judgement, the piece by Cranach also shows a smaller scene and two medallions with portraits of a man and a woman. Those two are shown in a grisaille fashion, looking like

---

25   Tacke "Lucas Cranach der Schnellste" 22. Several other works before and after 1518 with various patrons show the same crown. For instance, this is the case for Lucas Cranach the Elder: *Die Dreifaltigkeit*, around 1515, oil on limewood, 140 × 100, Leipzig, Museum der bildenden Künste, Inv.Nr. 248 or Lucars Cranach the Elder: *Die Heilige Dreifaltigkeit*, around 1530–1550, oil on wood, 41 × 28.7 cm, Innsbruck, Tiroler Landesmuseum Ferdinandeum, Inv.Nr. Gem. 117.

26   Luther Martin, *Die Schmalkaldischen Artikel*, ed. I. Dingel (Göttingen: 2014) 718–788, especially article 2,1.

27   Luther Martin, *Die sieben Bußpsalmen. Erste Bearbeitung*, ed. J.K.F. Knaacke et al., vol. 1 (Weimar: 1883) 154–220, here 173; Luther Martin, *Dictata super Psalmerium. Ps. LXXXIV–CL*, ed. J.K.F. Knaacke et al., vol. 4 (Weimar: 1886) 1–462, here 450; Ellwein E. (ed.), *D. Martin Luthers Epistel=Auslegung, Band 1, Der Römerbrief* (Göttingen: 1963) 36; Angenendt A., *Geschichte der Religiosität im Mittelalter* (Darmstadt: 2009). Hamm B., *Religiosität im späten Mittelalter. Spannungspole, Neuaufbrüche, Normierungen*, Spätmittelalter, Humanismus, Reformation 54 (Tübingen: 2011) 440–441.

stonework. The heads are shown sideways in a style that can be described as almost Renaissance-like. In lack of evidence, resemblance to members of the Schmitburg family – such as Heinrich and his wife – can not be deduced. Regarding a function as mere décor, they show that Cranach and his patron for that painting were open to new ideas concerning painting, thereby maybe also open to new ideas regarding other aspects of life such as faith.[28] The small scene at the top of the piece shows a family kneeling in front of a little chapel, praying. Only the oldest man of the group looks up just as Mary, mother of God, and her son Jesus appear in the clouds. The man kneeling is the same man who is also dying – which would make the small scenery the prequel of the bigger one. In the context of the painting, the appearance of Mary does not mean she will act in intercession for the man who sees her. She is not here to plead his case, but to notify him that his time on earth is up. According to popular belief of the time, Mary would appear to those who would die soon so they could prepare themselves – for instance by re-reading the *ars moriendi* or calling for a priest. What may seem as an obviously Catholic statement, is – just like the papal crown – nothing that Luther and his allies questioned at the time. Though Protestantism later stopped recognizing Mary as a person of worship – sola Jesus, only Jesus should be venerated – in 1518 Luther was still to develop this idea. Until then, he was but an admirer of the Virgin and even praised her at great length in his commentary on the "Magnificat".[29]

There is but one detail left. Going from the bottom to the top, it might be necessary to go back to the very bottom of the piece again and take a close look at the left corner to see a certain person, often forgotten by recipients. There, the notary, not bothered by the already grieving wife, the people already sorting possessions or even the death of his client, finishes the dying man's last will. As mentioned, this will can be interpreted as the way out of the sin of greed. But Cranach and his workshop did not only depict a man with pen and paper, scribbling some black lines. Instead, they actually managed to inscribe

[28] Rabenau K., "Die Bedeutung der Bilder für die persönliche Frömmigkeit und den Gottesdienst", in Guratzsch H. (ed.) *Vergessene altdeutsche Gemälde. 1815 auf dem Dachboden der Leipziger Nikolaikirche gefunden – 1997 anläßlich des 27. Deutschen Evangelischen Kirchentages präsentiert*, exh. cat., Museum der bildenden Künste Leipzig (Heidelberg: 1997) 20–25, here 23. Discussing the idea of the medallions being added later Preising "'Brille des Todes'" 34–35.

[29] Luther Martin, *Das Magnificat verdeutschet und ausgelegt*, ed. J.K.F. Knaacke et al., vol. 7 (Weimar: 1897) 546–601; Burger C., *Tradition und Neubeginn. Martin Luther in seinen frühen Jahren* (Tübingen: 2014) 129–144; Arnulf A., "Maria im lutherischen Kirchraum", in Lembke K. (ed.), *Madonna. Frau – Mutter – Kultfigur*, exh. cat., Niedersächsisches Landesmuseum (Dresden: 2015) 202–213; Preising "'Brille des Todes'" 31; Hamm „Religiosität im späten Mittelalter" 440.

the paperwork with readable words. In the man's last will, he offers his soul to God, his body to the ground and his possessions to those close to him. Looking for evangelical clues, this could be one. By offering his body to the ground the man accepts his inevitable mortality. By offering his soul to God the man accepts God as the only way to eternal life and gives himself into the grace of God. By offering his possessions exclusively to his next of kin the man may have asked for something out of line. Maybe under the influence of Luther and his treatises against indulgences and donating money to the church as an institution the dying man has decided not to give any money to the church. But then again, neither did he donate money to the poor. What seems like an obvious clue for Reformation ideas at first glance, could turn out to be too much of a stretch under closer examination.[30]

5 Catholic or Protestant? Ambivalent Times and Art

Every detail analysed alone as well as in correspondence to other parts shows no signs of alliance to either a traditionalist or Reformation side. Even more, the analysis underlined the ambivalence of the time. A time, in which only in retrospect clues can be interpreted for or against something. Interpretations of Scholars which tend to classify the piece as either obviously Catholic or as Protestantism hidden in plain sign are set to fail – this piece is as fluid, as ambivalent as the time in which it was created. A time of change, in which Luther may have been the (or at least one) spearhead of a movement, but not the initiator of said movement. More than that, ideas of change, of questioning traditional faith can be found even decades earlier. The times and ideas like indulgence and salvation changed. The rise of the *ars moriendi*, born out of the necessity of fearing an unguided and therefore bad death – resulting in the death of not only the body but the soul as well – led people to take matters into their own hands. Not only was it necessary to be prepared for the grim challenges that the devil would throw at them, maybe the fires of purgatory and hell were not as inevitable as they seemed before? Articulated in the ideas of a personal trial which could be influenced by withstanding some tasks and manifesting the own faith in God's grace, the trial would ultimately lead to being saved. Grace would come to all of God's creations.

By paying Cranach for such a piece, Heinrich Schmitburg was able to demonstrate his financial abilities and his social standing. Not only was he able

---

[30] Bünz, "Rekonstruktion des Epitaphs" 98; Niederkorn-Bruck, "Das Leben stirbt" 73; Preising, "'Brille des Todes'" 34.

to pay for a piece by an artist like Cranach to – unnecessarily – exchange an already existing epitaph. He also managed – merely two years before his own death – to display the family's social standing in it by including details like a doctor and by highlighting the core ideas of faith and salvation of the early sixteenth century. Both the patron and the artist managed to capture the changing of principles of faith. What may have seemed immutable before became questionable. The epitaph paid respect to those changes, manifesting the idea of both the father and the son Schmitburg as good Christians. While a lack of evidence forbids a retrospective speculation about the actual faith of the patron, the painting is a testament of a faith in God's mercy, that was shared by many, traditionalists and reformed thinkers alike. Just as many ideas-- which would later be understood as "typical" lutheran doctines – circulated well before Martin Luther even started to write, the painting is a testament to these widespread beliefs.

Ultimately, after close-reading the artwork, highlighting the social surroundings for both the painter and the patron, and after shaping a differentiated view on the piece as a symbol of a changing time, it is necessary to take a final look at the piece in the very physical context. Whilst it is possible to analyse every inscription and figure in great detail when looking at the work on its own, it is most important to picture it in its intended place. From 1518 on, it replaced an older epitaph in a church in Leipzig, installed in a nave.[31] Considering the rather small size of the piece installed in the gloomy setting of a sixteenth-century church, it seems doubtful that most church-goers would have been able to identify more than the general setting. Seeing Mary, the Trinity, the soul leaving the body being surrounded by both heavenly guardians and hellish minions, people would have recognized the general idea to realize: He who died this death, died a good death.

Bibliography

Primary Printed Sources

Ellwein E. (ed.), *D. Martin Luthers Epistel=Auslegung, Band 1, Der Römerbrief* (Göttingen: 1963).

Luther Martin, *Die sieben Bußpsalmen. Erste Bearbeitung*, ed. J.K.F. Knaacke et al., vol. 1 (Weimar: 1883) 154–220.

---

[31] Bünz "Rekonstruktion des Epitaphs" 97–100. About epitaphs in the time and context of the proto-reformation: Wulf „Protestantische Gemäldeepitaphien".

Luther Martin, *Disputatio pro declaratione virtutis indulgentiarum*, ed. J.K.F. Knaacke et al., Vol. 1 (Weimar: 1883) 229–238.

Luther Martin, *Ein Sermon von Ablaß und Gnade*, ed. J.K.F. Knaacke et al., Vol. 1 (Weimar: 1883) 239–246.

Luther, Martin, *Vorrede zu der unvollständigen Ausgabe der "deutschen Theologie"*, ed. J.K.F. Knaacke et al., Vol. 1 (Weimar: 1883), 152–153.

Luther Martin, *Dictata super Psalmerium. Ps. LXXXIV–CL*, ed. J.K.F. Knaacke et al., vol. 4 (Weimar: 1886) 1–462.

Luther Martin, *Das Magnificat verdeutschet und ausgelegt*, ed. J.K.F. Knaacke et al., vol. 7 (Weimar: 1897) 546–601.

Luther Martin, *Die Schmalkaldischen Artikel*, ed. I. Dingel (Göttingen: 2014) 718–788.

Secondary Literature

Angenendt A., *Geschichte der Religiosität im Mittelalter* (Darmstadt: 2009).

Ariès P., *Studien zur Geschichte des Todes im Abendland* (Munich: 1981).

Arnulf A., "Maria im lutherischen Kirchraum", in Lembke K. (ed.), *Madonna. Frau – Mutter – Kultfigur*, exh. cat., Niedersächsisches Landesmuseum (Dresden: 2015) 202–213.

Bätschmann O., *Ausstellungskünstler. Kult und Karriere im modernen Kunstsystem* (Cologne: 1997).

Brückner W., "Der gute Tod", in Kühne H. – Bünz E. – Müller T. (eds.), *Alltag und Frömmigkeit am Vorabend der Reformation in Mitteldeutschland*, exh. cat., Museum am Lindenbühl, Stadtgeschichtliches Museum Leipzig, Kulturhistorisches Museum Magdeburg (Petersberg: 2013) 91–92.

Buchwald G., *Reformationsgeschichte der Stadt Leipzig* (Leipzig; 1900).

Bünz E., "Kirchliches Leben und Laienfrömmigkeit im spätmittelalterlichen Leipzig", in Bünz E. – Kohnle A. (eds.), *Das religiöse Leipzig. Stadt und Glauben vom Mittelalter bis zur Gegenwart*, Quellen und Forschungen zur Geschichte der Stadt Leipzig 6 (Leipzig: 2013) 27–61.

Bünz E. – Kühne, H. (ed.), *Alltag und Frömmigkeit am Vorabend der Reformation in Mitteldeutschland. Wissenschaftlicher Begleitband zur Ausstellung 'Umsonst ist der Tod'*, Schriften zur Sächsischen Geschichte und Volkskunde 50 (Leipzig: 2015).

Burger C., *Tradition und Neubeginn. Martin Luther in seinen frühen Jahren* (Tübingen: 2014) 129–144.

Dixon C., "Luther's Ninety-Five Theses and the Origins of the Reformation Narrative", *English Historical Review* 132 (2017), 533–569 esp. 556.

Fleck L., *Entstehung und Entwicklung einer wissenschaftlichen Tatsache. Einführung in die Lehre vom Denkstil und Denkkollektiv* (Frankfurt [Main]: 1980).

Friedländer M.J. – Rosenberg J., *Die Gemälde von Lucas Cranach* (Berlin: 1932).

Haas A., "Tod und Jenseits in der deutschen Literatur des Mittelalters", in Gesellschaft für das Schweizerische Landesmuseum (eds.), *Himmel – Hölle – Fegefeuer. Das Jenseits im Mittelalter*, exh. cat., Schweizerisches Landesmuseum (Zurich: 1994) 69–78.

Hamm B., *Religiosität im späten Mittelalter. Spannungspole, Neuaufbrüche, Normierungen*, Spätmittelalter, Humanismus, Reformation 54 (Tübingen: 2011).

Heiland S., "Der Sterbende", in Guratzsch H. (ed.), *Vergessene altdeutsche Gemälde. 1815 auf dem Dachboden der Leipziger Nikolaikirche gefunden – 1997 anläßlich des 27. Deutschen Evangelischen Kirchentages präsentiert*, exh. cat., Museum der bildenden Künste Leipzig (Heidelberg: 1997) 54–56.

Hesse J., "Ars moriendi. Die Kunst, zwischen den Versuchungen der Teufel und den Ermahnungen der Heiligen heilsam zu sterben", in Gesellschaft für das Schweizerische Landesmuseum (eds.), *Himmel – Hölle – Fegefeuer. Das Jenseits im Mittelalter*, exh. cat., Schweizerisches Landesmuseum (Zurich: 1994) 262–265.

Höfler J., Der Meister E.S.. *Ein Kapitel europäischer Kunst des 15. Jahrhunderts. Textband* (Regensburg: 2007).

Plotzek J., "Ars moriendi, Neapel", in Plotzek J. et al. (ed.), *Ars vivendi – Ars moriendi* (München: 2011) 546–571.

Jung M., *Die Reformation. Theologen, Politiker, Künstler* (Göttingen: 2008).

Kemp W., Seele, in Kirschbaum E. (ed.), *Lexikon der christlichen Ikonographie. Band 4: Allgemeine Ikonographie. Saba, Königin von bis Zypresse. Nachträge* (Freiburg im Breisgau: 1972) 138–139.

Krems E., "Vom Hofkünstler zum Ausstellungskünstler: Künstler und ihre Mäzene in der Frühen Neuzeit und der Moderne", in Strobel J. – Wolf J. (ed.), *Maecenas und seine Erben. Kunstförderung und künstlerische Freiheit – von der Antike bis zur Gegenwart* (Stuttgart: 2015) 198–216.

Kühne H., "Frömmigkeit unterwegs", in Kühne H. – Bünz E. – Müller T. (eds.), *Alltag und Frömmigkeit am Vorabend der Reformation in Mitteldeutschland*, exh. cat., Museum am Lindenbühl, Stadtgeschichtliches Museum Leipzig, Kulturhistorisches Museum Magdeburg (Petersberg: 2013) 159–160.

Laager J. (ed.), *Ars moriendi. Die Kunst, gut zu leben und gut zu sterben. Texte von Cicero bis Luther* (Zurich: 1996).

Laukötter F., "Heilige Dreifaltigkeit", in Stamm R. (ed.), *Lucas Cranach der Schnellste*, exh. cat., Kunstsammlungen Böttcherstraße (Bremen: 2009) 88–89.

Lehrs M., "Der Künstler der Ars moriendi und die wahre erste Ausgabe derselben", *Jahrbuch der Königlich Preußischen Kunstsammlungen* 11 (1890) 161–168.

Nicolaisen J., "Der Hofmaler in der Handelsstadt – Aufträge und Auftraggeber Lucas Cranachs in Leipzig", in Guratzsch H. (ed.), *Vergessene altdeutsche Gemälde. 1815 auf dem Dachboden der Leipziger Nikolaikirche gefunden – 1997 anläßlich des 27.*

Deutschen Evangelischen Kirchentages präsentiert, exh. cat., Museum der bildenden Künste Leipzig (Heidelberg: 1997) 100–111.

Niederkorn-Bruck M., "Das Leben stirbt, wo es beginnt, und aufersteht, wo es zerrinnt. Der Tod und das Leben im Mittelalter", in Hameter W. – Niederkorn-Bruck M. – Scheutz M. (eds.), *Freund Hein? Tod und Ritual in der Geschichte*, Querschnitte Band 22 (Innsbruck – Vienna – Bozen: 2007) 60–81.

Noble B.-J., *The Lutheran Paintings of the Cranach Workshop. 1529–1555* (Ph.D. dissertation, Northwestern University: 1998).

Olds C.C., *Ars Moriendi: A Study of the Form and Content of fifteenth-century Illustrations of the art of dying* (Ph.D. dissertation, Pennsylvania University: 1966).

Preising D., "'Brille des Todes'. Das Einzelbild als Anleitung zu gutem Sterben im Spätmittelalter", in Preising D. – Rief M. – Vogt C. (eds.), *Der gute Weg zum Himmel. Spätmittelalterliche Bilder zum richtigen Sterben: das Gemälde ars bene moriendi aus der Sammlung Peter und Irene Ludwig*, exh. cat., Ludwiggalerie Schloss Oberhausen, Suermondt-Ludwig-Museum (Bielefeld – Berlin: 2016) 15–42.

Rabenau K., "Die Bedeutung der Bilder für die persönliche Frömmigkeit und den Gottesdienst", in Guratzsch H. (ed.) *Vergessene altdeutsche Gemälde. 1815 auf dem Dachboden der Leipziger Nikolaikirche gefunden – 1997 anläßlich des 27. Deutschen Evangelischen Kirchentages präsentiert*, exh. cat., Museum der bildenden Künste Leipzig (Heidelberg: 1997) 20–25.

Roeck B., *Der Morgen der Welt. Geschichte der Renaissance* (Munich: 2017).

Rudolf R., *Ars moriendi. Von der Kunst des heilsamen Lebens und Sterbens* (Cologne – Graz: 1957).

Scheffczyk L., "Himmel und Hölle: Kontinuität und Wandel in der Lehrentwicklung", in Greshake G. (ed.), *Ungewisses Jenseits? Himmel – Hölle – Fegefeuer*, Schriften der Katholischen Akademie in Bayern 121 (Düsseldorf: 1986) 41–42.

Schuchardt C., *Lucas Cranach des Aelteren Leben und Werke. Nach urkundlichen Quellen bearbeitet. Zweiter Theil* (Leipzig: 1851).

Schuchardt C., *Lucas Cranach des Aelteren Leben und Werke. Nach urkundlichen Quellen bearbeitet. Dritter Theil* (Leipzig: 1871).

Schuchardt G., "Cranach und Luther – Aspekte einer Partnerschaft", in *Cranach, Luther und die Bildnisse. Thüringer Themenjahr "Bild und Botschaft"*, exh. cat. Wartburg (Regensburg: 2015) 10–23.

Seiler R., *Mittelalterliche Medizin und Probleme der Jenseitsvorsorge*, in Gesellschaft für das Schweizerische Landesmuseum (ed.), *Himmel – Hölle – Fegefeuer. Das Jenseits im Mittelalter*, exh. cat. Schweizerisches Landesmuseum Zürich (Zurich: 1994) 117–124.

Smith J.C., *The Northern Renaissance* (London: 2004).

Stepner S., *Inscriptiones Lipsienses locorum publicorum academicorum pariter ac senatoriorum memorabiles* (Leipzig: 1686).

Tacke A., "Mit Cranachs Hilfe. Antireformatorische Kunstwerke vor dem Tridentiner Konzil", in Brinkmann B. (ed.), *Cranach der Ältere*, exh. Cat., Städel Museum (Ostfildern: 2007) 81–89.

Tacke A., "Lucas Cranach der Schnellste. Ein Künstler als Werkstattleiter", in Stamm R. (ed.), *Lucas Cranach der Schnellste*, exh. cat., Kunstsammlungen Böttcherstraße (Bremen: 2009), 12–28.

Vogel J., "Zur Cranachforschung", *Zeitschrift für bildende Kunst, Neue Folge* 18 (1907) 219–226.

Vögele J. – Spanier L., "Stadt, Krankheit und Tod. Zur Entwicklung der Sterblichkeit in historischer Perspektive", in von Hülsen-Esch A. – Westermann-Angerhausen H., *Zum Sterben schön. Alter, Totentanz und Sterbekunst von 1500 bis heute. Band 1: Aufsätze*, exh. cat., Museum Schnütgen, Goethemuseum, Kunsthalle Recklinghausen (Regensburg: 2006) 211–226.

Warnke M., *Hofkünstler. Zur Vorgeschichte des modernen Künstlers* (Cologne 1985).

Wegmann S., *Auf dem Weg zum Himmel. Das Fegefeuer in der deutschen Kunst des Mittelalters* (Ph.D. dissertation, Universität Regensburg: 2000).

Wegmann S., "Das nicht erloschene Fegefeuer. Zum Cranach-Retabel in der Nikolaikirche zu Jüterbog", in *Johann Tetzel und der Ablass*, exh. cat. Jüterbog (Berlin: 2017) 45–56.

Wulf I., *Protestantische Gemäldeepitaphien im Raum Wittenberg und in angrenzenden Territorien. Zur Entwicklung und Funktion des Gemäldeepitaphs vom Beginn der lutherischen Reformation bis zur Veröffentlichung des Konkordienbuches. 1517–1580* (Ph.D. dissertation, Freie Universität Berlin: 2011).

PART 4

Violence and Diseases

∴

CHAPTER 12

The Moment of Death during the Thirty Years' War

Sigrun Haude

1   Introduction

Death was ubiquitous during the Thirty Years' War (1618–1648). Violence, starvation, and epidemic diseases caused a staggering amount of human loss in large parts of the German lands.[1] This escalation of fatalities raises the question how contemporaries approached their moment of death during this perilous time. Historians have studied death from a variety of perspectives. Whereas Philippe Ariès explored the relationship between attitudes toward death and awareness of self from the middle ages to modern times, Craig Koslofsky traced ritual changes around death that occurred during the Reformation. Finding that the dead were increasingly separated from the living, he considered the social implications of this move.[2] Several collections of articles – with a wide chronological scope, sometimes from ancient to modern times – addressed issues of deathbed rituals, theology, burial, grief, and mourning, as well as the artistic representations of death.[3] The ways in which the war affected people's approach to death, however, has hitherto received little attention.[4]

This chapter, which focuses on situations heightened by the war – including pestilence, torture, and martyrdom, explores the topic from the point of view

---

1   See Haude S., *Coping with Life during the Thirty Years' War (1618–1648)* (Leiden: 2021).
2   Ariès P., *The Hour of Our Death* (New York: 1981); Koslofsky C.M., *The Reformation of the Dead. Death and Ritual in Earl Modern Germany, 1450–1700* (New York: 2000).
3   Becker H. – Einig B. – Ullrich P.-O. (eds.), *Im Angesicht des Todes. Ein interdisziplinäres Kompendium*, 2 vols. (St. Ottilien: 1987); Class M. – Reiß A. – Rüther S. (eds.), *Vom Umgang mit den Toten. Sterben im Krieg von der Antike bis zur Gegenwart* (Leiden – Boston: 2019); von Hülsen-Esch A. – Westermann-Angerhausen H. (eds.), *Zum Sterben schön. Alter, Totentanz und Sterbekunst von 1500 bis heute, Aufsätze* (Regensburg: 2006). In this last collection, Heike Düselder's contribution, "'Wer so stirbt, der stirbt wohl!' Der Umgang mit der Sterbestunde im Spiegel von Leichenpredigten" 238–249, which explores funeral sermons from the sixteenth to the eighteenth century to determine how the dying dealt with the hour of death, is particularly relevant. On England, see Houlbrooke R. (ed.), *Death, Ritual, and Bereavement* (London: 1989) and idem, *Death, Religion and the Family in England 1480–1750* (Oxford: 1998).
4   See, however, Kaiser M., "Zwischen 'ars moriendi' und 'ars mortem evitandi'. Der Soldat und der Tod in der Frühen Neuzeit", in Kaiser M. – Kroll S. (eds.), *Militär und Religiosität in der Frühen Neuzeit* (Münster: 2004) 323–343, who explores the religious concepts upon which soldiers could draw as they encountered death.

of the dying and the community they left behind. The evidence comes from funeral sermons, autobiographical accounts, and religious writings on death.

Funeral sermons (*Leichenpredigten*) are a particularly rich source for the study of death.[5] Beyond providing a sermon, with the biblical text often geared toward the situation and (if male) occupation or position of the deceased, these writings also included that person's curriculum vitae or résumé, of which the last section narrated the final illness and approach to death. Funeral sermons were not written for everyone but primarily for members of the nobility and the middle class, with government officials, military leaders, and ministers counting prominently among them. Notably, even though this genre did not include the whole spectrum of society, sermons were also written for women and children (typically related to the above mentioned sorts of men). While funeral sermons experienced a heyday during the seventeenth century and were especially associated with Lutherans, the genre reaches back to classical times. Funeral sermons were also written, although in much smaller numbers, for Roman Catholics.[6]

When examining *Leichenpredigten* during the Thirty Years' War, one finds, on the one hand, continuity with early modern ways of viewing and responding to the imminence of death. On the other, the war also fueled different concerns or magnified the usual anxieties surrounding death. The following analysis will begin with a discussion of the commonalities and then examine several cases in the context of the war.

---

5 On funeral sermons, see Lenz R., *Leichenpredigten. Quellen zur Erforschung der Frühen Neuzeit* (Marburg: 1990); Moore C., *Patterned Lives. The Lutheran Funeral Biography in Early Modern Germany* (Wiesbaden: 2006); Brunner B., "Die gedruckte Leichenpredigt als Erbauungsbuch – eine Erfolgsgeschichte des 17. Jahrhunderts", *Medium Buch* 1 (2019) 87–105; idem, "Heilige Stimmen. Die kommunikative Funktion der Toten in protestantischen Funeralschriften der Frühen Neuzeit", *Jahrbuch für Kommunikationsgeschichte* 24 (2022) 29–55.

6 Boge, B. – Bogner, R.G. (eds.), *Oratio Funebris. Die Leichenpredigt der frühen Neuzeit. Zwölf Studien*, Chloe. Beihefte zum Daphnis 30 (Amsterdam: 1999). On differences between Lutheran and Catholic funeral sermons, see Moore, *Patterned Lives* 32–33. The exploration of distinct messages of Lutheran and Catholic funeral sermons is an important subject that transcends the limits of this chapter. Most of the characteristics listed in the following discussion apply to Lutheran and Catholic approaches to death but there are also differences, including the consideration of purgatory, prayers for the dead, Mary, the saints, and the angels that play important roles for Catholics. All this, as well as the complicated role of works in one's life, deserves a more extensive treatment than can be offered here. On Reformed funeral sermons (their paucity and scarce biographical sections), see Moore C., *Patterned Lives* and Burnett, A.–N., "'To Oblige My Brethren:' The Reformed Funeral Sermons of Johann Brandmüller", *The Sixteenth Century Journal* 36 (2005) 37–54.

2   Continuities

Among the continuities, confession of one's sins, followed by absolution and holy communion, as well as reconciliation with the dying's enemies played important roles in one's preparation for death. No issue, however, was more important than to realize the unambiguous truth: the best way to meet death safely was to live one's entire life in Christ and not to turn to Him merely when one was at death's door. A life of continual prayer devoted to God represented the single secure way to enter into the heavenly kingdom and to counter the fear of death. The biographical sections of the funeral sermons carefully examined whether the deceased lived up to this goal. While these concerns were long-standing, the situation of war heightened the urgency of a life lived in accordance with God since 'the sword of war' could fell anyone at any time and 'without respect of persons'.[7]

The demonstration of patience (*Geduld*) constituted a second key element. The résumé following a sermon unfailingly highlighted whether the dying approached his or her death patiently or whether the person showed signs of restlessness and maybe even a desire to hurry death along. When Ludolf von Münchhausen lay on his deathbed, the minister Theodor Stedingk noted: 'Je mehr die Kranckheit zugenommen/ je mehr sich seine gedult herfür gethan' ('The more the illness intensified, the more [von Münchhausen's] patience came to the fore').[8] Indeed, patience was the only proper way in which to approach death since it acknowledged God as the one who held everything in his hands. Dying and death occurred on God's timetable. He could not be rushed nor slowed down to allow a loved one more time if this went against the Lord's will. Impatience denied God his sovereignty. Even medical men, who were regularly called to the bedside of the dying, could not alter God's decision. Thus, when the physicians had exhausted their medicines, the ministers

---

7   '… das Kriegsschwerdt/ ohne ansehen der Person/ jetzt disen/ jetzt jenen frisset/ …' Löher Bernhard, *Zwo Christliche Predigten Gehalten Vber der Leich Weilund deß Durchleuchtigen Hochgebornen Fürsten vnd Herren/ Herren Magni/ Hertzogen zu Würtemberg vnd Teckh/ Graven zu Mümpelgart/ Herren zu Heydenheim/ etc. Welcher Freytags den 26. Aprilis dises 1622. Jahrs/ in dem; zwischen rc. Jhr. Durchl. Herren Maximiliano, Hertzogen zu Ober: vnd NiderBayern/ rc. vnd rc. Herren Georg Friderichen Marggraven zu Baden vnd Hochberg/ rc. Fürstl. Gn. bey Oberreißheim vorgangenem Treffen/ auff Württembergischen Grund vnd Boden vmbkommen* […] (Stuttgart, J.W. Rößlin: 1622) (22) 23.
8   Stedingk Theodor, SORS MISERANDA VITÆ. *Das ist: Eygentliche Beschreibung Des Müheseehligen menschlichen Lebens in dieser Welt: Leichenbegräbnis von Ludolff von Münchhausen, Erbsasse zu Oldendorf und Reimeringhausen, gestorben 21. 9. 1640; am 12. 1. 1641 beigesetzt, die Schrift der hinterlassenen adeligen Witwe und Erben zum Trost* (Rinteln, P. Lucius: 1641) 39.

took over in guiding the dying toward the only efficacious medicine: true penitence and confession.

A third major concern consisted of approaching death with a sound mind ('bei vollem Verstand').[9] Unobstructed awareness was important so that a person could participate in the last preparation toward death – by reciting prayers, confessions, and songs. Being prepared for death ideally took place along two temporal trajectories: first, the long-term, i.e., life-long grounding of one's life in prayer and in the service to Christ (as discussed above), and, second, the generally short-term, final period leading up to one's death, which consisted of perpetual prayers, reading of biblical texts, spiritual conversations, and more. If the person on the deathbed could no longer speak, gestures of one's hand or head stood in for the mute tongue to signal one's devotion.[10] Those of old age prayed for a comprehending mind before death and that dementia would not overtake them. It was essential that one was able to confirm fully, loudly, and clearly one's commitment to God; slipping away unconsciously without grasping the religious importance of the last days and hours was considered most calamitous.

3 The War's Influences on the Moment of Death: Military Men

While these essential components continued to play a substantial role in the approach to death, the war not only caused great suffering but also affected what was considered the proper setting for the dying and thus engendered severe concerns about one's death and what came thereafter. Melchior von Reichau, war officer of Württemberg, war councilor, and chief bailiff of Blaubeuren and a man with a long and distinguished career, is a case in point.[11] In the first

---

9 See, for example Otto Nicolaus, *Christliche Leichpredigt/ fuer Burchardt von Benthen, Patrizier in Hannover, am 8. 1. 1642 verstroben und am 16. 1. 1642 beigesetzt. Prediger M. Nicolaus Otto, Pfarrer an der Kreuzkirche in Hannover* (Rinteln, P. Lucius: 1642) 45.

10 Walther Ludolf, *Christi grosse Freundlichkeit: Aller gläubigen Hertzen Labsal vnd Erquickung. Das ist: Christlicher Leich=Sermon/ fuer Elisabeth Dorenwald, Frau von Ludolff von Anderten. Patrizier von Hannover. Gestorben am 14. Jan. 1641. Morgends zwischen 9. vnd 10. Vhren sanfft vnd seelig bey gutem Verstande in wahrem Glauben an Christum eingeschlaffen* [...] (Rinteln, Petrus Lucius: 1641) 46.

11 Cuenen Johannes, *Christliche Leich Predigten/ Bey der Gegräbnuß deß Weyland WolEdlen/ Gestrengen vnd Vesten/ Melchior von Reichaw auff Corschwitz/ rc. der hochlöblichen Vnion/ vnd Fürstl. Würtemb. Bestelten Obristen/ KriegsRath/ vnd Obervogt zu Blawbeyren/ Gehalten die eine/ den 18. Maij/ Anno 1620. Zu Stuttgardten in der Spittalkirchen/ da die Leich Christlich vnd ehrlich zur Erden bestattet worden: Durch Tobiam Lottern/ der H. Schrifft Doctorn vnd StiffsPredigern zu Stuttgardten. Die ander aber hernach den 26.*

Leichenpredigt, the preacher, Tobias Lotter, took into account von Reichau's military profession and his arduous life, and underscored that the deceased's nearly forty years in the military amounted to nothing but an ongoing battle, in which he suffered many wounds, illnesses, and adversity. Lotter suggested that these hardships were almost certainly the reason for von Reichau's death at the age of fifty-two.[12] It is the second sermon, however, penned by the superintendent and minister, Johann Cuen, that spoke to a prevalent fear among the military, namely the prospect of dying on the battlefield. Cuen counted it as a particular blessing that von Reichau was able to die in his own bed rather than on the battlefield. While Cuen here puts his finger on a major fear among those who fought, civilians caught up in the military action also shared the dread of not dying in one's bed, where one would be surrounded by family, friends, and neighbors, and where one prepared oneself spiritually for the final hour. This dread was articulated in a prayer book concerning war, where the penitent entreated God:

> So es nun dein göttlicher Wille ist/ vnnd ich Gnade finde für deinen Augen/ so laß mich ja nit von der scherffe des schwerdts sterben/ daß mein Leichnam nicht vnter den Erschlagenen lige/ sondern laß mich zu seiner Zeit auff meinem Lager in Fried vnd Ruhe diese Welt gesegnen/ vnd mein Leben selig beschliessen.[13]

The dying's wish was to end his or her life peacefully, meditatively, honorably, and in harmony with God. War disrupted this desired bond not only by depriving one of the physical, meaningful space in which properly to approach death, but also by replacing the quiet and dignity of the death chamber with the noise and violence of the battlefield. Moreover, a quick death was often

---

Maij/ zu Blawbeyren/ Durch M. Johannem Cuenen/ Superintendenten vnd Pfarrern daselbsten (Stuttgart, J.W. Rößlin: 1620).

12 Cuenen, *Predigten* 60–65. On the vulnerability of soldiers' bodies, see Dinges M., "Soldatenkörper in der Frühen Neuzeit. Erfahrungen mit einem unzureichend geschützten, formierten und verletzten Körper in Selbstzeugnissen", in van Dülmen R. (ed.), *Körpergeschichten. Studien zur historischen Kulturforschung V* (Frankfurt a. M.: 1996) 71–98.

13 Scherertz Sigismund, *Kriegs Gebet vnd Andachten. Für die so mit schwerer Kriegsnoth von Gott heimgesucht sind* (Lüneburg, Stern: 1626) fol. Cxi r (XII. 'Gebet furchtsamer Hertzen/ die in Kriegsnoth blöde vnd verzagt sind/ vnd sich für dem Schwerdt fürchten', Nr. 6). 'If it is your divine will/ and I find mercy in your eyes/ then please do not let me die through the sharpness of the sword/ so that my corpse will not lie among the slain/ but when it is time let me bless this world from my bed in peace and quiet/ and let me end my life in a blessed way.' On Scherertz, see Bitzel A., *Anfechtung und Trost bei Sigismund Scherertz. Ein lutherischer Theologe im Dreißigjährigen Krieg* (Göttingen: 2002).

considered a 'bad death' ('böser Tod') because it caught people unexpectedly and unprepared.[14]

Cuen addressed another important issue that spoke both to the military's fear of being killed in battle and to their efforts to guard against it, namely their use of protective magic. In the case of von Reichau, the preacher rejected any charge that the deceased ever used such forbidden charms to make his body indestructible.[15] The fact that these possible activities were even mentioned in his résumé and that the minister saw the need to rebuff them, hints at how widespread such practices were among officers and soldiers. In his 1626 *Kriegsbüchlein für Christliche Soldaten* (*Military Manual for Christian Soldiers*), Pastor Sigismund Scherertz of Lüneburg responded to the question whether soldiers were allowed to resort to *Wundsegen*, a magic formula to stop a wound from bleeding and to help in the healing process, with a clear 'no':

> NEin. Denn es ist wider das erste vnd ander Gebot/ vnd beweget Gott zu grossem Zorn. Etliche Kriegesleute haben viel Aberglaubens im Streit/ da sich einer S. Georgen/ [...] befihlt/ Einer diesem/ der ander dem Heiligen [...]. Diese allesamt sind in fehrlichem Stande/ Denn sie gläuben nicht an Gott/ sondern versündigen sich vielmehr mit Vnglauben vnnd Mißglauben an Gott/ vnnd wo sie stürben/ müsten sie auch verlohren seyn.[16]

At the end of his little book, however, Scherertz granted one would be lucky to find three or four in a company of soldiers, who fully trusted in God's power to do all things and who eschewed magic remedies. Still, he concluded, even

---

14 This led to questions, especially during the war when people often perished in an instant, whether any sudden death was a bad death. See Knolle Antonius, *Vnsterblich Ehren=Gedächtnüs/ Klag=TRawer= vnd Leich=Predigten/ Fuer die Fuerstin Sophia, Markgraefin zu Brandenburg etc., gestorben am 23. 11.1646, von Hohann Albrecht Mintzeln 1648 gedruckt. 5. Leichenpredigt, von M. Antonius Knolle, Ekklesiast und Professor.* Herzog August Bibliothek, 95.22 Quodl. 20 (Hof, Mintzel: 1648) 217. On the subject of a "bad death", see Krusenstjern B.v., "Seliges Sterben und böser Tod. Tod und Sterben in der Zeit des Dreißigjährigen Krieges", in von Krusenstjern B. – Medick H. (eds.), *Zwischen Alltag und Katastrophe. Der Dreißigjährige Krieg aus der Nähe* (Göttingen: 1999) 469–496, and Düselder, "'Wer so stirbt, der stirbt wohl!'"

15 Cuenen, *Predigten* (15) 97.

16 Scherertz, *Kriegs Gebet* 142–143: 'No. It is against the first and second commandment/ and incites God to great wrath. Quite a few military people take recourse to much superstition during a battle. Thus, someone signs himself over to St. George/ [...] another to this and another to that saint [...]. All of these are in a dangerous state/ because they do not believe in God/ but rather fall into sin through disbelief and wrong belief toward God/ and when they die/ they would be lost'.

if the men did not believe as they should, 'we (ministers) nevertheless have to teach and make it known for the benefit of those (however few they might be)', who abstain from magic and place their trust in God.[17]

These passages point to an important underlying theme both among the military and the civilians, namely the fear of death during war. Soldiers dreaded death by the sword and prayed for the courage to make it through the conflict, but the rest of the populace, too, feared brutal death at the hand of armies and marauders. It is important to note, however, that, as people approached death in early modern times, most feared not so much death itself but that which came thereafter. They knew death only ended one's earthly life and that, if one did it right, something much better would follow. Why, then, was fear articulated so widely in funeral sermons, autobiographical accounts, and prayers? Undoubtedly, the war with its accompanying violence and hardships hastened one's end and jeopardized one's proper preparation toward death. People were terrified since the war not only shortened one's life to the point that one ran out of time for amending one's sinful ways; it also robbed one of the final chance – when one was on one's deathbed – to make everything right with God.

In the funeral sermons, the language of fear is juxtaposed with that of safety. Ministers tried to offset the anxieties of the dying (and their surrounding community, for that matter) by emphasizing a gentle and calm death, and by holding out that God would lead them to a 'safe haven'.[18] Moreover, learning to trust God's benevolent plan constituted another way to counter fear.[19]

4 The War's Influences on the Moment of Death: Civilians

The war did not only affect the lives of military men and their preparation for death. Magdalena von Reder (1594–1641), wife of Christoph von Reder, the governor of Friedland, Reichenberg and Seidenberg, provides a fascinating

---

17 Scherertz, *Kriegs Gebet* 147–148: 'Doch obs der Hauffe nicht thut/ müssen wir dennoch solches lehren vnd wissen/ vmb derer willen (wie wenig derselbigen auch sind) die es thun werden'.
18 Baldovius Johannes, *Leichenpredigt fuer Otto Schmidt, Sohn von Peter Schmidt, fuerstlicher Brauns. Lueneburg. Amptmann zu Nienburg an der Weser, am 3.2.1643 gestorben* (Rinteln, Peter Lucius: 1643) 46: 'Damit mag sich auch vnser hertzbetrübter Herr Amptmann trösten vnd gedencken/ er habe seinen lieben Otten auch nicht verlohren/ sondern jhn vor sich in einen sichern Port vnd Ort gebracht/ Gott der HERR hat jhn wieder zu sich genommen/ der jhn jhm gegeben hatte/ da ist er wol versorget'.
19 Scherertz, *Kriegs Gebet* 148.

example of a woman who suffered under the repercussions of war and who approached death in her own way.[20] The noble woman was first married at fourteen and became a widow in 1632 after twenty-four years of marriage. Whereas the minister, David Arndt, described this union in muted terms, Magdalena's second marriage to Christoph von Reder was clearly imbued with passion and deep love. Her new husband, also a widower, had fought in Denmark before he married Magdalena in Poland in 1634, where they had fled because of the war.[21]

Magdalena was an emigrant, who had been forced to flee her domain and 'look at it from the outside'. Living in exile and 'misery' (i.e., away from home), being barred from her home and territory, and subsisting on scarce provisions often prompted her to have gloomy thoughts. Eventually, however, she cast her lot with God and, so the minister, placed all her hopes in him. On Sundays she was the first person in church and the last to leave, and she deeply treasured God's word. During her long illness, she showed great devotion and in time surrendered entirely to God's will, saying: 'wie ers mit jhr schaffen möchte/ also solt jhr auch wollgefallen' ('However He wanted to deal with her, she would delight in it').[22]

After this fairly typical résumé of her life, Arndt offered a more unusual image of the faithful woman. Far from the passive recipient of pious truths at the hand of the minister, Magdalena was vigorously engaged in theological questions:

> Jnsonderheit kan vnd muß Jch allhier bey jhrer Liebe gegen Gottes Wort nicht verschweigen/ daß sie sehr begierig gewesen in Erkändnis GOttes vnd des HErrn JEsu/ darin das Ewige Leben stehet/ jmmer weiter

---

20 Arndt David, REFRIGERIVM CHRISTIANVM. Aller gedultigen Creutzträger Glaubens/ Liebes vnd HoffnungsBurgk/ ... Bey dem Christ= vnd HochAdelichem Begräbnuß der Weyland Wollgebornen Gnädigen Frawen/ Frawen MAGDALENÆ, Frawen von Redern/ geborne von Hundin/ Deß auch Wollgebornen Gnädigen Herrn Herrn CHRISTOPHORI, Herrn von Redern/ Herrn auff Friedland Reichenberg vnd Seidenberg; Groß Strelitz/ Tost vnd Weiß Kretschen etc. etc. Hertz vnd Vielgeliebten Gemahlin. Welche den 1 Januarij dieses jtzlauffenden 1641. Jahres zwischen 2. vnd 3. Vhren nach Mittag/ in wahrem Erkändnuß vnd standhaffter Bekändnuß jhres Erlösers Christi JEsu allhier in Schwerin/ als in jhrem langwirigen Exilio, sanfft vnd selig eingeschlaffen/ vnd hernach den 13. Febr. in vnser Evangelischen Kirchen beygesetzet worden. Auß dem 19. Capittel des grossen Creutzträgers Hiobs auffgerichtet (Alten Stettin, Georg Rheten: 1641) (30).
21 Arndt, REFRIGERIVM CHRISTIANVM 83.
22 Arndt, REFRIGERIVM CHRISTIANVM 85–86.

zuzunehmen/ daher sie auch bald diese/ bald ein andere Frage aus Gottes Wort erörtert.[23]

Arndt narrated that Magdalena would visit him with her husband and ask 'wenn sie mit jhrem hertzliebsten Eheschatz vnd Herren zu mir kommen/ viel Schrifftmässige Fragen/ so zur Seeligkeit nütz vnd heylsam auffgeben [...] Vnd wie jhre höchste Frewde gewesen von Gottes Wort zu reden/ also ist sie hergegen Spinnfeind gewesen/ allem vnnützen Geschwetz' ('many scriptural questions about what would be useful and beneficial for salvation [...] It was her greatest joy to talk about the Word of God, and so she despised any idle gossip').[24] Whether with admiration, exasperation, or regret, the minister noted that their meal was often forgotten over these discourses.

Arndt's testimony about Magdalena von Reder is noteworthy in several respects. Whereas typically the religious behaviour of the dying is cast in rather generic terms that underline the dying's submissiveness to God's plan, Magdalena's character is rendered with much greater nuance and complexity. Considering her journey, it is perhaps no surprise that her 'surrendering' to God was not of the meek and passive kind. Because of her experience of exile and the hardships she had to endure, she went through a phase of struggle before she fully embraced God, according to Arndt. Magdalena wanted to *know* about God, and she saw herself participating in this acquisition of knowledge that was vital to her salvation. Not only did she inundate the minister with questions; she also expounded Scripture herself and delighted in theological conversations rather than dinner. Arndt reported that Magdalena, on the one hand, showed patience during her last illness and weakened state. While she did ask God for enough time to settle her affairs, this was a usual point of business among those approaching death. Thus, like others, she gave instructions regarding what should happen to her body after death. Her corpse was to be buried as soon as possible in an oak casket and with a Christian funeral service. Magdalena asked Arndt to hold the sermon and told him which scriptural text to use. The minister, however, also narrated that, in her last severe battle with death, 'she clung to the Lord Jesus so tightly and did not let go of Him until He

---

23   Ibidem 86: 'In particular, in all her love toward God's Word, I can and must not conceal here that she was very eager to increase her knowledge of God and the Lord Jesus/ upon which rests eternal life/ therefore, she explicated from God's Word now this/ and then another question'.
24   Ibidem.

gave her the eternal blessing'.[25] As noted earlier, the highest praise belonged to those who approached death with patience and fully surrendered to God's will. Magdalena's wrestling with Jesus until He bestowed his grace upon her speaks less to her patience and instead underlines her persistent determination especially during this last stage of her earthly life. To a certain extent, her resolve and fortitude may have grown out of her life situation. After all, she had left her home for religious reasons, and it is understandable that she had an existential interest in being on the right religious path.

Another departure from the typical résumé is the space that is given to Magdalena's grieving husband. Normally preachers briefly acknowledged the sorrow among those left behind, but then quickly moved on to the much greater joy of the deceased, who was now with God, and instructed the mourning to be happy for their loved one. Indeed, too much sorrow was considered un-Christian because it argued with God's decision and with one's own destiny. But in Magdalena's case, the husband and company around her bed were so distraught that they, including Arndt, fell on their knees and entreated God to heal her if it was his will. In apparent response to their prayers, Magdalena did gain some new strength, which she used to settle more of her affairs, but she rallied only for a short while before finally succumbing to death. Arndt noted the 'inordinate sadness' her passing caused her husband and voiced no criticism of such profuse emotions.[26]

Exile and hardship, two cardinal experiences during the war, made Magdalena more invested in both her religious journey and her hour of death. She needed to get this right; she could not simply repeat the religious formulas handed down by generations of ministers but was compelled in her innermost being to be engaged in the fundamental questions surrounding life and death.

5 Torture

The war had a substantial effect on the preparation and moment of death in other ways as well, for example through the exercise of torture. Such practices were widely known and feared during the war. Johann Valentin Andreæ, Lutheran minister in Calw, described what torture meant for those who lost

---

25 Ibidem 88: 'wenn wir ansehen jhren letzten Kampff/ den sie in dieser Welt gehalten/ darin sie den HErrn Jesum so fest ergriffen/ vnd jhn nicht gelassen/ biß er jhr den Ewigen Segen mit geteilet vnd gegeben'.
26 Ibidem 93: 'gar übermässige Trawrigkeit'. On suffering and consolation in early modern funeral sermons, see Lehmann S., *Jrdische Pilgrimschafft und Himmlische Burgerschafft. Leid und Trost in frühneuzeitlichen Leichenpredigten* (Göttingen: 2019).

their lives in this way.[27] Since an important rationale for applying torture concerned revealing hidden treasures, no one was safe from such atrocities, not even old men and women. Andreæ reported one episode during the burning of Calw in 1634, when roughly 83 people died of torture. A man of over eighty years, who had been judge for five decades, had been brutally tortured and murdered, together with many other distinguished citizens. '[Er hatte verdient], den Rest seiner Tage im Schoos der Ruhe hinzubringen; er mußte eines grausamen Todes sterben' ('He had deserved to spend the remainder of his days in the bosom of tranquility; (but) he was forced to die a horrible death').[28]

Torture deprived people of the ability to prepare for death, which was all-important during this period. The tormented may have lived a life that could stand up before God, but the period close to death with its religious and social rituals was essential to ending one's life well. Rather than being felled violently through outside forces, men and women yearned to die gently and peacefully, and all efforts at the deathbed were geared toward ensuring a calm soul at peace and ready for God. Torture did away with these proceedings and made any deliberate, spiritual approach to death impossible.[29]

6   Martyrdom

Closely linked to torture was the experience of martyrdom, which tested the preparation toward death in other ways.[30] Andreæ offered the story of Caspar Nicolaus, who, the minister underlined, was a simple-minded and common (*geringer*) man but who had 'a whole lot of religion':

> Jch kann hier nicht mit Stillschweigen übergehen Caspar Nicolaus, der zwar als ein einfältiger und geringer Mann anzusehen war, aber sehr viel Religion hatte [...]. Als nun dieser arme Mann in die Klauen der Feinde gerathen, und gefragt worden, ob er einer von den Schwedischen

---

27 Andreæ Johann Valentin, *Fragment aus dem dreißigjährigen Krieg, betreffend das Schicksal und die Einäscherung der Stadt Calw, geschehen den 10. Sept. 1634*, transl. J.A. Leppichler (Tübingen, Heerbrand: 1793).

28 Ibidem 42. On Andreæ, see Brecht M., *Johann Valentin Andreae, 1586–1654. Eine Biographie* (Göttingen: 2008).

29 For an examination of torture, see Silverman L., *Tortured Subjects. Pain, Truth, and the Body in Early Modern France* (Chicago: 2001).

30 For a thorough discussion of martyrdom in the context of religious persecution, see Gregory B., *Salvation at Stake. Christian Martyrdom in Early Modern Europe* (Cambridge: 1999).

Spitzbuben sey? antwortete er, er sey ein Christ, und könne nicht läugnen, daß er gut Schwedisch denke. Hierauf wurde er derb geschlagen. Er aber erschrak nicht im geringsten darüber, und bekannte, er lebe als ein Schwedischgesinnter, und sey bereit, als ein solcher zu sterben; worauf er am ganzen Leib viele Wunden bekommen, die aber nicht tödlich waren. Daher sengten sie ihn mit Feuer, und da er merkte, daß er jetzt sterben werde, so verharrte er mit unüberwindlichem Muth bis auf den lezten Hauch unter langwierigen Peinigungen, so lang ihm seine Zunge gehorchte, bey dem Christlichen und Schwedischen Bekenntnis, wobey er versichert wäre, daß er mit dem Schwedischen König den Himmel erwarten dörfe; und so starb er als ein frommer Märtyrer.[31]

Andreæ was intrigued and impressed by the naturalness with which Nicolaus, a 'simple man' after all, followed his faith – even to the point of death. The Lutheran minister described him as a man who unquestioningly obeyed and unfailingly carried out orders, but evidently he could not be coerced to go against his religion, despite the fact that he would have to leave three orphans behind. To Nicolaus, the only path forward was steadfast clinging to his faith, which amounted to martyrdom. After admonishing his readers that Nicolaus' name should not be forgotten 'among the simple followers of Christ' nor should his orphans be neglected, Andreæ tried to justify why he himself did not become a martyr, pointing out that he never entirely left his flock and only meant to dodge the enemy.[32]

This divide between those who embraced martyrdom joyfully and those who found it harder to lay down their lives for God can also be seen in Catholicism, for example among members of religious orders who became prime targets during the war. The renowned reformer and Benedictine abbot, Veit Höser, wrestled with the decision whether he should stay behind when the Swedish enemy attacked his abbey Oberalteich in Bogen (Regensburg diocese) and thus

---

31   Andreæ, *Fragment* 45–46: 'When the poor man fell into the claws of the enemy and was asked whether he was one of the Swedish rogues, he answered he was a Christian and could not deny that he was good Swedish-minded. Thereupon he was roughly beaten. But he was not in the least frightened about it and confessed that he lived as a Swedish-minded man and would be ready to die as such, whereupon he suffered many wounds all over his body, which were not lethal. Thus, they scorched him with fire, and when he realized that he was about to die, he remained – with invincible courage, through prolonged torments, until his last breath (as long as) his tongue complied – steadfast in his Christian and Swedish confession. Because of this he was assured that he could await heaven with the Swedish king. And, thus, he died a pious martyr'.

32   Ibidem 46, 50: 'Er verdient, daß weder sein Nahme unter den einfältigen Bekennern Christi verlösche, noch daß seiner 3 Waisen, die er hinterlassen, vergessen werde'.

become a martyr for his faith or whether he should flee. Höser, who died of the plague in 1634, was not a timid man and pulled off many hair-raising escapes, but in a letter to a fellow pater, he acknowledged he was no martyr:

> Ich muß Dir gestehen, ich wollte nicht mit den ersten zur Flucht gezwungenen Brüdern abhauen und wollte aber auch nicht mit den Allerletzten von allen inmitten der Feinde bleiben. [...] Ich hielt durch mit den Letzten, aber ich war nicht mehr unter den Allerletzten, die von den Schweden den Tod erlitten und damit als Blutzeugen ihre Beharrlichkeit bis zum Ende bewiesen haben. Schamrot vor Schande muß ich dies bekennen, da es doch des vollkommenen Hirten Pflicht ist, seine Seele für seine Herde hinzuopfern. Aber, ach! Ich bin kein vollkommener Hirte; ich wäre des zufrieden, wenn ich nur ein wenig gerecht, im letzten Grade, befunden würde.[33]

As spiritual leader, Höser may have felt particularly torn regarding his decision. On the one hand, the abbot wanted to be there to guide his community of brethren through this difficult and desolate period; on the other, as he himself stated, he regarded it as his Christian responsibility, especially as a religious guide, to set an example and become a martyr for his faith. In the end, Höser conceded that he fell short of the highest mark of a true believer.

In contrast, Friar Melchior von Straubing and his brethren of the Capuchin monastery in Landshut showed enthusiastic resolve to die for their faith, when Bernhard of Saxe-Weimar's Swedish armies captured Landshut in 1634:

> haben Wir uns alle zugleich dem allmächtigen Gott ganz und gar mit einer demütigen beicht, und Sakramentseinnahme aufgeopfert, in mainung unser leben unserem Erzfater, von deme Wir es auf eine Zeit lang empfangen, als wahre mündere Brüder und Kinder S: Francisci, und wahre Blutzeugen Christi unser heil: Regel gemäß, ihme unserm Gott, und Herren durch diese Wüetterich und tyranische Bluthund mit freuden

---

[33] Höser, V. *'Wallensteins Rache an Bayern: Der Schwedenschreck.' Veit Hösers Kriegstagebuch*, ed. R. Sigl (Grafenau: 1984) 167 (24 February 1634): 'I have to admit to you I did not want to abscond with the first brethren who were forced to flee, and neither did I want to remain with the very last in the midst of the enemies. [...] I endured with the last, but I was not among the very last, who suffered death at the hands of the Swedes and as blood witnesses have proven their persistence until the end. Blushing with shame I have to admit this since it is the duty of the perfect shepherd to sacrifice his soul for his flock. But, alas! I am no perfect shepherd; I would be satisfied if, in the last degree, I were found a little just'.

unser leben, und blosse häls darzustrecken, ihme widerum auß zugeben seynd bereitt= und willig gewesen.[34]

The friars readily opened their doors to the soldiers and kneeled down in front of them, while lifting their hands toward heaven and waiting to see 'welcher der erste unter uns seyn würde, das triumphierend= blutige Sigkreuzl dauon zu tragen' ('who would be the first among them to carry away the triumphantly bloody cross of victory').[35] In the end, martyrdom was denied Melchior and his brethren since the Swedes were so perplexed about the Capuchins' behavior that the occupiers let the friars go.

Torture, martyrdom, as well as dying on the battlefield have in common that the ensuing death was the result of outside violence, but people who died as martyrs were in a very different position than those meeting their end through a shot or the strike of a sword. As seen above, soldiers wrestled with the fear of dying in the right spiritual state, and wondered whether they would pass muster with God and be admitted to the heavenly kingdom. Martyrdom, however, eliminated this fear. When choosing the path of the martyr, Nicolaus virtually ensured his entry into heaven. Despite the fact that he had no time or quiet to prepare for death, to attend to its all-important rituals, or to see to those he left behind, especially his three children (no mention is made of a wife), his faith and action assured him a place in heaven. In other words, even though none of the "safety measures" or a "normal" approach to death could be followed, the act of martyrdom alone vouched for the bona fide of the believer.

Undergoing torture to the point of death represents a more complicated situation. Not giving in to the pressure of violence could amount to martyrdom, as it did with Nicolaus, but armies and marauders also tortured people indiscriminately and for the most mundane and practical reasons. Thus, not everyone who was tortured made a conscious decision to become a martyr, even though many died precisely because of religious antagonism during an ever more brutal conflict.

---

34 Straubing Melchior von, *Capucineren zu* (1634). Staatsbibliothek München, Handschriftensammlung, Cgm 2943, fol. 4 r: 'all of us offered ourselves to the omnipotent God in humble confession and taking of the sacraments, believing that we were ready and willing to hand in our lives, which we, as true brothers and children of St. Francis and real blood witnesses of Christ according to our blessed rule, had received for a while from our Patriarch, and we gladly stretched out our lives and our bare necks toward this hothead and tyrannical bloodhound [Bernhard of Saxe-Weimar]'.

35 Ibidem fols. 5 r–v.

7 Death in Epidemic Proportions

Finally, the war led to mass deaths especially due to epidemic diseases, which presents the question how people approached their end when it came upon them quickly and en masse. Widespread malnourishment and armies crisscrossing the country disseminating diseases only exacerbated conditions for plague outbreaks. The mounting losses of loved ones were particularly difficult for those left behind. Pastor Sigismund Scherertz of Lüneburg, the same minister who in 1626 wrote *Kriegsbüchlein für Christliche Soldaten* (*Military Manual for Christian Soldiers*), shortly thereafter lost seven of his eight children in a plague that left Lüneburg with almost 7,000 deaths that year. The funeral sermon, dedicated to his wife, Elisabetha, was given by their friend Matthias Händel while in exile in Adorf.[36]

The minister highlighted how vulnerable humans were when they came into the world and that life continued to be extremely volatile. Händel then addressed how parents ought to mourn such excruciating losses. He counseled a 'middle road' between excessive wailing and tearing out one's hair, on one hand, and iron endurance, on the other. Holy Scripture wanted pious parents to mourn the death of their offspring; indeed, it was better to mourn than to drink. But even though losing seven children one after another no doubt compounded the parents' pain, 'so muß man nicht trawren vnd zagen/ wie die Heyden/ die keine Hoffnung haben/ sondern fromme Eltern sind viel eines bessern aus Gottes Wort berichtet/ daß nemblich jhre liebe Kinder vor der Angst hinweg gerissen/ vnd also zu gewündschter Ruhe kommen/' ('one ought not lament and despair like the heathens/ who have no hope/ but pious parents learn something better from Scripture/ namely that their dear children have been rescued from the fear/ and thus have passed into the desired peace').[37]

Händel had known most of the children for years and had instructed several when he was still a schoolteacher. His biographical sketches of the five girls and two boys, ranging from two to seventeen years of age, addressed their religious dedication and scholarly aptitude. But we also learn about the instability and uncertainty of their lives, which forced them to flee from one place to another during the war. Ten-year old Regina was the most brilliant among

---

36 *Christlich Leichgedächtniß SJeben frommer Geschwister/ Welche Anno Christi 1626. zur Zeit der Pest/ sanfft vnd selig im HErrn Christo diese Welt gesegnet/ vnd in jhr himmlisches Vaterland/ der Seelen nach/ gelanget sind/ Des Ehrwürdigen Herrn* SIGISMUNDI SCHERERTZII *Pastoris zu S. Lambert in Lüneburg vielgeliebten Kinder/ Jn zweene kurtze einfältige Sermones Aus der Historia Jobs im 1. vnd 19. Capitel verfasset* (Lüneburg, Stern: 1628) fol. Aiij v.

37 Ibidem fols. Biv v.

her siblings. According to the minister, she was also the only one, who at first did not embrace the prospect of death:

> Vnd als sie der liebe Gott auch angegriffen/ hat sie sich erstlich etwas betrübt erzeiget/ vnd gesagt/ Sie wolte lieber bey jhren Eltern vnd in diesem Leben bleiben: Doch sich endlich gehorsam in die Creutzschule begeben/ fleissig gebetet/ vnd jhr Trostsprüchlein offt wiederholet: HERR Christ/ du trewer Heyland mein/ Jch leb/ oder sterb/ so bin ich dein/ Bin ich denn dein/ vnd du bist mein/ Wer wolt mir doch zu wider seyn.[38]

Concerning the others, Händel emphasized their patience and devotion as they were dying. No doubt, having been raised in a minister's home, these children knew their religious texts, but Händel highlighted several other features not uncommon in such writings, namely singing, joy, and even laughter. Fourteen-year old Elisabeth sang eagerly 'LORD Jesus Christ/ I know quite well/ that I have to die someday', until her eyes grew too dark to make out the letters. In the quiet before her death, Elisabeth turned to those surrounding her:

> hat sie dennoch mit sonderbarer Begierd das schöne Lied gesungen/ HERR Jesu Christ/ ich weis gar wol/ daß ich einmal muß sterben/ etc./ biß jhr/ kurtz vor jhrem Abschied/ die Augen verdunckelt/ vnd sie die Buchstaben im Buch nicht mehr kennen können. Vnd als sie für jhrem Ende etwas still war/ hat sie endlich mit lachendem Munde/ vnd gar lieblichen Worten die anwesenden angeredet vnd gesagt: Es wären alle jhre verstorbene Geschwister bey jhr/ hat ein jedes angeredet/ vnd gesagt/ wie sie so schön wären. Endlich aber mit sonderlicher Frölichkeit gesagt: Sihe mein HERR Christi/ kompstu noch auch dazu/ vnd wilst mich holen. Nun wollte ich zwar gern bey meiner lieben Mutter allhie bleiben/ vnd jhrer warten: Aber weil du mich abholen wilst/ so wil ich mich bald geschickt machen/ vnd dir gerne in Himmel folgen.[39]

---

[38] Ibidem fols. Civ v: 'When the loving God seized her as well/ she showed herself initially distressed/ and said/ she rather wanted to stay with her parents and in this life: But she finally went obediently into the school of the cross/ prayed diligently/ and repeated her comforting maxim: LORD Christ/ my faithful savior/ whether I live/ or die/ I am yours/ If I am yours/ and you are mine/ Who, then, would [dare] to be against me'.

[39] Ibidem fol. Civ r: 'with a laughing mouth she spoke to them in lovely words: All her dead siblings were with her/ she had addressed each one of them/ and had said/ how very beautiful they were. Finally, she spoke with particular joyfulness: See my LORD Christ/ you, too, are joining in/ and want to fetch me. Now, I would love to stay here with my dear mother/ and serve her: But since you have come to fetch me/ I will get myself ready soon/ and will follow you gladly into heaven'.

Elisabeth's testimony – that she was seeing those who had gone before her and was looking forward to joining them in the beyond – was echoed in the biographical sections of other funeral sermons.

A second funeral sermon on the death of the seven children, by minister Gottfried Bavarus, underscored that all these young girls and boys were marked by the pains of the war – none more so than Judith, the oldest. Her many wretched experiences taught her to observe God's word more diligently. She suffered such great terror and deadly danger during the war in Bohemia that it grieved her parents deeply. By the time she reached Lüneburg, where she found some peace, Judith had learned 'to sweeten her cup of tears' with her deep faith in Jesus Christ, confident that 'nothing could separate her from the love of God' (Rom. 8).[40]

In Judith's experience, this earthly life had only misery to offer. Like others who had suffered similarly, she was not only ready but in fact yearning for her union with God:

> Wie Sie den auch zum öfftern für den Tisch mit sonderbahrer Lust gebetet/ vnd in jhre Gebetbücher geschrieben hat das Sprüchlein Davids/ Psal.42. Wenn werde Jch doch dahin kommen/ daß ich Gottes Angesicht schawe. Vnd also/ ob Sie gleich noch jung/ Jhr verlangen/ das Sie nach jhrem Erlöser CHRisto trage/ deutlich gnug zu verstehen geben. Vnd wann Sie ist gefraget worden/ warumb Sie doch vnter allen Sprüchen der Schrifft/ so Sie wüste/ diese zwey/ Job am 19. vnnd im 42. Psalm betete/ hat Sie geantwortet: Jhr Hertz trüge sie mit sonderbahrer Frewd zu diesen Worten des H. Geistes.[41]

Whereas Job 19 articulates the deep sorrows suffered on earth, Psalm 42 expresses the longing to be with God.

---

40   Ibidem fols Fiv – G r: '[...] hat Sie doch diesen süssen Bawm JEsum Christum mit wahrem Glauben in alle Jhr Creutzwasser gesencket/ vnd damit verzuckert/ auch gewiß gewust/ daß sie nichts scheiden werde von der Liebe Gottes/ Rom.8'.

41   Ibidem fol G r: 'Several times she prayed with special passion for (those around) the (dinner) table / and wrote in her prayer books the verse of David/ Psalm 42. When will I come to the point that I can behold God's countenance? And even though she was still young/ she expressed clearly enough her desire for Christ, her Savior. And when she was asked / why, of all the bible verses she knew, she prayed Job 19 and Psalm 42, she responded: Her heart carried her with particular joy to these words of the Holy Spirit'.

8 The Community around the Dying

Repeatedly during this discussion, the community of the dying has come into view. Funeral sermons were in fact delivered and written with the bereaved family and friends in mind.[42] The authors not only described how the dying approached death, but also how the community around the deathbed mourned and noted how it ought to conduct itself in its grief. The offered consolations and admonitions were largely those presented in situations outside of the context of war, but the turmoil of war conferred upon them a much greater poignancy. Particularly noteworthy during the dismal situation of war is the emphasis on the joy that was to come. Preachers underscored that the deceased were now in a much better place. In von Reichau's second funeral sermon, the minister ended by underlining that von Reichau's death was a grave loss for the war effort and those left behind, but, for von Reichau himself, nothing better could have happened to him.[43] The minister's declaration was rooted primarily in the deceased's grueling military life that brought him countless injuries and much suffering, and less in a religiously informed view of life.

Besides conjuring up an image of the deceased as now residing in a much more peaceful and joyful place, ministers also emphasized that the dead were not lost to the family but had only gone ahead to ready the final resting place for their loved ones. Death did not sever the connection between the deceased and those left behind, as Judith and others on their deathbed illustrated when they communed with those who had gone before. There existed a continuum between the earthly and the heavenly communities, which could prove a great comfort to the grieving, and we often read of the wish and prayer that the still living would follow the deceased soon.[44]

---

[42] Cf. also the chapter by Benedikt Brunner in this volume.
[43] Cuenen, *Predigten* 101.
[44] Note Hillard von Thiessen, who views the deathbed situation as a "normative threshold" between the earthly life and the life yet to come. In this liminal phase, the latter can seep into the former, and competing norms are reset. von Thiessen H., "Das Sterbebett als normative Schwelle. Der Mensch in der frühen Neuzeit zwischen irdischer Normenkonkurrenz und göttlichem Gericht", *Historische Zeitschrift* 295 (2012) 625–659. Cf. also his chapter in this volume.

9 Conclusion

Approaches to death during this unsettled and unnerving time of war reveal several of the cardinal characteristics evident during the early modern period in general, but it has also become clear that the war supercharged anxieties around the moment of death.[45] There was the fear of a violent death on the battlefield or during an attack on civilians that thwarted a dignified and well-prepared departing at home surrounded by loved ones. Importantly, it was not death itself people were afraid of, but the circumstances under which they died and whether they were worthy enough to enter the heavenly kingdom. The use of torture represented a particularly gruesome example of destroying the honor and ritual of death. Some countered such forced upon cruelty and obstruction of the "proper death" by choosing martyrdom, which in a way changed the demands of a "good death". The willingness to die for one's faith immediately catapulted the dying to the front row of the penitent.

Fear, however, was not the only strong sentiment among the dying during this theater of war. Many who had suffered the adversities of the conflict – from exile, destitution, and savagery to illnesses – were ecstatic at the prospect of moving on to a better place. And so, they joyfully spent the last phase of their lives, singing songs, laughing cheerfully, and inviting their loved ones to be glad for them. They would all be together again soon.

Bibliography

Primary Printed Sources

Andreæ Johann Valentin, *Fragment aus dem dreißigjährigen Krieg, betreffend das Schicksal und die Einäscherung der Stadt Calw, geschehen den 10. Sept. 1634*, transl. J.A. Leppichler (Tübingen: 1793).

Walther Ludolf, *Christi grosse Freundlichkeit: Aller gläubigen Hertzen Labsal vnd Erquickung. Das ist: Christlicher Leich=Sermon/ fuer Elisabeth Dorenwald, Frau von Ludolff von Anderten. Patrizier von Hannover. Gestorben am 14. Jan. 1641. Morgends zeischen 9. vnd 10. Vhren sanfft vnd seelig bey gutem Verstande in wahrem Glauben an Christum eingeschlaffen […]* (Rinteln, Petrus Lucius: 1641) 46.

Christlich Leichgedächtniß SJeben frommer Geschwister/ Welche Anno Christi 1626. zur Zeit der Pest/ sanfft vnd selig im HErrn Christo diese Welt gesegnet/ vnd in jhr himmlisches Vaterland/ der Seelen nach/ gelanget sind/ Des Ehrwürdigen Herrn

---

[45] On fear, especially of God, see Bähr A., *Furcht und Furchtlosigkeit. Göttliche Gewalt und Selbstkonstitution im 17. Jahrhundert* (Göttingen: 2013).

SIGISMUNDI SCHERERTZII Pastoris zu S. Lambert in Lüneburg vielgeliebten Kinder/ Jn zweene kurtze einfältige Sermones Aus der Historia Jobs im 1. vnd 19. Capitel verfasset (Lüneburg, Sterne: 1628).

Otto Nicolaus, *Christliche Leichpredigt/ fuer Burchardt von Benthen, Patrizier in Hannover, am 8.1.1642 verstroben and am 16.1.1642 beigesetzt. Prediger M. Nicolaus Otto, Pfarrer an der Kreuzkirche in Hannover* (Rinteln, P. Lucius: 1642).

Cuenen Johannes, *Christliche Leich Predigten/ Bey der Gegräbnuß deß Weyland WolEdlen/ Gestrengen vnd Vesten/ Melchior von Reichaw auff Corschwitz/ rc. der hochlöblichen Vnion/ vnd Fürstl. Würtemb. Bestelten Obristen/ KriegsRath/ vnd Obervogt zu Blawbeyren/ Gehalten die eine/ den 18. Maij/ Anno 1620. Zu Stuttgardten in der Spittalkirchen/ da die Leich Christlich vnd ehrlich zur Erden bestattet worden: Durch Tobiam Lottern/ der H. Schrifft Doctorn vnd StifftsPredigern zu Stuttgardten. Die ander aber hernach den 26. Maij/ zu Blawbeyren/ Durch M. Johannem Cuenen/ Superintendenten vnd Pfarrern daselbsten* (Stuttgart, J.W. Rößlin: 1620).

Höser, V. 'Wallensteins Rache an Bayern: Der Schwedenschreck.' *Veit Hösers Kriegstagebuch*, ed. R. Sigl (Grafenau: 1984).

Baldovin Johannes, *Leichenpredigt fuer Otto Schmidt, Sohn von Peter Schmidt, fuerstlicher Brauns. Lueneburg. Amptmann zu Nienburg an der Weser, am 3.2.1643 gestorben. Von M. Johannes Baldovius gehalten* (Rinteln, Peter Lucius: 1643).

Arndt David, *REFRIGERIVM CHRISTIANVM. Aller gedultigen Creutzträger Glaubens/ Liebes vnd HoffnungsBurgk/ ... Bey dem Christ= vnd HochAdelichem Begräbnuß der Weyland Wollgebornen Gnädigen Frawen/ Frawen MADGALENÆ, Frawen von Redern/ geborne von Hundin/ Deß auch Wollgebornen Gnädigen Herrn Herrn CHRISTOPHORI, Herrn von Redern/ Herrn auff Friedland Reichenberg vnd Seidenberg; Groß Strelitz/ Tost vnd Weiß Kretschen etc. etc. Hertz vnd Vielgeliebten Gemahlin. Welche den 1 Januarij dieses jtzlauffenden 1641. Jahres zwischen 2. vnd 3. Vhren nach Mittag/ in wahrem Erkändnuß vnd standhaffter Bekändnuß jhres Erlösers Christi JEsu allhier in Schwerin/ als in jhrem langwirigen Exilio, sanfft vnd selig eingeschlaffen/ vnd hernach den 13. Febr. in vnser Evangelischen Kirchen beygesetzet worden. Auß dem 19. Capittel des grossen Creutzträgers Hiobs auffgerichtet* [...] (Alten Stettin, Georg Rheten: 1641).

Scherertz Sigismund, *Kriegs Gebet vnd Andachten. Für die so mit schwerer Kriegsnoth von Gott heimgesucht sind* (Lüneburg, Stern: 1626).

Stedingk Theodor, *SORS MISERANDA VITÆ. Das ist: Eygentliche Beschreibung Des Müheseeligen menschlichen Lebens in dieser Welt: Leichenbegräbnis von Ludolff von Münchhausen, Erbsasse zu Oldendorf und Reimeringhausen, gestorben 21. 9. 1640; am 12. 1. 1641 beigesetzt, die Schrift der hinterlassenen adeligen Witwe und Erben zum Trost* [...] (Rinteln, P. Lucius: 1641).

Knolle, Antonius, *Vnsterblich Ehren=Gedächtnüs/ Klag=TRawer= vnd Leich=Predigten/ Fuer die Fuerstin Sophia, Markgraefin zu Brandenburg etc., gestorben am 23. 11.1646, von Hohann Albrecht Mintzeln 1648 gedruckt. 5. Leichenpredigt, von M. Antonius Knolle, Ekklesiast und Professor* (Hof, Mintzel: 1648).

Löher Bernhard, *Zwo Christliche Predigten Gehalten Vber der Leich Weilund deß Durchleuchtigen Hochgebornen Fürsten vnd Herren/ Herren Magni/ Hertzogen zu Würtemberg vnd Teckh/Graven zu Mümpelgart/ Herren zu Heydenheim/ etc. Welcher Freytags den 26. Aprilis dises 1622. Jahrs/ in dem; zwischen rc. Jhr. Durchl. Herren Maximiliano, Hertzogen zu Ober: vnd NiderBayern/ rc. vnd rc. Herren Georg Friderichen Marggraven zu Baden vnd Hochberg/ rc. Fürstl. Gn. bey Oberreißheim vorgangenem Treffen/ auff Württembergischen Grund vnd Boden vmbkommen* […] (Stuttgart, J.W. Rößlin: 1622).

Primary Manuscript Sources

Straubing, Melchior von, 'Relatio Was sich in dem Schweden Krieg zu Lanndshut mit dennen Capucineren zu getragen' (1634). Staatsbibliothek München, Handschriftensammlung, Cgm 2943.

Secondary Literature

Ariès P., *The Hour of Our Death*, transl. H. Weaver (New York: 1981).

Bähr A., *Furcht und Furchtlosigkeit. Göttliche Gewalt und Selbstkonstitution im 17. Jahrhundert* (Göttingen: 2013).

Becker H. – Einig B. – Ullrich P.-O. (eds.), *Im Angesicht des Todes. Ein interdisziplinäres Kompendium*, 2 vols. (St. Ottilien: 1987).

Bitzel A., *Anfechtung und Trost bei Sigismund Scherertz. Ein lutherischer Theologe im Dreißigjährigen Krieg* (Göttingen: 2002).

Boge, B. – Bogner, R.G. (eds.), *Oratio Funebris. Die Leichenpredigt der frühen Neuzeit. Zwölf Studien*, Chloe. Beihefte zum Daphnis 30 (Amsterdam: 1999).

Brunner B., "Die gedruckte Leichenpredigt als Erbauungsbuch – eine Erfolgsgeschichte des 17. Jahrhunderts", in Beyer H. – Simon S. (eds.), *Medium Buch* (Wiesbaden: 2019) 87–105.

Brunner B., "Heilige Stimmen. Die kommunikative Funktion der Toten in protestantischen Funeralschriften der Frühen Neuzeit", Sonderdruck, *Jahrbuch für Kommunikationsgeschichte* 24 (2022) 29–55.

Burnett, A.N., "'To Oblige My Brethren:' The Reformed Funeral Sermons of Johann Brandmüller", *The Sixteenth Century Journal* 36 (2005) 37–54.

Class M. – Reiß A. – Rüther S. (eds.), *Vom Umgang mit den Toten. Sterben im Krieg von der Antike bis zur Gegenwart* (Leiden – Boston: 2019).

Dinges M., "Soldatenkörper in der Frühen Neuzeit. Erfahrungen mit einem unzureichend geschützten, formierten und verletzten Körper in Selbstzeugnissen", in van Dülmen R. (ed.), *Körpergeschichten. Studien zur historischen Kulturforschung V* (Frankfurt a. M.: 1996) 71–98.

Düselder H., "'Wer so stirbt, der stirbt wohl!' Der Umgang mit der Sterbestunde im Spiegel von Leichenpredigten", in von Hülsen-Esch A. – Westermann-Angerhausen H. (eds.),

Zum Sterben schön. Alter, Totentanz und Sterbekunst von 1500 bis heute, Aufsätze (Regensburg: 2006) 238–249.

Gregory B., *Salvation at Stake. Christian Martyrdom in Early Modern Europe* (Cambridge: 1999).

Haude S., *Coping with Life during the Thirty Years' War (1618–1648)* (Leiden: 2021).

Houlbrooke R., *Death, Religion and the Family in England 1480–1750* (Oxford: 1998).

Houlbrooke R. (ed.), *Death, Ritual, and Bereavement* (London: 1989).

Hülsen-Esch A. von – Westermann-Angerhausen H. (eds.), *Zum Sterben schön. Alter, Totentanz und Sterbekunst von 1500 bis heute, Aufsätze* (Regensburg: 2006).

Kaiser M., "Zwischen 'ars moriendi' und 'ars mortem evitandi'. Der Soldat und der Tod in der Frühen Neuzeit", in Kaiser M. – Kroll S. (eds.), *Militär und Religiosität in der Frühen Neuzeit* (Münster: 2004) 323–343.

Koslofsky C.M., *The Reformation of the Dead. Death and Ritual in Earl Modern Germany, 1450–1700* (New York: 2000).

Krusenstjern B. von, "Seliges Sterben und böser Tod. Tod und Sterben in der Zeit des Dreißigjährigen Krieges", in von Krusenstjern B. – Medick H. (eds.), *Zwischen Alltag und Katastrophe. Der Dreißigjährige Krieg aus der Nähe* (Göttingen: 1999) 469–496.

Lehmann S., *Jrdische Pilgrimschafft und Himmlische Burgerschafft. Leid und Trost in frühneuzeitlichen Leichenpredigten* (Göttingen: 2019).

Lenz R., *Leichenpredigten. Quellen zur Erforschung der Frühen Neuzeit* (Marburg: 1990).

Moore C., *Patterned Lives. The Lutheran Funeral Biography in Early Modern Germany* (Wiesbaden: 2006).

Silverman L., *Tortured Subjects. Pain, Truth, and the Body in Early Modern France* (Chicago: 2001).

Thiessen H. von, "Das Sterbebett als normative Schwelle. Der Mensch in der frühen Neuzeit zwischen irdischer Normenkonkurrenz und göttlichem Gericht", *Historische Zeitschrift* 295 (2012) 625–659.

CHAPTER 13

Death Disrupted: Heresy Executions and Spectators in the Low Countries, 1550–1566

Isabel Casteels

1   Introduction

On the first Sunday after 15 August 1550, the inhabitants of Antwerp swarmed the streets and squares of their city.[1] It was the day of the procession of the Assumption of Mary, the most important religious *Ommegang* celebrated in Antwerp.[2] The pageant, in which important religious and civic corporations such as craft guilds had their own specified status and place, followed a fixed trajectory throughout the city and was meant to broadcast order and unity within the community. The civic authorities of Antwerp had selected this day for another type of display: a public execution. On the scaffold was Jan Lievens from Ghent, a baker, accused of being baptized as an adult, an act suggesting the heresy of Anabaptism.[3] As punishment, Lievens was to be burned until dead, after which the fire would be put out and his head would be mounted on a pole in the gallows' field. Everything went according to plan, until, describes one contemporary chronicler, 'als dese in het vier gaen soude, doen was daer eenen Lackenbereyders Knecht die hem quamp cussen, hem vermanende dat hy vromelyck soude stryden tot der doot (when he was about to go into the fire, there was a clothmaker's apprentice who came to kiss him, encouraging him to fight piously until death)'.[4] With this last-minute interference with

---

[1]   I would like to thank Louise Deschryver, the members of the reading group for Early Modern History at KU Leuven, the editors of this volume and the participants of the conference on the Moment of Death organized by the editors for their valuable contributions and suggestions for this chapter.

[2]   On the importance of procession culture in Antwerp see Marnef G., *Antwerp in the Age of Reformation. Underground Protestantism in a Commercial Metropolis, 1550–1577* (Baltimore: 1996) 86–88. See also Ramakers, B. *Spelen en figuren: toneelkunst en processiecultuur in Oudenaarde tussen Middeleeuwen en Moderne Tijd* (Amsterdam: 1996).

[3]   Genard P., "Personen te Antwerpen in de XVIe eeuw voor het feit van religie vervolgt", *Antwerpsch Archievenblad* 8 (1871) 1–471, 390 and 393.

[4]   Loon G. van (ed.), *Antwerpsch chronykje, in het welk zeer veele en elders te vergeefsch gezogte geschiedenissen sedert den jare 1500 tot het jaar 1574 zoo in die toen vermaarde koopstad als de andere steden van Nederland* (Leiden, Pieter vander Eyk: 1743) 48.

Lievens' execution, the clothmaker disrupted the carefully staged ritual and risked his life.

In the early modern 'theatre of death', the last moments on the scaffold were of the utmost importance. For governments staging executions, exemplary behavior from the patient – the term commonly used to indicate someone about to be executed – underscored their authority and the righteousness of the ritual of justice.[5] In heresy executions, even more was at stake. When not only worldly but also godly authority was challenged, a renouncing of dissident beliefs before death was needed to restore order and to allow the heretic to be reintegrated into the Christian community.[6] On the other hand, historians of the Reformation have underscored the agency of religious dissidents in shaping their rituals of death on the scaffold.[7] By resisting authorities, Protestants were able to fashion their own martyrdom on the scaffold, using their last moments as a powerful model for religious identity formation and confessionalization. In both strands of research, however, the execution audience is of secondary importance. Although historians have pointed out that executions needed to appeal to an audience's sense of justice in order to be successful,[8] the actions of execution spectators and the impact they had on the ritual of justice is rarely the focus of scholarly attention.[9]

---

5   Sharpe J.A., "Last Dying Speeches: Religion, Ideology and Public Execution in Seventeenth-Century England", *Past and Present* 107 (1985) 144–67; Spierenburg P. *The Spectacle of Suffering: Executions and the Evolution of Repression, from a Preindustrial Metropolis to the European Experience* (Cambridge: 1984); Foucault M., *Surveiller et punir: naissance de la prison* (Paris: 1975).

6   Nicholls D., "The Theatre of Martyrdom in the French Reformation", *Past and Present* 121 (1988) 49–73.

7   Gregory B., *Salvation at Stake: Christian Martyrdom in Early Modern Europe* (Cambridge: 1999); Murphy E.K.M., "Musical Self-Fashioning and the 'Theatre of Death' in Late Elizabethan and Jacobean England", *Renaissance Studies* 30 (2016) 410–429; Deschryver L., "You Only Die Once: Calvinist Dying and the Senses in Lille and Tournai During the Dutch Revolt", *Early Modern Low Countries* 4 (2020) 35–57; Dillon A., *The Construction of Martyrdom in the English Catholic Community, 1535–1603* (Routledge: 2002). The paradigm of confessionalization, first put forward by Heinz Schilling, is disputed but still influential. For a recent discussion see for example Hill K. (ed.), "Cultures of Lutheranism: Reformation repertoires in early modern Germany", *Past and Present. Supplements* 12 (2017).

8   Lake P. – Questier M., "Agency, Appropriation and Rhetoric under the Gallows: Puritans Romanists and the State in Early Modern England", *Past and Present* 153 (1996) 64–107; Cohen E., "Symbols of Culpability and the Universal Language of Justice: The Ritual of Public Executions in Late Medieval Europe", *History of European Ideas* 11 (1989) 407–416; Blok A., "The Symbolic Vocabulary of Public Executions" in Collier J.F. – Starr J. (eds.), *History and Power in the Study of Law: New Directions in Legal Anthropology* (Ithaca: 1989) 31–55.

9   Friedland P., *Seeing Justice Done: The Age of Spectacular Capital Punishment in France* (Oxford: 2012) does focus on perception, but mostly stresses that audiences enjoyed watching executions. Dülmen R. van, *Theatre of Horror: Crime and Punishment in Early Modern Germany*

This contribution will address this lacunae in historiography and show that in the context of the Reformation in the Low Countries, spectators regularly interfered with executions for heresy.[10] Although these interventions have been noticed by historians of the Reformation and Revolt in the Low Countries, they have often been interpreted as early, spontaneous outbursts of Reformed sympathies and general resistance against the strict heresy legislation, as a kind of prelude for the outbreak of Protestant violence that raged through the Low Countries during the Iconoclast Fury of 1566.[11] However, by far most inhabitants of the Low Countries in this period were Catholics. Indeed, as noted by Judith Pollmann, Catholic spectators paid a great deal of attention to the theatre of death, as they looked for signs of the sacred in the executions of heretics.[12]

This contribution aims to analyze the impact of such audience interventions. It does so by tracing descriptions of such incidents in a wide variety of sources, including legal administration documents, government correspondences, eyewitness accounts and chronicles, and martyrological writings. In the 1550s, martyr books started to circulate widely in the Low Countries, a center of both heresy persecution and book production. Incidents during executions were also a focus of the many chronicles, diaries and eyewitness accounts that were written in this period. Their writers were often part of the urban middle groups and show a particular interest for the order and peace in their cities.[13]

(Oxford: 1990) mentions audience engagement in the German context in the case of ritual failure, such as the breaking of the rope during executions or attacking the hangman in the case of botched beheadings.

10 There is hardly any research on audience behavior in the late medieval period. For Italy, Prosperi A., *Crime and Forgiveness: Christianizing Execution in Medieval Europe* (Cambridge, MA: 2020) has drawn attention to violent audience participation in political contexts in the Italian city states, but for the Low Countries, this research is lacking.

11 Schelven A.A. van, "Het begin van het gewapend verzet tegen Spanje in de 16ᵉ Nederlanden", *Jaarboek van de Maatschappij der Nederlandse Letterkunde* (1915) 126–156; Vrankrijker A. de, "Voorboden van oproer in de Zuidelijke Nederlanden in de jaren 1561–1562", *Bijdragen voor Vaderlandse Geschiedenis en Oudheidkunde* 5 (1935) 153–168; Duke A., "Building Heaven in Hell's Despite: The Early History of the Reformation in the Towns of the Low Countries", in idem, *Reformation and Revolt in the Low Countries* (London: 1990) 71–100, 75–76; Arnade P., *Beggars, Iconoclasts and Civic Patriots: The Political Culture of the Dutch Revolt* (Ithaca – Londen: 2008) 73–74; Decavele J., *De dageraad van de reformatie in Vlaanderen (1520–1565)* (Leuven: 1975) 398–432; Woltjer J., "Public Opinion and The Persecution of Heretics in The Netherlands, 1550–1559" in Pollmann J. – Spicer A. (eds.), *Public Opinion and Changing Identities in the Early Modern Netherlands: Essays in Honour of Alastair Duke* (Leiden: 2007) 87–106.

12 Pollmann J., *Catholic Identity and the Revolt of the Netherlands, 1520–1635* (Oxford: 2011), 54.

13 Pollmann J., "Archiving the Present and Chronicling for the Future in Early Modern Europe", *Past and Present* 230 (2016) 231–252; Caers B. – Demets L. – Gassen T. van (eds.), *Urban History Writing in North-Western Europe (15th–16th centuries)* (Turnhout: 2019).

Finally, these incidents were discussed in detail between local and central authorities. Whereas the carrying out of justice was a task for the local magistrates, in such troubled cases the central government became involved.

The argument is twofold. First, contrasting the description of these events challenges the idea that such incidents during executions were spontaneous outbursts of Protestants' sympathies. The symbolic violence used and contemporary discussions within the Reformed communities indicate that audience interventions were strategic and performative. Second, the chaos that surrounded these events facilitated the emergence of diverging narratives on their meaning, which created a context of uncertainty and anxiety among onlookers. The changing expectations and anticipation of new audience interferences caused local magistrates to take precautionary measures and adjust their execution policy accordingly. Although only a handful of executions were actually disrupted, the perception of these interventions and the atmosphere of anxiety they created still shaped the entire experience of attending and staging executions in this period. As such, this contribution serves as a reminder that the moment of death remained a highly unstable and unpredictable event in early modern Europe, despite all rituals and rules attempting to regulate it.

2 From Consolation to Rescue Attempts

The organization of heresy persecution in the Low Countries was complex and multilayered, requiring the cooperation of several levels of authority with overlapping jurisdictions.[14] The base for prosecution were the anti-heresy edicts published by Charles V (1500–1558) and his son Philip II (1527–1598) throughout the sixteenth century, which criminalized specific actions that indicated heresy, such as being baptized as an adult. The local magistrates and provincial courts were responsible for their reinforcement, sometimes with the help of inquisitors. In the period between the start of heresy persecutions in 1521 and the eruption of Protestant violence with the Iconoclast Fury of 1566, at least 1300 executions were carried out for violating the anti-heresy legislation, making the Low Countries the epicenter of European heresy persecution.[15]

---

14 Gielis G. – Soen V., "The Inquisitorial Office in the Sixteenth-Century Habsburg Low Countries: A Dynamic Perspective", *Journal of Ecclesiastical History* 66 (2015) 47–66; Goosens A., *Les inquisitions modernes dans les Pays-Bas méridionaux 1520–1633*, 2 vols. (Brussels: 1997/1998).

15 Numbers based on Monter W., "Heresy Executions in Reformation Europe, 1520–1565", in Grell O. – Scribner B. (eds.), *Tolerance and Intolerance in the European Reformation* (Cambridge: 1996) 48–64; and Duke, "Building Heaven" 71.

Approximately one third were carried out in the years between 1550 and 1566. Initially, repression was mainly directed towards the Anabaptists, but in the 1550s, Calvinism started to become a bigger threat.

Indeed, the early example of the clothmaker kissing Jan Lievens on the scaffold concerned an execution for Anabaptism. Historian James Tracy mentions a similar event in 1557, taking place in the town of Haarlem, in the province of Holland.[16] Here, around three hundred spectators attended an execution, several of whom tried to kiss and console prisoners convicted of Anabaptism, who were being escorted to the execution scene.

In consoling the condemned at the stake, spectators drew on repertoires of consolation and assistance in death coming from the *ars moriendi* tradition. From the fourteenth century onwards, the 'art of dying' had become increasingly important, elaborately explained in the very popular manuals that appeared on the topic.[17] A good death meant dying in exemplary fashion in the company of friends and family, showing repentance for your sins and enduring suffering in a steadfast manner. The importance of dying an exemplary death soon extended beyond the deathbed to the scaffold. *Ars moriendi* theologian Jean Gerson himself started a campaign for allowing criminals confession before their execution, reintegrating them into the Christian community and allowing a burial in sacred ground after their death.[18] Executions provided the perfect context to prepare for a good death – which should be repenting, steadfast, and exemplary to onlookers. In contrast to other ways of dying, the convicted criminal knew exactly when and where death would happen. Even more than unplanned deaths, executions thus came to be increasingly scripted, planned, and staged.

Not only for the condemned, but also for those witnessing the execution, this had important implications. Just like the *ars moriendi* propagated, dying was not something the criminal did alone, but in the company of the execution audience, assisting, comforting, and consoling the criminal and encouraging confession and penance. The clergy assisted in allowing criminals confession

---

16   Tracy J.D., *Holland Under Habsburg Rule, 1506–1556: The Formation of a Body Politic* (Berkeley: 1990) 200–201.

17   The original *ars moriendi* texts were composed around 1415 and published in Southern Germany. Their title came to be the name of the genre of death literature. As many death manuals were illustrated, they reached a wide European audience. In 1534, Erasmus of Rotterdam published his own *ars moriendi* account, which quickly became popular. See Pabel I.M., *Humanism and Early Modern Catholicism: Erasmus of Rotterdam's Ars Moriendi in Early Modern Catholicism* (Toronto: 2001).

18   Gerson J., "Requete pour les condamnés a mort" in Mgr. Glorieux (ed.), *Oeuvres complètes* (Paris: 1966) 341–343.

before death at least from the early sixteenth century onwards.[19] In the Italian city states, lay brotherhoods were founded with the specific purpose of assisting those about to die, whose elaborate manuals still survive.[20] Not only the clergy and brotherhoods, but also the audience in general took on this role, by, for example, saying a *pater noster* for the soul of the convicted criminal.[21] With the onset of the Reformation, those dying on the scaffold as martyrs adapted the *ars moriendi* tradition into a Protestant equivalent, and even used their deaths to exemplify good Protestant dying behavior.[22] The role of Reformed spectators, then, changed accordingly: whereas traditionally the audience had encouraged repentance, in the new Reformed confessional culture they encouraged steadfastness and adherence to the Reformed faith in the face of death.

Whereas such instances of audience consolation during executions of Anabaptists can still be seen as spontaneous or individual actions, the audience interference during executions of Calvinists seemed to be more coordinated. First and foremost, the appropriation of the execution soundscape by psalm singing came to be a widespread form of interference by the audience.[23] This seems to have been the case, for example, with the execution of Calvinist minister Christoffel Fabritius in Antwerp in 1564. Reports of the event make clear that unrest started among the audience when several onlookers started singing psalms.[24] The contents of the psalms might have influenced the crowd as

---

19　A chapter on this practice was one of the few original contributions included in Damhoudere J. de, *Praxis rerum criminalium* (1554) which was otherwise a plagiarized version of the earlier sixteenth century law treatise by Philip Wielant. See also the diary of Thomas Munters, whose brother was involved in consoling criminals before their deaths, for many examples of this practice. Grauwels, J., *Dagboek van Gebeurtenissen. Opgetekend door Christiaan Munters 1529–1545* (Assen: 1971).

20　Prosperi, *Crime and Forgiveness*; Terpstra N., *The Art of Executing Well: Rituals of Execution in Renaissance Italy* (Kirksville: 2008). For the Low Countries see Kauffman C.J., *Tamers of Death: The History of the Alexian Brothers from 1300 to 1789* (New York: 1976).

21　Grauwels, *Dagboek van Gebeurtenissen* 85–86.

22　Gregory, *Salvation at Stake* 120–142. For France, see also Friedland, *Seeing Justice Done* 89–116. On the reformation of the *ars moriendi* in general see Resch C., "Reforming Late Medieval Ars Moriendi: Changes and Compromises in Early Reformation Manuals for Use at the Deathbed", in Flæten J. – Rasmussen T. (eds.), *Preparing for Death, Remembering the Dead* (Göttingen: 2015), 153–172 and for the importance of death rituals in confessionalization see Deschryver, "You Only Die Once".

23　Murphy, *Musical Self-Fashioning* and Lambert E M., *Singing the Resurrection: Body, Community, and Belief in Reformation Europe* (Oxford: 2018).

24　*Recuil de ce que portent les trois diverses informations prinses juridicquement* […] in: Genard P., "Personen te Antwerpen in de XVIe eeuw voor het feit van religie vervolgt", *Antwerpsch Archievenblad* 9 (1872) 1–471, 206.

well. For example, in Rotterdam in 1558, riots among the audience began with a woman throwing her shoe.[25] Significantly, shoe throwing is mentioned in Psalm 60:8 and 108:9, psalms which came to be widely known among Calvinists in this period because of the vernacular psalm books in which they had recently been put to music.[26] Not only by singing, but also by chanting and shouting could audiences control the execution soundscape. In Middelburg in 1564, an audience had gathered during the proclamation of the verdict of two heretics, which were public events as well. Members of the audience started consoling the condemned in public after their death sentences had been pronounced – saying that they were wronged but 'dat zy geen sorghe en zouden hebben want zy nyet sterven en zouden (that they need not worry because they would not die)'.[27]

However, the comment of the spectators during the Middelburg proclamation might also have referred to the worldly lives of the condemned. By 1564, local authorities were confronted with increasingly violent attempts to 'save' Protestants from deaths on the scaffold. From 1561 onwards, forced prison breaks had started to take place in West Flanders.[28] In Belle, a prisoner was forcibly released from his guards when they were transferring him to another prison in April 1561. In November 1561, book seller Jan Hacke escaped from his prison in Meesen with outside help. A few months later, in May 1562, the preacher Willem Damman was freed from the episcopal prison in Ypres. Outside of Flanders, we find similar stories. In 1564, Margaret of Parma informs the King that a heretic escaped from prison in Valenciennes, with the help of the daughter of a prison guard.[29] Although the prisoner escaped, the girl that had helped him was captured and executed on the market square. In Antwerp in early 1565, the sisters Barbara and Madarda Catz, together with Simon

---

25   Versyden J.D., "Memorie oyer het oproer in 1558" in Unger J. – Bezemer W. (eds.), *De oudste kronieken en beschrijvingen van Rotterdam en Schieland* (Rotterdam: 1895) 223–226, 224.
26   Datheen Petrus, *De Psalmen Davids, ende ander lofsanghen, wt den Fransoyschen Dichte In Nederlandschen overghesett, Doer Petrum Dathenum* [...] (Heidelberg, Michael Chiraet: 1566).
27   Letter from Margeret of Parma to city of Middelburg, 7.11.1564, in: Pekelharing K.R., "Bijdragen voor de geschiedenis der Hervorming in Zeeland 1524–1572", *Archief* VI, uitgegeven door het Zeeuws Genootschap der Wetenschappen (1866) 225–316, 267–269.
28   See Decavele, *De dageraad* 398–432; Schelven, "Het begin van het gewapend verzet".
29   Gachard, L.P. (ed.), *Correspondance de Philippe II sur les affaires des Pays-Bas, Publiée d'après les originaux conservés dans les Archives royales de Simancas*, 5 vols. (Brussels: 1851) vol. 1, 333. See also Le Boucq P.J., *Histoire des troubles advenues à Valenciennes à cause des hérésies: 1562–1579* (Brussels: 1864) 9.

Dhondt, escaped with the help of accomplices.[30] Not every attempt succeeded. In 1562 some people had tried in vain to free a certain Philippe Desbonnes from his prison cell in Armentières.[31] In July 1566, however, an armed group did succeed in freeing two Calvinists from prison in the same city, incited by the illegal Calvinist hedge sermons that started to take place that summer all over the Low Countries.[32]

The most dramatic form of audience interference was the freeing of convicted heretics from the stake only moments before their deaths. This happened for example in Rotterdam in 1558, when five prisoners accused of Anabaptism were to be executed in front of the city hall.[33] The first prisoner, Jan Hendriks, was already hanged when he suddenly started to move. The audience broke through the ring of guards, cut down the hanged man, and freed the other prisoners as well. The hangman had to flee into one of the houses adjacent to the market square; the bailiff and city magistrates hid in the city hall.[34] In Valenciennes in April 1562, the audience attacked the scaffold on which two Calvinists, Philippe Mallart and Simon Faveau, were already standing, about to be burned. After initially returning the condemned to the safety of the prison hall, the guards could only stand and watch how the spectators managed to free the prisoners and get them out of the city.[35] The episode was all the more painful because this execution was ordered by the Governess Margaret of Parma herself. With the execution of Fabritius in Antwerp in 1564, a similar rescue attempt took place. Besides the singing of psalms, audience members also started to throw rocks, hitting some of the guards and even the bailiff.[36] In this case, however, an improvised stabbing by the hangmen prevented a rescue.

30   Genard P., "Ordonnantien van het Antwerpsch magistraat, rakende de godsdienstige geschillen der XVIe eeuw", *Antwerpsch Archievenblad* 2 (1865) 374–378.
31   Vrankrijker, "Voorboden van oproer" 163.
32   Hernighem A. van, *Eerste bouck van beschryfvinghe van alle gheschiedenesse (1562–1572)*, ed. A.L.E. Verheyden (Brussel: 1978) 17; Le Barre P. de – Soldoyer N., *Mémoires de Pasquier de le Barre et de Nicolas Soldoyer*, ed. A. Pinchart 2 vols. (Brussels – The Hague: 1859) vol. 1, 89.
33   Versyden, "Memorie oyer het oproer in 1558" 223–226; Geesink W., "Een terechtstelling van Anabaptisten te Rotterdam gestoord in 1558", *Rotterdams Jaarboekje* 2 (1890) 233–252; Hoop Scheffer J.G. de, *Inventaris der Archiefstukken berustende bij de Vereenigde Doopsgezinde Gemeente te Amsterdam*, 4 vols. (Amsterdam: 1883), vol. 1, 384–389; 393–394.
34   Versyden, "Memorie oyer het oproer" 224.
35   Paillard C. (ed.), *Histoire des troubles religieux de Valenciennes 1560–1567, publié daprès des documents inédits*, 4 vols. (Brussels – The Hague: 1874).
36   Information from Meesteren Pauwels Schuermans, 5.10.1564, in: Genard, "Personen te Antwerpen" 194.

3   A Violent Crowd?

Facing such insubordinate behavior, the city magistrates that staged the executions responded resolutely. The day after the disrupted execution of Fabritius, the city magistrate issued an ordinance summoning the instigators of the unrest to present and justify themselves in court.[37] In Middelburg, too, the magistrate tried to track down the 'principale roerers en bewegers, om, die gevonden, te straffen en punieren naer heurl. verdienste (principal instigators and troublemakers to, when found, be chastised and punished according to their merit)'.[38] In Valenciennes, governess Margaret of Parma ordered the Count of Boussu to trace the culprits, 'comme ces turbateurs sont gens de petite estoffe, il seroit facile avec une bande ou deux de gendarmerie les brider et chastier (because the troublemakers are low class people, it will be easy to chase and punish them with a band or two of gendarmerie)'.[39] If the authorities succeeded in tracking down spectators that interfered, they punished them harshly. In Antwerp, the urban magistrate itself took the responsibility for this. The clothmaker who kissed Jan Lievens, a man named Peter Vanden Broecke, was captured on the spot and put to death himself by fire only a few days later.[40] One of the 'rascals' who was accused of throwing stones during the execution of Fabritius was executed by the sword.[41]

In other cases, however, such events called for interference from higher levels of government. After the rescue from the stake in Rotterdam, the Council of Holland took charge of punishing the culprits because the urban government was held accountable for their failure to keep peace and order.[42] The day after the event, two deputies travelled to the council residing in The Hague to explain what happened and to excuse the magistrate. After that, several officials from the Council went to Rotterdam to investigate the matter. In total, nine spectators were sentenced. Punishments included performing *amende honorable*, paying a fine, public flogging, and banishment. For two of them, punishment was more severe: they were decapitated, with their heads

---

[37]   Genard, "Ordonnantien" 366–368.
[38]   Letter of Magistrate of Middelburg to Margaret of Parma, 8.11.1564, in: Pekelharing, "Bijdragen voor de geschiedenis" 270.
[39]   Paillard, *Histoire des troubles* 200.
[40]   Loon, *Antwerpsch chronykje* 48.
[41]   Ordinance proclaimed by Antwerp Magistrate on 9 October 1564, in Genard, 'Ordonnantien" 373–374.
[42]   Hoop Scheffer, *Inventaris der Archiefstukken* vol. 1, 384–389; 393–394.

displayed on spikes and their bodies on the wheel.[43] One of the condemned was sentenced to stand on the scaffold and watch the executions of the others. The hangman of the Council of Holland travelled to Rotterdam to carry out the sentences. Two culprits apparently got away: they were banned in absence.

Perhaps to prevent such interventions from higher up, the *emotions* were usually downplayed by the local authorities responsible for the execution, framing insubordinate audiences as irrational, emotional mobs. According to the Antwerp city councilors, incidents during Fabritius' last moments were caused by 'jonck gespuys ende geensins volck van fatsoene (young rascals and in no way decent people).[44] The Middelburg council assured governess Margaret of Parma that they were 'nyet min verwondert en zyn dan Uwe Alt.; want wy van te vooren noyt gelycke insolentie hier en hebben weten useren (no less surprised by such inconvenience than your highness, because never ever has such insolence taken place here before)'.[45] In Valenciennes, the interfering spectators were described as 'gens de petite qualité', that is, 'people of little quality'.[46]

However, the serious measures and severe punishments for disrupting executions make clear that Protestant coreligionists went through great lengths and put their own lives at stake to make their points. Indeed, there are strong indications that these instances of audience interference were not spontaneous or emotional outbursts of violence, but strategic and coordinated actions by the heretics' coreligionists. As mentioned above, audience interventions, especially in the case of executions in which Calvinists were involved, seem to have been well organized. Both in Valenciennes and Antwerp, groups had gathered already the night before at the prisons where the convicts were held. In Valenciennes, the Calvinist congregation had even offered a petition to the city council asking for the release of Faveau and Mallart. Moreover, the rioting audiences actually succeeded in smuggling the prisoners out of the city, which would most likely not have been possible without considerable organization.

Indeed, by the beginning of the 1560s, Calvinism in the Low Countries had taken on an increasingly organized and militant character.[47] In multiple

---

43   The Hague, National Archives, 3.03.01.01 (Hof van Holland) inv. nr 5654, fol. 290 vo. The criminal sentences from 1539–1811 are accessible online.
44   For instance in: Genard, "Personen te Antwerpen" 9, 252.
45   Pekelharing, "Bijdragen voor de geschiedenis" 269.
46   Paillard, *Histoire des troubles* 191.
47   Gelderen M. van, *The Political Thought of the Dutch Revolt 1555–1590* (Cambridge: 1992); Marnef G., "The Dynamics of Reformed Religious Militancy: The Netherlands 1566–1585", in Benedict P. (ed.), *Reformation, Revolt and Civil War in France and the Netherlands 1555–1585* (Amsterdam: 1999) 51–68. For the role of the preachers in this movement see also

towns, congregations 'under the cross' had formed, the most important one in Antwerp. In the same period, Calvinists started to preach out in the open – sometimes even carrying weapons to these hedge sermons. The early Reformed congregations under the cross fiercely debated the legitimacy of the use of violence. The official Reformed policy was one of non-resistance. The Anabaptist attacks on authority had shocked inhabitants of the Low Countries in the 1530s, and new Reformed communities were careful in avoiding association with them. Important church leaders, like Calvin himself, and the Dutch Stranger Churches in Protestant countries like England and some German principalities, likewise argued against the use of violence towards government officials. But they had the luxury of relative safety – for Calvinists in the Low Countries, persecution was a much bigger threat.

Therefore, the legitimacy of using violence against persecutors of faith was a much more pressing and practical matter in the Low Countries. Trying to adhere to the official policy of non-resistance, the congregation explored some creative solutions. For example, it was suggested that freeing prisoners was allowed, but only without using violence (the advice was to use fake keys), or it was allowed to rescue coreligionists with violence only when they were in custody of an inquisitorial officer, who was not recognized as government official. Although treatises on Reformed thought from the first half of the 1560s continued to insist on non-resistance, the Antwerp congregation decided in May 1562 that it was allowed to free co-religionists from prison – even by force.[48] Apparently, one of the leading figures of the Antwerp congregation, Herman Moded, immediately put this new policy into practice by freeing a prisoner from his guards on the Antwerp Vismarkt only a few days later.[49] Still, as we have seen, violent releases of prisoners already took place in the months preceding this decision. It makes more sense to interpret this decision as an attempt to justify actions that were happening anyway.

The extent to which the release of prisoners was discussed within the congregation further adds to the interpretation that such attacks were strategically planned and organized, instead of sudden outbursts of violence. Moreover, in the case of heresy executions, the highly ritualized display of authority offered an opportunity for Reformed onlookers to stage a performance themselves. Given the importance of the *ars moriendi* traditions mentioned above, the

---

Crew P.M., *Calvinist Preaching and Iconoclasm in the Netherlands 1544–1569* (Cambridge: 1978).

48 Braekman É.M., "Anvers – 1562: Le premier synode des Eglises réformées", *Bulletin Société d'Histoire du Protestantisme Belge* 102 (1989) 25–37.

49 Schelven, "Het begin van het gewapend verzet" 140.

moment of death was a highly symbolic event to interfere with. Doing so, spectators seem to have been drawing from repertoires of late medieval popular protest and revolts.[50] The freeing of prisoners from the stake in Valenciennes is telling. Contemporary accounts relate how suspicious groups of men wearing long robes with hoods, had been entering and disappearing again from the market, while singing psalms.[51] They had also assembled in front of the prison where the convicts were held, again singing psalms. But instead of freeing the prisoners right away, the group apparently waited until the actual execution was taking place before they made their move. This certainly increased the shock effect of the escape for both rulers and inhabitants of the Low Countries. The event quickly found its way into contemporary personal diaries and chronicles, not only in Valenciennes itself, but also in other cities of the Low Countries, now popularly known as the *Journee des Maubrulez*; or 'the day of the ill-burned'.[52] Similarly, the prison break in Armentières in 1566 was all the more shocking for contemporaries because it took place on the same day the bishop of Arras visited the town to give a sermon, and the holy sacrament was carried through town during a procession.[53]

Material and spatial structures of authority were appropriated during such attacks. In Haarlem, someone attacked soldiers guarding the execution with a wooden board to be used for the pyre.[54] In Valenciennes, before setting the prisoners free, the spectators first destroyed the scaffold, including the protective ring around it. During Fabritius' execution, spectators were throwing stones that were lying on the market square to be used for the construction of the new town hall. Of course, these items could just accidentally have been the closest thing at hand. However, the fact that their use is emphasized in eyewitness accounts suggests that the symbolism was meaningful to contemporaries.

---

50   Boone M., "The Dutch Revolt and the Medieval Tradition of Urban Dissent", *Journal of Early Modern History* 11 (2007) 350–375. On repertoires of urban resistance in the Low Countries see Serneels H., "Making Space for Resistance: the Spatiality of Popular Protest in the Late Medieval Southern Low Countries", *Urban History* (2021) 1–16.
51   Paillard, *Histoire des troubles* 156–157.
52   Manteau M. – Chavatte P.I., *Chronique de Mahieu Manteau et de Pierre-Ignace Chavatte*, ed. Eugène Debièvre (Lille: 1911) 32; D'Outreman Henry, *Histoire de la ville et comté de Valentiennes: Divisée en IV. parties* … ed. Pierre D'Outreman (Douai, Veuve de Marc Wyon: 1639) 200.
53   Hernighem, *Eerste bouck* 17; Le Barre P. de – Soldoyer N., *Mémoires de Pasquier*, vol. 1, 89; Vaernewyck M. van, *Van die beroerlicke tijden in die Nederlanden en voornamelijk in Ghendt: 1566–1568*, ed. Ferdinand Vanderhaeghen, 4 vols. (Gent: 1873) vol. 1, 16; Loon, *Antwerpsch chronykje*, 78.
54   Tracy, *Holland under Habsburg rule* 200–201.

4   Martyr Books and Execution Spectators

The martyrological writings that circulated in the Low Countries from the end of the 1550s onwards might have been fueling these violent audience interventions. Brad Gregory has rightly argued that these martyrological writings primarily seem to emphasize the suffering and endurance of martyrdom.[55] Indeed, most of all the ideal of steadfastness was emphasized, and when execution audiences featured in these narratives, their role was one of witnesses to the martyr's faith. However, taking a closer look at these stories reveals that consolation, too, was an interaction between audience and martyr that could be initiated by audience members to encourage the patient at the stake. The stories told in the most important collection of Anabaptist martyrologist writings, the *Offer des Heeren*, which was published in 1562, do indeed follow this script. One example are the letters of Anabaptist Hans van Overdam, who was burned at the stake in Ghent in 1550. During his transfer from one prison to another, tells Overdam, as many people came up to him 'gelijck water dat vanden Berghen neder loopt (as water flowing down from a mountain)', wishing him good luck, telling him that God would save him.[56] Similarly, a song describing the execution of several Anabaptists in 1551 mentions an onlooker shouting to the friar consoling the patients, 'Hoort ghy Antechristen verwoet / Staet achter wten wege / Laet de vrouwen spreken soet (hear you, Antichrist, step back and let these women speak)'.[57]

It is interesting to note that the martyrological accounts circulating among Reformed readers in the Low Countries emphasized audience interventions on behalf of the patient at stake much more than their other European counterparts. The *Mémoires* of the Spanish humanist and reformer Francisco de Enzinas (ca. 1518–1552) posthumously published in 1558, is a case in point.[58] In his treatise, Enzinas described in detail the spectators revolting against the officers during heresy executions in Leuven in 1543, which he witnessed himself during his stay in the Low Counties. According to the *Mémoires*, the Leuven theology students made fun of the judges, and one of them even punched a

---

55   Gregory, *Salvation at Stake* 134–138.
56   Cramer S. – Pijper F., *Het offer des Heeren, de oudste verzameling doopsgezinde martelaarsbrieven en offerliederen* (The Hague: 1904) vol. 2, 104.
57   Ibidem, 518.
58   Enzinas F. de, *Mémoires de Francisco de Enzinas: Texte latin inédit, avec la traduction française du XVIe siècle en regard 1543–1545*, ed. Ch.-Al Campan, Jean Baptiste François Blaes (Nendeln: 1862–1863) 13, 16; On the author, see: Vermaseren B.A., "Autour de l'edition de l'Histoire de l'estat du Pais Bas, et de la religion d'Espagne, par F. de Enzinas dit Dryander", *Bibliothèque d'humanisme et renaissance* 27 (1965) 463–494, 463.

guard in the face. One year later, Calvinist reformer Adriaen van Haemstede (ca. 1525–1562) published his *Historie der Vroome Martelaren*. Describing the execution of Adriaen Coreman and Hendrick Snoelaecke in Antwerp in 1559, Van Haemstede writes 'dewijle dat de Scherprechter besich was haer aen den pael te binden, heft God almachtich terstont sulcken beroerte onder den volcke gesonden datse met eenen roep riepen "slaet doot, slaet doot!" (while the hangman was binding them to the pole, God almighty sent such unrest among the audience that they cried with one voice "kill him, kill him!")'.[59] According to the account of Fabritius' death, added to the 1565 edition of Haemstede's martyr book, the audience was so loud, that no one could hear the words of Fabritius himself anymore.

It seems hardly a coincidence that violent audience interventions increased rapidly in the years after the publication of these martyr books. These martyrological writings not only presented an example or model for both martyr and audience, but also carried a message of legitimizing audience unrest or violence as an expression of God's will. Indeed, commenting on audience unrest during the execution of Cornelis Halewijn in 1559, Haemstede laments the 'blintheyt van den Raet ende Overheyt van Antwerpen, die niet aen en sien hoe dat God haer verstoort ende vreese aen iaecht, om dat sy tegen hem ende synen Gesalfden opstaen (blindness of the Council and Government of Antwerp, who do not see how it is God that disturbs and frightens them, because they oppose Him and His anointed ones)'.[60] Paradoxically, then, these martyr books likewise tended to downplay the agency of spectators themselves, just like the authorities did. The goal was mainly to display the agency of the martyr, as an example of good death, and the role of audiences in these narratives is supportive. Not a man-made strategically planned rescue attempt, but the hand of God was at work here.

5   Anticipating the Audience

Despite the authorities' efforts to downplay the risk of audience attacks and to keep up appearances that they were in control of their cities, the measures they started to take clearly suggest that authorities increasingly anticipated violent audience behavior to take place. Thus, in Rotterdam, before the problematic

59 Haemstede A.C. van, *De Gheschiedenisse ende den doodt der vromer Martelaren, die om het ghetuyghenisse des Evangeliums haer bloedt ghestort hebben, van den tijden Christi af, totten Jare M. D. Lix. toe, by een vergadert op het kortste* (Antwerp: 1559) 446–447.
60 Haemstede, *De Gheschiedenisse* 454.

execution of five Anabaptists in 1558, the city government had issued a proclamation 'Dat niemand de justitie en zoude beletten ofte resisteren met woorden of werken, op pene van lijf en goed (that no one would obstruct or resist justice with words or deeds, on punishment of life and goods)'.[61] Similarly, in Valenciennes the magistrates added a special clause to the verdicts of Mallart and Faveau:

> sy interdisons et deffendons à tous bourgeois manans et habitans de ceste ville de non venir armez ny enbastonnez veoir faire ladicte exécution, saulf ceulx ordonnez par messrs. de la justice, ny faire quelque esmotion ou donner empeschement à icelle, sur paine de la vye.
>
> (We forbid and prohibit all citizens and inhabitants of this city from coming armed or fortified to the aforementioned execution, except those ordered by the court, or to cause any disturbance or impediment to it, on pain of the law).[62]

But warnings alone did not assure the city governments. Indeed, all along the way from the city gates up to the condemned at the stake, preventive measures were put in place to keep potentially violent spectators at a safe distance from the execution. The main entrances to the cities were usually closed when trouble was expected.[63] This would not only prevent 'strangers' from coming in, but also troublemakers from going out in case something should happen. Places of execution were increasingly guarded. In normal circumstances, only the hangman with some city officials would be enough to ensure an orderly execution, but more often also the civic militia was enlisted to keep the peace. However, members of the civic militia itself sometimes held Calvinist sentiments and was not always likely to actually interfere should spectators attack.[64] Therefore, higher levels of authorities did not always trust to leave it up to the urban magistrate to guard potentially troubling executions. This was the case in Valenciennes in 1562: there, the governess had ordered the Count of Boussu, knight of the Order of the Golden Fleece, to oversee the execution with his own soldiers.[65] Sometimes the entire market square was closed off, to prevent

---

61 Versyden, "Memorie over het oproer" 223–224.
62 Sentence de mort contre Simon Fauveau et Philippe Mallart du 27 avril 1562, in: Paillard, *Histoire des troubles* vol. 2, 188–190.
63 Ibidem, 193.
64 Grayson J.C, "The Civic Militia in the County of Holland, 1560–81: Politics and Public Order in the Dutch Revolt", *BMGN – Low Countries Historical Review* 95 (1980) 35–63.
65 Paillard, *Histoire des troubles*, vol. 2, 200.

audiences from getting close to the scaffold. In other cases, the guards formed a ring around the execution place. Another ring, made of boards and spikes, was used to close off the scaffold.[66] Even on the execution platform itself, the condemned was often separated from the spectators by a small wooden house they had to enter and in which the burning took place.[67]

Moreover, in addition to the spatial separation of spectators and patient, there was a temporal dimension to these measures, such as carrying out executions very early in the morning or even in the middle of the night. The reason for this might have been that not many spectators would be present at the market square at that moment. Moreover, executions took place very shortly after the proclamation of the verdict. This prevented the heretic's coreligionists to organize themselves and set up a rescue attempt. The most extreme form of preventing audiences to interfere were the 'secret' executions the Antwerp government was carrying out on a large scale between 1557 and 1566.[68] Here, heresy executions were not even carried out in public anymore, but in the basement of the city prison, in the middle of the night.

Finally, the authorities tried to stay in control of the execution soundscape. When audiences started singing more often during executions, authorities made sure soldiers would drum and march during the event to drown out the chanting mass. Moreover, often the mouths of prisoners were blocked with a wooden ball or nailed down with a tongue screw.[69] This had not only the practical advantage of preventing the condemned to sing or speak, but also carried symbolic connotations. The piercing or cutting out of the tongue was a traditional punishment for blasphemy. As mentioned above, this measure was effective in preventing the condemned to stage a martyr's death, but again, also the prevention of communication between the condemned and the audience was at stake. In Valenciennes, for example, the rescue attempt of 1562 supposedly started when Faveau cried 'ôh Pere Eternel', the beginning of Psalm 94, which seemed to be a sign for the audience to start the attack.[70]

66 Versyden, "Memorie oyer het oproer" 200. Paillard, *Histoire des troubles:* 'les bailles plantées sur le marchié et le bois disposé'.
67 See for example Haemstede, *De Gheschiedenisse* 453–454. This practice is mentioned in many accounts of executions, for example in Ypres, Ghent, Antwerp, Leuven.
68 Casteels I., "Drownings in the Dark: The Politics of Secret Executions in Antwerp, 1557–1565", *Early Modern Low Countries* 5 (2021) 75–97.
69 Examples in martyrologies are numerous. Already in the 1530s this practice was in use, but the policy was made official only in 1571. See Gachard (ed.), *Correspondance de Philippe II* vol. 2, 687–8.
70 Rahlenbeck C., "Les Chanteries de Valenciennes", *Bulletin de la Commission pour l'histoire des Églises Wallonnes* III (1888) 121–159, 154. See also Vrankrijker, "Voorboden van oproer" 166–167.

The reason usually put forward by authorities for these measures was to prevent 'heresy contamination'. Heresy was regarded as a contagious disease that spread through the air or via contact with the heretic. Not only the government adhered to the idea that religious beliefs were 'contagious', but martyrological accounts also often mention the spreading of true faith by the mere presence of the martyr.[71] During executions especially, ashes from the burning of a martyr were thought to be inhaled by the spectators, thus becoming infused with religious ardor. Although such ideas were widespread, the focus on the discourse of contamination in both contemporary sources and historiography might obscure the fact that such measures were also meant to keep the audience from interfering during the execution. Indeed, it was very difficult for urban governments to downright acknowledge that this was the case – it would severely undermine their authority to admit they were not in control of their executions.

6 The Afterlife of the Last Moments

Even when direct intervention was no longer possible, audiences could still seize control over the meaning and afterlife of the moment of death. When speech or psalm singing were drowned out by noisy soldiers, the last words of the condemned were publicized in different ways. Even the so-called secret executions were not secret, but publicized as well, and recast as symbol of terror and oppression.[72] The precautionary measures taken by authorities to separate audiences from condemned only stimulated this process. After all, when no spectator could actually hear or accurately see how a martyr died, there was more room for postmortem interpretation.

Similarly, the measures taken by the authorities to take control of the execution soundscape were turned upside down by Reformed audiences. Louise Deschryver suggests that in Antwerp in 1566, Calvinists even adopted a militant character during their funeral rituals, making noise with drums and pipes – as a mirroring of the soldiers that tried to drown out the psalm singing during executions.[73] Many stories circulated in which martyrs were miraculously still able to speak after their tongue was pierced.[74] Even the tongue screws used to

---

71 For example in Crespin J., *Le Livre des Martyrs* […] (Geneva: Jean Crespin, 1554) 625–626.
72 See Casteels, "Drownings in the Dark".
73 Louise Deschryver, *No Rest for the Wicked. Death, Senses, and the Reformation in Sixteenth-Century Antwerp* (Ph.D. dissertation, Leuven University: forthcoming 2024) chapter 3.
74 Examples in van Haemstede, *De Gheschiedenisse* 170; 406; Crespin, *Le Livre des Martyrs* 639–640; Cramer – Pijper, *Het offer des Heeren* 575–577.

deprive the martyr from speech were reinvented as memorial objects of piety and resistance.[75] According to his martyrology, the tongue screw used on Hans Bret was picked up from the ashes after his execution and carefully kept by his friends. It survives until this day.[76] In martyrological writings, precautionary measures taken by urban magistrates were framed as sign of impotence, not of power. The account of executions in Leuven by Enzinas ridicules the increasingly elaborate 'theatrical' staging of these executions, calling them 'spectacles' and 'farces', in which the judges were 'the main characters of the tragedy'.[77] The famous martyrologist Jean Crespin, born in the French-speaking border region of the Low Countries, habitually describes the ceremonial character of public executions as 'mysteries', or 'farces', thus degrading their meaning.[78]

One of the cases cited above shows this dynamic particularly well: the execution of Fabritius and its afterlife.[79] Fabritius' rescue was prevented by his stabbing, but the battle over Fabritius' last moments was not over yet. Anticipating that his coreligionists might try to collect his remains for clandestine burial, the authorities left Fabritius' disfigured body on the market square for 'four or five hours', as bait. When no one showed up, they decided to throw his remains in the river Scheldt, instead of the more usual display on the gallows field, to 'verhueden dat die van sulcke seckten zyn groot werck makende vande dooden oft heure reliquien, als men heeft bevonden van Joannes Hus en andere (avoid that those of this sect make a great deal out of the dead or their relics, as was the case for Jan Hus and others)'.[80]

The attack during Fabritius' execution seriously eroded the authority of the Antwerp government, and the culprits had to be punished. A few weeks after the event, the magistrate sentenced to death one Robbert du Briel from

75 Braght T.J. van, *Het bloedigh tooneel der doops-gesinde, en weereloose Christenen, die om het getuygenisse Jesu hares salighmaeckers geleden hebben en gedoodt zijn van Christi tijdt af tot dese onse laetste tijden toe* (Amsterdam: Jacob Braat, 1660). Compare this with the memory of the tongue screw of Mayken Wens in: Pollmann J., "Met grootvaders bloed bezegeld. Over religie en herinneringscultuur in de zeventiende-eeuwse Nederlanden", *De Zeventiende Eeuw. Cultuur in de Nederlanden in interdisciplinair perspectief* 29 (2013) 154–175, at 159. For France, see Nicholls, "The Theatre of Martyrdom" 58.
76 Now in the collection of the Catherijnenconvent Utrecht.
77 Enzinas, *Mémoires de Francisco de Enzinas*, v. 13, 16, 71.
78 Nicholls, "The Theatre of Martyrdom" 57–58. See also Tucker J., *The Construction of Reformed Identity in Jean Crespin's "Livre des Martyrs"* (London: 2017).
79 Casteels I. – Deschryver L. – Soen V., "Introduction: Divided by Death? Staging Mortality in the Early Modern Low Countries", *Early Modern Low Countries* 5 (2021) 1–16.
80 Genard, "Personen te Antwerpen" 194. The Czech theologian Jan Hus was celebrated in reformed culture as a fifteenth-century protomartyr and his story is accounted in many martyrologies. Enzinas describes the same practice of throwing the ashes in the river after the executions he witnessed in Leuven.

Valenciennes for disrupting justice. In Du Briel's punishment, too, the symbolic battle continued. One contemporary chronicler emphasizes that Du Briel was the first prisoner to be decapitated in front of the new town hall – it is unlikely that this was a coincidence, since Du Briel was being punished for pelting the stones used for the construction of the new town hall during the execution of Fabritius.[81] The chronicler also mentions how Du Briel's body was displayed on the gallows' field with stones hanging around his body. However, another chronicler reports that Du Briel's body remained on the gallows' field for years, 'sonder dat het van eenighe vogelen geraeckt werde, geheel ende ongeschent blyvende (without it being touched by any birds, remaining intact and undamaged)'.[82] Interestingly, this story seems to echo Catholic doctrines connecting bodily incorruptibility with purity and piety, suggesting Du Briel's execution was unjust.

The battle shifted from mortal remains to the legacy of Fabritius' death. Apparently, even before the execution itself took place, some monks that had been present during Fabritius' examination of faith made public that Fabritius, who was a former Augustinian monk, had renounced his sins and had begged to return to his order. Only a few weeks after the execution, Fabritius' fellow Calvinist preacher Joris Wybo responded by publishing his own account of Fabritius' death, which was printed by Dirck Buyter in Vianen.[83] Wybo published a song about Fabritius too, also printed in Vianen.[84] In these publications, Wybo emphasizes that Fabritius stayed loyal to his Reformed ideas to the end, and that the rumors about his reconciliation with the Catholic church were false.

Shortly after, a small leaflet was printed in Antwerp by Jan Verwithaghen, containing two letters supposedly written by Fabritius, 'naer zijn eyghen handtschrift, ghelijck die in der Overheyts handen bewaert is (by his own hand, as they are kept by the authorities)'.[85] According to the anonymous editor of the pamphlet, the letters served 'om allen den ghenen, die tonrecht ende valschelijck inde historie Christophels Smits onlancx uutghegaen,

---

81 Loon, *Antwerpsch chronykje* 61.
82 Weert N. de, "Chronycke van Nederland, besonderlyck der stadt Antwerpen, sedert den jaere 1097 tôt den jaere 1565" in C. Piot (ed.), *Chroniques de Brabant et de Flandre, Collection de chroniques belges* (Bruxelles: 1879) 72–172, 144.
83 Joris Wybo, *Historie en gheschiedenisse van de verradelicke gevangkenisse Christophori Fabritij* (Vianen, Dirck Buyter: 1564).
84 Wybo, Joris, *Een nyeuwe geestelicke liedeken gemaect van een vrome martelaar genaempt Christophorus Fabricius, tot Antwerpen verbrant* [Vianen, Dirck Buyter: 1565]. No copies survive of the first edition.
85 [Vossenhole, Jan?] *Somighe seyndtbrieven Christophori Smits, de welcke int iaer Vierentsestsich den vierden Octobris t'Atwerpen verbrant is* (Antwerpen, Joannes Withagius: 1564).

beschuldicht ende aengheteekent sijn, te excuseren ende the ontschuldighen (to excuse and justify all those that were unjustly and falsely accused and alleged in the recently published history of Christophel Smit)'. In the letters, we read how happy Fabritius had been with the visits of the monks and how sorry he was for his sins, thus asserting that Fabritius had indeed renounced his heretical faith before his death. Later that year, the fight continued, when Wybo again responded to these letters in the second enlarged version of the *Historie en gheschiedenisse* of 1565, by stating that some 'papists and libertines' had revived 'slanderous gossips' by publishing forged letters in Fabritius' name, which they had read out loud on the stock exchange market and subsequently published.[86] We read the same in the enlarged second edition of Van Haemstede's *Historie der Martelaren*, which also included the account of Fabritius' death and was published by the same printer, Goossen Goebens in Sedan.[87] The story of Fabritius was also translated into French by the influential Walloon Calvinist minister Guido de Brès, who stayed in Sedan in that period, which translation was also printed by Goebens.[88]

In his treatise, Wybo identified the medical doctor Adriaen van Vossenhole as the 'grooten montspeelder ende guychelaer (big mouthplayer and phoney)' that had spread the false rumors.[89] According to Wybo, Vossenhole would do better to stick to his medical profession instead of playing the inquisitor, 'met eene sake hem te moeyen, dear af hy geen verstant en heeft (interfering with things he does not know anything about)'.[90] Van Vossenhole, in turn, could of course not tolerate these allegations. As late as 1569, he replied by publishing *Apologia*.[91] In this pamphlet, he copied the sentences of Wybo's *Historie* that concerned him, and meticulously refuted them one by one. He also stressed that he and Fabritius had always been on excellent terms. Decades after his

86 Joris Wybo, *Historie ende gheschiedenisse van de verraderlijcke ghevanghenisse Christophori Fabritii ende Oliverii Bockij, waer van den eenen tot een ellendighe verlossinge ghecomen is, ende den anderen wredelijck vermoort ende ten viere op gheoffert*, [Sedan, Goosen Goebens: 1565].

87 Haemstede, *Historie der Martelaren* ed. 1566, 615.

88 Guy De Brès, *Histoire notable de la trahison et emprisonnement de deux bons et fideles personnages en la ville d'Anvers*, [Sedan, Goosen Goebens: 1565]. De Brès was the author of the Belgic Confession, the most important doctrine for the Dutch reformed churches, which was published in 1561. De Brès was executed himself in Valenciennes in 1567, in the aftermath of the Iconoclast Fury.

89 Wybo, *Historie ende gheschiedenisse* fols. 144–146.

90 Wybo, *Historie ende gheschiedenisse* fol. 147.

91 Vossenhole, Adriaan van, *Apologia, dat is een verantwordinge tegen de ghene die van hem in een boecxken gheintituleert, Historie ende gheschiedenisse Christophori Fabritij gheschreven* [Cologne, Gottfried Hirtshorn: 1569].

death, the legacy of the last moments of Fabritius continued to attract attention. In 1582, Wybo's *Historie en gheschiedenisse* was reprinted in Antwerp, and again in 1593, 1610 and 1611, in the by then Calvinist cities of Haarlem and Amsterdam.[92]

7   The Uncertainty and Instability of Ritual

Such stories mattered and influenced the perception of contemporary execution spectators. Describing the disturbed execution of Fabritius, Antwerp chronicler Josse De Weert notes 'waer aff naerder staet in 't boeck der Martelaeren (on this there's more in the book of Martyrs)'.[93] Nowhere in his chronicle does De Weert reveal himself as a radical Protestant, suggesting that such narratives reached beyond Reformed communities alone. The circulation of such dissident interpretations of death contributed greatly to the aura of anxiety that increasingly surrounded executions in this period. Already with the onset of the Reformation, the alternative, Protestant scripts of dying created a rupture in the ritual. Witnessing a heresy execution in this period meant that you would be uncertain until the moment of death what would happen – whether they would repent or not, whether grace would be granted, and even what the method of execution would be. This materialized dramatically in the presence of two execution tools on the scaffold: a pyre for burning and a sword for the 'merciful' beheading.[94]

Even more unsettling for the spectators were the disruptions. Indeed, rather than spontaneous outbursts of general resistance against heresy persecution, these interventions were strategic interventions. However, most inhabitants of the Low Countries were, like De Weert, religiously and politically somewhere in the middle between dogmatic Catholicism on the one hand, and radical Protestantism on the other.[95] To be sure, doubts about the effectiveness and

---

92   Wybo, Joris, *Historie ende geschiedenisse vande gevangenisse der vromer mannen, Christophori Fabritii, dienaer des goddelicken woordts binnen Antwerpen, ende Oliverii Bockii van Heydelberch* (Antwerpen, Jasper Troyen: 1582); Wybo, Joris, *Historie ende gheschiedenisse van de verraderlijcke ghevanghenisse Christophori Fabritij ende Oliverij Bockij* (Amsterdam, Cornelis Claesz: 1593); Ibidem (Amsterdam, Jan Evertsz II Cloppenburgh: 1611).
93   Weert, "Chronycke van Nederland" 144.
94   For example with the execution of Cornelis Halewijn: Haemstede, *De Gheschiedenisse* 453–454.
95   See Woltjer J., *Friesland in hervormingstijd* (Leiden: 1962); Pollmann J., *Catholic Identity and the revolt of the Netherlands, 1520–1635* (Oxford: 2011); Pollmann J., *Een andere weg naar God: de reformatie van Arnoldus Buchelius (1565–1641)* (Amsterdam: 2000).

righteousness of heresy prosecutions and critique of the church and clergy were not limited to Protestants alone, but most people dreaded the violent and radical attacks on authority even more. These attacks made a huge impression on the inhabitants of the Low Countries. As became clear throughout this contribution, such events were recorded in detail in many chronicles, diaries, and eyewitness accounts.

Not only did chroniclers describe the disturbed executions, but the interest in executions in general increased greatly in the 1560s. Some chroniclers even started writing with the explicit goal of recording all justice taking place in their cities. A fascinating example are the books written by Ypres burgher Augustijn van Hernighem.[96] In the course of his life, Van Hernighem wrote seven books, covering a period of 33 years. Not only does he announce in the first section of every book that he will record 'alle justicie dier metter doot ghebuert hier binder stede ghedaen (all justice by death done here within this city)', he also meticulously numbers every single execution he writes about in the margins of his manuscript. It seems hardly a coincidence that he started his account in 1562, with chronicling the first armed hedge preaches taking place in Boeschepe, just outside Ypres, which was led by Gheleyn Damman, the brother of the Willem Damman, who had been released from prison around this same period.[97] Van Hernighem's obsession with capital punishment is exceptional, but not unique. The sheer number of such accounts that are written in this period already indicate how chaotic and troubled contemporaries perceived their times to be. For most of the spectators, the entire experience of watching executions thus became fraught with anxiety – the unsettling of a ritual that used to symbolize order and justice.

Much like urban governments, inhabitants themselves increasingly anticipated violence. In Rotterdam, tells one contemporary chronicler, already before the execution of the three Anabaptists in 1558 took place, 'hebben alle de borgers hierontrent wonende, hun deuren vast toegesloten (all the burghers living around here have closed their doors shut)'.[98] Another chronicler, looking back on execution that had taken place during his childhood years in Middelburg in the 1560s, writes 'soo ick se hebbe sien hanghen, naedat sy al doot én gestorven waeren, en de sentencie volbrocht was – want de kinderen, gelijck ick was, niet weleer mochte(n) commen sien om de oploopen, die in(t) dooden van sulke

---

[96] Van Hernighem, Augustyn. "Beschrijving der stad Yper", deel 1, 2, 5–7., 1562–1595. State Archives Kortrijk. Fonds Goethals-Vercruysse, ms. 296. Books 4 and 7 have not been published as editions; book 3 is lost.
[97] Van Hernighem, *Eerste bouck* 14.
[98] Versyden, "Memorie over het oproer" 224.

lieden toe geschieden (I saw them hanging there like that, after they were dead and deceased, and the sentence had been carried out – because the children, like I was, were not allowed back then to come watch because of the commotion that happened when killing such people)'.[99] Sometimes even the mere fact that a Protestant minister came to watch an execution was recorded, as was the case in Ypres in 1566. No troubles took place during the execution, but chronicler Augustyn van Hernighem mentioned anyway that Pieter Hazaert came to the city to watch justice being carried out.[100]

Still, there is no evidence that Catholic audiences themselves interfered or tried to stop such attacks, as was the case in France. There, many instances are known where enraged Catholics – even children – took the executions of Protestants into their own hands, lynching the condemned before the execution.[101] Although the 'rites of violence' during the French Wars of Religion might have been the exception rather than the rule, it is still noteworthy that the pattern in the Low Countries was precisely the opposite.[102] Only on a few occasions did Catholic burghers organize resistance against Protestants, for instance in Nijmegen, where a Calvinist preacher was even chased out of the city.[103] Indeed, Judith Pollmann has argued that this 'Catholic passivity' in the Low Countries was mainly due to the attitude of the priests.[104] Reform was considered a matter of the church, in which the laity played no role. In France, however, priests actively engaged their flocks in the fight against heresy. The same might be true, then, for heresy persecution. If religious reform was a matter for the church, legal persecution was a matter for the government. Indeed, it seems that most Catholic spectators in the Low Countries did simply not

---

99 Joossen P., *De kroniek van Pieter Joossen Altijt recht Hout*, ed. R.T. Fruin (Middelburg: 1909).
100 Van Hernighem, *Eerste bouck* 25.
101 Zemon Davis N., "The Rites of Violence: Religious Riot in Sixteenth-Century France", *Past and Present* 59 (1973) 51–91; Crouzet D., *Les Enfants bourreaux au temps des guerres de Religion* (Paris: 2020); Murdock G. – Roberts P. – Spicer A. (eds.), *Ritual and Violence: Natalie Zemon Davis and Early Modern France, Past and Present Supplement 7* (Oxford: 2012). For England, see also Walsham A., "Skeletons in the Cupboard: Relics after the English Reformation", *Past and Present* 206 (2010) 121–143.
102 Roberts, P. "French Historians and Collective Violence", *History and Theory* 56 (2017) 60–75.
103 For the situation in Nijmegen see Hageman M., *Het kwade exempel van Gelre: De stad Nijmegen, de Beeldenstorm en de Raad van Beroerten, 1566–1568* (Nijmegen: 2005).
104 For a discussion about the 'passivity' of the clergy in the Low Countries see Pollmann, *Catholic Identity*; and the various contributions in "Discussion on Catholic Identity and the Revolt of the Netherlands", *BMGN* 126 (2011).

see it as their job to interfere with the course of justice. Instead, the role of the spectator was one of compassion.[105]

Even if chronicles show anger and frustration about Reformed violence in their writings, they looked towards the authorities for an answer, instead of taking matters into their own hands. Brussels chronicler Jan de Pottre remarks for exemple: 'Dat comt er afvan de nuwe predicanten te laeten preken van de nuwe ende quade secte [...] Ick duecht dat sij aen de corde van de galge verberren sullen (That's what you get when you let these new preachers preach of these new and evil sects [...], may they burn on the rope of the gallows)!'[106] However, precisely because of the violent attacks during executions by Protestants, urban magistrates became increasingly reluctant to enforce the laws. It was simply too dangerous and the disruption of *concordia* and urban peace were considered more of a threat than heresy. Also here, the other execution spectators seemed to trust their authorities' policies. According to chronicler Marcus van Vaernewijck, reflecting on the decision of the Ghent magistrate in 1566 to release some heretics from prison,

> [...] oft zoude moghen ghedaen zijn om den trouble vanden volcke te mijden, die nu den stock in dhandt hadden ende naer de justicie niet vele en vraechden, meenende dat haer zake ghoet ende recht was, zoo haer die predicanten buten eenpaerlic in bliesen, up avonture dat zij niet met eenen psalmzanck, de vanghenesse zelve up en liepen ende zulcke ghevanghenen uut lieten, ghelijck alreede tot Aermentiers gheschiet was, [...] dwelc al waert in dien ghevalle niet onwijselic, maer zeer discretelic vander wet ghedaen was; want een medecijn of cijrurgien verzoet oft verstranct zijn medicijnen, drancken, electuarien, suppositorien oft ander medicanten, naer dat hij ziet die qualiteijt vander ziecte, passie ofte quetsuere vanden pacient, alzoo die edel justicie, als een wijse meestersse, doet haer kueren ende weerct an dlichaem der ghemeente, [...] somtijts met incisie oft snijden ende ooc somtijts veel zoeter ende gracelicker.

> [...] that they did this to prevent trouble from the people, who now have the stick in their hands and do not ask for justice, because they think their cause is righteous and just, or so their preachers keep teaching them, so as to prevent the danger that they will come up to the prisons while

---

105 On the importance of compassion in experiencing the passion of Christ see for example Roodenburg H., "Empathy in the Making: Crafting the Believer's Emotions in the Late Medieval Low Countries", *BMGN – Low Countries Historical Review* 129 (2014) 42–62.

106 Pottre Jan de, *Dagboek van Jan de Pottre, 1549–1602*, ed. B. de St. Genois (Gent: 1861) 25.

singing psalms and release the prisoners, which already has happened in Armentières [...] In such cases, this is not unwise, but rather very discreetly done by the authorities. As a doctor sweetens or strengthens his medicine according to the qualities of the disease, so does noble Justice, as a wise mistress, cure the body of the community [...], sometimes with cutting and incisions, but also sometimes with sweetness and grace.[107]

8 Conclusion

Burghers like Vaernewijck had good reason to be scared. Protestant violence erupted fully during the Iconoclast Fury of 1566, during which churches, monasteries, and statues of saints were destroyed. In the years following the Iconoclast Fury, the danger of witnessing executions increased even more. In addition to various pacification strategies, part of the Habsburg response to the troubles in the Low Countries was to punish those who had participated in the Fury of 1566 and officials that had failed to prevent it.[108] Soldiers from the royal army, led by Duke of Alba, usually guarded those executions. Unlike the civic militias, they did not hesitate to attack the audience in case of troubles, sometimes killing bystanders in the process.[109]

Audience interventions profoundly changed the experience and practice of executions in the Low Countries in the early 1560s. To be sure, only a handful of executions in this period were disturbed by audience interventions. Most executions that took place in the Low Countries were carried out in an orderly fashion. Still, the executions that *were* disturbed had much more impact than the orderly ones. Their histories were recounted many times in stories, books, songs, and letters and their legacies were important for confessional identity formation. These disturbances were not outbursts of a general resistance against heresy persecution. Instead, they were strategically employed by Protestant minorities. Local governments increasingly anticipated such disturbances to take place and adjusted their execution policies accordingly. For many inhabitants of the Low Countries, executions came to be highly unstable events, surrounded by anxiety.

As such, the Low Countries underscore the importance of an often-overlooked actor in the shaping of executions: the audience. Contemporary

---

107 Vaernewyck, *Van die beroerlicke tijden* vol. 1, 34–35.
108 Soen V., "The Beeldenstorm and the Spanish Habsburg Response (1566–1570)", *BMGN: Low Countries Historical Review* 131 (2016) 99–120.
109 See for example Vaernewyck, *Van die beroerlicke tijden* vol. 3, 147–50.

sources show a bias against the importance of execution audiences. For governments, stressing the agency of audiences undermines their authority, whereas the discourse of emotional and irrational mobs serves as a legitimation of far-reaching repression. For martyrological writings, the agency lies with the martyr at stake, providing an example of a good death. These biases echo in historiography. On the one hand, a Foucauldian model, in which the early modern public execution is analyzed as display of sovereign majesty, is still influential.[110] On the other hand, historians of the Reformation mainly stress the importance of exemplary martyr behavior.[111]

However, chronicles, eyewitness reports, and diaries, reveal a greater importance of audience behavior as a shaping factor in executions. The anxiety around the moment of death during the Wars of Religion, then, might be one of the reasons why executions came to be increasingly theatrical over the course of the sixteenth century. The more uncertainty and anxiety there was, the more rules and rituals were needed. Even with the most stylized, staged, and scripted of deaths such as the ones on the scaffold, an orderly moment of death was never certain.

Bibliography

Primary Printed Sources

Braght Thieleman Janszoon van, *Het bloedigh tooneel der doops-gesinde, en weereelooseChristenen, die om het getuygenisse Jesu hares salighmaeckers geleden hebben en gedoodt zijn van Christi tijdt af tot dese onse laetste tijden toe* (Amsterdam, Jacob Braat: 1660).

Crespin Jean, *Le Livre des Martyrs* [...] (Geneva, Jean Crespin: 1554).

D'Outreman Henry, *Histoire de la ville et comté de Valentiennes: Divisée en IV. parties ...* ed. Pierre D'Outreman (Douai, Veuve de Marc Wyon: 1639).

Damhoudere Joos de, *Praxis rerum criminalium* [...] (Antwerp, Jean Bellère: 1554).

Datheen Petrus, *De Psalmen Davids, ende ander lofsanghen, wt den Fransoyschen Dichte In Nederlandschen overghesett, Doer Petrum Dathenum* [...] (Heidelberg, Michael Chiraet: 1566).

Enzinas Francisco de, *Histoire de l'estat du Pais Bas, et de la religion d'Espagne* (Sainte-Marie, François Perrin: 1558).

---

110 A recent example is Ward R., *A Global History of Execution and the Criminal Corpse* (London: 2015).

111 For example in Gregory, *Salvation at stake*.

Enzinas F. de, *Mémoires de Francisco de Enzinas: Texte latin inédit, avec la traduction française du XVIᵉ siècle en regard 1543–1545*, ed. Ch.-Al Campan, Jean Baptiste François Blaes (Nendeln: 1862–1863).

Gachard, L.P. (ed.), *Correspondance de Philippe II sur les affaires des Pays-Bas, Publiée d'après les originaux conservés dans les Archives royales de Simancas*, 5 vols. (Brussels: 1851).

Haemstede Adriaan Cornelisz van, *De Gheschiedenisse ende den doodt der vromer Martelaren, die om het ghetuyghenisse des Evangeliums haer bloedt ghestort hebben* [...] (S.l. s.n.: 1559).

Hernighem A. van, *Eerste bouck van beschryfvinghe van alle gheschiedenesse (1562–1572)*, ed. A.L.E. Verheyden (Brussel: 1978).

Joossen P., *De kroniek van Pieter Joossen Altijt recht Hout*, ed. R.T. Fruin (Middelburg: 1909).

Le Barre P. de – Soldoyer N., *Mémoires de Pasquier de le Barre et de Nicolas Soldoyer*, ed. A. Pinchart 2 vols. (Brussels – The Hague: 1859).

Loon Gerard van (ed.), *Antwerpsch chronykje, in het welk zeer veele en elders te vergeefsch gezogte geschiedenissen sedert den jare 1500 tot het jaar 1574 zoo in die toen vermaarde koopstad als de andere steden van Nederland* (Leiden, Pieter vander Eyk: 1743).

Pottre J. de, *Dagboek van Jan de Pottre, 1549–1602*, ed. B. de St. Genois (Gent: 1861).

Vaernewyck M. van, *Van die beroerlicke tijden in die Nederlanden en voornamelijk in Ghendt: 1566–1568*, ed. Ferdinand Vanderhaeghen, 4 vols. (Gent: 1873).

Primary Manuscript Sources

The Hague, National Archives, 3.03.01.01 (Hof van Holland) inv. nr 5654, fol. 290 vo.
State Archives Kortrijk. Fonds Goethals-Vercruysse, ms. 296.

Secondary Literature

Arnade P., *Beggars, Iconoclasts and Civic Patriots: The Political Culture of the Dutch Revolt* (Ithaca – Londen: 2008).

Blok A., "The Symbolic Vocabulary of Public Executions" in Collier J.F. – Starr J. (eds.), *History and Power in the Study of Law: New Directions in Legal Anthropology* (Ithaca: 1989) 31–55.

Boone M., "The Dutch Revolt and the Medieval Tradition of Urban Dissent", *Journal of Early Modern History* 11 (2007) 350–375.

Braekman É.M., "Anvers - 1562: Le premier synode des Eglises réformées", *Bulletin Société d'Histoire du Protestantisme Belge* 102 (1989) 25–37.

Caers B. – Demets L. – Gassen T. van (eds.), *Urban History Writing in North-Western Europe (15th–16th centuries)* (Turnhout: 2019).

Casteels I. – Deschryver L. – Soen V., "Introduction: Divided by Death? Staging Mortality in the Early Modern Low Countries", *Early Modern Low Countries* 5 (2021) 1–16.

Casteels I., "Drownings in the Dark: The Politics of Secret Executions in Antwerp, 1557–1565", *Early Modern Low Countries* 5 (2021) 75–97.

Cohen E., "Symbols of Culpability and the Universal Language of Justice: The Ritual of Public Executions in Late Medieval Europe'", *History of European Ideas* 11 (1989) 407–416.

Coussemaker C.E.H. de, *Troubles religieux du XVIe siècle dans la Flandre Maritime, 1560–1570*, 4 vols. (Torhout: 1876).

Cramer S. – Pijper F., *Het offer des Heeren, de oudste verzameling doopsgezinde martelaarsbrieven en offerliederen* (The Hague: 1904).

Crew P.M., *Calvinist Preaching and Iconoclasm in the Netherlands 1544–1569* (Cambridge: 1978).

Crouzet D., *Les Enfants bourreaux au temps des guerres de Religion* (Paris: 2020).

Decavele J., *De dageraad van de reformatie in Vlaanderen (1520–1565)* (Leuven: 1975).

Demets L., "Spies, Instigators, and Troublemakers: Gendered Perceptions of Rebellious Women in Late Medieval Flemish Chronicles", *Journal of Women's History* 33 (2021) 12–34.

Deschryver L., "You Only Die Once: Calvinist Dying and the Senses in Lille and Tournai During the Dutch Revolt", *Early Modern Low Countries* 4 (2020) 35–57.

Deschryver L., *No rest for the wicked. Death, senses, and the Reformation in sixteenth-century Antwerp* (Ph.D. dissertation, Leuven University: forthcoming 2024).

Dillon A., *The Construction of Martyrdom in the English Catholic Community, 1535–1603* (Routledge: 2002).

Duke A., "Building Heaven in Hell's despite: The Early History of the Reformation in the Towns of the Low Countries" in idem *Reformation and revolt in the Low Countries* (London: 1990) 71–100.

Dülmen R. van, *Theatre of Horror: Crime and Punishment in Early Modern Germany* (Oxford: 1990).

Friedland P., *Seeing Justice Done: The Age of Spectacular Capital Punishment in France* (Oxford: 2012).

Foucault M., *Surveiller et punir: naissance de la prison* (Paris: 1975).

Geesink W., "Een terechtstelling van Anabaptisten te Rotterdam gestoord in 1558", *Rotterdams Jaarboekje* 2 (1890) 233–252.

Gelderen M. van, *The Political Thought of the Dutch Revolt 1555–1590* (Cambridge: 1992).

Genard P., "Ordonnantien van het Antwerpsch magistraat, rakende de godsdienstige geschillen der XVIe eeuw", *Antwerpsch Archievenblad* 2 (1865).

Genard P., "Personen te Antwerpen in de XVIe eeuw voor het feit van religie vervolgt", *Antwerpsch Archievenblad* 8 (1871) 1–471.

Gerson J., "Requete pour les condamnés a mort" in Mgr. Glorieux (ed.), *Oeuvres complètes* (Paris: 1966) 341–343.

Gielis G. – Soen V., "The Inquisitorial Office in the Sixteenth-Century Habsburg Low Countries: A Dynamic Perspective", *Journal of Ecclesiastical History* 66 (2015) 47–66.

Goosens A., *Les inquisitions modernes dans les Pays-Bas méridionaux 1520–1633*, 2 vols. (Brussels: 1997/1998).

Grauwels, J., *Dagboek van Gebeurtenissen. Opgetekend door Christiaan Munters 1529–1545* (Assen: 1971).

Grayson J.C, "The Civic Militia in the County of Holland, 1560–81: Politics and Public Order in the Dutch Revolt", *BMGN – Low Countries Historical Review* 95 (1980) 35–63.

Gregory B., *Salvation at Stake: Christian Martyrdom in Early Modern Europe* (Cambridge: 1999).

Hageman M., *Het kwade exempel van Gelre: De stad Nijmegen, de Beeldenstorm en de Raad van Beroerten, 1566–1568* (Nijmegen: 2005).

Hernighem A. van, *Nederlandsche historie 1572–1591*, 2 vols. (Gent: C. Annoot-Braeckman, 1864).

Hill K. (ed.), "Cultures of Lutheranism: Reformation repertoires in early modern Germany", *Past and Present*. Supplements 12 (2017).

Hoop Scheffer J.G. de, *Inventaris der Archiefstukken berustende bij de Vereenigde Doopsgezinde Gemeente te Amsterdam*, 4 vols. (Amsterdam: 1883).

Kauffman C.J., *Tamers of Death: The History of the Alexian Brothers from 1300 to 1789* (New York: 1976).

Lake P. – Questier M., "Agency, Appropriation and Rhetoric under the Gallows: Puritans Romanists and the State in Early Modern England", *Past and Present* 153 (1996) 64–107.

Lambert E.M., *Singing the Resurrection: Body, Community, and Belief in Reformation Europe* (Oxford: 2018).

Le Boucq P.J., *Histoire des troubles advenues à Valenciennes à cause des hérésies: 1562–1579* (Brussels: 1864) 9.

Manteau M. – Chavatte P.I., *Chronique de Mahieu Manteau et de Pierre-Ignace Chavatte*, ed. Eugène Debièvre (Lille: 1911).

Marnef G., *Antwerp in the Age of Reformation. Underground Protestantism in a Commercial Metropolis, 1550–1577* (Baltimore: 1996).

Marnef G., "The Dynamics of Reformed Religious Militancy: The Netherlands 1566–1585" in Benedict P. (ed.), *Reformation, Revolt and Civil War in France and the Netherlands 1555–1585* (Amsterdam: 1999) 51–68.

Monter W. "Heresy executions in Reformation Europe, 1520–1565" in Grell O. – Scribner B. (eds.), *Tolerance and Intolerance in the European Reformation* (Cambridge: 1996) 48–64.

Murdock G. – Roberts P. – Spicer A. (eds.), "Ritual and violence: Natalie Zemon Davis and Early Modern France", *Past and Present*. Supplements 7 (Oxford: 2012).

Murphy E.K.M., "Musical Self-Fashioning and the 'Theatre of Death' in Late Elizabethan and Jacobean England", *Renaissance Studies* 30 (2016) 410–29.

Nicholls D., "The Theatre of Martyrdom in the French Reformation", *Past and Present* 121 (1988) 49–73.

Pabel I.M., *Humanism and Early Modern Catholicism: Erasmus of Rotterdam's Ars Moriendi. In Early Modern Catholicism* (Toronto: 2001).

Paillard C. (ed.), *Histoire des troubles religieux de Valenciennes 1560–1567, publié d'après des documents inédits*, 4 vols. (Brussels – The Hague: 1874).

Pekelharing K.R., "Bijdragen voor de geschiedenis der Hervorming in Zeeland 1524–1572", *Archief VI, uitgegeven door het Zeeuws Genootschap der Wetenschappen* (1866) 225–316.

Pollmann J., "Archiving the Present and Chronicling for the Future in Early Modern Europe", *Past and Present* 230 (2016) 231–252.

Pollmann J., "Met grootvaders bloed bezegeld. Over religie en herinneringscultuur in de zeventiende-eeuwse Nederlanden", *De Zeventiende Eeuw. Cultuur in de Nederlanden in interdisciplinair perspectief* 29 (2013) 154–175.

Pollmann J., *Catholic Identity and the revolt of the Netherlands, 1520–1635* (Oxford: 2011).

Pollmann J., *Een andere weg naar God: de reformatie van Arnoldus Buchelius (1565–1641)* (Amsterdam: 2000).

Prosperi A., *Crime and Forgiveness: Christianizing Execution in Medieval Europe* (Cambridge MA: 2020).

Rahlenbeck C., "Les Chanteries de Valenciennes", *Bulletin de la Commission pour l'histoire des Églises Wallonnes* III (1888) 121–159.

Ramakers, B. Spelen en figuren: toneelkunst en processiecultuur in Oudenaarde tussen Middeleeuwen en Moderne Tijd (Amsterdam: 1996).

Resch C., "Reforming Late Medieval Ars Moriendi: Changes and Compromises in Early Reformation Manuals for Use at the Deathbed", in Flæten J. – Rasmussen T. (eds.), *Preparing for Death, Remembering the Dead* (Göttingen: 2015), 153–172.

Roberts, P. "French Historians and Collective Violence", *History and Theory* 56 (2017) 60–75.

Roodenburg H., "Empathy in the Making: Crafting the Believer's Emotions in the Late Medieval Low Countries", *BMGN – Low Countries Historical Review* 129 (2014) 42–62.

Schelven A.A. van, "Het begin van het gewapend verzet tegen Spanje in de 16[e] Nederlanden", *Jaarboek van de Maatschappij der Nederlandse Letterkunde* (1915) 126–156.

Serneels H., "Making Space for Resistance: the Spatiality of Popular Protest in the Late Medieval Southern Low Countries", *Urban History* (2021) 1–16.

Sharpe J.A., "Last Dying Speeches: Religion, Ideology and Public Execution in Seventeenth-Century England", *Past and Present* 107 (1985) 144–67.

Soen V., "The Beeldenstorm and the Spanish Habsburg Response (1566–1570)", *BMGN: Low Countries Historical Review* 131 (2016) 99–120.

Spierenburg P. *The Spectacle of Suffering: Executions and the Evolution of Repression, from a Preindustrial Metropolis to the European Experience* (Cambridge: 1984).

Terpstra N., *The Art of Executing Well: Rituals of Execution in Renaissance Italy* (Kirksville: 2008).

Tracy J.D., *Holland Under Habsburg Rule, 1506–1556: The Formation of a Body Politic* (Berkeley: 1990).

Tucker J., *The Construction of Reformed Identity in Jean Crespin's "Livre des Martyrs"* (London: 2017).

Unger J. – Bezemer W. (eds.), *De oudste kronieken en beschrijvingen van Rotterdam en Schieland* (Rotterdam: 1895).

Vermaseren B.A., "Autour de l'edition de l'Histoire de l'estat du Pais Bas, et de la religion d'Espagne, par F. de Enzinas dit Dryander", *Bibliothèque d'humanisme et renaissance* 27 (1965) 463–494.

Vrankrijker A. de, "Voorboden van oproer in de Zuidelijke Nederlanden in de jaren 1561–1562", *Bijdragen voor Vaderlandse Geschiedenis en Oudheidkunde* 5 (1935) 153–168.

Walsham A., "Skeletons in the Cupboard: Relics after the English Reformation", *Past and Present* 206 (2010) 121–143.

Ward R., *A Global History of Execution and the Criminal Corpse* (London: 2015).

Weert N. de, "Chronycke van Nederland, besonderlyck der stadt Antwerpen, sedert denjaere 1097 tôt den jaere 1565" in C. Piot (ed.), *Chroniques de Brabant et de Flandre, Collection de chroniques belges* (Bruxelles: 1879) 72–172.

Woltjer J., "Public Opinion and The Persecution of Heretics in The Netherlands, 1550–1559" in Pollmann J. – Spicer A. (eds.), *Public Opinion and Changing Identities in the Early Modern Netherlands: Essays in Honour of Alastair Duke* (Leiden: 2007) 87–106.

Woltjer J., *Friesland in hervormingstijd* (Leiden: 1962).

Zemon Davis N., "The Rites of Violence: Religious Riot in Sixteenth-Century France", *Past and Present* 59 (1973) 51–91.

CHAPTER 14

Deaths in Hospitals and Care Institutions in Sixteenth- and Seventeenth-Century London

Vanessa Harding

1   Introduction

All major cities in western Europe attracted religious foundations, including hospitals, in the early Middle Ages. In many cases they also acquired a wider array of other refuges to care for foundlings, orphans, the sick and elderly, and the insane in the later Middle Ages. Some hospitals and many almshouses in Protestant Europe survived the Reformation and continued to play an important part in the overall landscape of end-of-life care, dying and death in early modern cities. London, by far the largest city in early modern Britain and for centuries England's political, economic and governmental capital, was well-endowed with such foundations, established by the charity of individuals or groups but often sustained by corporate or civic bodies. This chapter sets out to identify the provision of hospitals and other care institutions in early modern London, their inmates, and their role in caring for the dying, as a contribution to understanding the circumstances in which a sector of the urban population faced and experienced death.

The prompt for this enquiry was the observation that institutions played a far larger part in death and burial in later seventeenth-century Paris than they did in London, at a time when the two cities may have been nearly equal in size, and both faced serious challenges in the form of high immigration, endemic and epidemic mortality, and population turnover. The Parisian equivalent of the London *Bills of Mortality*, the *État des Baptêmes*, which begin in 1670, show that nearly a quarter of all burials in Paris were attributed to a hospital or other residential institution. The great Hôtel-Dieu accounted for nearly a fifth of all burials, though some of these may have been gathered from elsewhere.[1] In London, by contrast, the Bills of Mortality had no separate return for hospital and institutional burials, except for those in the City's pesthouse,[2] but other

---

[1] État des Baptêmes, 1670: Paris, Bibliothèque Nationale, Printed books, reserve, L k/7 6745.
[2] *A collection of the yearly bills of mortality, from 1657 to 1758 inclusive, together with several other Bills of an earlier date* (London, A. Millar: 1759).

evidence indicates that they formed only a small fraction of the burial total, less than 5 per cent.

This contrast was noted by the demographer Sir William Petty, who attributed the high death toll in the Parisian hospitals to lower standards of medical care, which is perhaps debatable, but also more plausibly to differences in poverty levels: the fact that twenty times as many poor people 'chuse to lie sick in Hospitals rather than in their own houses […] shews the greater poverty or want of means in the people of Paris than those of London'.[3] Early modern London and Paris clearly had different cultures of hospitalisation and enclosure of the poor, which surely derived from differences in tradition, the role of the state, and religious belief.

Still, the number dying in a hospital or other charitable foundation in London was not negligible, and they should certainly play a part in our examination of the moment of death in early modern cities. After all, deaths in institutions, at least those where spiritual support was on hand, might have offered the dying person an experience closer to the ideal death promoted by the *ars moriendi* literature than might have been available in a domestic setting. Such deaths certainly fitted with the literature's focus on the death of adults and on the desirability of conscious preparation for death. Hospitals attended to spiritual as well as physical health, in many cases employing chaplains or clerics; almshouses too focused on living in charity and preparing for death.

2   Hospitals and Almshouses

To understand who died in hospitals and other institutions in early modern London, it is helpful to differentiate between those which largely expected their inmates to leave alive, and those which did not. The former included the sick hospitals – hospitals in the modern understanding of the word – and the latter, the numerous almshouses, hospices, and refuges for the poor (usually elderly or infirm, but not necessarily sick on entry). For the former, the occurrence of death was incidental but unavoidable, if frequent; for the latter, end-of-life care (or care to the end of life) was a key part of their mission. The pesthouses or plague hospitals form perhaps a separate category: they were intended to offer cure, but it is likely that in fact the great majority of their patients died.

---

3   Petty William, *Two essays in Political Arithmetic concerning the people, housing, hospitals &c. of London and Paris* (London, J. Lloyd: 1687) 7–8.

The principal sick hospitals were St Bartholomew's in Smithfield and St Thomas's in Southwark, with their subsidiaries. Both were medieval religious foundations reconstituted under the City of London's direction after the Reformation, with a specific remit to care for the sick and aged poor.[4] The remaining medieval leper hospital foundations were transferred to St Bartholomew's in 1549: of these, the Lock in Southwark and Kingsland in Hackney continued to be used, principally for venereal patients, after 1622.[5] The refounded St Bartholomew's was intended to care for some one hundred patients, but the number had increased to around 200 by the early seventeenth century.[6] St Thomas's accommodated 260 patients in c.1550.[7] Both had around 350 patients in the early eighteenth century.[8] There was also Bethlem Hospital for the insane, which could be considered a sick hospital in that it likewise aimed at cure and discharge, though its inmates were normally mentally rather than physically ill. It probably housed fifty to sixty inmates in the sixteenth century, rising to c.150 by the early eighteenth.[9]

The expansion of St Bartholomew's, St Thomas's and Bethlem partly compensated for a net loss of sick-hospital places in the mid-sixteenth century. The large medieval hospital of St Mary Spital outside Bishopsgate was closed down at the Reformation, and the Savoy, established in the early sixteenth century, though refounded after closure, soon lost all pretence of serving as a sick hospital or even as an overnight hostel for the homeless.[10]

Pesthouses and plague hospitals in London were a minor feature of London's response to plague, certainly when compared with the major *lazzaretti* of Italian cities, and in spite of pressure from central government to develop a hospital-quarantine system rather than a home-based one. The City of London established a pest-house of moderate size in the northern suburb in the 1590s, and several suburban parishes, including St Martin in the Fields and St Margaret Westminster, did so in the seventeenth century. The parish pesthouses were in some cases associated with almshouses or other provision for the poor; some

---

4   Barron C.M. – Davies M.P., *The Religious Houses of London and Middlesex* (London: 2007) 153, 173.
5   Barron – Davies, *The Religious Houses of London and Middlesex*, 175–176; Siena K.P., *Venereal Disease, Hospitals and the Urban Poor: London's 'foul wards' 1600–1800*, Rochester studies in medical history, 4 (Rochester: 2004) 64, 67.
6   Strype John, *A Survey of the Cities of London and Westminster* (London, A. Churchill, J. Knapton, R. Knaplock, J. Walthoe, E. Horne, B. Tooke, D. Midwinter, B. Cowse, R. Robinson, and T. Ward: 1720) (https://www.dhi.ac.uk/strype/) Bk. 1 ch. 26 184–188.
7   Ibidem, 188–190.
8   Ibidem, 187, 188.
9   Ibidem, 197.
10 Barron – Davies, *The Religious Houses of London and Middlesex* 160–163, 182–184.

were used for plague cases in the years when it was low-level but endemic, others were only used in epidemic years. The numbers accommodated obviously varied, with capacity expanded by sheds and tents as necessary.[11]

There was however a wide range of other institutions caring for the poor towards the end of life. Sarah Lennard-Brown's recent study of almshouses in medieval London draws a distinction between older hospital-style foundations, often with monastic origins or organisation, and the smaller-scale almshouses that proliferated after the Black Death for laymen and women, with their culture of mutual care and charitable living.[12] A few of these institutions, with ties to intercessory or chantry practices, did not survive the Reformation, but several more were founded between 1550 and 1600. On Lennard-Brown's showing there were about thirty-five almshouses with some 320–360 places (some of them were for couples) by 1600. Most of those founded before the Reformation were directly associated with city guilds (known in London as Livery Companies),[13] and accommodated decayed members and sometimes their wives or widows.[14]

The seventeenth and early eighteenth centuries saw several new almshouse foundations, most of them private, though some were committed to the management of Livery Companies. More of them were in the outer suburbs and environs of London. The largest of these was Sir Thomas Sutton's Hospital in the former precinct of the Charterhouse, for eighty pensioners living together in collegiate fashion.[15] Other comparatively large foundations included Sir Robert Jeffreys' almshouse in Shoreditch, run by the Ironmongers' Company, which held at least forty-four; Aske's hospital in Hoxton, run by the Haberdashers, for twenty poor men, later expanded; and Sion College, inside the city wall, for ten men and ten women. Most of the rest were for twelve or

---

11 Columbus A., *The Response to Plague and the Poor in the Suburban Parishes of Early Modern London, c. 1600–1650* (Ph.D. dissertation, Birkbeck, University of London: 2021) 211–228.

12 Lennard-Brown S., *Almshouses of London and Westminster: their Role in Lay Piety and the Relief of Poverty, 1330–1600* (Ph.D. dissertation, Birkbeck, University of London: 2020) 11–17.

13 The guilds or companies, to which all male citizens belonged, were significant foci of charitable benefaction for the support of members. An elite segment of the membership of most guilds was entitled to wear a livery of gown and/or hood on company occasions. In 1500 there were about 70 recognised companies, of which at least 47 had a livery section, but the term Livery Company is generally used to cover them all: Thrupp S., *The Merchant Class of Medieval London* (Chicago: 1948) 42.

14 Lennard-Brown, *Almshouses of London and Westminster* 29.

15 Porter S., *The London Charterhouse: a History of Thomas Sutton's Charity* (Stroud: 2009); Strype, *A Survey of the Cities of London and Westminster* Bk. 1 ch. 27 205–210.

fewer, sometimes only two or four.[16] Several parishes established almshouses, usually also with the help of private endowment, which they assigned to their own poor, both men and women, though almshouses specifically for poor widows were a notable feature.[17] It is hard to calculate the number of places in all these, but it seems likely that although the number of ordinary almshouse places certainly increased, it did not keep pace with London's burgeoning population, which by 1700, at over half a million, was perhaps 2 ½ times what it had been in 1600.

One significant development, however, was the growth of hospitals and almshouses dedicated to poor, maimed and decayed soldiers and sailors, reflecting the growth of these professions and their importance to the state and society. Some of these institutions blur the distinction between sick hospitals and long-term refuges, offering both immediate treatment for injuries sustained in service, and accommodation for the permanently disabled and those deserving consideration on account of long or arduous service.

Concern for maimed soldiers as an object of charity dated at least from the Elizabethan period, given the high involvement of English troops in Ireland and the Low Countries. Both St Bartholomew's and St Thomas's treated injured soldiers at times, and there was a close connection between battlefield surgery and surgical practice in hospitals. The ordinances of Sutton's Hospital at Charterhouse, which were shaped to meet the ambitions of the early Stuart state, identified maimed and disabled soldiers as one of the categories eligible for admission.[18] The Parliamentary side in the civil wars of the mid-seventeenth century was proactive in the creation of field hospitals. A Committee for Sick and Maimed Soldiers was established in 1642, taking over the premises of the by now largely neglected Savoy Hospital for that purpose, and later establishing another hospital at Parson's Green to the west of London.[19] With continuing military and especially naval engagements in the later seventeenth century, concern for veterans culminated in the establishment of the two new royal hospitals at Chelsea and Greenwich, for disabled soldiers and seamen respectively.

---

16   Strype, *A Survey of the Cities of London and Westminster* Bk. 1 ch. 27 212, 224; Bk. 1 ch. 4 146.
17   Ibidem, Bk. 2 ch. 2 19–20; Bk. 2 ch. 4 79; Bk. 2 ch. 7 110.
18   Herne Samuel, *Domus Carthusiana, or, An account of the most noble foundation of the Charter-House near Smithfield in London both before and since the reformation: with the life and death of Thomas Sutton, esq., the founder thereof, and his last will and testament* (London, Richard Marriott and Henry Broome: 1677) 132–133.
19   'Hospitals: Hospital of the Savoy', in *A History of the County of London: Volume 1, London Within the Bars, Westminster and Southwark*, ed. William Page (London: 1909) 546–549. British History Online http://www.british-history.ac.uk/vch/london/vol1/pp546-549; Strype, *A Survey of the Cities of London and Westminster* Bk. 1 ch. 27 210–212.

Both were elaborate foundations, with impressive premises and organisation, each accommodating about 400 pensioners.[20]

In addition to these, and similarly reflecting the importance of maritime activity to the nation and its capital, Trinity House of Deptford, in charge of lighthouses and pilotage, established an almshouse at Deptford, for fifty-nine 'poor decayed Masters or Pilots, and their Widows', in 1671, and another for twenty-eight of the same in Mile End in 1695.[21] The East India Company established an almshouse for fourteen seamen, 'disabled in their Service by Age or Accidents', in Poplar in the mid-seventeenth century; one Captain Fisher established almshouses for six seamen's widows in Dog Row, Stepney, in 1711.[22]

There may be a connection between the revisions of settlement law in the 1660s and 1690s and the development of hospital and infirmary care then and thereafter. It seems likely that the 1690s was a crucial decade, with considerable distress resulting from war and taxation; this was the period at which St Bartholomew's and St Thomas's ceased to provide free care for venereal patients, but it was also one in which the laws on settlement and entitlement to relief were given further precision.[23]

3   Inmates

This brief run-though of the various care institutions of early modern London gives some sense of who their inmates must have been, and therefore who was likely to die there. While the surviving sources give comparatively little direct information on the moment of death of any individual in one of these places, we can establish some of the circumstances which framed the individual experience, such as the cultures of individual institutions, the causes of death, where known, and the characteristics of the inhabitants.

The almshouses catered principally for the elderly: several had a minimum age for admission, such as Charterhouse (50 years, or 40 for maimed soldiers), or Jeffreys' almshouse (56 years), but mostly simply specified 'aged', which in common use usually meant 60 or more. Some were for men only, a few for women only, others had some of each, or offered places to married couples.

---

20 Strype, *A Survey of the Cities of London and Westminster* Bk. 1 ch. 27 214–219.
21 Ibidem 212, 219,
22 Strype, *A Survey of the Cities of London and Westminster* Bk. 4 ch. 2 44, 49; ibidem, Appendix 1 ch. 12 101, 103.
23 Siena, *Venereal Disease* 75, 85.

Charterhouse required incoming pensioners to be sober in mind and healthful of body, to be certified by the surgeon with the approbation of the physician. Other almshouses might admit those already infirm, but probably all excluded those known to be suffering from venereal disease.[24] Some of the later hospitals as we have seen were specifically for the physically disabled servicemen, and Bethlem, of course, admitted only those deemed insane.

The main sick hospitals took in people with a variety of complaints. An order of 1569 to 'take up' or detain beggars appointed that all who were 'aged, impotent, sick, sore, lame, or blind' were to be taken to St Bartholomew's or St Thomas's.[25] However, the majority of the patients were probably suffering from physical injuries including wounds, surgical emergencies (the treatment for cutting for the stone was developed at St Bartholomew's and St Thomas's), and venereal disease. The latter accounted for a significant number of patients at both hospitals. St Bartholomew's devoted an average of fifty-seven beds to venereal patients between 1622 and 1666 (at the Lock and Kingsland), while St Thomas's had some forty venereal beds in the main hospital in the early seventeenth century and about fifty-two by the 1660s. Venereal patients were largely seeking treatment, not end-of-life care, and both hospitals claimed to discharge large numbers as 'cured', though inevitably some would die under or as a result of treatment.[26]

The main common feature of most hospitals of whichever kind, however, is that their inmates were poor and dependent on charity for the provision of care. This meant that comparatively few would be in a position to make a will or testament. There were some exceptions to this: the qualification for Sutton's Hospital or Charterhouse was that pensioners be 'Gentlemen by Descent, and in Poverty, Souldiers that have born Arms by Sea or Land, Merchants decayed by Pyracy or Shipwreck, or Servants in Houshold to the King and Queens Majesty', and there are a dozen or more wills for Charterhouse brothers, some of which detail more than minimal assets.[27] Likewise the inhabitants of Chelsea and Greenwich Hospitals included some of sufficient substance to make a will.[28] But for the most part, for hospital patients and almshouse inmates, we lack

---

24 E.g. Strype, *A Survey of the Cities of London and Westminster* Bk. 1 ch. 27 208–209; Herne, *Domus Carthusiana* 133.
25 Strype, *A Survey of the Cities of London and Westminster* Bk. 1 ch. 26 178.
26 Siena, *Venereal Disease*, 67–84; Strype, *A Survey of the Cities of London and Westminster* Bk. 1 ch. 26 187, 188.
27 Herne, *Domus Carthusiana* 132–133; Kew, London, The National Archives (TNA), PROB 11/139/628, 11/163/244, 11/212/466, 11/245/127, 11/253/5, 11/264/11, 11/304/290, 11/388/261, 11/405/34.
28 E.g. TNA, PROB 11/446/169, 11/484/150.

the useful information that willmaking and probate can offer the study of death, dying, and the deathbed. Again, this contrasts with Paris, where many of those who died in hospitals were of higher status. The Hôtel-Dieu took care to ensure that dying inmates were able to make wills, and maintained a register of their testaments.[29]

4   Mortality in Hospitals and Almshouses

If we ask, how many died in hospitals and institutions, and what did they die of, the answer is partly already provided by understanding who was there and why.

Numbers of deaths in hospitals of all kinds are generally hard to find. The so-called 'Death books' of St Bartholomew's, though mandated in the seventeenth century, do not begin until 1762.[30] The modest totals of dead recorded in the *Bills of Mortality* for the parishes of St Bartholomew the Less or St Thomas Southwark in which those hospitals lay cannot include all the dead from the hospitals, though at least some burials from St Thomas's were recorded in the parish register as 'brought from the hospital'.[31] That said, Strype's 1720 edition of John Stow's Survey of London includes some useful statistics for the hospitals in the early eighteenth century: discharges, deaths, and persons remaining in care. St Bartholomew's and St Thomas's each buried between around 120 to 200 people a year in the early eighteenth century, while discharging a far higher number.[32]

Other institutions sometimes have their own records. Sutton's Hospital at Charterhouse had its own burial ground, in which some seventeenth-century pensioners requested burial, but the register appears to date from 1748 only. It was noted in 1676 that on average nine out of the eighty pensioners died in any year – 'Whence an Observation was made of the Healthfulness and Sweetness of the Place. To which another Observation may be made, of the Advantage

---

29   Register of testaments at the Hôtel-Dieu: Paris, Archives de l'Assistance Publique, Hôpitaux de Paris, cat 6358 (layette 330, liasse 1413(1)).
30   Medvei V.C. – Thornton J.L., *The Royal Hospital of St Bartholomew, 1123–1973* (London: 1974) 303.
31   *A collection of the yearly bills of mortality*; Parish registers of St Thomas, Southwark: London, London Metropolitan Archives (LMA), P71/TMS/1358/A, P71/TMS/1358/b, P71/TMS/1359.
32   Strype, *A Survey of the Cities of London and Westminster* Bk. 1 ch 26.

of a regular, temperate Course, for Length of Days'.[33] In fact this is not such a favourable mortality rate, considering that the major cause of death in early modern London, infant and neonatal mortality,[34] is excluded, and that the hospital dispersed its inmates to the country in time of plague, but it is interesting that it was so perceived.

Deaths in smaller almshouses seem to have been included in the general totals for the parish in which they lay, so that only those parishes with surviving registers that give information on individuals buried have any hope of capturing any details. One such is the parish of St Helen Bishopsgate in the city of London, in which lay two almshouses, the Leathersellers' Company's, for four men and three women, and the Skinners' Company's, for six poor people. The parish register records the burials of sixty Leathersellers' or Skinners' almspeople between 1593 and 1697, but the register probably fails to identify quite a few pensioners as such.[35] The same is true of the register of St Olave Hart Street, in which lay Sir John Milbourne's almshouse, founded in 1534 for fourteen poor men and their wives and run by the Drapers' Company, and the almshouse established by the Bayning family c.1638 for ten poor people. The register records the burials of 166 almsmen and women, or people from the almshouses, between 1558 and 1684, but again this seems likely to be an underestimate: there are long periods when only the names of the dead are given.[36]

Deaths in the sick hospitals presumably tracked the more severe ailments for which people were admitted, especially wounds and injuries, internal complaints needing surgical intervention, such as the stone, and venereal disease. It was noted that in the reign of Edward VI (1547–53) in St Bartholomew's there were 'healed of the Pox, Fistulas, filthy Blains and Sores, to the Number of Eight Hundred; and thence safe delivered [...]; besides Eight Score and Twelve that dyed there in their intolerable Miseries'.[37] Plague victims were not normally admitted, and it seems unlikely that gastric and respiratory complaints, from which many Londoners died, made up a significant proportion of deaths in the sick hospitals. On the whole the few wills of hospital patients are not illuminating on cause of death: testators described themselves (or were described) as

---

33 LMA, ACC/1876/PS/01/007; TNA, PROB 11/139/628; Strype, *A Survey of the Cities of London and Westminster* Bk. 1 ch. 27 p. 210.

34 Graunt John, *Natural and political observations mentioned in a following Index and made upon the Bills of Mortality* (London, Thomas Roycroft: 1662) 14.

35 *The registers of St Helen's, Bishopsgate, London*, ed. W.B. Bannerman (London: 1904).

36 *The registers of St Olave, Hart Street, London, 1563–1700*, ed. W.B. Bannerman (London: 1916).

37 Strype, *A Survey of the Cities of London and Westminster* Bk. 1 ch. 26 185.

'weak', 'sick and weak of body', 'sick of the sickness wherof he died', 'in a dying condition'.[38] Those at least had some foresight and time to prepare themselves for death, including dictating a will, and by implication had companions or attendants with whom they could communicate. Many hospital patients, however, must have been overtaken by unconsciousness or incapacity before being able to make their wishes known.

'Aged' was a standard category for cause of death in the seventeenth-century Bills of Mortality, accounting for about 7 per cent of all deaths. The statistician John Graunt thought that it would not be given as a cause of death except for those aged 70 or more.[39] It seems likely that most of the deaths in almshouses would have fallen into this category, unless some other identifiable disease or ailment was present. Some of the almspeople buried in St Olave Hart Street and St Helen Bishopsgate were said to be aged, or an 'old man' or 'old woman'; a few other causes of death were noted, including cough, consumption, and dropsy.[40] This is consistent with evidence from other registers that suggests that dropsy, palsy, and consumption were quite prevalent causes of death among the old.[41] The burial of three of the Drapers' Company's almsmen in one week in February-March 1653 suggests some infectious disease, but no cause is given. A couple of plague deaths in the almshouse are recorded in the epidemic of 1593; in 1665, the first plague death in St Olave's parish occurred in the Drapers' almshouse, and a further three died there shortly after.[42]

Several Charterhouse pensioners described their state at the time they made their wills: 'being visited by the hand of God with much weakness through many infirmities of my body'; 'aged weak and infirm of body'; 'sick and weak'; 'infirm and lame in my limbs'. All of these, however, had time to make proper wills, written, signed and witnessed, usually with the aid of a scrivener; none is obviously a deathbed will.[43] As 'gentlemen', and in some cases with goods worth leaving, the Charterhouse brothers may have been more likely to make precautionary wills, like the one who declared himself as 'fast stricken in years yet of good health of body and perfect mind and memory'.[44]

---

38   TNA, PROB 11/273/511, 11/286/385, 11/371/285, 11/452/282.
39   Graunt, *Natural and political observations ... upon the Bills of Mortality* 17.
40   *The Registers of St Helen's, Bishopsgate*; *The Registers of St Olave, Hart Street*.
41   E.g. Forbes T.R., *Chronicle from Aldgate: Life and Death in Shakespeare's London* (New Haven: 1971).
42   *The Registers of St Olave, Hart Street* 126–127, 185, 200.
43   TNA, PROB 11/139/628, 11/201/279, 11/297/296.
44   TNA, PROB 11/212/468.

5 End-of-Life Care and the Moment of Death

Obviously there was quite a wide range of experience of end-of-life care, to which the institution's mission, staff, and premises contributed.

One of the objectives of the medieval almshouse was to offer the inmates the chance of a good death, supporting their spiritual journey towards it. To this end, inmates were expected to live in charity, and to contribute mutual care, including nursing care.[45] This ethos of mutual charity survived the Reformation, and is reiterated in the statutes of some later almshouse foundations. Several Charterhouse wills mention fellow-pensioners, and some ask them to bear the testator's corpse to burial exactly as a medieval fraternity might have done.[46] The physical layout of almshouses favoured the private and tranquil deathbed: almost all were organised as individual dwelling units grouped together, sometimes within a gated enclave or precinct, or around a shared space or garden.[47]

Most of the larger institutions also made provision for spiritual welfare, with one or more pastors, chaplains, or priests attached. Godly living was expected and regular attendance at divine service was often required.[48] While parish clergy were important in making wills for their parishioners, however, this seems to be less of a function in the hospitals, though admittedly numbers are very small. One of the few examples where a cleric was involved in making a will for a hospital patient is that of David Ap David, a patient at St Thomas's, whose nuncupative will of 25 May 1574 was witnessed by Richard Tyler, 'minister of the said parish', presumably visiting the sick man.[49] This contrasts with willmaking at the Hotel-Dieu in Paris, where a register of wills was kept from 1644, each will prefaced with the words 'Before us the priests and chaplains of the Hotel-Dieu' and concluding with the signatures of testator and witnesses.[50]

For larger or more formally organised hospitals and institutions, such as the sick hospitals, or the new hospitals at Chelsea and Greenwich, ordinances and accounts give some sense of the medical assistance provided: the appointment of surgeons or physicians, apothecaries, matrons and nursing sisters. St Bartholomew's had three surgeons, a matron, and twelve sisters, who also

---

45   Lennard-Brown, *Almshouses of London and Westminster* 277–279.
46   E.g. TNA, PROB 11/139/628.
47   Lennard-Brown, *Almshouses of London and Westminster* 171, 213, 241, 245.
48   E.g. Strype, *A Survey of the Cities of London and Westminster* Bk. 1 ch. 27 224.
49   TNA PROB 11/56/295.
50   Register of testaments at the Hôtel-Dieu: Paris, Archives de l'Assistance Publique, Hôpitaux de Paris, cat 6358 (layette 330, liasse 1413(1)).

received board and livery.[51] Chelsea had a salaried physician, surgeon, apothecary, and surgeon's mate, and twenty-five matrons.[52]

Ordinances do not tell us about the quality of care given, or the balance of discipline and treatment. Encouragingly, though, in some cases the experience was good enough to evoke gratitude. Gilbert Anderson, a seaman, in St Thomas's Hospital in 1673 after having his leg shot away, assigned all his wages to his surgeon Mr John Shorey, who was evidently present as he made the statement.[53] In 1659, Thomas Harris, tailor, a patient in St Bartholomew's Hospital, left 'unto my loving nurse or sister of the ward wherein I now lie the sum of five shillings to buy her a pair of gloves to wear in remembrance of me'.[54] In 1667/8, Robert Bliss, seaman, on his deathbed in St Thomas's Hospital, left the residue of his estate to 'my welbeloved friend Joan Symons, sister of the King's ward in St Thomas's hospital aforesaid'.[55] This suggests that these individuals were present and attentive to the dying, and perhaps too that their assistance at the last moment could be expected. In this, hospital experience paralleled the domestic: older women probably provided the majority of all nursing care at the time, both at home and in institutions. Parish almswomen may indeed have been called on to do so in return for their pensions, attending not just other almspeople but the poor of the parish as well. They were more likely than either clergy or medical professionals to be there at the moment of death.[56]

6   Conclusion

Given the scarcity of wills for hospital and almshouse inmates, this is probably as close as we can come to the moment of death for the majority of such people, who formed a small but not insignificant number of the dying in early modern London. While the scale of provision of hospital and almshouse care did not match the huge population growth of the sixteenth and seventeenth

---

51 Strype, *A Survey of the Cities of London and Westminster* Bk. 1 ch. 26 184–185.
52 Ibidem, ch. 27 214–215.
53 TNA, PROB 11/343/56.
54 TNA, PROB 11/286/385.
55 TNA, PROB 11/326/188.
56 Harkness D.E., "A View from the Streets: Women and Medical Work in Elizabethan London", *Bulletin of the History of Medicine* 82.1 (2008) 52–85; Earle P., "The Female Labour Market in London in the late 17th and early 18th centuries", *Economic History Review*, 2nd ser., 42 (1989) 328–353; Mortimer I., "The Triumph of the Doctors: Medical Assistance to the Dying, c. 1570–1720", *Transactions of the Royal Historical Society* 15 (2005) 97–116.

centuries, there is nevertheless evidence for concern for to the elderly poor and for endeavours to target relief effectively. Some at least of London's enormous wealth was channelled towards this category of the poor population, and to new needs arising from London's, and England's, involvement in maritime and military activity. The topic also fits into larger narratives of changing charitable concerns, evolving attitudes the poor, and the medicalisation of death.

Bibliography

Primary Printed Sources

A collection of the yearly bills of mortality, from 1657 to 1758 inclusive, together with several other Bills of an earlier date (London, A. Millar: 1759).

Graunt John, *Natural and political observations mentioned in a following Index and made upon the Bills of Mortality* (London, Thomas Roycroft: 1662).

Herne Samuel, *Domus carthusiana, or, An account of the most noble foundation of the Charter-House near Smithfield in London both before and since the reformation: with the life and death of Thomas Sutton, esq., the founder thereof, and his last will and testament* (London, Richard Marriott and Henry Broome: 1677).

Petty William, *Two essays in Political Arithmetic concerning the people, housing, hospitals &c. of London and Paris* (London, J. Lloyd: 1687).

Strype John, *A Survey of the Cities of London and Westminster* (London, A. Churchill, J. Knapton, R. Knaplock, J. Walthoe, E. Horne, B. Tooke, D. Midwinter, B. Cowse, R. Robinson, and T. Ward: 1720) (https://www.dhi.ac.uk/strype/).

The Registers of St Helen's, Bishopsgate, London, ed. W.B. Bannerman (London: 1904).

The Registers of St Olave, Hart Street, London, 1563–1700, ed. W.B. Bannerman (London: 1916).

Primary Manuscript Sources

État des Baptêmes, 1670: Paris, Bibliothèque Nationale, Printed books, reserve, L k/7 6745.

Paris, Archives de l'Assistance Publique, Hôpitaux de Paris, cat 6358 (layette 330, liasse 1413(1)).

The National Archives, London

PROB 11/139/628, 11/163/244, 11/212/466, 11/245/127, 11/253/5, 11/264/11, 11/304/290, 11/388/261, 11/405/34, PROB 11/446/169, 11/484/150, 11/273/511, 11/286/385, 11/371/285, 11/452/282, 11/201/279, 11/297/296, 11/212/468, 11/56/295, 11/343/56, 11/326/188.

London Metropolitan Archives (LMA)
Parish registers of St Thomas, Southwark: P71/TMS/1358/A, P71/TMS/1358/b, P71/TMS/1359.

Secondary Literature

'Hospitals: Hospital of the Savoy', in *A History of the County of London: Volume 1, London Within the Bars, Westminster and Southwark*, ed. William Page (London, 1909), 546–549. *British History Online* http://www.british-history.ac.uk/vch/london/vol1/pp546-549.

Barron C.M. – Davies M.P., *The Religious Houses of London and Middlesex* (London: 2007).

Columbus A., The Response to Plague and the Poor in the Suburban Parishes of Early Modern London, c. 1600–1650 (Ph.D. dissertation, Birkbeck, University of London: 2021).

Earle P., "The Female Labour Market in London in the late 17th and early 18th centuries.", *Economic History Review*, 2nd ser. 42 (1989) 328–53.

Forbes T.R., *Chronicle from Aldgate: Life and Death in Shakespeare's London* (New Haven: 1971).

Harkness D.E., "A View from the Streets: Women and Medical Work in Elizabethan London", *Bulletin of the History of Medicine* 82.1 (2008) 52–85.

Lennard-Brown S., Almshouses of London and Westminster: their Role in Lay Piety and the Relief of Poverty, 1330–1600 (Ph.D. dissertation, Birkbeck, University of London: 2020).

Medvei V.C. – Thornton J.L., *The Royal Hospital of St Bartholomew, 1123–1973* (London: 1974).

Mortimer I., "The Triumph of the Doctors: Medical Assistance to the Dying, c. 1570–1720", *Transactions of the Royal Historical Society*, 15. (2005), 97–116.

Porter S., *The London Charterhouse: a History of Thomas Sutton's charity* (Stroud, Amberley: 2009).

Siena K.P., *Venereal Disease, Hospitals and the Urban Poor: London's 'foul wards' 1600–1800*, Rochester studies in medical history 4 (Rochester: 2004).

CHAPTER 15

Fleeing the Deathbed: Sensory Anxieties and the Persecution of Non-Catholic Dying Practices in Antwerp, 1560s–1570s

Louise Deschryver

1   Introduction

On 4 May 1571, Antwerp's magistracy issued a rather unusual, but highly interesting ordinance. The city authorities were searching for information on a man called Hans Vanderthoren, who had mysteriously disappeared from his own sickbed a few weeks before. The ordinance stated that, as Hans' end had seemed to be drawing near, his wife and attending neighbours had told him to call for the parish priest to assist him in his final hours and administer the last rites. Hans had agreed. By the time the priest had arrived, however, it seems the dying man had changed his mind. He bluntly refused to receive Extreme Unction and sent the cleric away. Consequently, the latter alerted the authorities of Hans' peculiar deathbed behaviour. On April 19, the day after Palm Sunday, a city government official knocked on the front door. He was let in and brought to the sick chamber by Hans' wife, where they discovered an empty bed. Hans' wife told the visitor she could not tell where her husband had gone, nor when he would be back. Rather remarkable, for a man who had been considered to be on the brink of death.[1]

We can safely assume Hans had not dragged his dying body out of his house to go on an enjoyable stroll. After the eventful visit of his parish priest, Hans and his loved ones presumably knew trouble was coming their way and smuggled him out of the house. Indeed, as this chapter will show, in mid-sixteenth-century Antwerp refusing to partake in Catholic funerary rituals could buy you a one-way ticket to the scaffold. In the late 1560s and 1570s, both the city's secular and clerical authorities had come to consider lay deathbed behaviours as meaningful markers that crystallized Catholic, Lutheran and Calvinist identities, and as such a prime site for detecting hubs of heresy within the city walls. Lay believers, too, increasingly considered deathbed

---

[1] Génard P., "Ordonnantien van het Antwerpsch Magistraat, rakende de godsdienstige geschillen der XVIᵉ eeuw", *Antwerpsch Archievenblad* 2 (1865) 460–463.

practices to signal one's confessional identity in this life and the next, and thus to immediately influence the fate of the soul in the afterlife. This chapter argues that the way in which both Antwerp's authorities and lay inhabitants understood and expressed these confessional differences was through the senses and the body. As famously argued by John van Engen, the late medieval Church provided lay believers with 'multiple options' for embodying their faith, either favouring traditions of inner spirituality or outward sensuousness.[2] However, by the middle of the sixteenth century, these sensory devotional behaviours no longer just signified one's personal style of worship, but gradually became affixed to growing confessional identities, in particular through public sensory practices during heresy executions and eruptions of iconoclastic violence. As such, by the late 1560s, all devotional sensing (of, for example, candles, crucifixes, church bells, incense, the Sacrament) had become imbued with unprecedented politico-confessional meaning.[3] Hans and his loved ones knew this – even more, it was the very reason for his renouncement of the Last Sacraments – and made sure to avoid further inquiries by hiding him away.

In further disentangling Hans' unorthodox deathbed story, and those of other laypeople from Antwerp, this chapter deepens our understanding of the moment of death as a site of sensory strife during the religious struggles of the sixteenth century. In this article, I investigate who was persecuted for non-Catholic dying in Antwerp's 1560s and 1570s. In studying those believers who died outside of the Catholic Church during a time of severe post-mortem persecution I show that confessional subversion was rarely a straightforward choice even for devoted members of the city's Protestant communities. Most importantly, however, I argue it was essentially through the body and the senses that one did or did not die within a certain confession, and that the authorities' battle for Catholic orthodoxy on the deathbed was equally

---

2   Van Engen J., "Multiple Options: The World of the Fifteenth-Century Church", *Church History* 77.2 (2008) 257–284.
3   Deschryver L., "You Only Die Once: Calvinist Dying and the Senses in Lille and Tournai During the Dutch Revolt", *Early Modern Low Countries* 4.1 (2020) 35–57. For literature on the reformation of the senses, see Baum, J., *Reformation of the senses: the paradox of religious belief and practice in Germany* (Urbana: 2019); Baum, J., "From Incense to Idolatry : The Reformation of Olfaction in Late Medieval German Ritual", *Sixteenth Century Journal* 44.2 (2013) 323–344; Christ M., "Sensing Multiconfessionality in Early Modern Germany", *German History*, 40.3 (2022) 317–339;, Hahn P., "Lutheran Sensory Culture in Context", *Past and Present* 234 (2017) 90–113; Hahn P., "The reformation of the soundscape: Bell-ringing in early modern Lutheran Germany", *German History* 33.4 (2015) 525–545; Missfelder, J.-F., "Sounds and Silences of Reformation: Zurich, 1524–1571", in Knighton T. – Mazuela-Anguita A. (eds.) *Hearing the City in Early Modern Europe* (Turnhout: 2018), 135–144; Milner M., *The Senses and the English Reformation* (Farnham: 2011).

centred around lay believers' bodies. This made perfect sense, in a world in which sensory perception was considered an intensely physical process, imbuing permeable human bodies with either salutary or devilish affects. Indeed, concepts such as 'holiness', 'idolatry' or 'heresy', which modern researchers tend to understand as purely cognitive or doctrinal ideas, for early modern people were deeply embodied states of being, which entered the body (and thus affected the soul) through the eyes, ears, nose, mouth, and skin.[4] Taking into consideration pre-modern sensory traditions and anxieties, this chapter shows, is indispensable for understanding how during the Reformation 'the moment of death' was increasingly turned into a pressure cooker of confessional identity formation.

In the Low Countries, historiography on death during the Dutch Reformation has mostly focussed on the persecution and execution of so-called heretics.[5] While invaluable in their contribution to our understanding of heresy persecution during the Dutch Reformation, they do not tell us a lot on the embodied death experience of the average Dutch lay person. Although a great number of sixteenth-century Protestants died on the scaffold or at the stake, far more of them preferred to die at home, if at all possible. In Antwerp in the second half of the sixteenth century, we know many of them did. This chapter investigates those decades during which Antwerp's (non-martyr) Protestant dying were persecuted most heavily, namely in the late 1560s and early 1570s, by the joint forces of the Duke of Alba and Franciscus Doncker. The former was governor-general of the Low Countries and as such the representative of King Philip II's royal authority in the Netherlands.[6] The latter was a canon of the

---

4   Woolgar C.M., "What Makes Things Holy? The Senses and Material Culture in the later Middle Ages", in MacDonald R. – Murphy E.K.M. – Swann E. (eds.), *Sensing the Sacred in Medieval and Early Modern Culture* (Abingdon – New York: 2018) 60–78; Woolgar C.M., *The Senses in Late Medieval England* (New Haven: 2006); Wauters W., *De beroering van de religieuze ruimte. De belevingswereld van kerkgangers in de Antwerpse Onze-Lieve-Vrouwekerk, ca. 1450–1566* (Ph.D. dissertation, KU Leuven: 2021).

5   However, on this topic, too, a recent systematic study is lacking. Valuable contributions to the still scattered field of executions in the early modern Low Countries are Goosens A., *Les inquisitions modernes dans les Pays-Bas méridionaux (1520–1633)* (Brussels: 1998); Spierenburg P.C., *Judicial Violence in the Dutch Republic: Corporal Punishment, Executions and Torture in Amsterdam 1650–1750* (Ph.D. dissertation, University of Amsterdam: 1978); Van Dijck M.F., *De pacificering van de Europese samenleving: repressie, gedragspatronen en verstedelijking in Brabant tijdens de lange zestiende eeuw* (Ph.D. dissertation, University of Antwerp: 2007). For recent publications on executions during the Revolt, see Casteels I., "Drownings in the Dark: The Politics of Secret Executions in Antwerp, 1557–1565", *Early Modern Low Countries* 5.1 (2021) 75–97 and her contribution in this volume.

6   On the Duke of Alba's policies in the Low Countries, see Janssens G., "Le Duc d'Albe: artisan de la paix et initiateur de la bonne gouvernance aux Pays-Bas", in De Moreau de

Our Lady cathedral and one of the most powerful (and zealous) members of Antwerp's clerical establishment.[7] It is their persecution policy that provides us, for these years solely, with judicial documentation on non-Catholic dying in private houses across Antwerp, which this chapter combines with information provided by urban chroniclers. By the middle of the 1570s, Doncker had died, Luis de Requesens had replaced the duke of Alba as governor-general of the Low Countries, plague wreaked havoc across Antwerp's churchyards and the Dutch Revolt had reached a new phase of military confrontation. The persecution of non-Catholic dying in Antwerp was no longer a priority and the city's judicial sources again remain silent on inhabitants refusing the Last Sacraments. By the late 1570s, the tumultuous sixteenth-century history of Antwerp took a new turn, once more, and the foundations were laid for what would become a Calvinist Republic in the city between 1581 and 1585. In 1585, the city was eventually reconquered by Alexandre Farnese and firmly put back under the control of Philip II and the Catholic Church.

2   The Dying Chamber as a Route to Building a Tridentine Urban Community

The men and women who died in Antwerp in the second half of the sixteenth century had lived through a particularly turbulent introduction of the Reformation in their city. While in the first decades of the century global trade had turned Antwerp into a booming metropolis, dissident Lutheran (in the 1520s), Anabaptist (in the 1530s) and Calvinist (in the 1540s) ideas reached the city with remarkable speed. There, they caught the attention of an ever-growing, highly international citizenry, and started to simmer beneath the hustle and bustle of everyday life. Already in the 1520s, illegal gatherings were organised, small incidents of iconoclasm took place and Lutheran-inspired sermons could be heard from enthusiastic Antwerp clergymen (in particular

---

Gerbehaye C. – Dubois S. – Yante J.M. (eds.), *Gouvernance et administration dans les provinces belgiques (XVI–XVIIIe siècles). Ouvrage publié en hommage au Professeur Claude Bruneel*, Archives et Bibliothèques de Belgique/Archief- en bibliotheekwezen in België 99 (Brussel: 2013) 131–152; Janssens G., "Le duc d'Albe et l'execution des décrets du Concile de Trente aux Pays-Bas: raison d'état et dévouement religieux en temps de guerre (1567–1573)", in Soen V. – François W. (eds.), *The Council of Trent: Reform and Controversy in Europe and Beyond (1545–1700) – 2: Between Bishops and Princes* (Leuven: 2013) 279–296.

7 Marnef G., "Een kanunnik in troebele tijden. Franciscus Doncker, voorman van de contrareformatorische actie te Antwerpen (1566–1573)", in Put E. – Marinus M.-J. – Storme H. (eds.), *Geloven in het verleden: Studies over het godsdienstig leven in de vroegmoderne tijd, aangeboden aan Michel Cloet* (Leuven: 1996) 327–338.

at the Augustinian monastery).[8] Antwerp's clergy struggled to get a grip on the growing circulation of 'heretical' ideas within their parishes, which were large and increasingly overcrowded.[9] The secular urban authorities, for their part, were mostly concerned with protecting Antwerp's booming trade and the wealth it procured.[10] Eventually, their half-hearted attempts to quell the religious unrest with occasional public executions stimulated rather than eradicated the formation of Protestant Churches under the Cross. As Guido Marnef has shown, by the early 1550s especially the organisation of both a Dutch and a Walloon underground Calvinist consistory within the city was well under way.[11] By 1565, these consistories had obtained too strong a position within the city for the magistrate to be able to intervene without 'endangering the political and social fabric of the city', Marnef argued.[12] With its massive trading interests, inadequate religious institutions and high levels of anonymity, by the middle of the sixteenth century Antwerp had become the largest centre of Protestantism in Low Countries.

By the 1560s, the Low Countries had grown rife with confessional tension. In those same years, political dismay at the stern policies of Habsburg overlord Philip II reached an all-time high, too. The convergence of both these dynamics created an explosive cocktail of open rebellion and resulted in the so-called "Iconoclastic Fury" sweeping across the Low Countries in the summer of 1566.[13] On August 20, Antwerp's churches were ravaged. In the immediate aftermath, both Lutheran and Calvinist deputies from Antwerp's consistories managed to obtain unprecedented rights of public worship from stadtholder William

---

8   Marnef G., "Antwerpen als bakermat van het Lutheranisme in de zestiende-eeuwse Nederlanden: van de vroege jaren twinig tot de Calvinistische Republiek (1577–1585)", *Bulletin de la Société Royale d'Histoire du Protestantisme Belge* 146.2 (2017) 13–54.

9   Wauters, *De beroering van de religieuze ruimte* 18–24; Kint A., *The Community of Commerce: Social Relations in Sixteenth-Century Antwerp* (Ph.D. dissertation, Columbia University: 1995) 147–149.

10 Christman V., *Pragmatic Toleration. The Politics of Religious Heterodoxy in Early Reformation Antwerp, 1515–1555* (Rochester, 2015).

11 Marnef G., "De Nederlandse Geloofsbelijdenis in context: De Confession de Foy en het vroege gereformeerd protestantisme in de Nederlanden", *Theologia Reformata* 55 (2012) 237–243.

12 Marnef G., *Antwerpen in de tijd van de Reformatie: ondergronds protestantisme in een handelsmetropool 1550–1577* (Antwerp: 1996) 124.

13 Marnef G., "The Dynamics of Reformed Religious Militancy: The Netherlands, 1566–1585", in Benedict P. – Marnef G. – Van Nierop H. (eds.), *Reformation, Revolt and Civil War in France and the Netherlands 1555–1585* (Amsterdam: 1999) 51–68; Scheerder J., *Het Wonderjaar te Gent, 1566–1567*, Decavele J. – Janssens G. (eds.), Verhandelingen van de maatschappij voor geschiedenis en oudheidkunde te Gent 36 (Ghent: 2016) 29–40.

of Orange.[14] As a result, from fall 1566 to spring 1567, Antwerp's Protestants were able to publicly dispose of their dead according to their own rites, and gained unprecedented possibilities for developing and embodying their own funerary repertoires in the public sensescape.[15] This experiment with religious pluralism was short-lived, however. Governor-general Margaret of Parma had never agreed to Orange's concessions. By March, 1567, she was able to send Habsburg troops to Antwerp's walls, and swiftly defeated the ill-prepared army of Reformed 'rebels' that had gathered in the nearby village of Oosterweel. In the following weeks hundreds of Protestant families (estimations suggest around three thousand people) fled Antwerp.[16] On April 28, 1567, Parma solemnly entered the city and with a ritual procession complete with crucifixes and thousands of lit candles powerfully reclaimed Antwerp's sensescape both for the Catholic faith and the Spanish Habsburg king.[17] A few months later, in October 1567, the Duke of Alba replaced her as governor-general of the Low Countries.[18] His stern punishment of the 1566 upheavals, followed by the first

14   William of Orange, *Correspondance de Guillaume le Taciturne, prince d'Orange*, ed. L.-P. Gachard, 6 vols. (Brussels – Leipzig – Ghent: 1850) 2, 215–218; Bousard T., *Rust in vrede? Begrafenissen en religieuze controversen in Antwerpen en Brugge tijdens de Nederlandse Opstand (1565–1585)* (Master's thesis, KU Leuven: 2013) 15–16; Marnef, *Antwerpen in de tijd van de Reformatie* 129–130.

15   Margaret of Parma never acknowledged or ratified the Antwerp agreements. In the chaotic days after the Fury she had conceded the Dutch nobility could allow Protestant sermons to continue where they had been held before the Fury (*extra muros*), on the condition the nobles would help her re-establish order. Orange in Parma's opinion far exceeded these concessions by actively allowing not just *intra muros* preaching, but exercise of Protestant worship (including baptisms, marriages and burials) as a whole. See Soen V., "Habsburg Political Culture and Antwerp defiant: Pacification Strategies of Governors-General during the Dutch Revolt (1566–1568)", in Kavaler E. – Van Bruaene A.-L. (eds.), *Netherlandish Culture in the Sixteenth Century: Urban Perspectives* (Turnhout: 2017) 167–185; Soen V., *Vredehandel: Adellijke and Habsburgse verzoeningspogingen tijdens de Nederlandse Opstand* (Amsterdam: 2012) 59–65.

16   Marnef, *Antwerpen in de tijd van de Reformatie* 145–146; Janssens G., *Brabant in het verweer: loyale oppositie tegen Spanjes bewind in de Nederlanden van Alva tot Farnese 1567–1578* (Heule: 1989) 163.

17   *Chronycke van Antwerpen sedert het jaer 1500 tot 1575; gevolgd van eene beschryving van de historie en het landt van Brabant, sedert het jaer 51 vóór J.-C., tot 1565 na J.-C., volgens een onuitgegeven handschrift van de XVIe eeuw* (Antwerpen: 1843) 138–139; Janssens G., "De ordonnantie betreffende de pacificatie van de beroerten te Antwerpen (24 mei 1567): breekpunt voor de politiek van Filips II ten overstaan van de Nederlanden", *Handelingen van de Koninklijke Commissie voor de Uitgave der Oude Wetten en Verordeningen van België / Bulletin de la Commission Royale pour la Publication des Anciennes Lois et Ordonnances de Belgique* 50 (2012) 113–115.

18   Janssens G., "Le Duc d'Albe: artisan de la paix et initiateur de la bonne gouvernance aux Pays-Bas", in De Moreau de Gerbehaye C. – Dubois S. – Yante J.M. (eds.), *Gouvernance et*

military invasion of the Low Countries by William of Orange in 1568, marked the definitive beginning of the Dutch Revolt.

Both Parma and Alba as governor-general strove to put an end to the practice of non-Catholic dying that had taken hold in Antwerp after the Fury. Both considered sensory rituals to be of vital importance in this policy, too, both as a powerful force of re-sacralisation and as a telling indicator of lay believers' religious orthodoxy. Shortly after her arrival in Antwerp, Parma summoned the archbishop of Cambrai, Maximilien de Berghes, to the city, to have him ritually reconsecrate the Our Lady Cathedral, its ruined high altar and its churchyard.[19] While consecration rituals of churches after the iconoclastic violence of 1566 have received most historiographical attention, historians tend to overlook the massive importance of reconciliation rituals for the parish churchyards. Yet, as Andrew Spicer pointed out, it is precisely this part – and *de iure*, only this part – of churches' *immunitas ecclesiae* that was profaned during the upheavals of 1566–1567.[20] In Catholic eyes, the Lutheran and Calvinist bodies that had been interred in the churchyards throughout the city had annihilated the protective and sacred touch of the churchyard's soil. According to two Catholic chroniclers, 'countless citizens' had come to witness the reconciliation of Antwerp's oldest churchyard on May 15, 1567, and to hear the sermon held by the archbishop afterwards. They described the five wooden crosses, each with three candles, that were installed during the consecration process, too.[21] These crosses not only were a strong visual sign in reclaiming

---

        administration dans les provinces belgiques (XVI–XVIIIe siècles). Ouvrage publié en hommage au Professeur Claude Bruneel, Archives et Bibliothèques de Belgique/Archief- en bibliotheekwezen in België 99 (Brussel: 2013) 135.

19   Van Haecht Godevaert, *De Kroniek van Godevaert van Haecht over de troebelen van 1565 tot 1574 te Antwerpen en elders*, ed. Rob van Roosbroeck, 2 vols. (Antwerp, 1929) 1, 220; *Chronycke van Antwerpen*, 137; Bertrijn Geeraard, *Chronijck der Stadt Antwerpen toegeschreven aan den notaris Bertrijn Geeraard*, ed. Gust Van Havre (Antwerpen: 1879) 234; Antwerp, Felixarchief, PK 108: Van Wesenbeke Jan, *Chronyke van het voorgevallene binnen de stad Antwerpen van het jaar 1567 tot 1580, voor afgegaen door eenige onderhandelingstuks met den hertog van Alba, gecollecteerd by Jan van Wesenbeke Chronyke*, 12. See also Spicer A., "After Iconoclasm: Reconciliation and Resacralization in the Southern Netherlands, c. 1566–1585" *Sixteenth Century Journal* 44.2 (2013) 410–425.

20   Spicer A., "Consecration and Violation: Preserving the Sacred Landscape in the (Arch)diocese of Cambrai, c. 1550–1570", in Delbeke M. – Schraven M. (eds.), *Foundation, Dedication and Consecration in Early Modern Europe* (Leiden: 2011) 268–271.

21   Bertrijn, *Chronijck der Stadt Antwerpen* 234; Van Wesenbeke, *Chronyke* 12. Both writers' chronologies, however, are not correct: the consecration took place on May 15, 1567, and not July 15, 1568. Moreover, both claim it was suffragan bishop de Cuyper who consecreated the churchyard, while earlier (and chronologically more accurate) reports confirm it was de Berghes, see Van Haecht, *De Kroniek van Godevaert van Haecht*, 1 220; *Chronycke*

the churchyard exclusively for members of the Catholic faith (even more so by the candles lit on top of them), they also had a purifying function. Just as church buildings were ritually purified with twelve crosses anointed with holy oil, these crosses could annihilate the pernicious powers of the heretical bodies in the Churchyard of Our Lady.[22] The candles visually reminded the faithful of the crosses' sanctity, but also enhanced their apotropaic powers.[23]

After the reconciliation of the city's churchyards, the canons of the Our Lady Cathedral were determined to never again allow their soil to be contaminated with the bodies of heretics. Under the impulse of canon Franciscus Doncker, and with the support of the new governor Duke of Alba, death rituals became a spearhead in the policy of reinstating Catholic orthodoxy.[24] First and foremost, as the synod of Cambrai had stated in April 1567, no one was to die without receiving the Last Sacraments (Eucharist, confession, Extreme Unction). The synodal acts impelled secular priests to teach the laity on the last rites, 'which brought no small use to the people' and administer it to all.[25] This was not an easy undertaking in the notoriously overcrowded parishes of Antwerp. At Alba's instigation, then, in September 1568, the Antwerp magistracy issued an ordinance reinstating the ancient custom in which six neighbours of a dying man or woman solemnly accompanied their parish clergy in bringing the Sacrament (the Host, being the body of Christ) and holy oil to the deathbed, while carrying lit torches in their hands. After having become

---

    van Antwerpen, 137. It is likely Bertrijn used Wesenbeke's writings to compile his chronicle and copied the latter's mistakes.

22   Spicer, "After Iconoclasm" 423.

23   Gauthier C., *L'encens et le luminaire dans le haut Moyen Âge occidental. Liturgie et pratiques dévotionnelles* (Ph.D. dissertation, Free University of Brussels: 2008) 50, 56, 229, 243–246.

24   Janssens G., "Le duc d'Albe et l'execution des décrets du Concile de Trente aux Pays-Bas: raison d'état et dévouement religieux en temps de guerre (1567–1573)", in Soen V. – François W. (eds.), *The Council of Trent: Reform and Controversy in Europe and Beyond (1545–1700) – 2: Between Bishops and Princes* (Leuven: 2013) 279–296; Marnef G., "Een kanunnik in troebele tijden. Franciscus Doncker, voorman van de contrareformatorische actie te Antwerpen (1566–1573)", in Put E. – Marinus M.-J. – Storme H. (eds.), *Geloven in het verleden: Studies over het godsdienstig leven in de vroegmoderne tijd, aangeboden aan Michel Cloet* (Leuven: 1996) 327–338.

25   'Extremae unctionis sacramentum, cum non paruam hominibus adferat utilitatem, docere pastores volumus unctionem illam licite omnibus in mortis periculo constitutis ministrari posse, etiam illis qui decimum quartum annum non compleuerint.' In *Synodvs dioecesana Cameracensis, celebrata anno Domino millesimo quingentesimo sexagesimo septimo, mense octobri. Præsidente R.P.Dn. Maximiliano à Bergi […] Accessit quoque titulorum & capitum index vt lectoris commodo omni ex parte foret consultum* (Brussels, Michiel de Hamont: [1568]) 15r–16r; Spicer, "Consecration and Violation" 266.

'interrupted during and due to the troubles', the ordinance stated, during this ritual these neighbours should once again revere the Sacrament as it ought to be. They were also expected to keep a close eye on all passers-by, and report those who did not pay the Sacrament the appropriate respect.[26] Thus, in seeking to bring Tridentine Catholicism to Antwerp, Alba both forced its citizens to embody Catholic funerary rituals and considered citizens' bodies to carry revealing signals of lingering heresy. At the same time, reinstating social control mechanisms around the deathbed allowed the clerical authorities to track down those houses where they were not wanted. Rather than trusting families to claim 'death had been too swift to call him in time' (as Penny Roberts has shown was an excellent excuse to avoid deathbed idolatry in early modern France) several families were now held responsible for the sensory orthodoxy of the same deathbed.[27]

As a second part of the battle for the dead, a decree was issued in May 1569 that all men and women who had died without receiving the Last Sacraments would be refused burial in their parish churchyard.[28] Instead, their bodies would be dragged through Antwerp's streets with a rope around their necks and be buried beneath a newly built gallows outside the city walls (among Antwerp inhabitants quickly known as 'Doncker's gallows'). There they would lie between those of (self-)murderers, thieves and other executed convicts. Furthermore, all of the deceased's worldly goods were to be confiscated. Finally, if the authorities had proof of the moribund having been ill for longer than twenty-four hours and still having failed to call the parish clergy, the body would be hanged from the gallows instead of being buried underneath it.[29]

---

26   Génard, "Ordonnantien van het Antwerpsch Magistraat" 423.
27   Roberts P., "Contesting Sacred Space: burial disputes in sixteenth-century France", in Gordon B. – Marshall P. (eds.), *The Place of the Dead: Death and Remembrance in Late Medieval and Early Modern Europe* (New York – Cambridge: 2000) 131–148.
28   Remarkably, the official ordinance instating these measures has never been unearthed by historians. The most immediate reference to its introduction is to be found in the urban chronicle written by Antwerp painter Godevaert van Haecht (*De Kroniek van Godevaert van Haecht*, 2, 89), however, without a clear reference to the level of government instating these punishments. Bousard does not refer to any official documentation on the ordinance (Bousard, *Rust in vrede?* 23–24) and I have not been able to trace it in Antwerp urban regulations (Génard P., "Index der gebodboeken, berustende ter Secretary der stad Antwerpen", *Antwerpsch Archievenblad* 1 (1864) 120–464) nor in royal legislation collections (Terlinden C. – Bolsee J. (eds.), *Liste chronologique provisoire des édits et ordonnances des Pays-Bas: règne de Philippe II (1555–1598)*, Commission Royale pour la Publication des Anciennes Lois et Ordonnances de la Belgique (Brussels: 1912). Further research into the matter is being undertaken.
29   After a short trial period in Antwerp, by the end of the month Alba extended this measure to the rest of the Low Countries, too, see Bousard, *Rust in vrede?* 23–24; Marnef, "Een Antwerpse kanunnik in troebele tijden" 328–329.

With these haptic rituals of public desecration, Antwerp's secular and clerical authorities highlighted the (non-)participation in sensory deathbed rituals as the supreme marker of one's confessional affiliation. In line with late medieval *ars moriendi* theology, which considered the last hours as conclusive for the determination of the fate of one's soul, the deathbed in sixteenth-century Antwerp became a site of ultimate compliance or defiance, of nailing one's confessional colours to the mast.[30]

Forcing dying men and women and their families to die a Catholic death fitted within the wider attempt of royal and clerical authorities to bring as many doubtful believers as possible back into the seat of the mother Church. It is very likely this strategy was rather successful – at least in the sense that it made a great number of Protestant families resort to Nicodemite dying practices to safeguard their family's honour, home and livelihood. This we can gather from the numbers of so-called 'pardonist' families in Antwerp. Indeed, in 1570, the rigorous post-mortem punishments were complemented by a long-awaited general pardon, issued by the Duke of Alba on behalf of King Philip II. On July 16, in a lavish Tridentine ceremony in the Our Lady Cathedral of Antwerp, Alba announced that all who had strayed from orthodox devotion and wished to revoke their 'heretic' delusions, were given three months to go see their parish priest. There, they were to abjure their blasphemies and to accept the Tridentine *Professio Fidei*, after which they received an absolution for all errors in the form of a pardon letter, and could register for judicial reconciliation too. Bishop Sonnius reported no less than 14 128 'pardonists' for the city of Antwerp alone, making up for the second-highest urban reconciliation rate in the Low Countries (second only to Tournai with 28 358 reconciliations).[31] Many Antwerp citizens were thus willing and prepared to (outwardly) re-join the Catholic Church, in return for so much-needed peace and quiet after the upheavals of the 1560s.

---

30 On the genre of late medieval *ars moriendi*, see Chartier R., "Les arts de mourir, 1450–1600", *Annales. Histoires, Sciences Sociales* 31. 1 (1976) 51–75; Lips E.J.G., "Om Alle Menschen Wel Te Leren Sterven". Een onderzoek naar het publiek en de receptie van Nederlandstalige Ars moriendi-teksten in de vijftiende en vroege zestiende eeuw", *Nederlands Archief voor Kerkgeschiedenis/Dutch Review of Church History* 66.2 (1986) 148–179; Binski P., *Medieval Death: Ritual and Representation* (London: 1996).

31 Soen V., *Geen pardon zonder Paus! Studie over de complementariteit van het koninklijk en pauselijk generaal pardon (1570–1574) en over inquisiteur-generaal Michael Baius (1560–1576)*, Verhandelingen van de Koninklijke Vlaamse academie van België voor wetenschappen en kunsten 14 (Brussels: 2007) 194–223; Soen V., "The Beeldenstorm and the Spanish Habsburg Response (1566–1570)", *BMGN: Low Countries Historical Review* 131.1 (2016) 113–117. For the text of the pardon, see *Grace et pardon general, donne par le Roi nostre sire. A cause des troubles passez* (Brussels, Michiel de Hamont, 1570).

3 Resilient Bodies: Lingering Protestant Deathbed Practices and How (Not) to Sense the Last Sacraments

And yet, regular protest actions reminded both Antwerp's clergy and laity of the deep aversion to Catholic sensory (death) rituals that lingered in some parts of the urban population. The aforementioned ordinance trying to enforce outward respect for the Sacrament in the street was issued and re-issued, but according to the Antwerp (and Lutheran) painter Godevaert van Haecht, passers-by still dove away into alleys or turned their backs in order to avoid having to look at or kneel before the Sacrament. Some people, he claimed, even urinated before it, in an open display of bodily protest.[32] In his extensive contemporary chronicle, Van Haecht also rather gleefully reports other ways in which some of his fellow-citizens challenged Catholic restoration efforts. In February 1568, he writes, some 'tricksters' had taken up the habit of calling a clergyman for non-existing dying chambers, resulting in clerics fruitlessly searching for the house in which their presence was required.[33] In April 1570, he noted down a piece of anti-clerical gossip that was going about the city, saying that on his way to a deathbed, the parish priest of Saint-George had fought with undeferential passers-by not once, but twice. Reportedly, he had slapped one man in the face after he refused to honour the Sacrament, and had yelled 'You rogues, go to the gallows' to three others who had refused likewise.[34]

Obstructive actions against Catholic funerary rituals extended to individual deathbed behaviours, too, no matter how risky. Indeed, in spite of the gruelling desecration of 'heretic' corpses and the harsh repercussions for the families of those who refused to receive the Last Sacraments, in Antwerp between 1569

---

32   Philip II of Spain, *Correspondance de Philippe II sur les affaires des Pays-Bas* [*1558–1577*]: pub. d'après les originaux conservés dans les Archives royales de Simancas; précédée d'une notice historique et descriptive de ce célèbre dépôt et d'un rapport à M. le ministre de l'intérieur, ed. L.-P. Gachard, 4 vols. (Brussels – Leipzig – Ghent: 1851) 2, 676–677, 682–683; Génard, "Ordonnantien van het Antwerpsch Magistraat" 423; Génard, "Index der gebodboeken" 292; Van Haecht, *De Kroniek van Godevaert van Haecht*, 2, 47, 107–108; Van Wesenbeke, *Chronyke* 62.

33   'Ende deestyt geschiede 't, dat eenighe pastoors uytgestreken werden van scalcken, die haer riepen om met den sacrament te comen en vloden heymelyck van haer; ende en conden de papen 't huys, daer den siecken sou syn niet vinden', Van Haecht, *De Kroniek van Godevaert van Haecht*, 2, 9.

34   Ende op den 9 dach April so gesciede 't dat een pastoor van St. Joriskerck met syn sacrament buyten der stat geweest hebbende, ontmoette eenen man die 't sacrament niet en eerde, waerom den paep hem met der ander handt sloech en den man en dorst hem niet weeren. Daerna al gramme synde, ontmoeyten hem 3 gesellen die 't oock niet en eerden en hy en dorst die niet slaen, maer riep so: Rabauwen gaedt al na de galge', Van Haecht, *De Kroniek van Godevaert van Haecht*, 2, 126.

and 1575 at least twenty-one people died as 'heretics'.[35] It is very likely their number was far higher. First, the fact that in 1569 Alba and Doncker thought it opportune to threaten the laity with the gallows' field, suggests there was still a significant problem of non-Catholic deaths in Antwerp two years after the city's Protestant communities had lost their rights of worship. Second, all twenty-one cases I was able to trace in Antwerp's judicial archives and chronicles only ended up in historical records because something went wrong during illegal burial practices. On May 3, 1569, for example, passers-by stumbled upon the dead body of an unidentified male in the churchyard of Saint-Andrew, after the basket in which it had been buried at night stuck out of the ground.[36] Similarly, on July 6 of that same year, an illegally buried man was discovered in a garden in Deurne, outside the city walls.[37] Again on July 29, a body was removed from the city walls, after two dogs had caught scent of it and had started to unearth it.[38] We can only guess how many bodies remained undetected by Antwerp's sixteenth-century authorities – and thus absent from the city's judicial records. However, if we can believe Antwerp's new bishop Franciscus Sonnius, in 1575 'a great number of people [still] lived and died in the city without receiving the Sacraments of the Church'.[39]

He seems to have been quite right. A closer examination of the deceased 'heretics' we do know about, suggests Protestant dying practices occurred across all social classes and quarters of Antwerp. Of the twenty-one bodies that were buried beneath or hanged from Antwerp's gallows for heretical dying between 1569 and 1575, I have been able to trace the occupation for twelve. They ranged from textile worker to wealthy merchant and included a fisherman, a confectioner, a broker, and a silver smith – to name but a few.[40] For most cases, we have some information of the context in which the bodies were discovered. Interestingly, these data suggest the socio-economic background of believers influenced their ways of avoiding Catholic 'idolatry' in their final moments.

---

35   See Appendix 321–322.
36   Génard, "Ordonnantien van het Antwerpsch Magistraat" 423; Van Haecht, *De Kroniek van Godevaert van Haecht* 2, 87–88.
37   Van Haecht, *De Kroniek van Godevaert van Haecht* 2, 95.
38   Van Haecht, *De Kroniek van Godevaert van Haecht* 2, 96.
39   Philip II of Spain, *Correspondance de Philippe II sur les affaires des Pays-Bas [1558–1577]: pub. d'après les originaux conservés dans les Archives royales de Simancas; précédée d'une notice historique et descriptive de ce célèbre dépôt et d'un rapport à M. le ministre de l'intérieur*, ed. L.-P. Gachard, 4 vols. (Brussels – Leipzig – Ghent: 1858) 3, 305.
40   With six of the twelve identified professions relating to craftwork, Antwerp's middling classes seem to be well-represented. For a detailed analysis of the socio-economic backgrounds of Antwerp's Protestant communities after the Fury, see Marnef, *Antwerpen in de tijd van de Reformatie* 179–261.

The deceased 'heretics' that were picked up from Antwerp's poorest quarters seem to have simply desisted from calling for a parish priest. In the overflowing streets and homes of, for example, the parish of Saint-Andrew, their deaths had a good chance of never being noticed, or of being too low-profile to cause much consternation.[41] They could appeal to (quite literal) underground networks for Protestant burial. Indeed, in December 1574, the Calvinist mason Jasper Sterx was caught red-handed with two other men, as they were burying a deceased female coreligionist in her basement at night.[42] According to Van Haemstede, Sterx was an elder of the Antwerp Calvinist church and had buried other members of his faith 'honourably, without any papish superstition'– thus suggesting a certain degree of institutionalised clandestine burial practice organized by the Calvinist consistory.[43] These kinds of practices were risky and not always successful, as we can tell from the aforementioned discovered bodies in the churchyard and city walls of Saint-Andrew, and from two unidentified female bodies who according to Antwerp's judicial records were picked up in the '*Blydenhoek*' and the '*Kakhoek*', two street corners in Antwerp's poorest neighbourhood.[44] However, the sources suggest that believers who appealed to them did not have much financial or social capital to lose in risking post-mortem punishments. Their confessional identity had probably become stronger than their wish for an honourable, public burial within the parish churchyard.

More affluent and influential Antwerp citizens sought to die according to their Protestant beliefs in Antwerp's re-Catholicised sensescape, too. They seem to have done so in more subtle and pragmatic ways than their poorer fellow citizens, incorporating some traditional *ars moriendi* rituals to avoid post-mortem punishment. This is illustrated beautifully in the case of the wealthy confectioner and 'treffelyck coopman (eminent merchant)' Dierick Bousyn.[45] Apparently, Bousyn had been assisted at his deathbed by the

---

41   Kint, *Community of Commerce* 117–126.

42   Génard P., "Personen te Antwerpen in de XVIe eeuw voor het feit van religie gerechtelijk vervolgd – Lijst van ambtelijke bijhoorige stukken. (vervolg)", *Antwerpsch Archievenblad* 13 (1876) 157–158, 191; Génard, "Tijdordelijke tafel" 94–95; Van Haecht, *De Kroniek van Godevaert van Haecht* 2, 328–329; Van Wesenbeke, *Chronyke* 208–209.

43   Van Haemstede Adriaan, *Historien oft gheschiedenissen der vromer martelaren, die om het ghetuyghenisse des Evangeliums haer bloet gestort hebben, van den tijde Christi af tot den jare LXXIX* (Dordrecht, [Jan Canin]: 1579) 621.

44   Génard, "Personen te Antwerpen" 13, 206; Génard, "Tijdordelijke tafel" 99; Thys A., *Historiek der straten en openbare plaatsen van Antwerpen* (Antwerp: 1879) 599–607; Meuleman A., "Historiek: Sint-Andriesplaats 23 – Dienst voor Stadsreiniging" *Tijdschrift van de Heemkundige kring Sint-Andrieskwartier Herleeft* 6.3 (1985).

45   Van Haecht, *De Kroniek van Godevaert van Haecht* 2, 124.

infamous Calvinist preacher Herman Moded before calling on the clergy of the Our Lady Cathedral to come and give him the Last Sacraments. These bluntly refused to oblige, saying they knew full well Bousyn had been part of the Calvinist rebellion on the Meir-bridge in 1567, and he only wished to be administered the Sacraments to secure his worldly goods. Consequently, Bousyn's wife and friends emptied his house and fled the city, leaving his dead body behind, where it was discovered by the authorities four days later.[46]

We know Bousyn was not the only moneyed Calvinist who attempted to combine both Calvinist and Catholic sensory rituals in his final hours in the hopes of safekeeping his reputation and his widow's livelihood. He was just one of the few who – due to his prominent reputation – was caught trying to do so. Indeed, not one month before his passing, an unnamed woman had very nearly succeeded with this very same coping strategy. At the order of the city margrave, she was disinterred from the Our Lady Churchyard six days after her burial, after the authorities had caught wind of her having had a Calvinist minister at her deathbed (possibly also Moded).[47] On the question of exactly how pernicious the presence of Catholic sensory funerary rites and paraphernalia were, then, there seems to have been no consensus among Antwerp's Reformed laity. Indeed, in spite of Calvin's continued condemnation of Nicodemite practices, even leading Reformed families such as Bousyn's could decide the presence of a Calvinist preacher at their deathbeds had armed them against the arrival of the Sacrament, oil, holy water, candles, incense, crucifixes, and saintly images later on.[48] That their calling for Catholic clergy in their last moments would automatically also result in their bodies being buried and commemorated with elaborate Tridentine funeral practice does not seem to have been a major issue for them, either. Several of these had indeed already been held for the unnamed woman before her disinterment.[49] Possibly, some of Antwerp's Protestants saw no greater threat in these idolatrous rituals than in complete

---

46 Bertrijn, *Chronijck der Stadt Antwerpen* 244; Van Haecht, *De Kroniek van Godevaert van Haecht* 2, 124; *Chronycke van Antwerpen* 217; Génard P., "Personen te Antwerpen in de XVIe eeuw voor het feit van religie gerechtelijk vervolgd – Lijst van ambtelijke bijhoorige stukken. (Vervolg. 1567–1570)", *Antwerpsch Archievenblad* 12 (1875) 438, 443, 475; Génard, "Personen te Antwerpen" 13, 167; Génard, "Tijdordelijke tafel" 73.

47 Bertrijn, *Chronijck der Stadt Antwerpen* 242; Van Haecht, *De Kroniek van Godevaert van Haecht* 2, 121; *Chronycke van Antwerpen*, 215; Génard, "Personen te Antwerpen" 12, 43; Génard, "Personen te Antwerpen" 13, 73.

48 Eire C., *War against the Idols: The Reformation of Worship from Erasmus to Calvin* (Cambridge: 1986) 234–275.

49 Van Haecht, *De Kroniek van Godevaert van Haecht*, 2, 121.

social ruin, as Protestant theology claimed no actions on the dead body could influence the fate of the soul, anyway.[50]

Socio-economic position thus seems to have influenced Antwerp's inhabitants' choices of deathbed demeanour. It is difficult to ascertain if gender might have equally shaped sensory dying practices in this context, but I would suggest it was less of a defining factor. Firstly, the sources for Antwerp show that both men and women underwent post-mortem punishments for actively refusing to die a Catholic: between 1568 and 1575 they record eleven men and nine women taken to the gallows' field for this crime.[51] These numbers somewhat differ from the gender pattern for heresy persecution as a whole throughout the sixteenth-century Low Countries, in which mostly males were persecuted as the perceived instigators of heretical subversion. However, the newly established Council of Troubles from fall 1567 deliberately decided to target heretics' surroundings too, thus appealing to social mechanisms of dissuasion to quell religious heterodoxy. This was not different for the new deathbed legislations issued at the end of the 1560s I discussed above. After the death of a 'heretic', the confiscation of worldly goods did not just target those possessions of the 'heretic' in question, but all the common household goods as well.[52] As such, the non-Catholic deaths of a husband and a wife could be equally detrimental to Antwerp families and their surroundings. However, further investigations are needed to verify this hypothesis, which is solely based on research data for Antwerp.

If we turn back to the wondrous case of Hans Vander Thoren's last hours with which this chapter commenced, we can understand better why he actively avoided dying as a Protestant martyr. Like many of his fellow believers, Hans – though constant in his beliefs and his aversion to Catholic sensory funerary rituals – was not prepared to sacrifice his body and his family to the glory of an exemplary death on Antwerp's scaffold. It is very likely that his flight was aimed at protecting his wife and children through dying outside of clerical scrutiny. As long as he could not provide the authorities with proof of *actually* having died without receiving the Last Sacraments in the end, his family might escape prosecution. To attain this, however, he had to get out of his house.

It is quite likely Hans – impaired as he was – had help carrying out this disappearance act. A dive into the city's criminal records confirms that Hans'

---

50 Karant-Nunn S.C., *The Reformation of Ritual: An Interpretation of Early Modern Germany* (Abingdon – New York: 2007) 172–173; Koslofsky C., *The Reformation of the Dead: Death and Ritual in Early Modern Germany, 1450–1700* (New York: 2000).

51 The sex of two bodies could not be ascertained, see Appendix.

52 On the Council of Troubles and its policies, see Verheyden A.L.E., *Le Conseil des troubles* (Flavion: 1981) and Goosens, *Les Inquisitions modernes* 108–113, 118–123, 167–169.

refusal to receive the Last Unction was indeed rooted in Calvinist beliefs, and he had been involved in Antwerp's Calvinist circles a few years before. In 1569, he had been persecuted by the city margrave for the possession of illegal Reformed writings, but thanks to capable lawyers, he had managed to escape a condemnation after a year of captivity in Het Steen, Antwerp's communal prison.[53] More telling is the fact that Hans' body eventually was discovered in the house of a supposed member of Antwerp's Calvinist consistory. As we can read in the urban ordinance with which this paper opened, one day after his disappearance, Hans – or rather, his corpse – had fallen from the second story window of a house in the *Hoochsetterstraete*, in the wealthy west of the city.[54] The house was rented by Jacques Bocquet, a textile worker, who (according to eyewitnesses) had pulled the body inside his house and subsequently left town with his wife and children. Further investigations revealed the couple to have had all kinds of beef and pork in their pantry (in the middle of Lent), to possess a psalter by a 'sectarian minister called Petrus Dathenus' (a very popular collection of psalms in Antwerp's clandestine Calvinist churches) and indeed to have hosted several illegal Calvinist gatherings in their home.[55] Supposedly, then, Hans' coreligionists stepped up after he had defied the Catholic priest, and took him to Bocquet's house – either to protect Hans and his family from persecution, or to not allow him the chance to recant and accept the Last Sacraments after all.

Hans' rejection of Catholic sensory deathbed rituals, then, had taken him straight towards Calvinist ones: to a house that was imbued with the spoken Word of Scripture, where a psalter lay ready for Calvinist communal singing, instead of Catholic clerical chanting. Nevertheless, something must have gone wrong while Hans was hiding away with the Bocquets. If we can believe Van Haecht, the dying man had been delusional with disease (Van Haecht believed it was plague) and had jumped from the window himself.[56] The attention this must have attracted to the house probably resulted in the Bocquet family's unforeseen flight from the city. Hans' unidentified corpse, meanwhile, was buried beneath the gallows – but not hung from them, in line with the above-mentioned post-mortem regulations. Three days later, however, the authorities realised the corpse had belonged to the missing Hans, who had not died too suddenly to receive the Last Sacraments, but had indeed actively

---

[53] Génard, "Tijdordelijke tafel" 62 and 97. For the extensive proceedings of the case of Vander Thoren, see Génard, "Personen te Antwerpen" 12, 326, 334–335, 366, 383.
[54] Thys, *Historiek der straten en openbare plaatsen van Antwerpen* 329–330; Marnef, *Antwerpen in de tijd van de Reformatie* 32–34.
[55] Génard, "Ordonnantien van het Antwerpsch magistraat" 460–463.
[56] Van Haecht, *De Kroniek van Godevaert van Haecht* 2, 150–151.

refused them. As a result, his corpse was dug up again, and hung from the gallows instead.[57]

4 Conclusion

Hans and his non-Catholic dead fellow citizens, as it turns out, were quite a remarkable group of Reformed believers. They were no fervent martyrs seeking to die a painful heroic death for the Reformed faith. Neither were they practical Nicodemites, accepting that the unusually fierce post-mortem persecution in Antwerp in the 1560s and 1570s simply forced them to die in the Catholic Church. Hovering somewhere between Catholic orthodoxy and Calvinist martyrdom, they were part of the ever elusive 'middle group believers' first studied by Dutch historian Jan Juliaan Woltjer in the 1960s.[58] Until today, historians building on Woltjer's work continue to struggle with questions on what drove these middle groups and how we can better understand this rather vague category of believers.[59] Often these questions turn out to be unanswerable, as sources so often tell us more on the extreme ends of the confessional spectrum than on contemporaries situated somewhere in between, anxiously trying not to put their head over the parapet. It should come as no surprise, then, that in historiography beyond the Low Countries, too, moderate or doubtful believers have been considerably less studied than their zealous Protestant and Catholic contemporaries.[60] The exceptional post-mortem heresy persecution installed by the Duke of Alba and Canon Doncker in mid-sixteenth-century Antwerp, however, has provided us with rare sources on non-martyrological and non-Catholic dying during the Reformation. The stories of imperfect, cross-confessional death practices in the 1560s and 1570s in Antwerp that have come down to us are rare, and most often incomplete.[61] Yet, they offer us priceless glimpses of laypeople whose devotional practices generally did not make it into historical record at all, precisely because they were no heroic Reformed martyrs, and neither were they exemplary Catholics.

---

57   Génard, "Personen te Antwerpen" 13, 169.
58   Woltjer J.J., *Friesland in hervormingstijd* (Leiden: 1962); Woltjer J.J., *Tussen vrijheidsstrijd en burgeroorlog. Over de Nederlandse Opstand 1555–1580* (Amsterdam: 1994).
59   Kooi C., *Reformation in the Low Countries, 1500–1620* (Cambridge: 2022) 102–104.
60   Racaut L. – Ryrie A., "Introduction: Between Coercion and Persuasion", in Racaut L. – Ryrie A. (eds.), *Moderate Voices in the European Reformation* (Aldershot: 2005) 1–12.
61   With the term 'cross-confessional' I refer to the combination of distinctive elements of different confessional cultural practices, in the framework of this paper Catholic and Calvinist deathbed rituals.

This chapter has argued that we need to interpret these stories with close attention to what they can tell us about embodied and sensory lay deathbed practices during the Reformation. Early modern men and women understood their souls to be embodied and their bodies to be permeable, susceptible to both divine and devilish affects entering the body through the senses. To decide whether or not a Catholic priest (bringing incense, holy oil, holy water, a crucifix, burning candles) could attend to one's deathbed was a question with great spiritual consequences, that could make one die in an embodied state of heresy, idolatry or of Christian purity – depending on one's take on what kind of power these rituals and objects held. This is not to say that these sensory considerations annihilated or outweighed all other factors influencing the dying practices of Antwerp's sixteenth-century laity. If anything, the case studies in this article show how even impassioned members of Antwerp's Reformed Churches struck sensory compromises on their deathbeds to protect their families and worldly goods. Indeed, most of the people who ended up on Antwerp's gallows for dying outside of the Catholic Church arrived there unintentionally, either because their illegally buried bodies were discovered or because word of their unorthodox deathbed behaviour had spread. Socio-economic position influenced people's deathbed behaviours, as did the severe political pressure exercised by the authorities to accept Catholic rituals – and probably also by the Antwerp consistory to resist it.

And yet, the dangers these Reformed believers were willing to expose themselves to in an attempt to protect themselves from Catholic funerary rites were considerable. They risked inviting the most persecuted Reformed preachers of the Low Countries into their homes and they risked having their bodies disappear after dying in the hopes it would not catch the attention of the parish priest (or Catholic fellow parishioners). Some of them turned away and insulted Catholic clergymen right to their faces. While Hans had run or been taken away from his dying chamber afterwards, his fellow citizen Bartholomeus Swyndrecht was either too weak to flee or simply did not try to do so after insulting his parish priest on his sickbed. His body was picked up at his own house after his death and brought to the gallows' field, seemingly without the slightest resistance.[62] I argue that we cannot understand these people's actions without taking fully into account the powerful anxieties surrounding sensory rituals in Antwerp at this time. Our understanding of lay (middle group) believers in the Reformation can benefit considerably, I believe, from actively renouncing the Descartian tendency to study devotional practices as

---

62   Génard, "Personen te Antwerpen" 12, 414–415 and 471; *Chronycke van Antwerpen* 204; Van Haecht, *De Kroniek van Godevaert van Haecht* 2, 88; Van Wesenbeke, *Chronyke* 59.

the derivative expression of confessional ideas. Rather, we should try to adapt the worldview of ordinary early modern men and women, according to which sensory stimuli such as the sight of the crucifix, the touch of a burning candle or the smell of incense literally carried within them ideas of idolatry/spirituality able to physically enter the body, and these ideas in turn could affect one's skills of sensory discernment for better or worse. Taking into consideration these pre-modern sensory notions is indispensable for understanding how during the Reformation 'the moment of death' was increasingly turned into a pressure cooker of confessional identity formation.

Appendix: Men and Women Prosecuted Post-mortem for Deathbed Heresy in Antwerp, 1569–1581

Date	Name	Sex	Address	Confession	Occupation	Prison/Home	Juridical sources	Chronicles
25 September 1568	Jean le Gillon	Male	parish of Saint-George	Calvinist	Silver smith	Prison	AA x, p. 17, 51–63, XII, p. 287, 290–297, 300–302, 305, 307, 440, XIV pp. 56–57	VH II p. 45; B p. 240
4 May 1569	Unknown	Male	parish of Saint-Andrew	Unknown	Unknown	Home	AA II, p. 436, XII p. 377, XIV p. 67	x
5 May 1569	Unknown	Female	Maalderijstraat, parish of Our Lady	Lutheran	Miller (wife of)	Home	AA XII p. 471	VH II p. 88
16 May 1569	Bartholomeus Swyndrecht	Male	Venusstraat, parish of Our Lady/Saint-James (borderstreet)	Calvinist	Broker	Home	AA XII p. 380, 414–415, 436, 471, XIV p. 69	AC p. 257
27 May 1569	Joos	Male	Vismarkt/Schipstraat, parish of Saint-Walburga	Unknown	Apprentice	Home	AA XII p. 383, 45, XIV p. 69	VH II p. 90; AC p. 205
5 July 1569	Unknown	Unknown	Unknown	Unknown	Unknown	Home	x	VH, II, 95
28 July 1569	Unknown	Male	Wijngaertstraat, parish of Our Lady	Unknown	Trader	Home	AA XII p. 387, XIV p. 69	VH, II, 96
29 July 1569	Unknown	Unknown	Unknown	Unknown	Unknown	Home	x	VH II, 96
24 August 1569	Unknown	Male	Kathelijnevest, parish of Our Lady	Unknown	Tailor	Home	AA XII p. 391, XIV p. 69	VH II p. 90; AC p. 211
31 January 1570	Unknown	Female	Unknown, parish of Our Lady	Calvinist	Unknown	Home	AA XII p. 430, XIV p. 73	VH II p. 121; AC p. 215, B p. 242

Date	Name	Sex	Address	Confession	Occupation	Prison/Home	Juridical sources	Chronicles
10 March 1570	Dierick Bousyn	Male	Peter Potstraat, parish of Our Lady	Calvinist	Trader	Home	AA XII p. 438, 443, 475, XIII p. 167, XIV p. 73	VH II p. 124; AC p. 217; B p. 244
May 1570	Adriana Gemert	Female	Unknown	Calvinist	Cloth weaver (wife of)	Prison	AA XII p. 389, 422–459, XIII p. 168, XIV p. 70	x
May–June 1570	Hans Raey	Male	Unknown	Unknown	Unknown	Home	AA XII p. 474, XIII p. 167, XIV p. 77	x
May–June 1570	Van Digne	Female	Vlasmarkt, parish of Our Lady	Unknown	Cloth dyer (widow of)	Home	AA XII p. 474, XIII p. 167, XIV p. 77	x
17 February 1571	Unknown	Male	Unknown	Unknown	Unknown	Home	x	AC pp. 242–243
4 May 1571	Hans vander Thoren	Male	Unknown	Calvinist	Unknown	Home	AA II pp. 460–462, XIII p. 169, XIV 62, 97	VH II pp. 150–151
24 December 1574	Neesken	Female	Lange Schipperskapelstraat, parish of Saint-Walburga	Calvinist	Unknown	Home	AA XIII pp. 205–206; XIV p. 99	VH II pp. 328–329
1575	Unknown	Female	Kakhoek, parish of Saint-Andrew	Unknown	Unknown	Home	AA XIII p. 206, XIV p. 99	x
1575	Unknown	Male	Unknown	Unknown	Unknown	Prison	AA XIII p. 206, XIV p. 100	x
1575	Unknown	Female	Unknown	Unknown	Unknown	Prison	AA XIII p. 206, XIV p. 101	x
1575	Unknown	Female	Blydenhoeck, parish of Saint-George	Unknown	Unknown	Home	AA XIII p. 206, XIV p. 102	x

Bibliography

Primary Printed Sources

Chronycke van Antwerpen sedert het jaer 1500 tot 1575 gevolgd van eene beschryving van de historie en het landt van Brabant sedert het jaer 51 voor J.-C. tot 1565 na J.-C. volgens een onuitgegeven handschrift van de XVIe eeuw (Antwerpen: 1843).

Grace et pardon general, donne par le Roi nostre sire. A cause des troubles passez (Brussels, Michiel de Hamont, 1570).

Philip II of Spain, *Correspondance de Philippe II sur les affaires des Pays-Bas [1558–1577]: pub. d'après les originaux conservés dans les Archives royales de Simancas; précédée d'une notice historique et descriptive de ce célèbre dépôt et d'un rapport à M. le ministre de l'intérieur*, ed. L.-P. Gachard, 4 vols. (Brussels – Leipzig – Ghent: 1851–1858).

Synodvs dioecesana Cameracensis, celebrata anno Domino millesimo quingentesimo sexagesimo septimo, mense octobri. Præsidente R.P.Dn. Maximiliano à Bergi [...] Accessit quoque titulorum & capitum index vt lectoris commodo omni ex parte foret consultum (Brussels, Michiel de Hamont: [1568]).

William of Orange, *Correspondance de Guillaume le Taciturne, prince d'Orange*, ed. L.-P. Gachard, 6 vols. (Brussels – Leipzig – Ghent: 1850–1857).

Van Haemstede Adriaan, *Historien oft gheschiedenissen der vromer martelaren, die om het ghetuyghenisse des Evangeliums haer bloet gestort hebben, van den tijde Christi af tot den jare LXXIX* (Dordrecht, [Jan Canin]: 1579).

Primary Manuscript Sources

Antwerp, Felixarchief, PK 108: Van Wesenbeke Jan, *Chronyke van het voorgevallene binnen de stad Antwerpen van het jaar 1567 tot 1580, voor afgegaen door eenige onderhandelingstuks met den hertog van Alba, gecollecteerd by Jan van Wesenbeke Chronyke*.

Secondary Literature

Baum, J., *Reformation of the senses: the paradox of religious belief and practice in Germany* (Urbana: 2019).

Baum, J., "From Incense to Idolatry: The Reformation of Olfaction in Late Medieval German Ritual", *Sixteenth Century Journal* 44.2 (2013) 323–344.

Bertrijn Geeraard, *Chronijck der Stadt Antwerpen toegeschreven aan den notaris Bertrijn Geeraard*, ed. Gust Van Havre (Antwerpen: 1879).

Bousard T., *Rust in vrede? Begrafenissen en religieuze controversen in Antwerpen en Brugge tijdens de Nederlandse Opstand (1565–1585)* (Master's thesis, KU Leuven: 2013).

Casteels I., "Drownings in the Dark: The Politics of Secret Executions in Antwerp, 1557–1565", *Early Modern Low Countries* 5.1 (2021) 75–97.

Christ M., "Sensing Multiconfessionality in Early Modern Germany", *German History*, 40.3 (2022) 317–339.

Christman V., *Pragmatic Toleration. The Politics of Religious Heterodoxy in Early Reformation Antwerp, 1515–1555* (Rochester, 2015).

Deschryver L., "You Only Die Once: Calvinist Dying and the Senses in Lille and Tournai During the Dutch Revolt", *Early Modern Low Countries* 4.1 (2020) 35–57.

Eire C., *War against the Idols: The Reformation of Worship from Erasmus to Calvin* (Cambridge: 1986).

Gauthier C., *L'encens et le luminaire dans le haut Moyen Âge occidental. Liturgie et pratiques dévotionnelles* (Ph.D. dissertation, Free University of Brussels: 2008).

Génard P., "Index der gebodboeken, berustende ter Secretary der stad Antwerpen", *Antwerpsch Archievenblad* 1 (1864) 120–464.

Génard P., "Ordonnantien van het Antwerpsch Magistraat, rakende de godsdienstige geschillen der XVIe eeuw", *Antwerpsch Archievenblad* 2 (1865) 308–472.

Génard P., "Personen te Antwerpen in de XVIe eeuw voor het feit van religie gerechtelijk vervolgd – Lijst van ambtelijke bijhoorige stukken. (Vervolg. 1567–1570)", *Antwerpsch Archievenblad* 12 (1875) 1–480.

Génard P., "Personen te Antwerpen in de XVIe eeuw voor het feit van religie gerechtelijk vervolgd – Lijst van ambtelijke bijhoorige stukken. (vervolg)", *Antwerpsch Archievenblad* 13 (1876) 1–214.

Génard P., "Tijdordelijke tafel der namen van personen te Antwerpen in de XVIe eeuw voor het feit van religie gerechtelijk vervolgd", *Antwerpsch Archievenblad* 14 (1877) 1–103.

Goosens A., *Les inquisitions modernes dans les Pays-Bas méridionaux (1520–1633)* (Brussels: 1998).

Hahn P., "Lutheran Sensory Culture in Context", *Past and Present* 234 (2017) 90–113.

Hahn P., "The reformation of the soundscape: Bell-ringing in early modern Lutheran Germany", *German History* 33.4 (2015) 525–545.

Janssens G., "De ordonnantie betreffende de pacificatie van de beroerten te Antwerpen (24 mei 1567): breekpunt voor de politiek van Filips II ten overstaan van de Nederlanden", *Handelingen van de Koninklijke Commissie voor de Uitgave der Oude Wetten en Verordeningen van België / Bulletin de la Commission Royale pour la Publication des Anciennes Lois et Ordonnances de Belgique* 50 (2012) 105–132.

Janssens G., "Le duc d'Albe et l'execution des décrets du Concile de Trente aux Pays-Bas: raison d'état et dévouement religieux en temps de guerre (1567–1573)", in Soen V. – François W. (eds.), *The Council of Trent: Reform and Controversy in Europe and Beyond (1545–1700) – 2: Between Bishops and Princes* (Leuven: 2013) 279–296.

Janssens G., "Le Duc d'Albe: artisan de la paix et initiateur de la bonne gouvernance aux Pays-Bas", in De Moreau de Gerbehaye C. – Dubois S. – Yante J.M. (eds.), *Gouvernance* *et administration dans les provinces belgiques (XVI–XVIIIe siècles). Ouvrage publié en hommage au Professeur Claude Bruneel*, Archives et Bibliothèques de Belgique/ Archief- en bibliotheekwezen in België 99 (Brussel: 2013) 131–152.

Janssens G., *Brabant in het verweer: loyale oppositie tegen Spanjes bewind in de Nederlanden van Alva tot Farnese 1567–1578* (Heule: 1989).

Karant-Nunn S.C., *The Reformation of Ritual: An Interpretation of Early Modern Germany* (Abingdon – New York: 2007).

Kint A., *The Community of Commerce: Social Relations in Sixteenth-Century Antwerp* (Ph.D. dissertation, Columbia University: 1995).

Kooi C., *Reformation in the Low Countries, 1500–1620* (Cambridge: 2022).

Koslofsky C., *The Reformation of the Dead: Death and Ritual in Early Modern Germany, 1450–1700* (New York: 2000).

Marnef G., "De Nederlandse Geloofsbelijdenis in context: De Confession de Foy en het vroege gereformeerd protestantisme in de Nederlanden", *Theologia Reformata* 55 (2012) 237–251.

Marnef G., "Een kanunnik in troebele tijden. Franciscus Doncker, voorman van de contrareformatorische actie te Antwerpen (1566–1573)", in Put E. – Marinus M.-J. – Storme H. (eds.), *Geloven in het verleden: Studies over het godsdienstig leven in de vroegmoderne tijd, aangeboden aan Michel Cloet* (Leuven: 1996) 327–338.

Marnef G., "The Dynamics of Reformed Religious Militancy: The Netherlands, 1566–1585", in Benedict P. – Marnef G. – Van Nierop H. (eds.), *Reformation, Revolt and Civil War in France and the Netherlands 1555–1585* (Amsterdam: 1999) 51–68.

Marnef G., *Antwerpen in de tijd van de Reformatie: ondergronds protestantisme in een handelsmetropool 1550–1577* (Antwerp: 1996).

Meuleman A., "Historiek: Sint-Andriesplaats 23 – Dienst voor Stadsreiniging" *Tijdschrift van de Heemkundige kring Sint-Andrieskwartier Herleeft* 6.3 (1985).

Milner M., *The Senses and the English Reformation* (Farnham: 2011).

Missfelder J.-F., "Sounds and Silences of Reformation: Zurich, 1524–1571", in Knighton T. – Mazuela-Anguita A. (eds.) *Hearing the City in Early Modern Europe* (Turnhout: 2018), 135–144.

Racaut L. – Ryrie A., "Introduction: Between Coercion and Persuasion", in Racaut L. – Ryrie A. (eds.), *Moderate Voices in the European Reformation* (Aldershot: 2005) 1–12.

Scheerder J., *Het Wonderjaar te Gent, 1566–1567*, Decavele J. – Janssens G. (eds.), Verhandelingen van de maatschappij voor geschiedenis en oudheidkunde te Gent 36 (Ghent: 2016).

Soen V., "Habsburg Political Culture and Antwerp defiant: Pacification Strategies of Governors-General during the Dutch Revolt (1566–1568)", in Kavaler E. – Van Bruaene A.-L. (eds.), *Netherlandish Culture in the Sixteenth Century: Urban Perspectives* (Turnhout: 2017) 167–185.

Soen V., "The Beeldenstorm and the Spanish Habsburg Response (1566–1570)", *BMGN: Low Countries Historical Review* 131.1 (2016) 99–120.

Soen V., *Geen pardon zonder Paus! Studie over de complementariteit van het koninklijk en pauselijk generaal pardon (1570–1574) en over inquisiteur-generaal Michael Baius (1560–1576)*, Verhandelingen van de Koninklijke Vlaamse academie van België voor wetenschappen en kunsten 14 (Brussels: 2007).

Soen V., *Vredehandel: Adellijke and Habsburgse verzoeningspogingen tijdens de Nederlandse Opstand* (Amsterdam: 2012).

Spicer A., "After Iconoclasm: Reconciliation and Resacralization in the Southern Netherlands, c. 1566–1585" *Sixteenth Century Journal* 44.2 (2013) 411–433.

Spicer A., "Consecration and Violation: Preserving the Sacred Landscape in the (Arch)diocese of Cambrai, c. 1550–1570", in Delbeke M. – Schraven M. (eds.), *Foundation, Dedication and Consecration in Early Modern Europe* (Leiden: 2011) 253–274.

Spierenburg P.C., *Judicial Violence in the Dutch Republic: Corporal Punishment, Executions and Torture in Amsterdam 1650–1750* (Ph.D. dissertation, University of Amsterdam: 1978).

Terlinden C. – Bolsee J. (eds.), *Liste chronologique provisoire des édits et ordonnances des Pays-Bas: règne de Philippe II (1555–1598)*, Commission Royale pour la Publication des Anciennes Lois et Ordonnances (Brussels: 1912).

Thys A., *Historiek der straten en openbare plaatsen van Antwerpen* (Antwerp: 1879).

Van Dijck M.F., *De pacificering van de Europese samenleving: repressie, gedragspatronen en verstedelijking in Brabant tijdens de lange zestiende eeuw* (Ph.D. dissertation, University of Antwerp: 2007).

Van Engen J., "Multiple Options: The World of the Fifteenth-Century Church", *Church History* 77.2 (2008) 257–284.

Van Haecht Godevaert, *De Kroniek van Godevaert van Haecht over de troebelen van 1565 tot 1574 te Antwerpen en elders*, ed. Rob van Roosbroeck, 2 vols. (Antwerp, 1929).

Wauters W., *De beroering van de religieuze ruimte. De belevingswereld van kerkgangers in de Antwerpse Onze-Lieve-Vrouwekerk, ca. 1450–1566* (Ph.D. dissertation, KU Leuven: 2021).

Woltjer J.J., *Friesland in hervormingstijd* (Leiden: 1962).

Woltjer J.J., *Tussen vrijheidsstrijd en burgeroorlog. Over de Nederlandse Opstand 1555–1580* (Amsterdam: 1994).

Woolgar C.M., "What makes things holy? The Senses and Material Culture in the later Middle Ages", in MacDonald R. – Murphy E.K.M. – Swann E. (eds.), *Sensing the Sacred in Medieval and Early Modern Culture* (Abingdon – New York: 2018) 60–78.

Woolgar C.M., *The Senses in Late Medieval England* (New Haven: 2006).

Index Nominum

Abbot, Robert   156
Albaleste, Charlotte   41
Andreæ, Johann Valentin   244–246
Antoinette (enslaved person)   92–93
Arndt, David   242–244
Augustine   145, 148
Avrigny, Guillaumette d'   45

Baumännin, Catharina   25*n*18, 28–29
Bavarus, Gottfried   251
Beer, Martin   144
Behaim, Lucas Friedrich   144
Benson, Joseph   95, 97
Berge, Joachim von   112–114
Bosch, Hieronymus   216
Bouchereau, Samuel   42
Bousyn, Dierick   314–315, 322
Bressuire, Moris de   43, 50
Broecke, Peter Vanden   265
Browne, Edward   61
Bruegel, Pieter the Elder   185
Burnet, Gilbert   143

Calderón, Rodrigo, Conde de la Oliva, Marqués de Siete Iglesias   21–23, 28–29
Cambell, Sir James   61–62
Canitz, Maria von   114–115, 117
Carpzov, Benedikt   26
Casaubon, Isaac   10
Catz, Barbara   263
Catz, Madarda   263
Charles of Austria   4
Charles IV (Holy Roman Emperor)   179
Charles V (Holy Roman Emperor)   260
Chiffoleau, Jacques   121
Christina (enslaved person)   93
Clement VIII (Pope, Ippolito Aldobrandini)   124
Cleve, Joos van   177, 180, 183–184
Conrart, Valentin   45
Cortéz, Hernán   96
Cranach the Elder, Lucas   211–227
Cruyce, Balthasar van der   50*n*45
Cuen, Johann   238*n*11, 239–240, 252*n*43

Daillé, Jean   39, 41–43
Damman, Willem   263, 278
Dathenus, Petrus   317
de Bonnyers, Marc   127
de Brébeuf, Jean   88
de Champlain, Samuel   96
de Lodève, Andéol   133, 134*n*73
de Ribas, Polonia   85
de Torres, Margarita   84–85
de Torres, Micaela   84–85
de Yrala, Gerónimo   85
Desbonnes, Philippe   264
Dissaudean, Mr.   42
Doncker, Franciscus   304–305, 309–310, 313, 318
Doolittle, Samuel   73
Du Moulin, Marie   45–48, 50–51, 55
Du Moulin, Pierre   45, 51, 53–55
Duke Jean V   121
Dun, Edward   1–2
Dunstall, John   66
Dunton, John   68, 73–74
Duplessis-Mornay, Anne de   41
Duplessis-Mornay, Elisabeth de   41
Duplessis-Mornay, Philippe   39–43, 46–47, 50*n*45, 51, 54–55
Dyhrn, Hans Christoph von   110–111

Eliot, John   91
Ephrem the Syrian   167
Eunica (enslaved person)   94

Fabritius, Christoffel   262, 264–266, 268, 270, 274–277
Faveau, Simon   264, 266, 271–272
Ferdinand I (Emperor of the Holy Roman Empire)   112
Fish, William   94–95
Francis of Assisi, O.F.M., Saint   28, 248*n*34
Frederik Hendrik, prince of Orange, stadholder of Holland   36, 43
Frisch, Johann Leonhard   147
Füssel, Martin   112–113

Gayle, Sarah Haynsworth   83
Gerhard, Johann   153
Gernler, Lucas   148
Girbigius, Matthaeus   110
Goes, Hugo van der   172, 179–180
Góngora y Argote, Luis de   22, 23n6
Graunt John   297
Gudula (Saint)   183
Guzmán, Gaspar de, Conde-Duque de Olivares   21

Hacke, Jan   263
Hackeney (family; Cologne)   183–184
Hakluyt, Richard   96
Händel, Matthias   249–250
Hedwig of Braunschweig-Wolfenbüttel   107
Hendriks, Jan   264
Henry II (King of France)   119
Henry IV (King of France)   39, 198
Henry VI (King of England)   193–195, 197–199, 207
Holbein, Hans the Elder   172n37
Holzschuher of Neuenbürg, Eustachius Carl   147
Höser, Veit   246–247
Houblon, James   143
Hulsius, Antonius   46

Isselburg, Peter   4

Jacobus (Saint; Apostle)   179
Jacobus de Voragine   180n63
Jaucourt, Jean de   41
Jeffreys, Sir Robert   291, 293
Jesus Christ   55, 110, 143, 151, 155, 157, 171, 177, 179, 181, 211, 223–225, 244, 251
Johannes (enslaved person)   93
John (Saint; Apostle)   169, 177, 179–180
John of Thessalonica (Archbishop)   180n63
Jones, Joseph   84
Joutaya (Wendat man)   88, 91
Jumel, Gilles   121
Jurieu, Pierre   51

Kaysersberg, Johann Geiler von   167
King Philip II (King of Spain). *See* Philip II (King of Spain)
Kleiner, Johann Georg   111–112

La Trémouille, duke de   43
Lalemant, Gabriel   90
Le Febvre, Barbe   137
Lievens, Jan   257–258, 261, 265
Lorrain, Paul   73
Louis XIV (King of France)   38, 45n28
Luther, Martin   6, 102, 104, 109, 214–215, 217, 224–227
Lydius, Jacob   48–50

Mallart, Philippe   264, 266, 271
Marci, Kornelius   145, 152
Margaret of Anjou (Queen of England)   193–201, 205–207
Margaret of Cortona O.F.S., Saint   28
Margaret of Parma   263–266, 307–308
Mary, Virgin   11, 135, 165–188, 225
Mather, Cotton   149–151, 154–155
Maximilian I (Holy Roman Emperor)   183, 184n72
Maximilian II (Emperor of the Holy Roman Empire)   112
Mayhew, Experience   89
Meckenem, Israhel van   172
Milbourne, Sir John   296
Moded, Herman   267, 315
Mornay, Françoise de   41

Nicolaus, Caspar   245
Nouhes de La Tabarière, Jacques de   41

Oldendorp, Christian   92, 94

Pacher, Michael   172
Paetz, Adriaen   51
Paul V (Pope, Camillo Borghese)   135
Pepys, Samuel   9, 11–12, 69
Peter (Saint; Apostle)   176, 179–180
Petty, Sir William   289
Philip II (King of Spain)   27n26, 260, 304–306, 311, 312n32, 313n39
Philip III (King of Spain)   21
Philip IV (King of Spain)   21
Pius V (Pope, Antonio Michele Ghislieri)   135
Poach, Andreas   104–106
Pömer, Christoph Jacob   145
Poynter, Elizabeth   95
Pseudo-Melito   180n63

INDEX NOMINUM

Ratzenberger, Matthäus   103–106
Rembrandt (Harmenszoon van Rijn)   185, 187*n*79
Richard (Duke of Gloucester)   196*n*8, 197
Richard Plantagenet, Duke of York   11, 193–208
Rivet, André   36, 38, 43–51, 53–55
Rivet, Frederick   47–50
Rose (enslaved person)   83–84
Rudolph II (Emperor of the Holy Roman Empire)   112

Saint-Germain, Jacques de   41
Sandoval y Rojas, Francisco Gómez, Duque de Lerma, Marqués de Denia, Cardinal   21
Saumaise, Claude   43
Scherertz, Elisabetha   249
Scherertz, Sigismund   239*n*13, 240, 241*nn*17, 19, 249
Schmitburg, Heinrich   212, 214, 216–217, 222, 225–227
Schmitburg, Valentin   212, 217
Schongauer, Martin   181
Schurman, Anna Maria van   45
Scudéry, Madelaine de   45
Selnecker, Nikolaus   107–109
Sendchal, Antony de, seigneur d'Auberville   41
Sixtus V (Pope, Felice Peretti di Montalto)   135
Smith, John   96

Sonnius, Franciscus   311, 313
Spalatin, Georg   217
Spiera, Francis   10
Stedingk, Theodor   237
Sterx, Jasper   314
Strype, John   290*n*6, 295
Sutton, Sir Thomas   291–292, 294–295

Taylor, Jeremy   63*n*15, 70
Taylor, Thomas   152
Toledo, Fernando Álvarez de (Duke of Alba)   143, 281, 304–305, 307–311, 313, 318
Tonnerawanont (Wendat man)   87

Ursula Magdalena, Lady of Dyhrn and Schönau   111

Vanderthoren, Hans   302
Vane, Henry   11–12
Villarnoül, Marthe de   41
von Münchhausen, Ludolf   237
von Reder, Christoph   241–242
von Reder, Magdalena   241–243
von Straubing, Melchior   247
Vossenhole, Adriaen van   276

Willem II, prince of Orange, stadholder of Holland   43, 46, 306–308
Wybo, Joris   275–277

Zwinger, Theodor   148